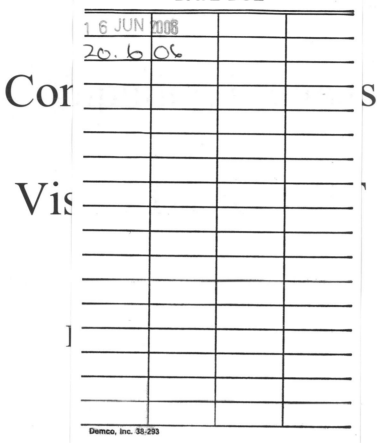

Cor   s

Vis

Published by
Payne-Gallway Publishers Limited
26-28 Northgate Street
Ipswich IP1 3DB
Tel: 01473 251097
Fax: 01473 232758
E-mail: info@payne-gallway.co.uk
Web site: www.payne-gallway.co.uk

Cover picture © 'Figure in Grass' by Susie Hamilton

Cover photography © Mike Kwasniak, 160 Sidegate Lane, Ipswich

Cover design by Direction Advertising and Design Ltd

First edition 2003

A catalogue entry for this book is available from the British Library

ISBN 1 903112 91 5

Printed in Great Britain by
W M Print Ltd, Walsall, West Midlands

Preface

Aim

This book has been written mainly for students of 'AS' or 'A' Level Computing. It assumes no knowledge of programming and covers everything needed to write a large program. Students on other courses of a similar standard, such as BTEC National, and first year HND and degree courses, should also find the material useful.

AS / A level Computing

Depending on the Examining Board, Computing students may need to produce a small project or write a number of programs for the 'AS' part of the course. For 'A' level a substantial piece of programming may be needed. The theory part of the course covers a number of important programming concepts, which are best learned through practical programming. Visual Basic .NET is an excellent, modern language through which to learn these concepts.

How the book is structured

The book is divided into three parts.

Part One goes through all the main programming concepts carefully. These need to be understood by all students.

Part Two covers a variety of topics which will prove useful in their project work. These topics include printing reports, interacting with Access databases, and object-oriented programming techniques.

Part Three goes through the main stages of producing a project to 'A' level standard by using a sample project based on a snooker club. All the programming concepts used in the sample project are covered earlier in the book.

The approach throughout is a very practical one. Parts One and Two include 50 sample programs, with step-by-step instructions explaining how to build them and explanations about how they work. In Part Three each stage in the design and coding of the full project is explained.

New to Visual Basic .NET

Visual Basic .NET introduced many changes to the language. For example:

Because Visual Basic .NET does not support printing output directly on a form, Chapter 4 explains how output can be displayed in other ways.

Console applications, which have a command interface only, are new to Visual Basic .NET.

The Visual Basic language is now infused with OOP (object-oriented programming). This approach is explained in Chapters 17 and 18 but you can still choose whether to create your own classes and objects. However everything else in the book can be understood without understanding these chapters.

Additional material – including a document covering Menus – is available on the publisher's web site www.payne-gallway.co.uk/vbnet

Table of Contents

Introduction

Visual Basic .NET

In recent years Visual Basic has become one of the world's most popular event-driven programming languages. An event-driven language is one that responds to events – clicking a button, selecting an item from a list, tabbing out of a control and so on. The most popular non-event-driven languages in schools and colleges during the 1980s and 1990s were BASIC and Pascal but these are being replaced by more modern languages. Visual Basic is likely to be one of the main teaching languages for the foreseeable future.

Visual Basic version 6 was replaced by Visual Basic .NET in 2002. It is part of Microsoft's Visual Studio .NET, a suite of tools and languages having a common graphical user interface. The .NET framework was introduced to create Web applications as well as the Windows applications that Visual Basic had long been designed for. Microsoft took this opportunity to clear up some inconsistencies and outdated features of Visual Basic, but more importantly made a series of major changes to the language.

How to use this book

The book is divided into three sections. **Part One** covers the key topics you are likely to need to produce a project to 'A' level standard. **Part Two** covers several topics which you may find useful in your project work and one topic, debugging (in Chapter 13), which you are encouraged to look at after you have done some of the work in Part One.

Part Three covers a sample 'A' level Computing project. It takes you step-by-step through analysing, designing and building a Visual Basic .NET application for a snooker club. All the coding concepts used in this project are covered in Part One and in Chapter 14 of Part Two.

The structure of each chapter in Parts One and Two is the same. There are one or more sections explaining the main concepts and up to four complete programs to illustrate them. Each program consists of step-by-step instructions telling you how to build it, interspersed with any essential explanation. These programs should be done as practical exercises – you don't learn much programming by only reading about it! There are 50 of these programs and they are summarised in Appendix A.

Take it from here...

All the chapters in Parts One and Two have a *Take it from here...* section. This contains suggestions for follow-up work related to the topics covered in the chapter. Visual Basic Help is likely to be a useful source for many of the answers. You are encouraged to do these if you have the time and interest. There is nothing in this section which *must* be understood to do the exercises at the end of the chapter or to understand the sample project.

Questions on the programs

Most of the chapter programs have suggestions for more practical work to develop a concept further or extend what the program does. It would be sensible to do these as soon as possible after completing the program in the main part of the chapter. These questions are graded using from one to three stars.

End of chapter exercises

All the chapters in Parts One and Two except Chapter 14 have exercises for you to build your own programs. Only a very few of these involve something new that has not been directly covered in the current or previous chapters. These exercises are also graded using from one to three stars.

Reusing your programs

A small number of sample programs or exercises are needed again for another program or exercise. These are as follows:

Program/exercise	Also required for
Program 2.4	Program 9.1
Program 3.4	Program 9.2
Chapter 4, exercise 3	Chapter 10, exercise 4
Program 10.1	Program 10.2
Program 17.1	Program 18.1

Code

In the 50 chapter Programs code extracts are nearly always presented in a shaded format as in the example below. When building a chapter Program you must type in all the shaded code. Occasionally a line or two of code is not shaded. This is usually to illustrate another way of coding the same thing or showing you an incorrect way of coding something. Do not type the unshaded code in.

```
Password = "secret"                              'initialise variables
Attempt = 0
Do                                               'start of loop
   Attempt = Attempt + 1
   InputPassword = InputBox("Enter password. This is attempt " & _
                 "number " & Attempt)
Loop Until (Attempt = 3) Or (InputPassword = Password) 'end of loop
```

This extract illustrates three important coding conventions:

- The 5th line of code has an underscore character (_) at the end. This means that the line has been broken into two lines because it is too long to fit into the page width of this book. When copying code into your program you *could* break it into two lines in the same way. Visual Basic .NET accepts the underscore character as the connection between the split lines, but note that there must be at least one space before it. On the other hand you can type the two lines as one line into your program, but remember to leave out the underscore. You cannot break a line of code in the middle of text that is in quotes.

- Three lines of code have an apostrophe (') followed by a short explanation of what the line means. Such explanations are called **comments** and must come after the apostrophe. In this book the code and the comments are formatted differently. Comments are in italics and are not bold. When you run your program Visual Basic .NET skips over the comments – they are there for human use only. If you are doing an assessed project using Visual Basic .NET you will be expected to write comments as appropriate. There are rather more comments provided in the code extracts in this book than you should write in your own programs, but they have the extra role here of teaching you how the code works. You do not have to copy these comments when you write the sample programs, but if you do you will certainly find them helpful when returning to your code later.

- The lines of code between the words **Do** and **Loop** are **indented**. Indenting code in a consistent way is an invaluable aid to understanding what you have written. Visual Basic .NET will attempt to indent for you as you type your code, but like commenting indents are there for human use only. In this book indents are two characters in size.

Web site

The publisher's web site contains a variety of support material on www.payne-gallway.co.uk/vbnet.

Students and teachers can download:

- Files needed for some of the practical work in Parts One and Two:

Folder/Program/File	Type of file	Required for
Collections folder. Contains 2 subfolders – Program 10-3 Controls Collection and Program 10-4 OwnCollection	Two Visual Basic .NET programs to illustrate Collections	Chapter 10 *Take it from here....* section, question 2
DegreeStudents.txt	Text	Chapter 12 exercise 1
Sales.txt	Text	Program 14.1
GardenCentreProducts.dat	Random access	Chapter 14 exercise 2
DegreeStudents2.txt	Text	Chapter 14 exercise 3
HolidayHomes.mdb	Access database	Programs 15.1, 15.3 Chapter 15 exercise 2
Alevels.mdb	Access database	Program 16.2
Vocational Students.mdb	Access database	Chapter 15 exercise 1, 2 Chapter 16 exercise 4
Repayments.mdb	Access database	Chapter 16 exercise 1
Hospital.mdb	Access database	Programs 15.2, 15.4 Chapter 16 exercises 2, 3
OOP Ski Trip	Visual Basic .NET Ski Trip program	Chapter 17 Chapter 18 exercises 1, 2

- A Word file listing all the changes from Visual Basic versions 5 and 6 to Visual Basic .NET that relate to the topics covered in Parts One and Two.

Teachers can also download:

- The Visual Basic .NET files for the 50 programs in Parts One and Two.

- The Visual Basic .NET files for the 72 End of Chapter Exercises.

- The Visual Basic .NET files for the project in Part Three.

- A Word file containing commentary and the full code for the *Questions on the Programs* sections.

Part One – Basic Topics

Chapter 1 introduces you to Visual Basic .NET's **programming environment** – the screen on which you build and run a program. You will learn to use the basic **Toolbox** and to adopt a standard way of referring to the controls you use from the Toolbox in your code.

Chapter 2 teaches you how to use several controls from the Toolbox – **text box, list box, combo box, button, check box, group box, timer** and **scroll bar**. Of these the text box is the one most commonly used in programs and it is also the easiest. You will use the list box a lot in your later work, so make sure you understand Program 2.1 well.

Chapter 3 introduces you to Visual Basic .NET's **data types** and how to declare and use **variables** that belong to these types. The concept of the **scope** of a variable is important, and you will learn the difference between **global** and **local** scope.

Chapter 4 shows you how to display and format the output your program produces in labels, message boxes and list boxes.

Chapter 5 introduces you to **console applications**. These are programs which have no controls; a command interface is used.

Chapter 6 takes you through the two **selection** constructs in Visual Basic – **If** and **Select Case**. You will also learn how to use two important **logical operators** – **AND** and **OR**.

Chapter 7 covers **loops**. Three important types of loop – **For...Next, Do While...Loop** and **Do...Loop Until** are covered.

Chapter 8 looks at how to handle **strings, dates** and **time**. String handling is the most common task in programming and Visual Basic .NET has a variety of methods and functions to do this. The case study in Part Three uses time a lot.

Chapter 9 covers **procedures**. All the events that you will have met so far have been coded as event procedures. Visual Basic has another type of procedure – the **general procedure**. Sometimes these procedures need to be passed one or more items of data to do their job. These items of data are known as **parameters**.

Chapter 10 covers **arrays**. An 'ordinary' array is a data structure in which you can store large quantities of data belonging to a particular data type. A **control array** is a special type of array which features prominently in the case study in Part Three.

Chapter 11 introduces you to **records**. A record is like a single row in a database table, containing data in a number of fields. An **array of records** is like the table itself, consisting perhaps of a great number of records.

Chapter 12 covers **files**. These are essential when you need to permanently store data entered through your program. The two main types of file – **text** files and **random access** files – are discussed. Random access files store their data as records and are generally preferable to text files. The case study in Part Three uses random access files a lot.

Chapter 1 – Introducing Visual Basic .NET

A Visual Basic .NET Project

Event-driven languages like Visual Basic .NET are built using one or more **forms**. On these you place a variety of **controls** and attach code to some or all of them to suit the purpose of your program. All except one of the programs you will do in Parts One and Two of this book have only one form; it's surprising how much you can pack into such a program. The sample 'A' level project in Part Three needs only four.

Figure 1.1 shows a form. In this program the user clicks the Start button and then types as fast as they can in the white area. The number of seconds that have elapsed ticks over on the right, and after 60 seconds they are told how many words they have typed in.

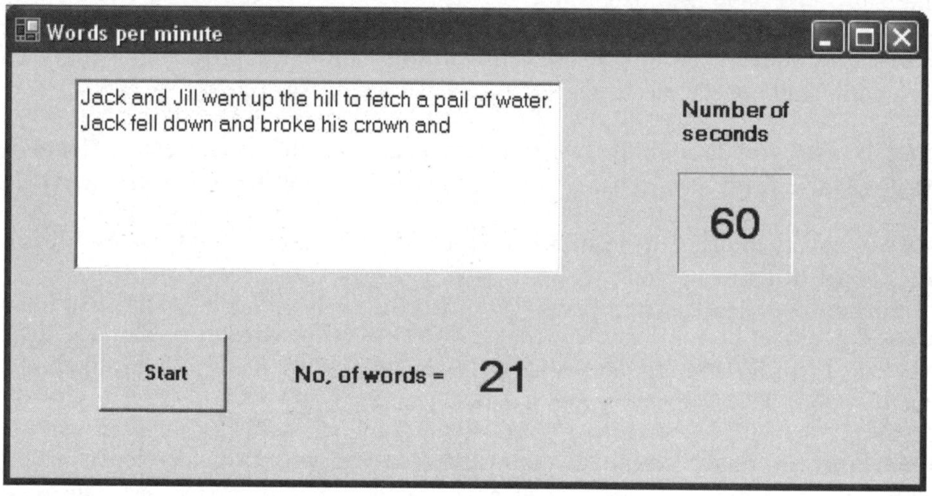

Figure 1.1: A program made up of one form

The example above is a **program**. It has one form with several controls and some code hidden from view which runs when the user clicks the Start button. Visual Basic .NET refers to a program as a **project**. From now on the two terms mean the same thing.

Building a folder system for your programs

Visual Basic .NET stores all the files for a given program or project inside a parent folder with several subfolders. Each chapter in this book has up to four complete programs and several exercises at the end which require further programs. One sensible way to store all the programs from this book is to have an overall folder containing all the programs and separate folders for each chapter. You can create these program folders from Windows or from within Visual Basic .NET.

1. In Windows create an overall folder named **VB NET Programs** or a name of your choice.

2. Inside this folder create a new folder named **Chapter 01**. If you wish, create folders at this stage for some of the later chapters too.

The programming environment

The programming environment of a language refers to the interface the programmer uses to build a program and then to run and test it. It is the screen in front of you, including all its menus, icons and buttons. This is often called an **Integrated Development Environment**, or **IDE** for short. Let's have a practical tour of Visual Basic .NET's IDE and at the same time build our first program.

Setting up your profile

1. Load Microsoft Visual Studio .NET from Windows and you'll get the Start Page window shown in figure 1.2. Make sure the **My Profile** link on the left is selected.

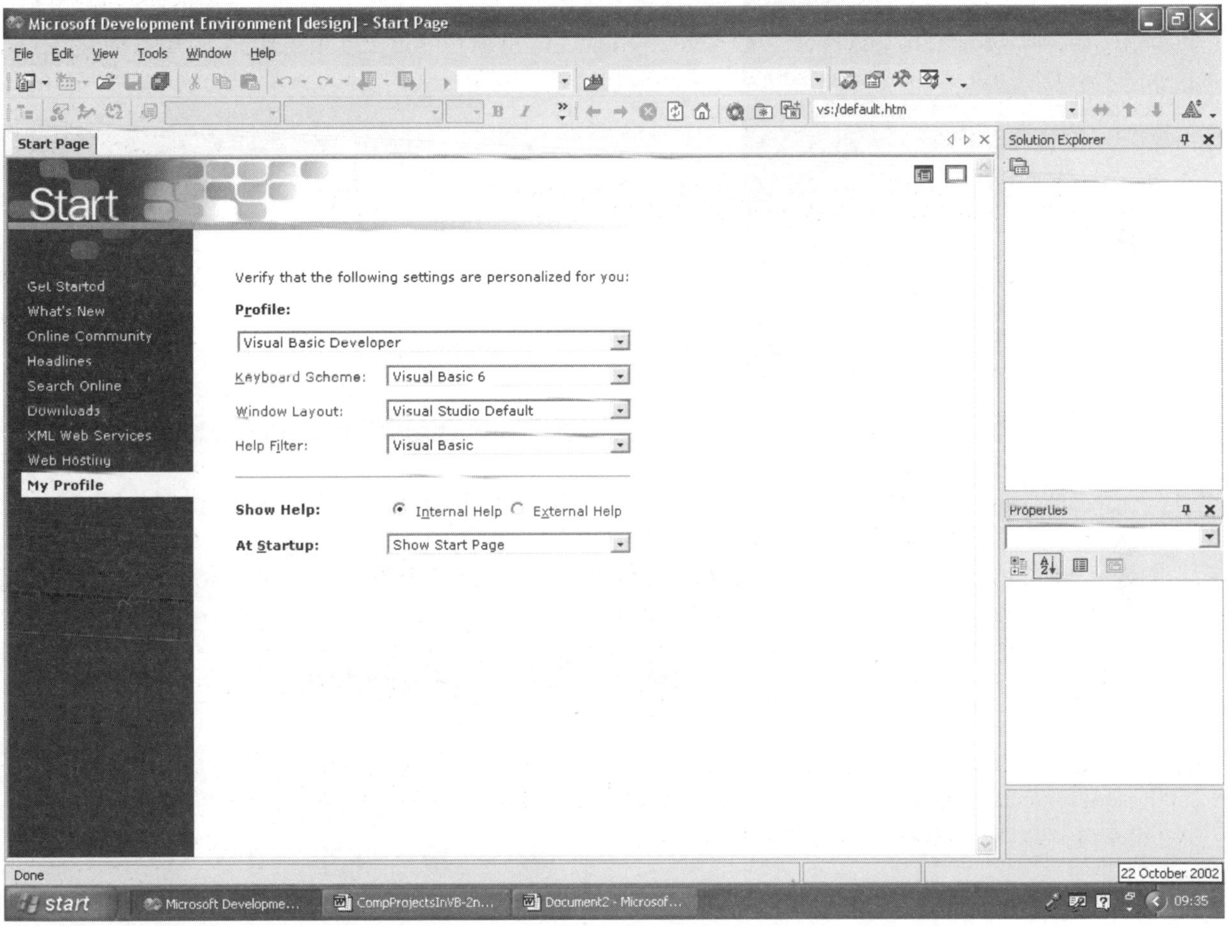

Figure 1.2: The Start Page window of Visual Studio .NET

2. The Introduction to this book explained that Visual Basic .NET is part of Visual Studio .NET. This Start page allows you to configure Visual Studio .NET for Visual Basic .NET use. Make the selections from the five combo boxes as shown in figure 1.2, starting with **Visual Basic Developer** from the top combo box.

Starting a new project

3. Click the **Get Started** link on the left side of the Start Page window. You should get a window similar to that shown in figure 1.3. The central part lists your recent projects (although you do not have any yet). If any of the other smaller windows shown in figure 1.3 are not displayed (Toolbox, Solution Explorer and Properties), get them from the View menu.

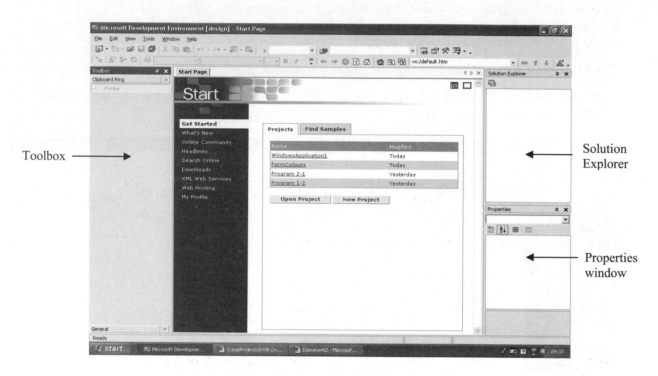

Figure 1.3: The Visual Basic .NET IDE

4. To create a new project click the **New Project** button or select **File/New/Project** from the menu. The New Project window shown in figure 1.4 appears.

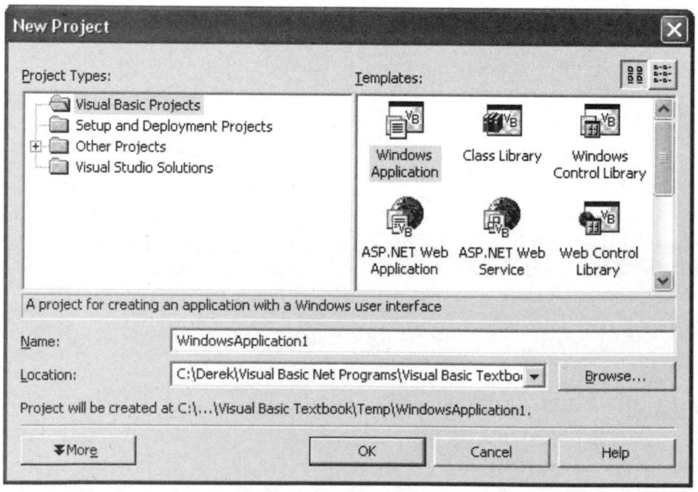

Figure 1.4: The New Project window

5. In figure 1.4 the list of Project Types on the left highlights Visual Basic Projects and Templates on the right highlights Windows Application. If they are not highlighted on your screen then click on them now.

6. The default name for a new project is Windows Application followed by a number. In Figure 1.4 this is WindowsApplication1 in the Name box. Change this to **First Program** as in figure 1.5. Visual Basic .NET will create a parent folder with this name to store the whole project.

7. In the Location box you specify the path to your parent Visual Basic folder. It was suggested earlier that you created a folder called **My VB Programs** and inside this a folder called **Chapter 01**. If the correct path is not shown in the Location box click **Browse** and select it in the usual Windows way. Now click **OK**.

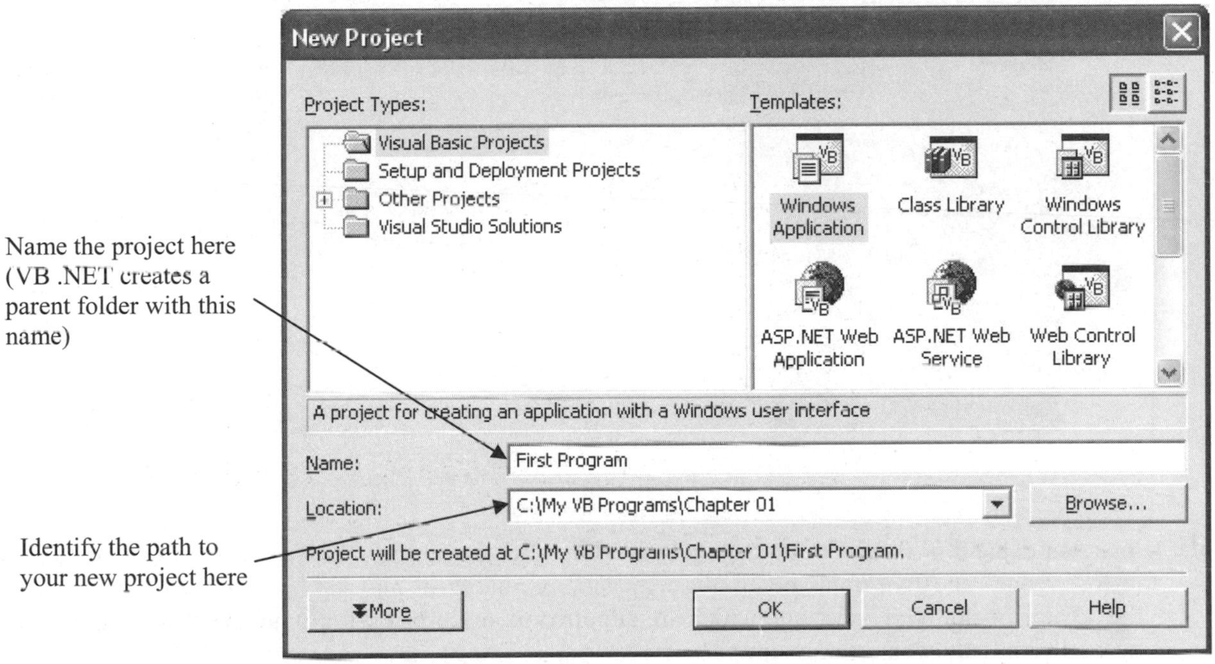

Figure 1.5: Naming a project and identifying its location

8. You now get the screen shown in figure 1.6. The three sections labelled Toolbox, Solution Explorer and Properties in figure 1.3 were empty, but now have some information in them. If your Properties window does not have the same information as that in figure 1.6 just click on the Form (which also has the effect of making its blue border darker).

The Page tabs

9. There are two pages available at present. Switch between the **Start Page** and the **Form1.vb [Design]** pages. The most important other page is the one with the program's code, as you will see shortly.

The Solution Explorer

A solution is the program or programs you have built to solve a particular problem, and the Solution Explorer displays its main components. To meet really big problems programmers may build several different projects. In all the work in this book only one project is used for a given problem.

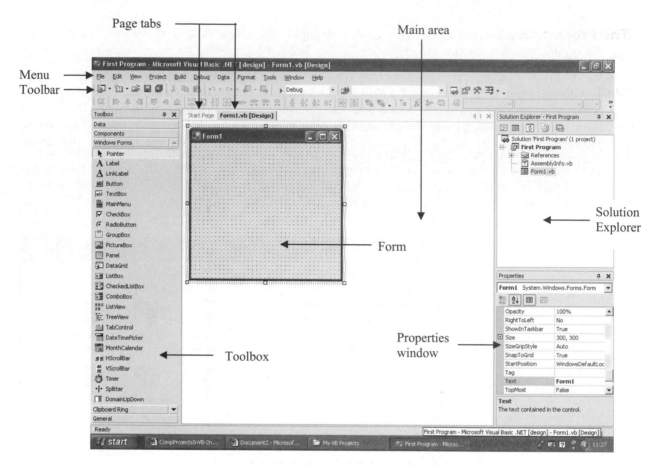

Figure 1.6: A new Visual Basic .NET project

10. You can expand or contract the display by clicking the small + or – buttons. Click the + button next to References and five items beginning with *System* will be displayed. These refer to basic parts of the Visual Basic .NET language which are supplied to any project. For example System.Drawing is needed when you want to draw graphics on a form.

The Toolbox

The **Toolbox** contains icons for each control you can put on your forms. There are three main groups of controls – Data, Components and Windows Forms. The Windows Forms group is by far the most important group. You will use the Data controls only in Chapters 15 and 16. The Components controls are not used at all in this book. Controls have technical and ordinary names. For example we might refer to a list box but its technical name, as shown in the Toolbox, is ListBox.

11. Click on the TextBox control and with the left mouse button down draw a rectangular shape on the form. Release the mouse button to get a text box drawn on the form with the word TextBox1 in it.

12. Practise placing a variety of controls on the form. Note how the name that appears with some of these controls reflects the type of control. Thus you get Label1, Button1, CheckBox1 and so on. Place the same type of control on the form again and the name will be Label2, Button2 etc.

13. Place a Timer control on the form. It is displayed instead in a lower part of the window called the **pane** area. Some controls are displayed here rather than on the form. Can you find the others?

The Properties window

When you place a control from the Toolbox onto a form it is an example of an **object**. The form itself is also an object. All objects can have **properties**, and most of these can be seen in the Properties window, which is below the Solution Explorer. **A property is a descriptive feature of an object.**

14. Select the form by clicking anywhere once on it outside the controls. Scroll through its 50 properties listed in the Properties window. Some of these are shown in figure 1.7. These are listed alphabetically but click on the **Categorized** icon and they are arranged by category.

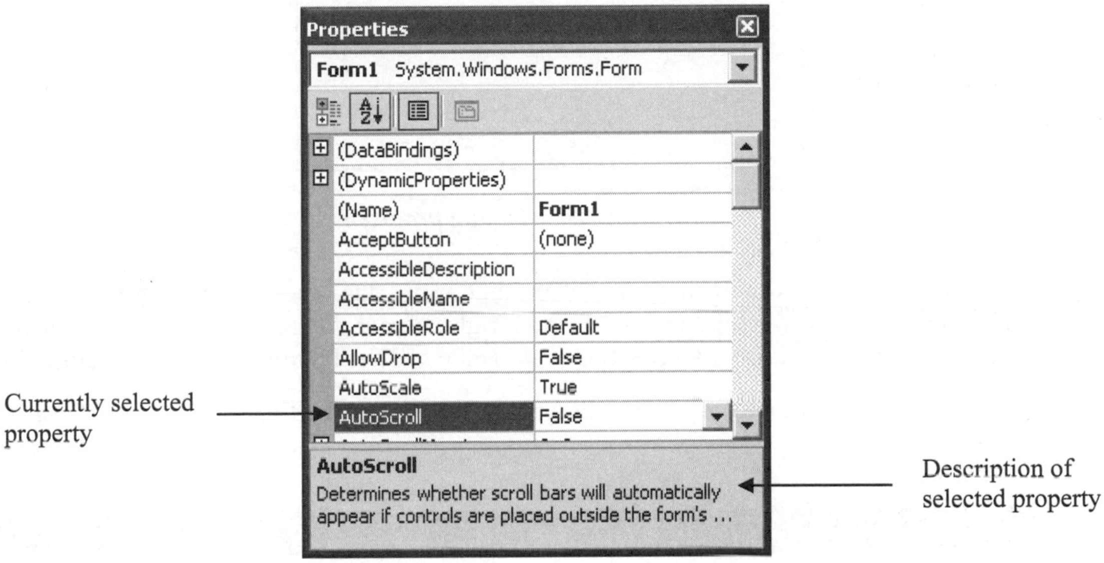

Currently selected property

Description of selected property

Figure 1.7: Some of the form's properties

15. Scroll through the properties and find the **Text** property. The default value is Form1. Change this to **My First VB Program**, press **Enter** and this will be displayed in the form's title bar.

16. Delete all the controls on the form and the Timer control below by selecting **Edit/Select All** from the menu and then **Edit/Delete**. Place a Label control to fill the top quarter or so of the form. The Properties window now displays the label's properties. Change its Text property from Label1 to **This program does nothing except display this label**.

17. Find the Font property of the label and click its ellipsis button (…). Change the font to point size **12 bold**.

Running the program

To run a program its code must be changed from the words you have written, commonly called **high-level** or **source code**, into something your computer can understand. Computers only understand 1's and 0's; this sort of code is called **binary** or **machine** code. The Visual Basic **compiler** changes the source code into binary code and stores this in the computer's memory so that the program can run. Although you haven't written any code in this program there is some background code created automatically by Visual Basic .NET that we haven't looked at yet.

18. To run the program click the **Start** button on the toolbar, or select **Debug/Start** from the menu, or press **F5**. Your running program should look like that in figure 1.8.

Figure 1.8: The running program

19. You will see two or three new windows at the bottom of the screen. Close these and close the program by clicking the 'x' button at the top right corner of each. You are returned to the programming environment. If you have an Output window at the bottom of the screen close this too.

20. Select **File/Close Solution** to close this program or **File/Exit** to finish your Visual Basic .NET session.

PROGRAM 1.1　　*Display your name*

> **Specification**　Display your name on a form in large letters

The previous program displayed a message in a label without you writing any code. In this one you will write code to display your name in a text box. Figure 1.11 shows the program.

Designing the form

1. Load Visual Studio .NET and you will get the Start Page shown in figure 1.3. Click **New Project** and in the New Project window type **Program 1-1** in the Name box and in the Location box select the path to your Chapter 01 folder (which will probably already be displayed). Click **OK**.

2. Make the provided form wider (about three-quarters of the width of the main area will do).

3. In the Properties window change the form's Text property from Form1 to **Print my name**. This text should now appear in the form's title bar.

4. From the Toolbox place a large label across the middle part of the form. Find the label's Font property in the Properties window. Click on the ellipses button (...) and in the Font window set the font to **30 bold**. When your name appears on the form let's have it in large letters!

5. The default value of the label's Text property in the Properties window is Form1. Delete this so that no text is displayed in the label.

Coding

Code may be executed when a particular event occurs. There are dozens of possible events but the commonest is when a control on a form is clicked. Another common event occurs just as the program's form is displayed. This event is called the Load event, and in this program when it happens your name should appear on the form.

6. Double-click anywhere on the form outside the label and you'll be given the code shown in figure 1.9. At present we are interested only in the two lines beginning with **Private Sub** and ending with **End Sub**. The rest of the code will be explained later in this chapter. These two lines are the code template for the form's Load event, which you can tell from the words Form1_Load.

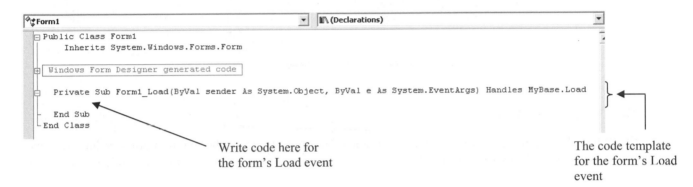

Figure 1.9: The code template for the form's Load event

When you double-click any control on a form, or the form itself, Visual Basic .NET supplies the code template for the event which the makers of the language think is the most commonly used one for that control. For a form they think the Load event should be the default one. Some controls have the Click event as their default one.

The first line of the code template contains several words inside a pair of brackets, *ByVal sender As System.Object, ByVal e As System.ArgEvents*. All code templates supply these but you will rarely need to use them. In this book they will be replaced by an ellipsis (**…**) when they are not needed in a program.

7. Between the two lines of the template type one line of code to tell Visual Basic .NET to display your name in the label. Put your own name between the quotation marks, but first stop typing as soon as you have written the period (.) after Label1 and look at the list of properties which pops up (see figure 1.10). This very useful feature is called **IntelliSense**. You can select a property from this list by double-clicking it or type the property name in yourself

```
Private Sub Form1_Load(...) Handles MyBase.Load
   Label1.Text = "Derek Christopher"
End Sub
```

The '=' sign means *store or assign the text inside the quotation marks into the Text property of the label*. Technically it is known as an **assignment statement**.

There is one other thing to note about the code: The line you have written is **indented**. Indenting code in a consistent way is a very important part of writing good code. It makes code easier to read, as you will appreciate when writing more complex code later. In this book indents are two characters in size.

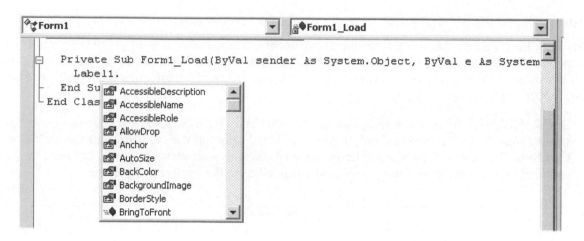

Figure 1.10: IntelliSense: The properties of a label

Running the program

8. Click the **Start** button on the toolbar or select **Debug/Start** from the menu. Your running program should look like that in figure 1.11. If the program does not run properly check the code you wrote in step 7 above.

Figure 1.11: Program 1.1 to display your name

8. Close the program by clicking the 'x' button, or click on the small icon to the left of your form's title bar and then click close, or simply press Alt + F4.

9. Select **File/Close Solution** to close this program or **File/Exit** to finish your Visual Basic .NET session.

end of Program 1.1

Naming controls

Many Visual Basic .NET programmers use a naming convention that adds a lower-case three-character prefix to the name they give a control. For example if the purpose of a text box is for the user to type in a person's salary then you might name it txtSalary. Whenever you come across this in your code you would know it was a text box from the txt prefix, and the 'Salary' part would give a strong clue as to its purpose.

Figure 1.12 lists the prefixes for most of the controls that you will need to refer to in code in the programs in this book.

Control	Prefix
Check box	chk
Combo box	cbo
Button	btn
Form	frm
Group box	grp
Horizontal scroll bar	hsb

Control	Prefix
Label	lbl
List box	lst
Menu	mnu
Radio button	rad
Text box	txt
Timer	tmr

Figure 1.12: Prefixes for naming controls

PROGRAM 1.2   *Change a message*

Specification   When a button is clicked the message "I LIKE Visual Basic" appears. When a second button is clicked the message changes to "I HATE Visual Basic"

The finished program can be seen in figure 1.13.

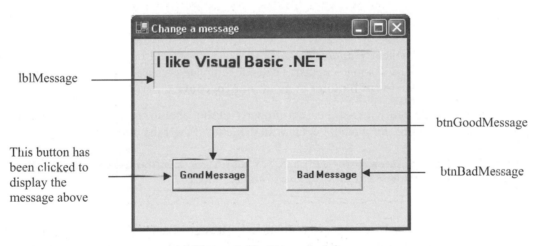

lblMessage

This button has been clicked to display the message above

btnGoodMessage

btnBadMessage

Figure 1.13: Program 1.2

Designing the form

1. If you are starting a new session load Visual Studio .NET. If you are continuing from the previous program the Start Page should be on your screen. Click **New Project** and in the New Project window type **Program 1-2** in the Name box. In the Location box select the path to your Chapter 01 folder (which will probably already be displayed). Click **OK**.

2. Make sure Form1 is selected and in the Properties window change its Text property from Form1 to **Change a message**.

3. Click on the Label control in the toolbox, and then with the mouse button down draw a rectangle in the upper part of the form.

4. Find the label's Name property in the Properties window and change it from Label1 to **lblMessage**, using the 'lbl' prefix as explained earlier. Note that this prefix begins with the *letter* 'l' and not the *number* 1.

5. Set the label's Text property to blank by deleting the default value Label1.

6. The default value for the label's BorderStyle property is None, meaning that no border will be shown when the program runs. To get the sunken border effect in figure 1.13 change this to **Fixed3D**.

7. Set the label's Font property to **14 Bold**.

8. Drag a button from the Toolbox and draw a rectangle at the bottom left of the form. Set its Text property to **Good Message**. Change its Name property to **btnGoodMessage**.

9. Place a second button at the bottom right of the form. Set its Text property to **Bad Message**. Change its Name property to **btnBadMessage**.

Coding

10. Double-click on the Good Message button and you'll get the code template for its Click event shown below. The Click event is the one Visual Basic .NET associates most commonly with a button. Recall what was said after step 6 in the previous program about replacing the information in the brackets on the first line with an ellipsis (**...**) in this book.

```
Private Sub btnGoodMessage_Click(...) Handles btnGoodMessage.Click

End Sub
```

The words after the brackets, *Handles btnGoodMessage.Click*, reinforces the fact that any code will be executed if btnGoodMessage is clicked. The code template plus any code that is written inside the template, is known as an **event handler** or an **event procedure**.

11. Type the line of code below to set the Text property of the label to the message you wish to output. Remember that the prefix for a label begins with the letter 'l', not the number 1.

```
Private Sub btnGoodMessage_Click(...) Handles btnGoodMessage.Click
   lblMessage.Text = "I LIKE Visual Basic .NET"
End Sub
```

12. Return to the form either by clicking the **Form1.vb [Design]** Page tab (see figure 1.6) or the **View Designer** button in Solution Explorer's small toolbar (you will need to hover the mouse over this button to see its name displayed). Double-click the Bad Message button on the form to get its code template

13. Type in a line of code similar to that in step 11 to output the appropriate message when the button is clicked:

```
Private Sub btnBadMessage_Click(...) Handles btnBadMessage.Click
   lblMessage.Text = "I HATE Visual Basic .NET"
End Sub
```

Running the program

14. Click the **Start** button on the toolbar or select **Debug/Start** from the menu. Click on each of the two buttons to check that the message changes. Close the program.

A look at the hidden code produced by Visual Basic .NET

Visual Basic .NET produces code templates for the various events associated with the controls on a form, but only when you ask for them. Some other code is always produced. Figure 1.14 shows all the displayed code. The first two lines and last line of code are always on a form. You do not need to understand what they mean, but to do so you would need to be familiar with Chapter 17.

```
Form1                                 ▼   (Declarations)                                          ▼

Public Class Form1
    Inherits System.Windows.Forms.Form

   Windows Form Designer generated code

    Private Sub btnGoodMessage_Click(ByVal sender As System.Object, ByVal e As System.EventArgs
        lblMessage.Text = "I like Visual Basic .NET"
    End Sub

    Private Sub btnBadMessage_Click(ByVal sender As System.Object, ByVal e As System.EventArgs)
        lblMessage.Text = "I hate Visual Basic .NET"
    End Sub

End Class
```

Figure 1.14: The displayed code in Program 1.2

15. Click on the + sign to the left of the grey shaded code *Windows Form Designer generated code*. This reveals about 70 lines of code that tell Visual Basic .NET which controls to put on the form and where to put them when the program runs. Scroll down until you come to the code relating to btnGoodMessage. Two of the lines of code set its Name and Text properties.

16. You will never need to modify this hidden code. To remove it scroll up to the top of the form and click the - button to the left of #Region.

17. Select **File/Close Solution** to close this program or **File/Exit** to finish your Visual Basic .NET session.

end of Program 1.2

Summary of key concepts

- A Visual Basic .NET **project** (program) is made up of one or more **forms**. All the files relating to a particular project are stored by Visual Basic .NET inside a parent folder named after the project.

- To build a program you place **controls** from the Toolbox onto a form. Controls are examples of **objects**. Most controls have many possible **event procedures**. The code inside these procedures is fired off when the particular event occurs. A common event is the Click event.

- Objects have **properties**. A property controls the appearance and behaviour of an object. A commonly used property of forms, labels and text boxes is the Text property.

- To **compile** a program is to change the **source code** you have written into **machine code** that the computer can understand.

- It is standard practice in this book to prefix the Name property of objects or controls that will be referred to in code by three letters to indicate the type of control, e.g. txt for a text box, btn for a button.

- The '=' sign is often used as an **assignment statement**. It assigns the item on its right to the item on its left, e.g. lblMessage.Text = "Hello"

Take it from here....

1. In Windows look inside any of the three parent folders for the programs in this chapter (First Program, Program 1-1 or Program 1-2). Find out the names of any subfolders and files that have been created for that project. Some of these are text-only files and can be opened in Notepad or WordPad. Open them and see if you can identify some of the pieces of information stored in them. One of the files is an application file (meaning it is executable from Windows). Double-click it to run the program.

2. Use Visual Basic .NET's Help to find out about the various properties of some of the controls you can put on a form. Select **Help/Index** from the menu and then type in the type of control, e.g. **Button, TextBox** etc.

3. The control just below the Label on the Toolbox is the LinkLabel control. Find out what this is used for and how you would use it on a form.

4. The **Object Browser** is part of the IDE which holds information about your project and about a host of features of the Visual Basic .NET language. Explore this feature by selecting **View/Other Windows/Object Browser** or just press the **F2** key.

5. The **Build** menu has four selections with the word Build or Rebuild. This menu is really only important when you have finished a major program and want to run it from outside the Visual Basic .NET programming environment. Find out about these Build selections.

Questions on the Programs

Program 1.1

***1**. Display your address in a second label when the program runs.

End of chapter exercises

***1**. Place a button on a form. When it is clicked the title bar of the form should display **Welcome to Visual Basic .NET**.

***2**. Place two buttons on a form and set their Text properties to **Show** and **Hide**. Place a label on the form and set its Visible property to **False** (which means it will be invisible when the program first runs). Clicking the Show button should make the label visible and display the message **Hello** inside it. Clicking the Hide button should remove the label and its message. When you set the Visible property in code you do not need quotation marks around the terms True or False.

**3. Write a program with a label and two buttons. Clicking the ForeColor button displays the message shown in figure 1.15 in a blue colour. Clicking the BackColor button displays a different message and colours the rest of the label yellow. Note that the message is centred within the label. Use the label's ForeColor and BackColor properties. To set these properties write Color.Red or Color.Yellow to the right of the assignment statement (=). IntelliSense is used when you write the dot after Color and you will have over 140 colours to choose from.

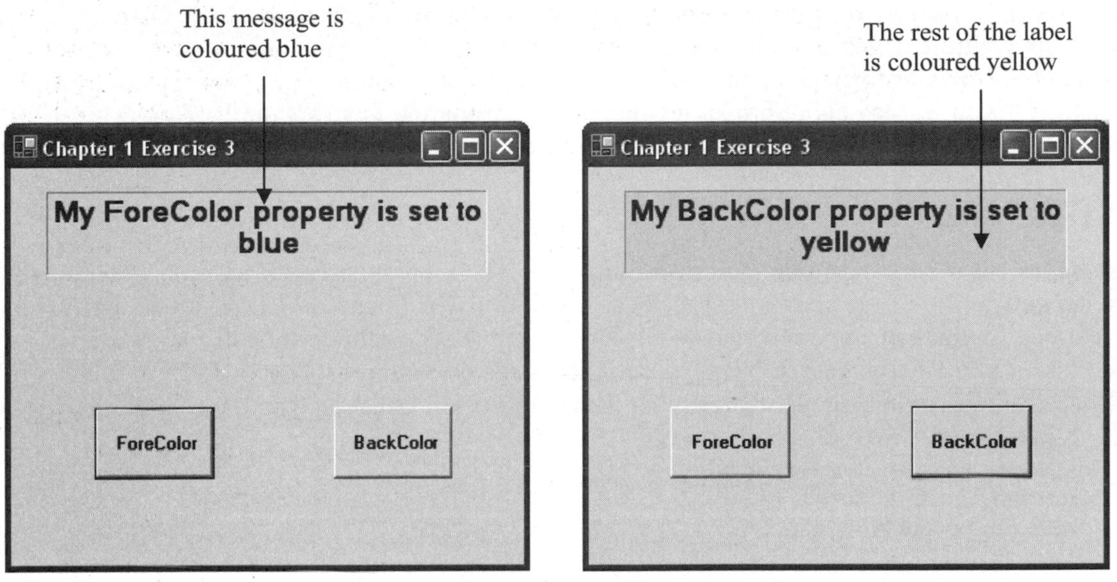

This message is
coloured blue

The rest of the label
is coloured yellow

Chapter 1 Exercise 3

My ForeColor property is set to blue

ForeColor   BackColor

Chapter 1 Exercise 3

My BackColor property is set to yellow

ForeColor   BackColor

Figure 1.15: Exercise 3

Chapter 2 – Working with Controls

In Chapter 1 you used two controls from the Toolbox – a label and a button. In this chapter you will use another six controls which will allow you to design a wide range of interfaces in your programs. To get these controls to work for you requires an understanding of some of their properties, methods and events. In Chapter 1 you learned about properties and events. A **method** is an action that you can perform on a control. For example the Clear method removes the contents of a control.

The Text Box

Text boxes are used for entering and displaying data. The property you will use most commonly is the **Text** property. One of the commonest methods you will use is **Focus**, which positions the cursor inside the text box. If you had a text box named txtName, then the code below would display whatever has been typed into it in a label named lblName, clear its contents by setting its Text property to blank (**""**), and finally put the cursor in the text box ready for the next piece of data to be typed in.

```
lblName.Text = txtName.Text
txtName.Text = ""
txtName.Focus()
```

The List Box

Use a **list box** if you want to select one or more items from a list of items. Figure 2.1 shows an example of its use - the query wizard in the database package Access. The list box on the left lists the fields that can be selected. When selected they are moved to the other list box on the right.

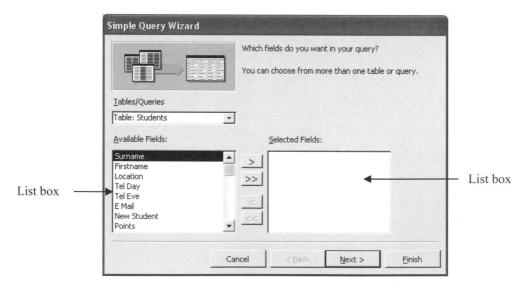

Figure 2.1

The following are the properties and methods of the list box that you will commonly use:

Properties

Items   Contains all the items in the list box. The first item is indexed (numbered) by Visual Basic .NET as 0, the next as 1 and so on.

Items.Count   Contains the number of items in the list box.

SelectedIndex   Contains the index or number of the item currently selected. For example, if the 6th item is selected ListIndex contains 5 (since the first item is numbered as 0). If no item is selected its value is -1.

Sorted   Specifies whether the items in the list box are sorted or not.

Text   Contains the currently selected item from the list box.

Methods

Items.Add   Adds an item to the list box, e.g *lstNames.Items.Add("Gary")*

Items.Clear   Removes all the items from the list box. e.g. *lstNames.Clear*

Items.RemoveAt   Removes an item from the list box. It must be followed by the index of the item to be removed, e.g. *lstNames.RemoveAt(lstNames.SelectedIndex)* removes the item currently selected.

Before starting the programs in this chapter you may wish to create a folder, **Chapter02**, in Windows for all the work you will be doing from the chapter.

PROGRAM 2.1   *A list box of countries*

Specification	Allow the user to enter the name of a country in a text box. Provide three buttons to add the name to a list box and to display all the names alphabetically, to delete a selected country from the list box, and to delete all the countries from the list box.

Designing the form

1.   If you are starting a new session load Visual Studio .NET. If you are continuing from the previous program the Start Page should be on your screen. Click **New Project** and in the New Project window type **Program 2-1** in the Name box. In the Location box select the path to the location of this project (e.g. C:\My VB Projects\Chapter 02). Click **OK**.

2.   Change the Text property of the form to **Using a List Box**.

3.   Drag a label, text box, three buttons and a list box onto the form and position them as shown in figure 2.2.

You can make the text box as wide as you like but you cannot change its height. If you change its Font property to a larger point size the height increases as appropriate. If you change its MultiLine property to True (so that text could go over more than one line) you have complete control over its height.

4.   Set the properties of these controls as shown in figure 2.3. Since the label will not be referred to in code there is no need to change its default Name property. The purpose of the Items property at design time is to populate the list box with items before the program runs. To do this click the small ellipsis button in the Items property and type the three countries listed in figure 2.3 into the String Collection Editor window as shown in figure 2.4.

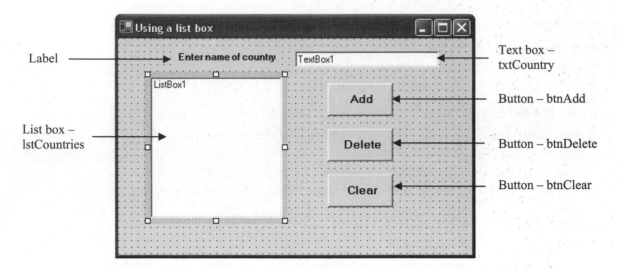

Figure 2.2: Design of program 2.1

Control	Property	Property setting
Text box	Name Text	txtCountry blank (i.e. delete *Text1*)
Button	Name Text	btnAdd Add
Button	Name Text	btnDelete Delete
Button	Name Text	btnClear Clear
List box	Name Sorted Items	lstCountries True Spain USA Austria

Figure 2.3: Design-time property settings for controls in program 2.1

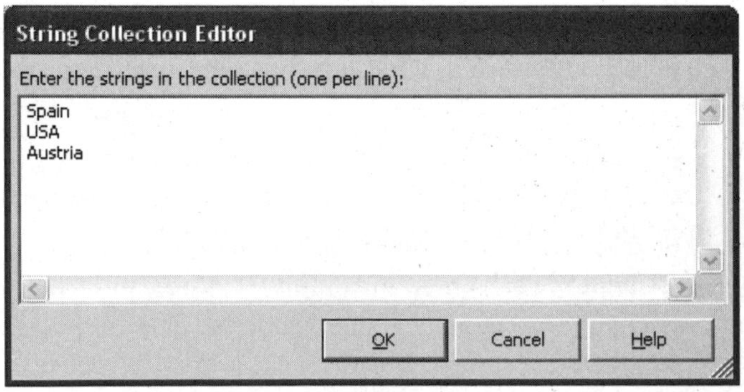

String Collection Editor

Enter the strings in the collection (one per line):

```
Spain
USA
Austria
```

OK   Cancel   Help

Figure 2.4: Entering countries into the Items property

Coding

In all the programs from now on the code will contain a number of **comments**. A comment must begin with an apostrophe (') and can come after some proper code on a particular line or be on its own line. Comments are ignored by the compiler. They are there to help other programmers understand your code, and to help you understand it as well! Many of the comments in this book, though, would not be needed by experienced programmers. You are advised to write the comments as well as the code.

5. Double-click the Add button to bring up its Click event procedure code template. Complete the code as shown below. The **Items.Add** method is used to add an item to the list box. The first comment spans two lines because it will not fit in this book on the same line as the code it refers to. You can write it over two lines as shown here or keep it on the same line.

```
Private Sub btnAdd_Click(...) Handles btnAdd.Click
    lstCountries.Items.Add(txtCountry.Text) 'Add contents of text box to
                                            'list box display
    txtCountry.Text = ""                    'clear the text box
    txtCountry.Focus()          'put cursor in text box ready for next country
End Sub
```

6. Get the code template for the Click event of the Delete button. You can do this directly from the Page tab containing the code rather than having to get to the form and double-click the button. From the Class Name combo box select **btnDelete** (figure 2.5). Then from the Method Name combo box select **Click**.

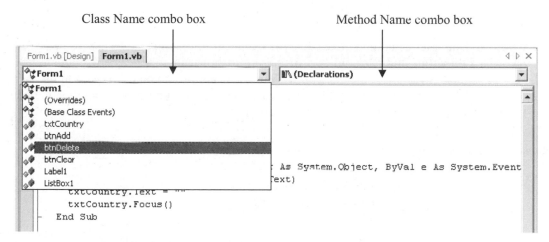

Figure 2.5: Using the Class Name and Method Name combo boxes to get an event code template

7. In the code template enter the line of code below. The Items.RemoveAt method is used to delete the item currently selected. The property SelectedIndex holds the index value of this item. If the third item is selected it holds the value 2 because indexing starts from 0.

```
Private Sub btnDelete_Click(...) Handles btnDelete.Click
    lstCountries.Items.RemoveAt(lstCountries.SelectedIndex) 'delete
                            'selected item from list of displayed items
End Sub
```

8. Get the code template for the Click event of the **Clear** button and enter the following:

```
Private Sub btnClear_Click(...) Handles btnClear.Click
   lstCountries.Items.Clear()      'delete all items displayed in list box
End Sub
```

Running the program

9. Click the **Start** button on the toolbar or select **Debug/Start** from the menu. Enter several country names into the text box and click the Add button after each one. The names will be displayed in alphabetical order in the list box because its Sorted property is set to True. If you fill the list box a scroll bar will automatically be added. Try out the Delete and Clear buttons.

end of Program 2.1

The Combo Box

The term **combo box** is short for 'combination box' because this control combines the features of the text box and the list box. You use exactly the same properties and methods described earlier for the list box to make a combo box work. A combo box is often called a drop-down list box. The two main differences between combo and list boxes are:

- With some types of combo box you can edit any of the displayed items or type in an item that is not listed.

- The standard combo box must be clicked to reveal its items. It therefore takes up less room on a form.

Figure 2.5 had two examples of combo boxes that you cannot edit. Examples of those you can edit can be found on Word's Formatting toolbar, and two of these are shown in figure 2.6. By clicking the small button the list of fonts is revealed. If the one you wish to use is not listed you can type it in the edit part of the combo box and Word might be able to switch to it. The list of font sizes does not include every number. Again you enter the number you want in the edit part.

Edit part of the combo box

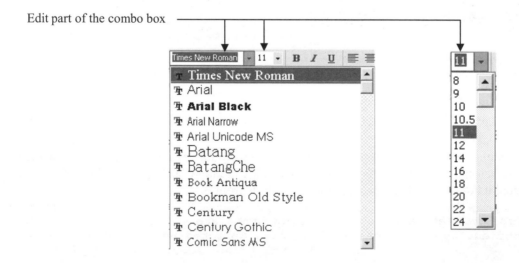

Figure 2.6: Combo boxes on Word's Formatting toolbar

The Radio Button

Radio buttons are used to allow the user to select one option from two or more options. A common example is Word's four options when you wish to print a document, as shown in figure 2.7. You can select only one of these four.

Note the following about the radio button:

Properties Apart from the Name and Text properties, the most useful property is **Checked**. It holds True if the radio button is selected or False if it is not selected. You need to understand about selection in Chapter 6 to use this property.

Methods You are most unlikely to use these.

Events The **Click** and the **CheckedChanged** events are the only ones you are likely to use. The Click event occurs when you click the button (i.e. when you select it) and the CheckedChanged event occurs when you check or uncheck it. CheckedChanged is the default event.

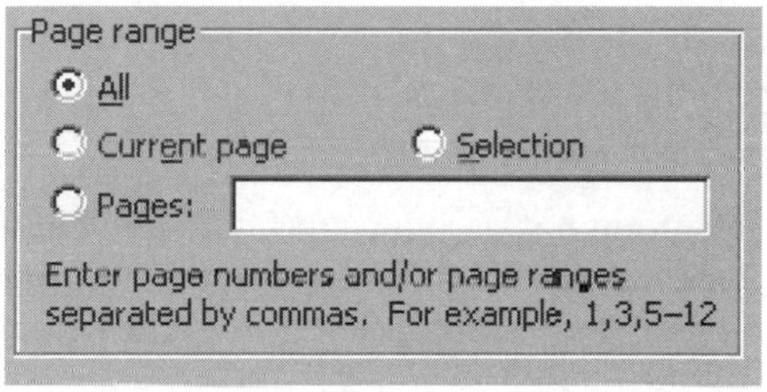

Figure 2.7: Radio buttons when printing from Word

The Check Box

The **check box** is similar to the radio button in that you can test its Checked property to see if it is selected. Unlike the radio button you can select more than one at a time. A common use of check boxes in Windows applications is setting general default values through the **Tools/Options** menu. Figure 2.8 shows an example from the spreadsheet Excel. All but two of the check boxes in this example have been selected.

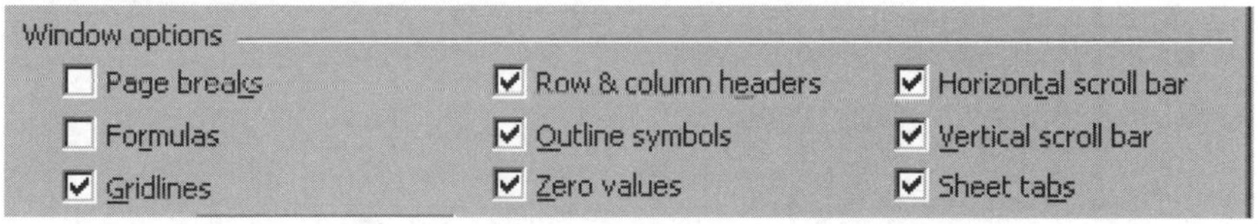

Figure 2.8: An example of the use of check boxes in Excel

The check box has similar properties and methods to the radio button. Like the radio button, the commonest events you're likely to use are CheckedChanged (the default event) and Click.

The Group Box

The **group box** is a rectangular shape in which you usually place other controls. In figure 2.7, for example, four radio buttons (and a text box) are contained inside a group box with the title Page Range. The advantages of using a group box are:

- You can reposition all the controls inside it at design time by moving the group box only.
- You can show or hide all the controls inside it at run-time by showing or hiding the group box only.
- If you want two or more groups of radio buttons, so that one can be selected from each group, then you *must* put each group into a group box. Without the group boxes you could only select one radio button from all the radio buttons on the form.

You are unlikely ever to use the group box's methods and events. The **Visible** property can be a useful one. It can hold True or False. Set it to False to hide the group box and all its controls. The sample project in Part Three uses this technique a lot.

PROGRAM 2.2   *Radio buttons, check boxes and group boxes*

Specification	Demonstrate the use of two groups of radio buttons and a group of check boxes

1. Open a new project and change the form's Text property from Form1 to **Radio buttons, check boxes and group boxes**.

2. Drag a group box control from the toolbox and position and size it as shown in figure 2.9. Change its Text property to **Gender**.

3. Place two radio buttons on the group box as shown in figure 2.9. Draw them as rectangles in order to reveal their default Text properties as RadioButton1 and RadioButton2. Change their Names to **radMale** and **radFemale** and their Text properties to **Male** and **Female**.

4. Move the group box a little and check that both radio buttons 'belong' to it by moving with it.

5. Place a label below the group box. Set its Name to **lblGender**, its Text property to blank and its BorderStyle to **Fixed3D**.

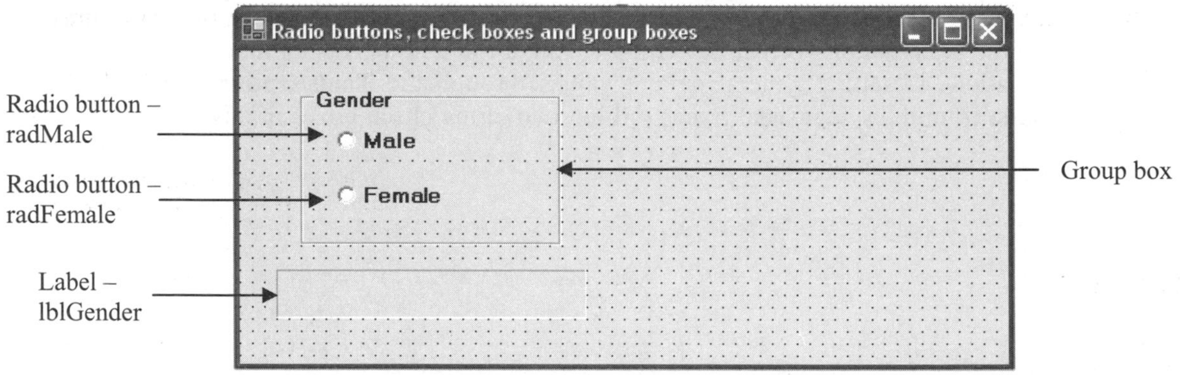

Figure 2.9: Design of Program 2.2 after step 5

6. Double-click the Male radio button to bring up the code template for its default event procedure, the CheckedChanged event. In this simple program it does not matter whether we use the Click or the CheckedChanged event. Type in the single line of code below for the label to inform us that the male button has been selected.

```
Private Sub radMale_CheckedChanged(...) Handles radMale.CheckedChanged
    lblGender.Text = "You selected Male"
End Sub
```

7. Get the code template for the Female radio button and enter a similar line of code:

```
lblGender.Text = "You selected Female"
```

8. Run the program and try out the two radio buttons.

9. Place another group box on the form and change its Text property to **Age** as shown in figure 2.10.

10. Place three radio buttons in this group box. Keep the default Names but change their Text properties to those in figure 2.10.

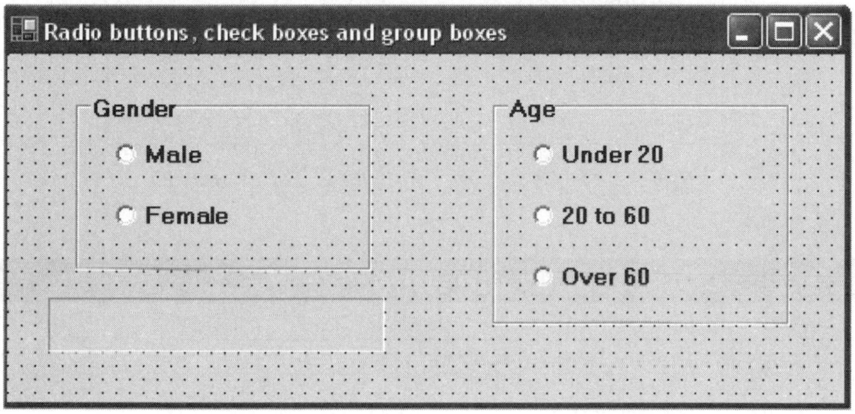

Figure 2.10: Design of Program 2.2 after step 10

11. Run the program to demonstrate that you can select one option from each of the two groups.

12. Place a third group box on the form and change its Text property to **Replies** as shown in figure 2.11.

13. Place three check boxes on this group box and set their Text properties as shown in figure 2.11.

14. Run the program and see that you can select one, two or all three check boxes.

end of Program 2.2

The Timer

The Timer is one of several toolbox controls that are not visible at run time. It only does one thing: it checks the system clock. It has no methods but two important properties. These are:

Enabled   This holds True or False. An enabled timer is able to carry out what you have coded in its Tick event (see below), but a disabled timer cannot.

Interval   This is measured in milliseconds. A value of 1000 represents 1000 milliseconds or 1 second.

The Timer only has one event, called the **Tick** event. An enabled timer runs the code in this event when the time represented by its Interval property has elapsed. For example an Interval value of 500 would call the Tick event every half a second.

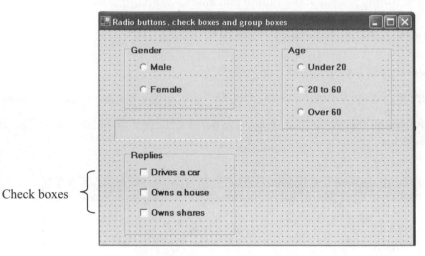

Figure 2.11: Design of Program 2.2 after step 13

Check boxes

PROGRAM 2.3   *Displaying the time*

Specification   Display the time to the nearest second on a form

1.   Open a new project. Set the form's Text property to **Display the time**. Place two labels on the form. Set the Text property of the left label to **The time is**. Set the Text property of the right label to blank, set its Name to **lblTime** and its BorderStyle property to **Fixed3D**. Figure 2.12 shows this design.

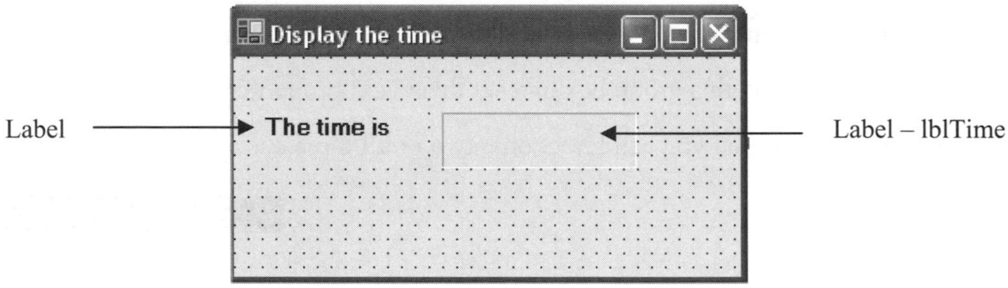

Label ⟶ ► The time is   ◄ ⟵ Label – lblTime

Figure 2.12: Design of program 2.3

2.   Place a timer control anywhere on the form. It appears in the pane at the bottom part of the Form design window. Set its Name to **tmrTime**. Set its Enabled Property to **True** and its Interval property to **1000** so that the Tick event is called every second.

3.   Double-click the timer to bring up the code template for its Tick event. Add the line of code that follows. This uses the Visual Basic **TimeString** property which returns the system time as hh:mm:ss in a 24-hour format.

```
Private Sub tmrTime_Tick(...) Handles tmrTime.Tick
    lblTime.Text = TimeString          'display current time in the label
End Sub
```

4. Run the program. You can't see the timer but the time should 'tick' away to the nearest second.

End of Program 2.3

The Scroll Bars

The Toolbox has a **horizontal scroll bar** and a **vertical scroll bar**. They are identical except for their orientation on a form. They are used to increase or decrease a value. They have starting and finishing values, represented by the two ends of the scroll bar, and either all the values in between or values at set intervals. A scroll box is moved between the two ends to set the value.

Scroll bars have no important methods but the most useful properties and events are:

Properties

Maximum The highest value, represented by the right side of a horizontal scroll bar or the bottom of a vertical scroll bar.

Minimum The lowest value.

Value The number represented by the current position of the scroll box – between Minimum and Maximum

Events

Scroll This is triggered as the user moves the scroll box. This is the scroll bar's default event.

PROGRAM 2.4 *Changing a form's colour using scroll bars*

Specification Use three horizontal scroll bars so that the form's colour changes as the user moves their scroll boxes.

To understand how this program works you need to understand the Visual Basic .NET function **RGB** (which stands for **R**ed, **G**reen, **B**lue). A function returns one item of data, in this case a number representing the colour required. The function provides a colour by mixing proportions of the three primary colours red, green and blue. Each of the three colours can have a value from 0 to 255. So the code

```
form 1's Backcolor = RGB(255, 0, 0)       'max red, no green, no blue
form 2's BackColor = RGB(0, 255, 0)       'max green, no red, no blue
form 3's BackColor = RGB(125, 125, 125)   'equal mixtures
```

would set the form 1's BackColor property to red and form 2's BackColor to green. Form 3 gets equal amounts of the three colours to produce a grey. The three numbers given to the function are called **arguments** or **parameters**.

1. Open a new project and set the form's Text property to **Change the form's colour**.

2. Place three labels and three horizontal scroll bars from the toolbox onto the form as shown in figure 2.13.

3. Change the Text properties of the labels to **Red**, **Green**, and **Blue** as appropriate.

4. Name the scroll bars **hsbRed**, **hsbGreen** and **hsbBlue**.

5. As the default **Minimum** property of a scroll bar is 0 leave this alone. Set the **Maximum** property of the scroll bars to **255**. To set all three at once select one of them, and with the Shift key pressed down select the other two. When you have two or more controls selected the Properties window lists those properties that the controls have in common.

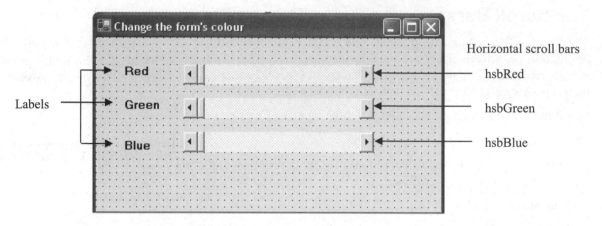

Figure 2.13: Design of program 2.4

6. Double-click the red scroll bar to bring up its default Scroll event code template. Type in the code to set the form's colour as follows:

Me refers to the form

ColorTranslator.FromOle is a method belong to System.Drawing

Underscore character to break a single line of code into two lines (must have at least one space before it)

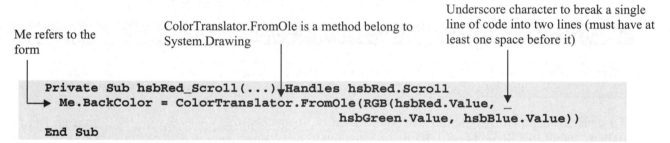

```
Private Sub hsbRed_Scroll(...) Handles hsbRed.Scroll
    Me.BackColor = ColorTranslator.FromOle(RGB(hsbRed.Value, _
                                hsbGreen.Value, hsbBlue.Value))
End Sub
```

There are four things to say about this code:

- You can split one line of code over two or more lines by using the underscore character. You do not have to use it in the example though; it is there because the line will not fit across the page in this book.

- Visual Basic .NET will not let you refer to the form by name (Form1). You must use the word Me instead.

- If you click the + button next to References in the Solution Explorer you will see one of the listed items is System.Drawing. This is part of Visual Basic .NET that handles graphics (including colouring). **ColorTranslator.FromOle** is one of its methods. This method must be given a number which it translates into the colour required.

- The number given to ColorTranslator.FromOle is supplied by the RGB function. The three parameters passed to RGB are the numbers (from 0 to 255) stored in the Value property of each of the scroll bars.

7. Double-click the green scroll bar to bring up its default Scroll event code template. Type in the same code as you entered for the red scroll bar's Scroll event in step 6.

8. Repeat step 7 for the blue scroll bar.

9. Run the program and as you move the scroll boxes the form's colour will change. Because each scroll bar has 256 possible values you can set the form to 256 x 256 x 256 = 16,777,216 colours!

One small drawback when you run the program is that when you set the form to a dark colour the labels may not be visible. Two ways round this are to use text boxes instead, or to reset the ForeColor property of the labels as the colour of the form changes (you need to understand the If statement covered in Chapter 6 for this).

This program will be used again in Program 9.1.

End of Program 2.4

Summary of key concepts

- The **text box** is used for entering and displaying data.

- The **list box** and **combo box** are used for displaying a list of items from which the user can select an item. With a combo box you can edit the items at run-time.

- Two or more **radio button**s allow the user to select an option. If the radio buttons are not grouped on a **group box** only one button on the form can be selected at once. When radio buttons are grouped on group boxes one button can be selected from each group. The **Checked** property holds True if the button is selected and False otherwise.

- Any number of **check box**es can be selected at the same time. The **Checked** property holds True if the check box is selected and False otherwise.

- A **group box** is often used to hold groups of radio buttons or check boxes. If a group box is moved or made invisible, then all its controls move or become invisible.

- A **timer** has a Tick event that is called after an elapse of time equivalent to its **Interval** property value. The **Enabled** property of the timer must be True for the Tick event to be called. An Interval value of 1000 represents 1000 milliseconds or 1 second.

- A Visual Basic .NET **function** returns a value. Some functions require **arguments** or **parameters** to be passed to them. The **RGB** function, which can be used to set the colour of an object, requires three numbers to be passed to it.

Take it from here...

1. The list box has a sister control called a **checked list box**. Find out how this differs from the ordinary list box.

2. How does the **Items.Remove** method of list and combo boxes differ from the **Items.RemoveAt** method?

3. The **DropDownStyle** property of the combo box has three settings. Experiment using each of these.

4. The **Panel** control can also be used to group controls such as radio buttons and check boxes. Find out how it differs from the group box control.

5. The **Appearance** property of the radio button has two settings. The default is Normal, which you used in Program 2.3. Find out how the other setting behaves.

6. Investigate the **SmallChange** and **LargeChange** properties of scroll bars.

7. Investigate the following controls on the toolbox – **TabControl**, **DateTimePicker**, **NumericUpDown**, **TrackBar** and **ProgressBar**.

8. The RGB function has a simpler sister function called **QBColor**. Investigate this function.

Questions on the Programs

Program 2.1

***1**. In Program 2.1 you could only select one item from the list box. The **SelectionMode** property allows you to select more than one. It has two types of multi-selection. Try out both types.

**2. Add labels below the list box to display the number of countries currently in the list box and the name of the country currently selected.

Program 2.2

***1**. Add another label below the Age group box to indicate which of the radio buttons is currently selected.

***2**. Make the Age group box (and the label in question 1 above if you did this question) invisible when the program runs. When the user first selects a gender option make the group box (and label) appear.

Program 2.3

***1**. Change the Enabled property of the Timer to **False** so that the time is not displayed when the program starts. Add two buttons. Clicking one of these should start the timer (and therefore start displaying the time). Clicking the other should stop the timer.

Program 2.4

***1**. To the right of each scroll bar place a label to display the current position of the bar's scroll box (i.e. a value from 0 to 255).

***2**. To see the difference between the Scroll and Change events change the first line of **hsbRed**'s Scroll event so that it is a Change event. Run the program and move the scroll box in this scroll bar.

End of chapter exercises

***1**. Use a vertical scroll bar to simulate volume control on a radio. Use three radio buttons which will position the scroll box at one-third, half and two-thirds the volume when the relevant one is clicked. Figure 2.14 shows the program.

**2. Build a program using two list boxes as shown in figure 2.15. One of these, called lstEmployees, lists all the employees in a firm. The other, called lstExcursion, lists those employees taking part in the firm's annual outing. Populate lstEmployees at design time using its Items property. When the program runs the user can click a button to copy the selected name from lstEmployees to lstExcursion. A second button should let them delete a name from lstExcursion in case they have made a mistake. Display the number of people on the firm's excursion.

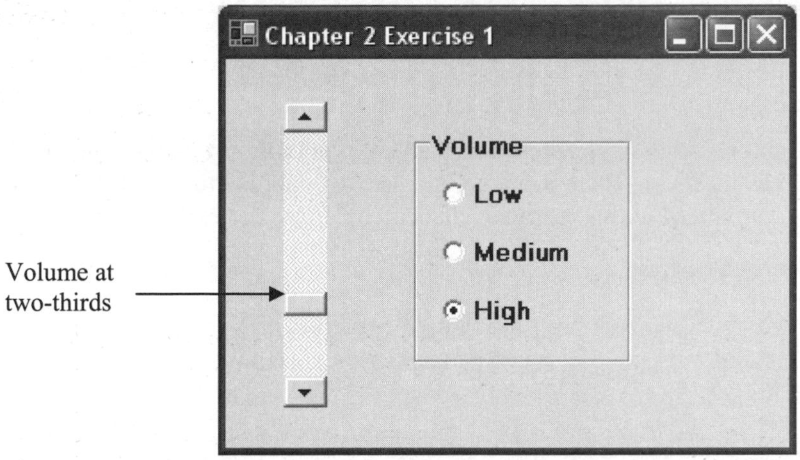

Figure 2.14: Exercise 1

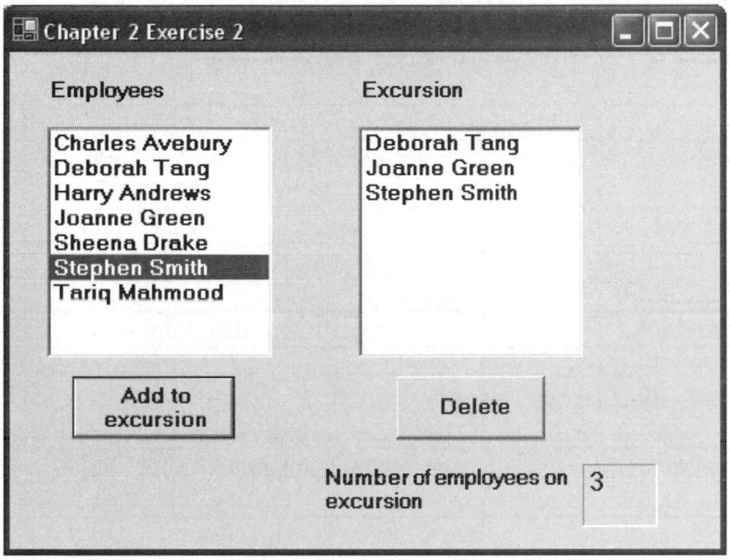

Figure 2.15: Exercise 2

**3. Build a program to implement the two list boxes shown in figure 2.1. Items can be moved between the two list boxes. At this stage you will only be able to move one item at a time rather than the two or more which this actual example allows. In figure 2.1 the lower two buttons, which move items from the right list box to the left one, are dimmed because there are no items to move in this direction. Find out which button property allows this and disable the appropriate button on your form. As soon as an item is moved into the right list box allow the button to be used. (You won't be able to enable it when the right list box becomes empty again without knowing about selection, covered in Chapter 6.)

Chapter 3 – Working with Data

Variables

When a program runs, any data that it uses must be stored in RAM. A **variable** is a name made up by the programmer to identify the address in RAM where a particular piece of data is stored. Our programs so far have managed to avoid using variables but this restricts what can be done. For example the code

```
lblNumber.Text = txtNumber.Text
```

displays in the label lblNumber whatever the user has typed into the textbox txtNumber. But to *store* what is in the textbox and use what is stored after the user has typed something else into the text box, we would need a variable.

Data Types

Every variable must be of a given **data type**. The main data types you will use in your Visual Basic .NET work are summarised in figure 3.1.

Data type	Used for storing...	Possible stored values	Storage required (bytes)
Short	Whole numbers, e.g. 8, 453	-32,768 to +32,767	2
Integer	Whole numbers	-2,147,483,648 to +2,147,483,647 (approx. –2 billion to +2 billion)	4
Long	Whole numbers	Very large range	8
Single	Numbers with decimal places, e.g. 4.76, 98.00	Very large range, from very small to very large	4
Double	Same as Single	Much larger range than Single	8
Decimal	Numbers with decimal places, especially currency values	Very large range	16
Char	A single character	Any Unicode character in the range 0 – 65,535	2
String	One or more characters	Any Unicode characters	2 per character
Date	Dates and time	Dates from 1 Jan. 100 to 31 Dec. 9999 Time from 0:00:00 to 23:59:59	8
Boolean	True or false values	True, False	2

Figure 3.1: Summary of the main data types

Declaring variables

To declare a variable means to tell Visual Basic two things about it:

- Its name or **identifier**.
- Its **data type**.

The Dim statement

Use the keywords **Dim** and **As** when you declare a variable. The code below declares three variables of different data types.

```
Dim Number As Integer
Dim Payment As Decimal
Dim DateOfPayment As Date
```

Note:

- Always use meaningful identifiers. The three variables could have been declared as A, B and C but these would tell you nothing about what they are used for storing.
- Identifiers cannot have spaces. When you use two or more words you could join each by an underscore, e.g. date_of_payment, or you could omit the underscores and make each start with an upper-case letter, e.g. DateOfPayment. In this book underscores are not used and single-word variable identifiers will begin with an upper-case letter (except when naming controls with their prefix).

You can declare more than one variable of the same data type in the same line of code. For example

```
Dim FirstNumber, SecondNumber, ThirdNumber As Integer
```

declares three Integer variables. Each one is separated by a comma.

Option Explicit and Option Strict

Although you are allowed to use variables in your code without declaring them first, a good rule of programming is **declare variables before using them**. In Visual Basic .NET you do this by setting the **Option Explicit** statement to **On**. In earlier versions its default value was Off and you had to set it to On for a given program by writing *Option Explicit* as the first line of code, or set it for all programs through the **Tools/Options** menu. In Visual Basic .NET its default value is On so you do not need to do anything. However should you wish to set it to Off just write *Option Explicit Off* as the first line of code. You have to do this for each program; you cannot set it through **Tools/Options** for all programs.

Suppose you used the three-line declaration at the top of this page with the default Option Explicit On, and later assigned the following values to your variables:

```
Number = 24             'programmer assigns value to variable
Payment = txtPay.Text   'value assigned from user input
Name = txtCustomer.Text 'value assigned from user input
```

The variable *Name* has not been declared and an error would be reported when you try to run the program.

Option Strict is a new feature of Visual Basic .NET. Look at the following code:

```
Dim Number As Integer
Number = txtNumber.Text   'assign to Number what the user types
                          'into the text box txtNumber
```

Whatever number the user types into the text box is stored in its Text property as text. For example the number 35 is stored as *character* 3 followed by character 5. The code tries to store this in the Integer variable *Number*. With Option Strict set to On this data conversion (from text to Integer in this case) is not allowed. When set to Off it is allowed. Although some consider it good programming practice to convert data types rather than rely on automatic conversion, **in this book the program examples assumes that Option Strict is Off unless the program states it is On**. Program 3.4 is the only one in the book where it is set to On, to show you how to carry out data conversions. In the example just used above you would use the CInt function (meaning **C**onvert to **Int**eger) to store the contents of the text box in the Integer variable Number:

```
Dim Number As Integer
Number = CInt(txtNumber.Text)
```

Option Strict's default setting is Off so you do not need to do anything in your code to use this setting.

PROGRAM 3.1   *Add two numbers*

Specification   Allow the user to enter two numbers and display their sum.

You could get input from the user using two text boxes, but this program will introduce you to another method of getting simple input, the **input box**. Figure 3.1 shows the output from the program, displayed in the label lblTotal.

1.   Open a new project and get to its Code window either by clicking the **Form1.vb** page tab or the **View Code** button in the Solution Explorer window.

2.   Place two labels on the form as shown in figure 3.2. Set the Text property of the left one to **The sum of the two numbers is** and set the right one to blank. In figure 3.1 both labels have their BorderStyle property set to Fixed3D, but this is really so that you can see them more easily in the figure. Name the right label **lblTotal**.

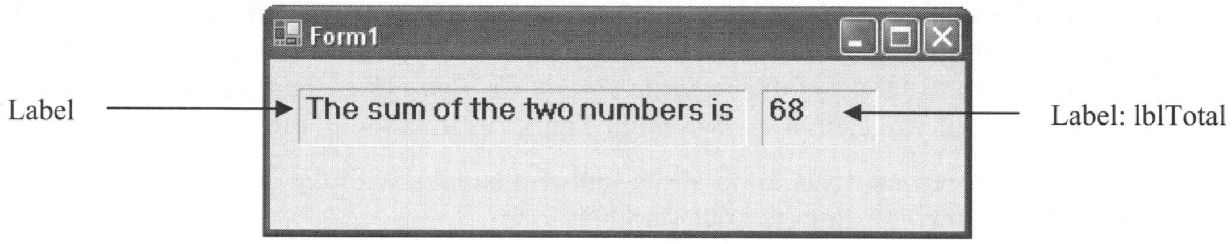

Figure 3.2: Output from Program 3.1

3.   We need three variables, two to store the numbers entered by the user and a third to store their sum. Declare them below the section *Windows Form Designer generated code* as in figure 3.3. The Short data type is used, which can stores values from -32768 to +32,767 (see figure 3.1).

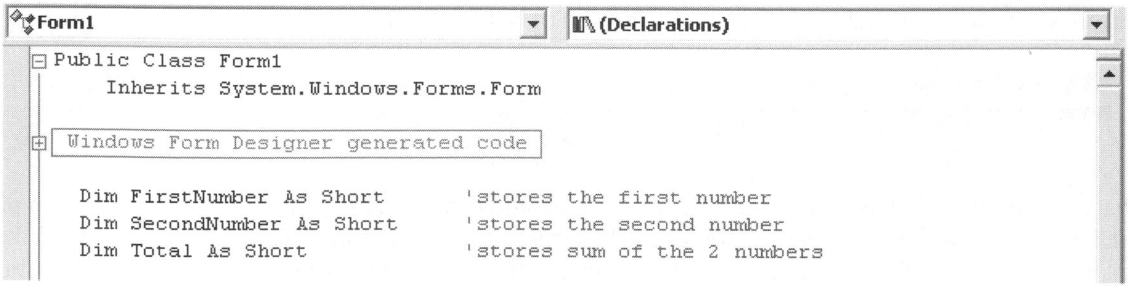

Figure 3.3: Declaring the three variables

4. Click the **Form1.vb[Design]*** page tab or the **View Design** button in the Solution Explorer to get to the form in design view. Double-click anywhere on the form to bring up its default Load event code template. Type in the code below:

```
Private Sub Form1_Load(...) Handles MyBase.Load
    FirstNumber = InputBox("Enter your first number")
    SecondNumber = InputBox("Enter your second number")
    Total = FirstNumber + SecondNumber
    lblTotal.Text = Total
End Sub
```

Note:

- The words in brackets after InputBox will be displayed in the input box.
- Whatever the user types into an input box is assigned directly to a variable. For example the number the user enters into the first input box is stored in *FirstNumber*.
- FirstNumber + SecondNumber adds the contents of the two variables (and not their names!)

5. Run the program. The input box below will appear first (figure 3.4). Type in a small number and click **OK**. Another input box appears asking for the second number. Type in another small number, click **OK** and you will then get the sum of the two numbers displayed in the label.

Figure 3.4: The first input box

6. Run the program again and this time enter a number that is too big for FirstNumber to hold (any number over 32767), a situation called **overflow**. You will get a run-time error message as in figure 3.5. Click **Break** and you'll be taken back to the code, with the line that caused the error highlighted in green.

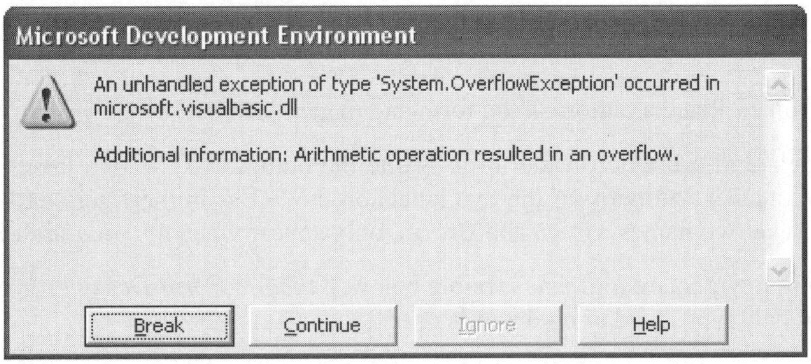

Figure 3.5: The run-time error message indicating overflow

7. You are in what is called debug mode. Try deleting some of the code and you will not be able to. Debug mode does not allow it. Select **Debug/Stop Debugging** from the menu. In the Output window at the bottom there is the message that *Arithmetic operation resulted in an overflow.*

8. Change the data type of each of the three variables from Short to **Integer**. Integers can hold much larger numbers (see figure 3.1). Run the program again using numbers too large for Short but within the Integer range.

> *end of Program 3.1*

Scope of variables

The **scope** of a variable refers to the part of the program that can use it. There are two main types of scope:

- **global**
- **local**

Global scope

A form variable with global scope can be used anywhere on the form, i.e. in any of its event procedures. In program 3.1 the variables were declared outside the single (Form_Load) event and this gives them global scope throughout Form1. The code inside the form's Load event used them, and so could code in any other event procedure we might have on Form1. If the program has more than one form then all the forms can reference the global variables declared on any form.

Local scope

Local variables are declared inside an event procedure and can be used only by code inside that procedure. In program 3.1 we could have declared the variables inside the form's Load event instead of outside. A good rule is **always declare variables with as narrow a scope as possible**. It will lead to fewer errors.

It is possible to give a global variable and a local variable the same identifier (name). Program 3.2 shows what happens in this situation.

PROGRAM 3.2   *Illustrating global and local scope*

Specification   Demonstrate the difference between a global variable and a local variable

1. Open a new project. Place a button on the form and name it **btnOK**.

2. Place four labels and a button on the form. Name the button and the two labels on the right as in figure 3.6. Set the Text property of the two labels on the left as in the figure and for the two on the right to blank. The two names, Green and Brown, only appear when the program runs.

3. In the Code window declare a global variable below *Windows Form Designer generated code*. This is of the String data type, used to hold words or text.

```
Dim Surname As String          'declare global variable
```

4. In the form's Load event procedure make sure the code is as follows:

```
Private Sub Form_Load(...) Handles MyBase.Load
  Surname = "Green"              'Store Green in the global variable
  lblGlobal.Text = Surname       'and display it in label lblGlobal
End Sub
```

5. In the Click event procedure of the button declare a local variable, using the same identifier as the global one, and display its contents:

```
Private Sub btnOK_Click(...) Handles btnOK.Click
  Dim Surname As String          'Declare local variable
  Surname = "Brown"              'Store Brown in it
  lblLocal.Text = Surname        'and display this in label lblLocal
End Sub
```

6. Run the program. The name 'Green' is displayed in the upper label since the global variable is being accessed by the form's Load event. Click the button and 'Brown' is displayed in the lower label since the local variable is now being used (figure 3.6).

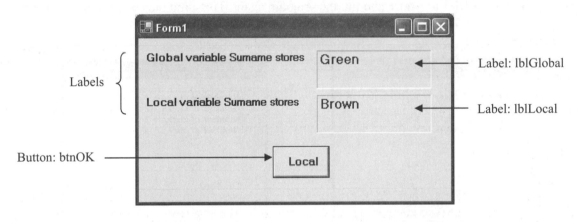

Figure 3.6: Output from Program 3.2

end of Program 3.2

Static variables

Variables no longer exist when they go out of scope. A global variable ceases to exist when the form is closed and a local variable ceases when its event procedure has finished. Sometimes you need to keep the value stored in a local variable until the next time the event in which it is declared is called. You need to declare the local variable as **static** as the next program shows.

PROGRAM 3.3   *Using a static variable*

Specification	Demonstrate the use of a static variable

1. Open a new project. Place a button on the form and name it **btnOK**.

2. Place a list box on the form and name it **lstOutput**.

3. Make sure the button's Click event code is as follows:

```
Private Sub btnOK_Click(...) Handles btnOK.Click
   Dim Number As Integer                         'declare local variable
   Number = Number + 1                           'add 1 to Number
   lstOutput.Items.Add("Number of clicks = " & Number) 'display number
                                                 'of clicks in the list box
End Sub
```

Look carefully at what is displayed in the list box through the **Items.Add** method. **Number of clicks =** is inside quotation marks and this text is output directly. **Number** is a variable and so what it stores it output. The two parts are joined or **concatenated** to form a continuous display by the concatenation operator **&**.

4. Run the program and click the button a few times. The display will keep saying you have only clicked the button once (figure 3.7 left). Between each click Number ceases to exist and its contents are lost. Each time it is created again Visual Basic sets its default value to 0 and the code **Number = Number + 1** adds 1 to it.

5. Change the word **Dim** to **Static** and run the program again. This time the correct number of clicks is displayed (figure 3.7 right). The value of Number is not lost between clicks.

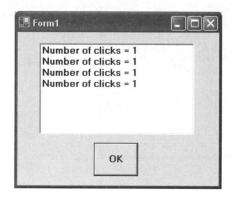 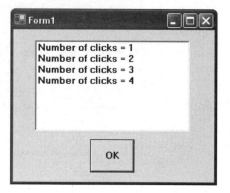

Figure 3.7: Program 3.3

end of Program 3.3

Constants

You can store a new value in a variable whenever this is appropriate. In program 3.3 the value of Number increased by 1 each time the user clicked the button. Instead of a variable use a **constant** when

* the user does not provide the value, and
* you don't want the value to change.

For example if the basic tax rate is 25p in the pound then you could declare it as a constant as follows. You must assign it a value as part of the declaration.

```
Const TaxRate = 0.25            'use = sign when declaring a constant
Const TaxRate As Single = 0.25  'if Option Strict is on you must also
                                'state its data type
```

If you try to assign to TaxRate another value such as 0.28 later in the program, an error results.

Arithmetic operations on data

Arithmetic can be done with variables belonging to all the data types listed at the start of this chapter except Char and String.

Types of operation

There are 8 of these, as listed in figure 3.8.

Operator	Visual Basic	Order of precedence
Addition	+	6=
Subtraction	-	6=
Multiplication	*	3=
Division	/	3=
Integer division	\	4
Modulus	Mod	5
Negation	-	2
Exponentiation	^	1

Figure 3.8: The arithmetic operators

The program below would produce the output shown in figure 3.9:

```
Private Sub Form_Load(...) Handles MyBase.Load
  Const A = 6
  Const B = 4
  lstOutput.Items.Add("A + B = " & A + B)
  lstOutput.Items.Add("A - B = " & A - B)
  lstOutput.Items.Add("A x B = " & A * B)
  lstOutput.Items.Add("A / B = " & A / B)
  lstOutput.Items.Add("A \ B = " & A \ B)
  lstOutput.Items.Add("A modulus B = " & A Mod B)
  lstOutput.Items.Add("A to the power B = " & A ^ B)
End Sub
```

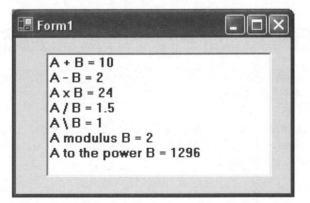

Figure 3.9

37

Note the following:

- Ordinary division (/) produces a number with a decimal place.
- Integer division (\) produces a whole number. The decimal part is removed.
- Modulus gives the remainder after the first number is divided by the second number, e.g. 12 Mod 5 = 2, 6 Mod 6 = 0, 6 Mod 8 = 6.

Order of precedence

This is shown in figure 3.8. It tells us the order in which Visual Basic carries out the operations. Look at the following program and the output in figure 3.10.

```
Private Sub Form_Load(...) Handles MyBase.Load
   Const A = 10
   Const B = 4
   Const C = 6
   lstOutput.Items.Add("B + C * A = " & B + C * A)
   lstOutput.Items.Add("A / B * C / B = " & A / B * C / B)
   lstOutput.Items.Add("(A / B) * (C / B) = " & (A / B) * (C / B))
End Sub
```

In the first expression C * A is done first rather than B + C. In the second expression the three operations are done in the order written since division and multiplication have equal precedence. In the third expression the divisions are done before multiplication because of the brackets.

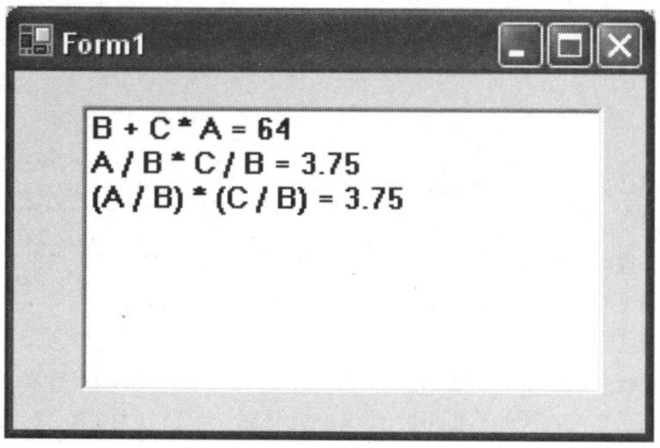

Figure 3.10

PROGRAM 3.4   *Calculating the average exam mark*

Specification   Allow the user to enter as many exam marks as they wish and display them in a list box. The program finishes when the user clicks a button to show the average mark

In this program we will set Option Strict to On (see page 31) to learn about data conversion. In addition to giving you practice with variables and calculations, this program will teach you more about how the interface of a form can behave at run-time.

1.   Open a new project and on the form place two labels, two text boxes, three buttons and a list box as shown in figure 3.11.

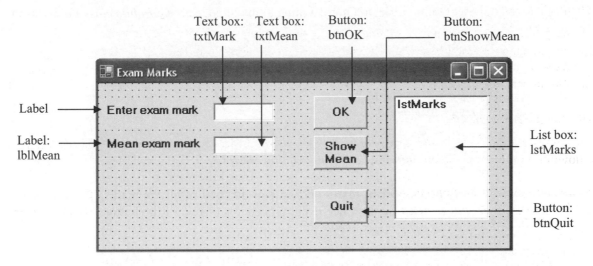

Figure 3.11: Design of program 3.4

2. Set the properties of these controls as listed in figure 3.12. Note:

- The **OK** button processes a mark but the user should not be able to click it until they have entered a mark. Setting its Enabled property to False does this. The same applies to the **Show Mean** button.

- Before the user enters a mark the text box (and label) to display the mean can be hidden. Setting their Visible property to False property does this.

Control	*Property*	*Property setting*
Form	Text	Exam marks
Label	Text	Enter exam mark
Label	Name Text Visible	lblMean Mean exam mark False
Text box	Name Text	txtMark Blank
Text box	Name Text Visible	txtMean Blank False
Button	Name Text Enabled	btnOK OK False
Button	Name Text Enabled	btnShowMean Show Mean False
Button	Name Text	btnQuit Quit
List box	Name	lstMarks

Figure 3.12: Design-time property settings for the controls in program 3.4

3. In the Code window set Option Strict to On by writing a line of code above *Public class Form1* as in figure 3.13.

```
Form1                                        (Declarations)
    Option Strict On
 Public Class Form1
        Inherits System.Windows.Forms.Form
```

Figure 3.13: Setting Option Strict On

4. Two variables will hold the number of marks entered and the total of all the marks. These must be global because they will be used by the Click event procedures of two of the buttons. Declare them below *Windows Form Designer generated code*:

```
Dim Total As Short              'stores running total of marks
Dim NumberOfMarks As Short      'stores number of exam marks entered
```

5. Since these two variables store running totals **initialise** them to 0 in the form's Load event:

```
Private Sub Form_Load(...) Handles MyBase.Load
   Total = 0
   NumberOfMarks = 0
End Sub
```

Strictly speaking this is not necessary since Visual Basic initialises Integers to 0 when it creates them. It is a good practice to adopt, however, since you may wish to initialise numbers, or variables of other data types, to something other than 0.

When the OK button is clicked the following must happen:

- The **Show Mean** button must be enabled so the user can click it to find the mean.
- The exam mark entered by the user must be removed.
- The cursor must be positioned ready for the next exam mark.

6. Type in the code below for the Click event of the **btnOK** button. With **Option Strict** On you cannot store what the user types in txtMark directly into the variable Number because they are different data types (text/string and Integer). The **CInt** (meaning **C**onvert to **Int**eger) function is used to convert from String to Integer.

```
Private Sub btnOK_Click(...) Handles btnOK.Click
   Dim Number As Integer
   Number = CInt(txtMark.Text)       'read exam mark.Use CInt to convert
   lstMarks.Items.Add(Number)        'copy it to list box
   Total = Total + Number            'add it to running total of marks
   NumberOfMarks = NumberOfMarks + 1 'increase number of marks by 1
   btnShowMean.Enabled = True        'enable the Show Mean button
   txtMark.Text = ""                 'clear out the old exam mark
   txtMark.Focus()                   'place cursor ready for next mark
End Sub
```

7. When the **Show Mean** button is clicked the text box (and label) to display the mean must be made visible. If the user clicks the **OK** button again there will not be a number to process and a run-time error will result. We should disable it. So type the following into the Click event of btnShowMean:

```
Private Sub btnShowMean_Click(...) Handles btnShowMean.Click
   Dim Mean As Double                  'declare local variable
   Mean = Total / NumberOfMarks        'calculate mean mark and
   txtMean.Text = Mean                 'display it
   txtMean.Visible = True              'show text box which displays mean
   lblMean.Visible = True              'and show its label
   txtMark.Enabled = False             'disallow more marks to be entered
   btnOK.Enabled = False               'and disable OK button
End Sub
```

The variable *Mean* is likely to require decimal places and must be declared as Single or Double. With Option Strict On it must be Double.

8. When the **Quit** button is clicked the program should close. In the Click event procedure for btnQuit type in:

```
Private Sub btnQuit_Click(...) Handles btnQuit.Click
   Me.Close()                          'removes form from memory
End Sub
```

Recall from page 26 that you cannot refer to the form by name (Form1). You must use **Me**.

9. Run the program and enter an exam mark. There's a problem – the OK button is disabled so the mark cannot be processed! We disabled it at design time so that the user could not accidentally click it before a mark had been entered. The **TextChanged** event for the text box where a mark is entered can handle this. This event occurs as soon as the first digit is typed in.

10. To get the code template for txtMark's TextChanged event select **txtMark** from the Class Name combo box (see figure 2.5) and then select **TextChanged** from the Method Name combo box. Enter the single line of code to enable the OK button:

```
Private Sub txtMark_TextChanged(...) Handles txtMark.TextChanged
   btnOK.Enabled = True
End Sub
```

11. Run the program. Enter a few marks and then click the **Show Mean** button. When the mean mark is displayed the OK button is disabled, so all you can do is click Quit.

end of Program 3.4

Summary of key concepts

- A **variable** is a name made up by the programmer to identify the address in RAM where a particular piece of data is stored.

- Every variable must be of a particular **data type**. The main data types are **Short**, **Integer** and **Long** (for storing whole numbers), **Single**, **Double** (both decimal numbers), **Decimal** (monetary values or numbers with a fixed number of decimal places), **Char** (a single character), **String** (text), **Date** (date and time) and **Boolean** (true or false).

- To declare a variable use the syntax **Dim** *identifier* **As** *data type,* e.g. Dim Number As Integer. You can declare two or more variables of the same data type using one line of code.

- When **Option Explicit** is **On** (the default value) you must declare variables before using them. When **Option Strict** is **Off** (the default value) Visual Basic will convert between data types where possible.

- To convert a string to an Integer use the **CInt** function.

- **Overflow** is caused by trying to store a number that is too large for its data type. It will result in a run-time error.

- The **scope** of a variable refers to the part of the program that can use it. **Global** variables on a form can be used by all procedures on a form. **Local** variables are declared inside a procedure and can only be used by code within that procedure.

- A good rule is to always declare variables with as narrow a scope as possible.

- Form global variables exist until the form closes. Local variables exist until the procedure in which they are declared finishes. However a **Static** local variable keeps its contents between calls to the procedure in which it is declared.

- A **constant** holds a value that cannot be changed during the program. The declaration syntax is **Const** *identifier = value,* e.g. Const Number = 20 if Option Strict is Off. If it is On you must also declare its data type, e.g. Const Number As Integer = 20.

- **Arithmetic operators** have an order of precedence. You can change the order by using brackets.

Take it from here...

1. Two data types not covered in this chapter are **Byte** and **Object**. Investigate these.

2. You could replace the word Dim when declaring a form's global variable with **Public** or **Private**. Find out how these would affect the variable's scope.

3. Visual Basic .NET distinguishes between **widening** and **narrowing** conversions when converting from one data type to another. Find out what these terms mean.

4. Visual Basic .NET has 12 functions for converting from one data type to another, including CInt that was covered in this chapter. Investigate these.

Questions on the Programs

Program 3.1

*1. Change the program to add three numbers rather than two.

Program 3.3

*1. Using your knowledge of scope, you may deduce that there is another way of displaying the correct number of times the user has clicked the button without using the keyword Static. Change the code to do this.

Program 3.4

*1. If the user enters a lot of exam marks it can be tiresome having to click the **OK** button after each one. It would be easier to press **Enter** instead. In the Properties window set one of the button's properties to allow this.

2. The user can enter one set of exam marks, find their average and then the program ends. Change it so that the user can enter as many sets of marks as they wish. Add a **Clear button to begin the new set of marks. Display only the current set of marks in the list box.

End of chapter exercises

*1. Allow the user to enter a series of numbers in a text box (like the exam marks in program 3.4). Clicking a button between numbers should display their running total. Use a static variable for the running total.

**2. Figure 3.14 shows the program in action. Allow the user to enter the numeric values for A, B and C. They can then click one of three radio buttons to display the result of the selected calculation.

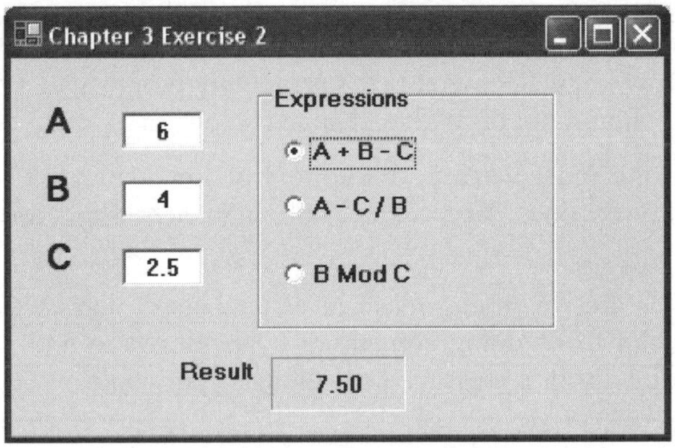

Figure 3.14: Exercise 2

**3. A motorist wishes to work out how many miles per gallon their car is doing. The motorist should enter three items of data – the car's mileage when the petrol tank was last filled, the number of gallons of petrol just put in to refill the tank, and the new mileage. Calculate the miles per gallon. Figure 3.15 shows the program.

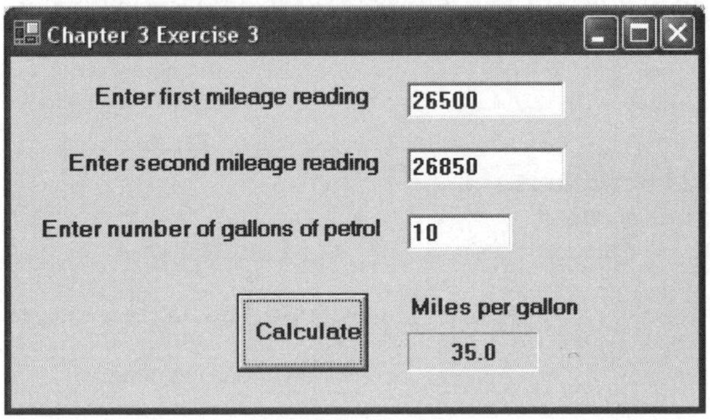

Figure 3.15: Exercise 3

Chapter 4 – Displaying and Formatting Output

Methods of displaying and formatting output

Earlier versions of Visual Basic had the very useful Print method which could be used to write output directly on a form. Visual Basic .NET does not support this but there are other ways of displaying output on the screen:

Label A label is useful when you need to display something short and simple, such as the result of adding some numbers, the current time or a text message of several words. Although you can display more than one line of output in a label, it is not a sensible means of displaying many lines because you cannot see any output that does not fit into it.

Text box A text box displays one line only, but if its MultiLine property is set to True, it can display two or more lines. Unlike a label you can view any hidden display by using the up and down arrow keys. Set a text box's ReadOnly property to True if you use it for output since the user should not be able to change its content.

List box A list box is the most versatile basic control for displaying output. Use its Items.Add method to add new lines. Vertical and horizontal scroll bars are provided automatically if needed.

Message box Message boxes are for giving users brief messages such as *Correct* or *Incorrect*, or to give them a choice of doing something by having Yes and No buttons. You can also display text directly in a message box, though you would not normally use it to display a lot of data.

Concatenating strings

Sometimes you need to **concatenate** or join two or more pieces of data together and output them as a single longer string. Use the ampersand or concatenation operator **&**. You met this in Program 3.3. The code below concatenates two names into one. It uses three ampersands to concatenate four items of data, two **literal** strings (in quotation marks) and two variables. The third item of data, the " ", is a single space to separate the two parts of the name. If FirstName stores Joe and Surname stores Brown then the output would be *Your name is Joe Brown.*

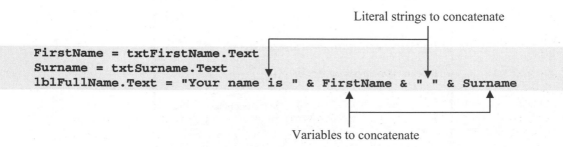

Literal strings to concatenate

```
FirstName = txtFirstName.Text
Surname = txtSurname.Text
lblFullName.Text = "Your name is " & FirstName & " " & Surname
```

Variables to concatenate

PROGRAM 4.1 *Using a label, text box and message box for display*

Specification Ask the user to enter two numbers. Display the result of adding, subtracting, multiplying and dividing the numbers in a label, a text box and a message box.

Figure 4.1 shows the program. Although the display in the label and text box looks identical, you cannot click inside the label. In the text box you can scroll through the data using the up and down arrow keys, although in this example it is not necessary since all the data is displayed.

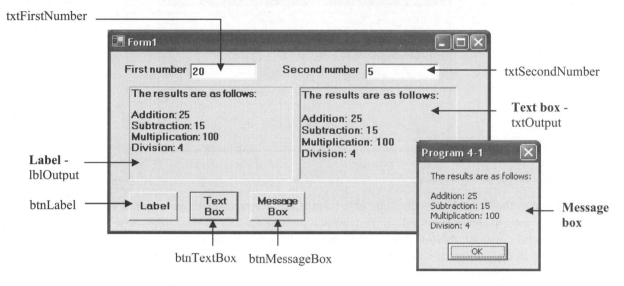

Figure 4.1: Displaying output in a label, a text box and a message box

1. Open a new project and build the form using figure 4.1. Set the MultiLine and ReadOnly properties of txtOutput to **True**. Set the BorderStyle property of lblOutput to **Fixed3D**. Note that you cannot design a message box; it is produced only through code.

2. Declare the three global variables needed, two for the numbers and one to store the concatenated string to display. Recall that these are declared just below the section *Windows Form Designer generated code.*

```
Dim FirstNum, SecondNum As Single
Dim Message As String
```

3. The Label button's Click event stores the numbers and concatenates and displays the output string:

```
Private Sub btnLabel_Click(...) Handles btnLabel.Click
  FirstNum = txtFirstNumber.Text               'store the 2 numbers
  SecondNum = txtSecondNumber.Text
  Message = "The results are as follows:"       'concatenate the string
  Message = Message & "Addition: " & FirstNum + SecondNum
  Message = Message & "Subtraction: " & FirstNum - SecondNum
  Message = Message & "Multiplication: " & FirstNum * SecondNum
  Message = Message & "Division: " & FirstNum / SecondNum
  lblOutput.Text = Message                      'display the string
End Sub
```

The output string is built up over 5 lines of code. The code **Message = Message &** means *concatenate to Message whatever follows the ampersand sign.* Alternatively these lines could have been written as one long line of code containing the eight ampersands.

4. Run the program. Enter two numbers and click the Label button. The output should look something like that in figure 4.2. The exact layout will depend on whether you have changed the Font property of the label and the label's width. Clearly it is not displayed in neat rows, as figure 4.1 shows.

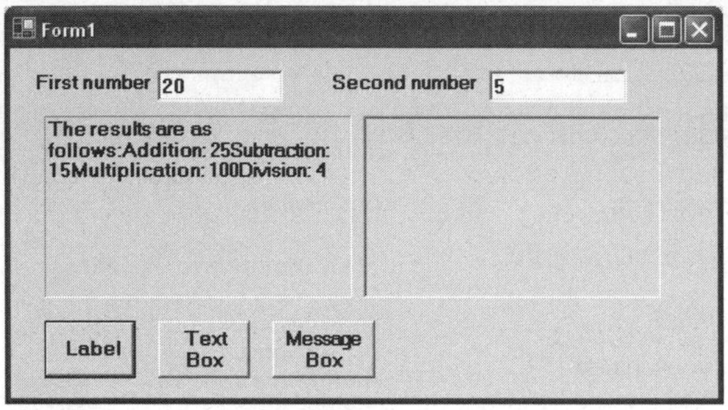

Figure 4.2

5. To achieve the right display use one of Visual Basic's **constants**. The constant **vbCrLf** combines a carriage return and a linefeed so that output continues on the next line. You can use the more meaningful constant **vbNewLine** for the same job. We need one of these constants at the end of each of the addition, subtraction and multiplication lines. We need two at the end of the heading line, *The results are as follows*, so that a blank line is produced between the heading and the rest of the output.

```
Message = "The results are as follows:" & vbNewLine & vbNewLine
Message = Message & "Addition: " & FirstNum + SecondNum & vbNewLine
Message = Message & "Subtraction: " & FirstNum – SecondNum & vbCrLf
Message = Message & "Multiplication: " & FirstNum * SecondNum & vbCrLf
Message = Message & "Division: " & FirstNum / SecondNum
```

6. Run the program again and check that the output is like that in figure 4.1.

7. Copy the code for the Label button's click event into the Text button's click event but change the last line so that output is displayed in the text box rather than the label.

8. We could use the same code again for the Message Box button. However let's learn one or two other constants that will work in message boxes but not in labels or text boxes, and learn another way of building up the concatenated string. Write the code below in this button's Click event.

```
Private Sub btnMessageBox_Click(...) Handles btnMessageBox.Click
  FirstNum = txtFirstNum.Text
  SecondNum = txtSecondNum.Text
  Message = "The results are as follows:" & vbCr & vbCr
  Message += "Addition: " & FirstNum + SecondNum & vbLf
  Message += "Subtraction: " & FirstNum - SecondNum & Chr(13)
  Message += "Multiplication: " & FirstNum * SecondNum & Chr(10)
  Message += "Division: " & FirstNum / SecondNum
  MsgBox(Message)
End Sub
```

Note:

- The constant **vbCr** means carriage return and **vbLf** means linefeed. In a message box both have the same effect as vbNewLine. **Chr(13)** is the same as vbCr and **Chr(10)** is the same as vbLf. Chr is a function which returns the character equivalent to the number in brackets after it. Chr(65), for example, returns 'A'. Chr(10) returns the linefeed character.

- **Message +=** is used several times instead of **Message = Message &**.as in step 5. This means *add or concatenate to Message whatever follows +=*. You could use the same construction to add one to a counter. For example in Program 3.3, which displays the number of times you click a button, you could have written Number += 1 instead of Number = Number + 1.

- To produce a message box call the **MsgBox** function with the item to be output in brackets after it. If the item is a literal string enclose it in quotation marks. An alternative is **MessageBox.Show** followed by the item in brackets. You can make a message box behave in many different ways by passing other data items inside the brackets. The *Take it from here...* section asks you about this.

9. Run the program and check that the output looks like that in figure 4.1. Then make the display label and text box only a centimetre or two in height and run it again. Confirm that you cannot see all the output in the label but you can scroll through the text box using the up and down arrow keys.

> **end of Program 4.1**

Displaying output in tables

Sometimes you may wish to display output as columns in a table like the example in figure 4.3. Although you can produce columns in labels, text boxes and message boxes, the list box is the best choice if you want to display a lot of data because scroll bars are provided if needed, as in figure 4.3.

Team	Played	Points
One Day Wonders	12	22
Uld Caledonians	12	21
Adventurers	11	21
Victors Forever	11	19
Live and Let Live	12	16
Champions All	10	14
Happy Hunters	11	14
Always Cheerful	11	13

Figure 4.3: Displaying tabular data in a list box

There are several ways of displaying data in a table. All methods need a fixed-width font such as Courier New so that each character has the same width. You need to work out how many characters to allocate to each column. Figure 4.4 shows the calculations used to produce the output in figure 4.3.

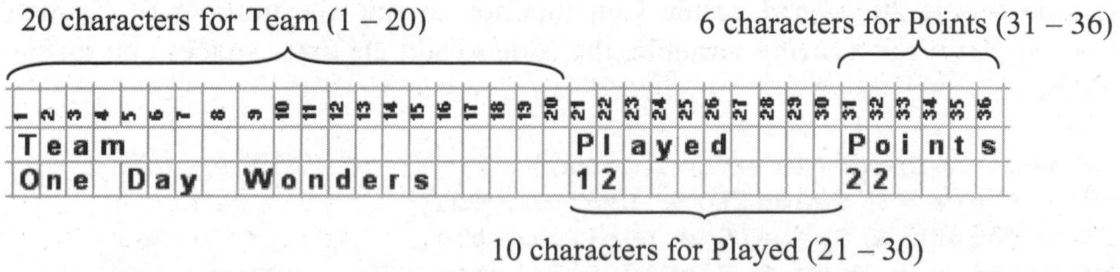

20 characters for Team (1 – 20)   6 characters for Points (31 – 36)

10 characters for Played (21 – 30)

Figure 4.4: Calculating the characters required for each column

Using String.Format

Technically **String.Format** is a method of Class String (Chapter 17 explains what a Class is). At this stage all you need to know is how to use it. To display the output in figure 4.3 you would declare a String variable as follows.

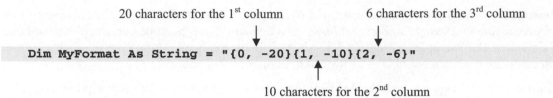

20 characters for the 1st column   6 characters for the 3rd column

```
Dim MyFormat As String = "{0, -20}{1, -10}{2, -6}"
```

10 characters for the 2nd column

Each column has a pair of curly brackets or braces and they are numbered 0, 1, 2 etc. The minus sign in front of the number of characters indicates that output should be left justified. If you omit the minus sign the output will be right justified.

To display the column titles in figure 4.3 you use String.Format and pass it both the format string declared above and the three items of data that will be matched on to the three parts of this string.

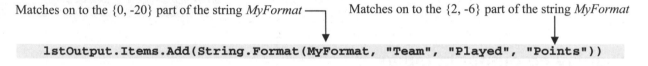

Matches on to the {0, -20} part of the string *MyFormat* ———   Matches on to the {2, -6} part of the string *MyFormat*

```
lstOutput.Items.Add(String.Format(MyFormat, "Team", "Played", "Points"))
```

Then assuming the variables *Team*, *Played* and *Points* hold the team name, number of games played and total points, you would display the details of a given team using the **Items.Add** method of the list box:

```
lstOutput.Items.Add(String.Format(MyFormat, Team, Played, Points))
```

Using the Space function

The **Space** function returns a string consisting of a specified number of spaces. For example the code below would produce the concatenated string *There are 10   spaces here*.

```
Message = "There are 10" & Space(10) & "spaces here"
```

In figure 4.4 the first team displayed, One Day Wonders, uses 15 of the 20 characters available for the Team column. We need to add 5 spaces to the string variable that stores the team name. 10 characters are allowed for the Played column. The team has played 12 games and used two of these characters, character *1* and character *2*, so 10 spaces must be added to this variable. The number of spaces to add can be calculated using the general expression

> Number of spaces to add = column width – number of characters used

For the team name this is 20 – 15. Use the **Len** function to find the number of characters in a string. Assuming *OneTeamDetails* is a String variable, the code to add the extra spaces and display the details of one team would be:

```
Team = Team & Space(20 - Len(Team))        'Add spaces to Team,
Played = Played & Space(10 - Len(Played))   'Played
Points = Points & Space(6 - Len(Points))    'and Points
OneTeamDetails = Team & Played & Points  'Concatenate the 3 items of data
lstOutput.Items.Add(OneTeamDetails)       'and display in list box
```

PROGRAM 4.2   *Tabular display in a list box*

Specification	Allow the user to enter the following details of the results of a running road race – competitor's number, name, club and time taken. Clicking a button should display these four items of data as a table in a list box.

The resulting display after entering the details of four runners can be seen in figure 4.5. The first line in the list box has left justified column headings. Each of the other lines displays the details of one runner.

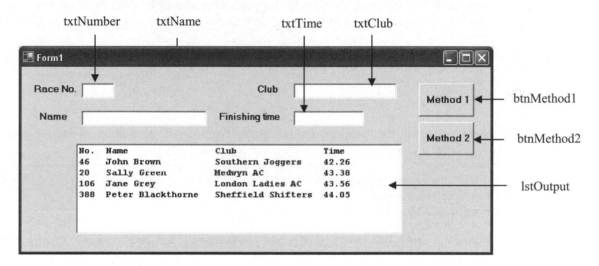

Figure 4.5: Program 4.2

Figure 4.6 shows the calculations made for the four columns in this program. The column headings and the details of the first runner displayed in figure 4.5 are used.

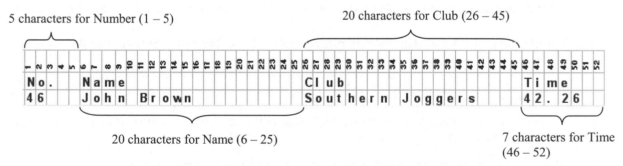

Figure 4.6: Calculating the column widths

1. Open a new project and design the form using figure 4.5. Set the Text properties of the four text boxes to blank. Set the Font property of the list box to **Courier New**.

Using String.Format

2. Below *Windows Form Designer generated* code declare a String variable to hold the format. This needs details of the columns inside four sets of braces (curly brackets).

```
Dim MyFormat As String = "{0,-5}{1,-20}{2,-20}{3,-7}"
```

3. Double-click anywhere on the form outside the controls to bring up its Load event template. When the program starts we want the column headings to be displayed as the first row in the list box:

```
lstOutput.Items.Add(String.Format(MyFormat,"No.","Name","Club","Time"))
```

4. In the Click event procedure for btnMethod1 declare local variables to hold the four items of data about a runner, and a further variable *OneRunnerDetails* to hold the concatenated details of the current runner. When the program runs the runner's time should be entered as minutes and seconds. For example 35.28 represents 35 minutes and 28 seconds and so the Single data type should be used.

```
Private Sub btnMethod1_Click(...) Handles btnMethod1.Click
   Dim Number, Name, Club, OneRunnerDetails As String
   Dim Time As Single
End Sub
```

5. Store the data items in the variables and use String.Format to display them. Write the code after the variable declarations in step 4.

```
Number = txtNumber.Text     'Store the 4 items of data about one runner
Name = txtName.Text
Club = txtClub.Text
Time = txtTime.Text
lstOutput.Items.Add(String.Format(MyFormat, Number, Name, Club, Time))
```

6. Clear the text boxes for details of the next runner and position the cursor for the first item of data:

```
txtNumber.Clear()          'Clear the 4 text boxes
txtName.Clear()
txtClub.Clear()
txtTime.Clear()
txtNumber.Focus()   'Position cursor for input of next runner's number
```

7. Run the program. Enter data for one runner and click the Method 1 button. The details should be displayed in columns.

The adding spaces method

8. In the Click event procedure for btnMethod2 declare the same five variables as in step 4 for the Click event of btnMethod1.

9. Store the data items in the variables. Write the first four lines of code in step 5.

10. Use the Space function to add the appropriate number of spaces to each of the first three items of data about the runner. Store and concatenate this data with the runner's time.

```
Number = Number & Space(5 - Len(Number))      'Add spaces to Number,
Name = Name & Space(20 - Len(Name))           'to Name
Club = Club & Space(20 - Len(Club))           'and to Club
OneRunnerDetails = Number & Name & Club & Time   'Concatenate with Time
```

11. Display the string in the list box:

```
lstOutput.Items.Add(OneRunnerDetails)      'Display in list box
```

12. Clear the text boxes and position the cursor. Use the same code as in step 6.

13. Run the program and check that this second method works.

end of Program 4.2

The Format function

So far we have looked at how to lay out the output. At a more detailed level you may wish to display individual items of data in a particular way. How many decimal places do you want, do you want a '£' symbol before your currency value and so on. The **Format** function is used for formatting numbers, currency, strings, dates and time. Give it two arguments:

- The expression to be formatted. This would usually be a numeric constant such as 45.86 or a variable.

- An indication, inside quotation marks, of how to format the expression. This could be a **named numeric format** or a **user-defined numeric format**.

The example below uses a variety of named and user-defined numeric formats and it produces the output shown in figure 4.7. If you wish to try this out put a list box on the form, name it lstOutput and type the code below in the form's Load event procedure.

```
Const Number = 52478.3296     'Declare a constant to hold the number
With lstOutput.Items
   .Add("Using named numeric formats")
   .Add("    General Number  " & Format(Number, "General Number"))
   .Add("    Fixed           " & Format(Number, "Fixed"))
   .Add("    Standard        " & Format(Number, "Standard"))
   .Add("    Percent         " & Format(0.175, "Percent"))
   .Add("    Currency        " & Format(Number, "Currency"))
   .Add("")
   .Add("Using user-defined numeric formats")
   .Add("    0               " & Format(Number, "0"))
   .Add("    0.00            " & Format(Number, "0.00"))
   .Add("    ###.00          " & Format(Number, "###.00"))
   .Add("    #,##0.0         " & Format(Number, "#,##0.0"))
   .Add("    ###.00          " & Format(Number, "###.00"))
   .Add("    £#,##0.00       " & Format(Number, "£#,##0.00"))
   .Add("    0.0%            " & Format(0.175, "0.0%"))
End With
```

There are two features to note about this code:

- It uses the **With...End With** structure for the 15 lines to add items to the list box. It a shorter alternative to writing lstOutput.Items.Add on each line.

- The tabular display (in figure 4.7) is achieved with spaces but without using the Space function. We used this function earlier because the number of spaces needed depended on the data input by the user. Here it is fixed by the programmer.

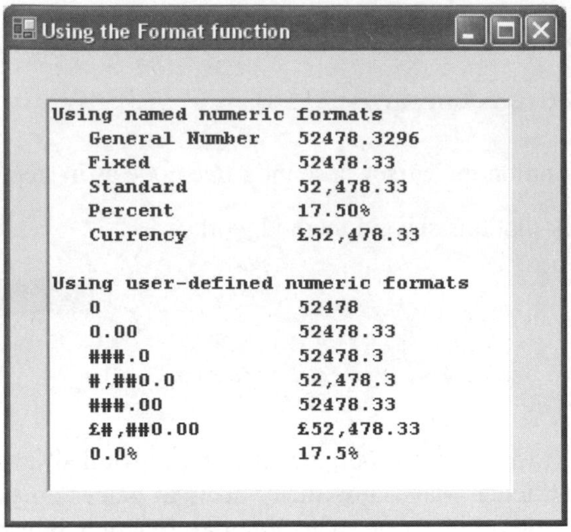

Figure 4.7

There are enough examples above for you to find or work out a format that covers most numeric outputs you are likely to require. Use them as a reference to return to when the need arises.

In program 3.4 if you had wished to output the average exam mark to one decimal place, you could not use any of the named formats as these output at least two decimal places. The third user-defined format above shows how to display one decimal place. So in the Click event for btnShowMean you would write:

```
txtMean.Text = Format(Mean, "0.0")
```

Summary of key concepts

- Labels, text boxes, list boxes and message boxes can all be used to display output. The most versatile is the list box.

- Joining strings together is called **concatenation**. Use the concatenation operator or ampersand (**&**).

- A **message box** can be displayed by calling the **MsgBox** function or the **Message.Show** method.

- A number of Visual Basic **constants** can be used for laying out displayed text. To output on a new line in a label, text box or a message box use **vbCrLf** or **vbNewLine**. A message box can also use **vbCr** and **vbLf** to do the same thing.

- Use a fixed-width font such as Courier New to produce a tabular display. Use **String.Format** or the **Space** function to produce the columns.

- The **Len** function returns the number of characters in a String variable.

- Use the **Format** function to display numbers and currency. Use a **named** or a **user-defined** format.

- To reduce the amount of code use **With…End With** when displaying a lot of items in a list box.

Take it from here…

1. There are three other functions for formatting numbers and currency – **FormatCurrency**, **FormatNumber** and **FormatPercent**. Investigate these.

2. There is an alternative concatenation operator to the ampersand – the plus sign (+). It only works in some situations. The following code would run properly (note that the last line has been commented out). If the last line is not commented out what happens when it runs? Explain the result.

```
Dim Number As Integer
Dim RoadName, Town As String
Number = 10
RoadName = "The High Street"
Town = "AnyTown"
lstOutput.Items.Add(Number & " " & RoadName & " " & Town)
lstOutput.Items.Add(RoadName + " " + Town)
'lstOutput.Items.Add(Number + " " + RoadName)
```

3. Investigate the **MsgBox** function and the **Message.Show** method for using message boxes. Although similar they are not the same.

Questions on the Programs

Program 4.2

****1.** Add a 5th item of data about each runner – their gender/age category (JM for junior male, JF for junior female, SM for senior male, SF for senior female, VM for veteran male and VF for veteran female). Display this between the Club and Time columns in the list box.

End of chapter exercises

***1.** Write a program using input boxes that asks the user to enter the first names and ages (whole numbers) of each of their two children. Display a message in a label or message box containing these names and their average age. For example if **Sally**, **Paul**, **13** and **10** had been entered into the input boxes then the message should be **Sally and Paul have an average age of 11.5 years**.

****2.** Write a program for a shop that hires products for one or more days. The user should enter 5 items of data about each hire transaction and these should then be displayed in a list box table as in figure 4.8. Input the transaction details through text boxes.

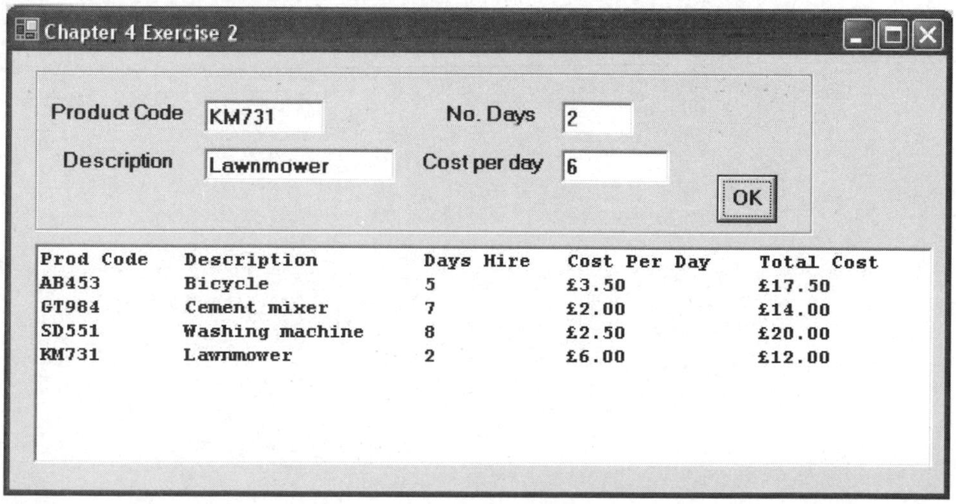
Chapter 4 Exercise 2
Product Code
KM731
No. Days
2
Description
Lawnmower
Cost per day
6
OK
Prod Code Description Days Hire Cost Per Day Total Cost
AB453 Bicycle 5 £3.50 £17.50
GT984 Cement mixer 7 £2.00 £14.00
SD551 Washing machine 8 £2.50 £20.00
KM731 Lawnmower 2 £6.00 £12.00

Figure 4.8: Exercise 2

***3.   Build a simple calculator as shown in figure 4.9. The user enters two numbers and then clicks one of the four arithmetic operators to display the result. The whole calculation is also displayed in the list box. Clicking the Clear button allows all this to be repeated. Since the calculator has no memory, to calculate 6 + 8 – 2 for example, the user would need to look in the list box or at the displayed result of 6 + 8 to find the first number (14) to enter for the next calculation.

In figure 4.9 the user has calculated the result of (14 + 2) x (8 - 10 / 5). First the part in the left brackets (14 + 2) has been calculated, then 10 / 5 in the right brackets (because division has precedence over subtraction). Then the result of 10 / 5 is subtracted from 8, and this result is finally multiplied by 6 (the result of the first calculation).

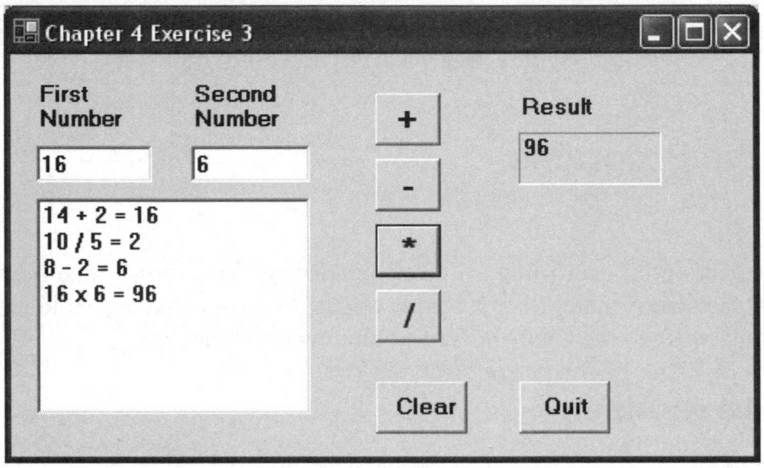

Figure 4.9: Exercise 3

Chapter 5 – Console Applications

What is a console application?

So far all the programs have had simple graphical user interfaces (GUIs) by using a form with one or more controls. These are called Windows applications but Visual Basic .NET offers a variety of other types. One of the simplest is a **console application**, an application that deals only in text. A console application runs in a command window, which was called the MS-DOS prompt in Windows 95/98 but in Windows NT/2000/XP is called the command prompt. Figure 5.1 shows an example. The user interacts with this program by entering data about the jackpot and the number of people sharing it. The program calculates the amount per person and displays it.

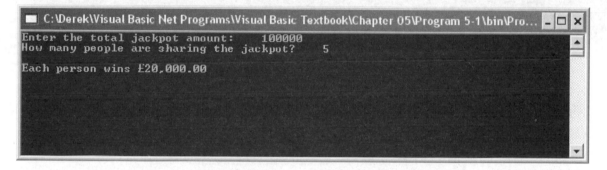

Figure 5.1: A console application

Why use console applications?

It is not that long ago that nearly all programming was done through a command interface. Rich visual languages such as Visual Basic have grown up only relatively recently. But why use such an 'old-fashioned' interface? One or more of the following reasons may apply to you:

- Students whose only experience of programming is Visual Basic or a similar language rarely appreciate that there still is a programming world beyond GUIs.

- If you are a student doing a Computing/Computer Science course you probably need to read, and perhaps write algorithms. A command interface is a more natural way of learning about this.

- When you are trying to code something quite complex the visual environment can get in the way. Your code may need to reference several controls and this can obscure the really relevant code. A console application lets you concentrate on the important bits.

However you can still skip this chapter and understand the rest of the book!

PROGRAM 5.1   *A simple console application*

Specification	Calculate the profit made from a local dance. Tickets cost £5.00 and £10.00. Ask the user how many of each have been sold. Also ask the user how much the band cost to hire, how much was spent on food and how much all the other costs came to in total. Output the total income (from ticket sales), the total expenditure and the profit. Also output the profit as a percentage of the income.

Figure 5.2 shows the program running. The complete code for the program is shown in figure 5.5.

```
C:\Derek\Visual Basic Net Programs\Visual Basic Textbook\Chapter 05\Program 5-1\bin\Pro...

How many £5.00 tickets sold? 150
How many £10.00 tickets sold? 100
Cost of band? 380
Cost of food? 620
Other costs 230

Total income is £1,750.00
Total expenditure is £1,230.00
Profit is £520.00
The profit of £520.00 represents 29.7% of the income
```

Figure 5.2: Program 5.1

1. Open a new project and in the New Project window select **Console Application** under Templates (see figure 5.3).

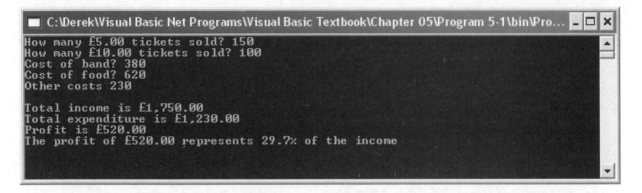

Figure 5.3: Opening a new Console Application

Since a console application has no forms the project opens with the code window. Every console application consists of at least one **module** and a procedure called **Main** as in figure 5.4. A procedure is like an event procedure in that it contains some code, but differs in that the code is not directly fired off by an event. A Visual Basic .NET module consists only of code and is stored as a separate file; Module1.vb is the default name. If you wish to rename the module you must do so in the Solution Explorer, not directly in the code. However you cannot rename the procedure Main since every console application expects one procedure with this name.

```
Start Page   Module1.vb                                    ◁ ▷ ×
                                              ▼   ▮▸ (Declarations)              ▼
  ☐ Module Module1                                                                ▲

  ☐     Sub Main()

        End Sub

  └ End Module
```

Figure 5.4: The code template with a new console application

2. Immediately under Sub Main() declare the variables needed. The Decimal data type is the most appropriate for the six monetary variables.

```
Sub Main()
   Dim FivePoundTickets, TenPoundTickets As Integer
   Dim CostOfBand, CostOfFood, OtherCosts As Decimal
   Dim Income, Expenditure, Profit As Decimal
```

3. To write to the console window use **Console.Write** followed by brackets containing what must be written. String literals must be inside quotation marks but variables must not. Assign data input by the user to a variable with **Console.ReadLine().** The code below stores the number of £5.00 tickets sold.

```
   Console.Write("How many £5.00 tickets sold? ")   'Write to console window
   FivePoundTickets = Console.ReadLine()            'Store user input
```

With Console.Write the cursor stays on the same line. You could use **Console.WriteLine** to position it on the next line. Figure 5.2 shows that the number sold has been typed in on the same line as the input prompt, and so Console.Write is used.

4. Display prompts and read the data for the £10.00 tickets, band, food and other costs. Figure 5.2 shows a blank line after the other costs have been read in. A Console.WriteLine() without anything in the brackets handles this.

```
   Console.Write("How many £10.00 tickets sold? ")
   TenPoundTickets = Console.ReadLine()     'read no. of £10 tickets
   Console.Write("Cost of band? ")
   CostOfBand = Console.ReadLine()          'read cost of band
   Console.Write("Cost of food? ")
   CostOfFood = Console.ReadLine()          'read cost of food
   Console.Write("Other costs ")
   OtherCosts = Console.ReadLine()          'read other costs
   Console.WriteLine()                      'produces a blank line
```

5. Calculate the income, expenditure and profit:

```
   Income = (FivePoundTickets * 5) + (TenPoundTickets * 10)
   Expenditure = CostOfBand + CostOfFood + OtherCosts
   Profit = Income – Expenditure
```

```
Start Page  Module1.vb*                                                          ◁ ▷ ✕
🔧Module1                              ▼  📄 (Declarations)                              ▼

⊟ Module Module1

⊟     Sub Main()
          Dim FivePoundTickets, TenPoundTickets As Integer
          Dim CostOfBand, CostOfFood, OtherCosts As Decimal
          Dim Income, Expenditure, Profit As Decimal
          Console.Write("How many £5.00 tickets sold? ")
          FivePoundTickets = Console.ReadLine()
          Console.Write("How many £10.00 tickets sold? ")
          TenPoundTickets = Console.ReadLine()
          Console.Write("Cost of band? ")
          CostOfBand = Console.ReadLine()
          Console.Write("Cost of food? ")
          CostOfFood = Console.ReadLine()
          Console.Write("Other costs ")
          OtherCosts = Console.ReadLine()
          Console.WriteLine()
          Income = (FivePoundTickets * 5) + (TenPoundTickets * 10)
          Expenditure = CostOfBand + CostOfFood + OtherCosts
          Profit = Income - Expenditure
          Console.WriteLine("Total income is {0}", Format(Income, "Currency"))
          Console.WriteLine("Total expenditure is {0}", Format(Expenditure, "Currency"))
          Console.WriteLine("Profit is {0}", String.Format("{0:C}", Profit))
          Console.WriteLine("The profit of {0} represents {1}% of the income ", Profit, Profit / Income * 100)
          Console.ReadLine()
      End Sub

⊾ End Module
```

Figure 5.5: The complete code for Program 5.1

6. Display the total income, expenditure and profit and the profit as a percentage of the income. You do not need to use the two underscores below; recall that an underscore splits one line of code over two lines. Note that the 0 and 0:C are inside braces (curly brackets).

```
Console.WriteLine("Total income is {0}", Format(Income, "Currency"))
Console.WriteLine("Total expenditure is {0}", Format(Expenditure, _
                                                "Currency"))
Console.WriteLine("Profit is {0}", String.Format("{0:C}", Profit))
Console.WriteLine("The profit of {0} represents {1} of the income ", _
          Format(Profit, "Currency"), Format(Profit / Income, "0.0%"))
```

Note three things in the code above:

- When non-literal strings are displayed using Console.WriteLine, *Income*, *Expenditure*, *Profit* and *Profit / Income*, you must mark their place in the literal string. Thus Income and Expenditure are marked with {0}. The last Console.WriteLine displays two non-literal strings – Profit is marked with {0} and Profit / Income with {1}.

- The named format Currency is used to display the income and expenditure. String.Format does the same thing and is used simply to remind you of an alternative method. "{0:C}" is the format used. The 0 is used in the same way Chapter 4 used it – to number the item to be formatted. There is only one item here, Profit, so it is numbered 0. The C means currency.

- A user-defined format is used to display the profit as a percentage of the income. This format, "0.0%" was the last example shown in figure 4.7.

7. Finally, to stop the program closing so that you can see it in the console window, write the following line. This will execute when you press **Enter**.

```
Console.ReadLine()
```

8. Run the program. Press **Enter** to close the program (or close the command window in the usual way).

end of Program 5.1

Summary of key concepts

- A **console application** has no forms and uses only text. It runs in a **command window**.

- Use **Console.Write** or **Console.WriteLine** to output data. The former keeps the cursor on the same line and the latter puts it on the next line.

- Use **Console.ReadLine** to read and store data.

Take it from here...

1. It is possible to use forms from a console application. However you would need to know how to create forms and their controls from code, which is only partially addressed in Chapter 17 through an unrelated topic. There seems little point using much of what you can do with forms from a console application – why not use a Windows application in the first place? Using message boxes is possibly one exception. For Program 5.1 display the last four lines shown in figure 5.2 again in a message box when the user presses Enter to close the program.

End of chapter exercises

Write console applications to solve the following:

***1**. Ask the user to input the price of a new car and the percentage discount it attracts. Calculate and display the price after discount.

***2**. Write a program to convert from degrees Fahrenheit (°F) to degrees Celsius (°C). The user should enter a temperature in °F. The formula is $°C = 5 / 9 (°F – 32)$. Display the result in the form *60 degrees Fahrenheit is 15.5 degrees Celsius.*

***3**. Calculate a cricketer's batting average for his last four innings. The user should input the number of runs scored in each of these innings. Display the answer to one decimal place.

Chapter 6 – Selection

What is selection?

Selection means that one or more lines of code may or may not be executed depending on whether a condition is true or false.

Types of selection in Visual Basic

Visual Basic has two selection constructs:

- **If**
- **Select Case**

The **If** construct has three variations:

- **If Then**
- **If Then…Else**
- **If Then…ElseIf** or **If Then…Else If**

If Then

The following code displays a message if a person is aged over 16::

```
Dim Age As Integer
Age = txtAge.Text
If Age > 16 Then                              'age greater than 16?
   lblOutput.Text "You are old enough to drive"
End If
```

- The '>' sign means 'greater than' and is an example of a **relational operator**. Visual Basic has several of these, which are listed in the *Summary of key concepts*.

- The condition to test is *Age > 16*. If it is true the message is printed, and if false the message is skipped.

- Because the condition is either true or false it is called a **boolean** condition. (Boolean was one of the data types listed at the start of Chapter 3.)

- An **If** must always have a matching **End If** to tell Visual Basic where the construct ends. It inserts this automatically when you press Enter after typing in the line containing If.

If Then…Else

The **Else** part of the construct is executed if the boolean condition is false. For example:

```
If Age > 16 Then                              'age greater than 16?
   lblOutput.Text = "You are old enough to drive"
Else                                          'age 16 or less
   lblOutput.Text = "You are too young to drive. You must be 17 years old"
End If
```

If Then...ElseIf

In the previous example there were two routes through the If construct. With three or more possible routes you can use **If Then...ElseIf**. For example:

```
If Age > 16 Then                               'age greater than 16?
   lblOutput.Text = "You are old enough to drive"
ElseIf Age = 16                                'age 16 exactly?
   lblOutput.Text = "You are too young to drive. You must be 17 years old" _
                    & " but you only have to wait less than a year."
Else                                           'age 15 or less
   lblOutput.Text = "You are too young to drive. You must be 17 years old"
End If
```

There are three routes through this example and two boolean conditions to test. If Age stores 16 the first condition *Age > 16* is false. The second one, *Age = 16*, is then tested, and since it is true the next line of code is executed. The Else part would be skipped.

You can write the ElseIf and its condition over two lines instead of one. The code above could be written as follows:

```
If Age > 16 Then                               'age greater than 16?
   lblOutput.Text = "You are old enough to drive"
Else
   If Age = 16                                 'age 16 exactly?
     lblOutput.Text = "You are too young to drive. You must be 17 years " _
                      & " old but you only have to wait less than a year."
   Else                                        'age 15 or less
     lblOutput.Text = "You are too young to drive. You must be 17 years old"
   End If         'end of If Age = 16
End If            'end of If Age > 16
```

This version has two End Ifs matching the two separate Ifs. The previous version had only one End If.

PROGRAM 6.1   *Deciding exam grades*

Specification   Ask the user to enter an exam mark from 0 to 100. Display the grade it represents Merit (60 or more), Pass (40 – 59), Fail (under 40)

1.   Open a new project, double-click on the form to bring up its Load event code template and type in:

```
Private Sub Form1_Load(...) Handles MyBase.Load
   Dim Mark As Integer
   Mark = InputBox("Enter an exam mark from 0 to 100")
   If Mark >= 60 Then                          'mark 60 or more?
     MsgBox("Merit")
   ElseIf Mark >= 40 Then                      'mark 40-59
     MsgBox("Pass")
   Else                                        'mark under 40
     MsgBox("A mark of " & Mark & " is a Fail")
   End If
End Sub
```

Note:

- Mark is declared as a local variable (though it could have been a global one since there is only one procedure on the form).

- The relational operator (>=) is used, meaning **greater than or equal to**. Note that the condition *Mark >= 60* is the same as *Mark > 59*.

2. Run the program three times and test each of the three routes through the If construct by entering, for example, marks of 70, 50 and 30.

end of Program 6.1

Testing multiple conditions

The boolean condition has so far consisted of one test. A multiple boolean condition has two or more tests and each one is either true or false. For this you need to use Visual Basic's **logical operators**. The two important ones are **And** and **Or**.

An AND condition

In the example below there are two conditions to test, *Age > 18* and *Gender = "F"*. Each of these is either true or false. **When you AND two or more conditions each one must be true for the overall condition to be true. If just one of them is false the overall condition is false.**

```
Dim Age As Integer
Dim Gender As String
Age = txtAge.Text
Gender = txtGender.Text
If (Age >= 18) And (Gender = "F") Then        'females 18 and over
   lblOutput.Text = "Allow into nightclub"
Else                                          'everybody else
   lblOutput.Text = "Do not allow into nightclub"
End If
```

The two conditions have brackets. This is optional, but as it can help readability the practice is used in this book.

An OR condition

Members of a ten-pin bowling club get an award if, during one season, they score at least 240 points on 5 or more occasions, or they score 200 points on 10 or more occasions:

```
Dim TwoForty As Integer      'VB does not allow identifiers 240 or 200
Dim TwoHundred As Integer    'since they must not start with a digit
      'Assume data has been input and stored in these 2 variables
If (TwoForty >= 5) Or (TwoHundred >= 10) Then
   lblOutput.Text = "Give award"
End If
```

When you OR two or more conditions, then if at least one of them is true the overall condition is true. They must all be false for the overall condition to be false.

PROGRAM 6.2 *Selecting cutlery*

Specification	Write a program for a mail order company selling cutlery. The user should select three things – a cutlery brand, one or more cutlery items (knife, fork, spoon) and a quantity – and then click a button for the price to be calculated. Before calculating the price the program must check that the user has selected all three things and output an appropriate message if they have not. (Question 2 on this program asks you to calculate the price.)

This program provides an opportunity to practice using some of the controls you covered in Chapter 2. Figure 6.1 shows the program in action. The user has selected a brand of cutlery but not the item(s) or quantity. If the Price button is then clicked the message in figure 6.2(a) appears. When all three things have been selected the satisfactory message in figure 6.2(b) appears. The Items are selected using check boxes. If the Full Set check box is selected the other three should automatically be selected. The Quantity is selected using radio buttons.

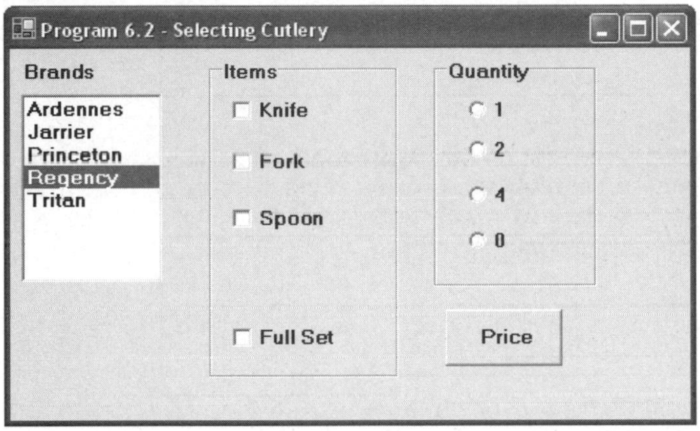

Figure 6.1: Program 6.2

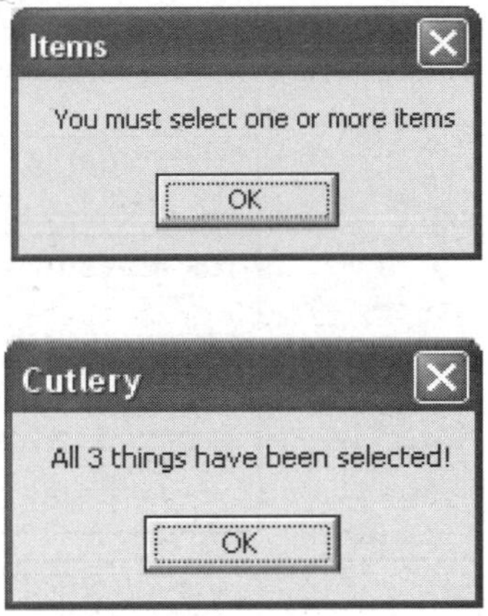

Figure 6.2 (a) above (b) below

1. Open a new project and design the form using figures 6.1 and 6.3.

We don't need variables in this program and only two event procedures need to be coded:

- When the Full Set check box is clicked the other check boxes must be selected automatically.
- When the Price button is clicked an appropriate message must be displayed.

2. Double-click the Full Set check box to get its default CheckedChanged event procedure. The **Checked** property of a check box indicates whether or not it has been selected, so type in the following:

```
Private Sub chkFullSet_CheckedChanged(...) Handles chkFullSet.CheckedChanged
  If chkFullSet.Checked = True Then    'full set selected
    chkKnife.Checked = True              'select other 3 check boxes
    chkFork.Checked = True
    chkSpoon.Checked = True
  Else                                 'full set not selected
    chkKnife.Checked = False             'Deselect other 3 check boxes or
    chkFork.Checked = False              'leave them deselected if in
    chkSpoon.Checked = False             'that state already
  End If
End Sub
```

Control	Property	Property setting
Form	Text	Program 6.2 – Selecting Cutlery
Label	Text	Brands
List box	Name	lstBrands
	Items	*See 5 brands in figure 6.1*
Group box	Text	Items
Group box	Text	Quantity
Check box	Name	chkKnife
	Text	Knife
Check box	Name	chkFork
	Text	Fork
Check box	Name	chkSpoon
	Text	Spoon
Check box	Name	chkFullSet
	Text	Full Set
Radio button	Name	radOne
	Text	1
Radio button	Name	radTwo
	Text	2
Radio button	Name	radFour
	Text	4
Radio button	Name	radEight
	Text	8
Button	Name	btnCalcPrice
	Text	Price

Figure 6.3: Property settings for the controls in program 6.2

3. Get the Click event procedure for the button and enter the code below. As there are three things the user must select, there are four routes through the **If** construct. Two **ElseIf**s and an **Else** handle this. Note that as **Visual Basic does not allow comments on the same line as a joining underscore character** the comments below on the ElseIfs are written on the previous line.

```
Private Sub btnCalcPrice_Click(...) Handles btnPrice.Click
  If lstBrands.Text = "" Then                'has a brand been selected?
    MsgBox("You must select a brand", , "Brand")
              'brand has been selected but has an item been selected?
  ElseIf (chkKnife.Checked = False) And _
         (chkFork.Checked = False) And _
         (chkSpoon.Checked = False) Then  'NB ElseIf could be on one line
    MsgBox("You must select one or more items", , "Items")
            'brand and item selected but has a quantity?
  ElseIf (radOne.Checked = False) And _
         (radTwo.Checked = False) And _
         (radFour.Checked = False) And _
         (radEight.Checked = False) Then  'NB ElseIf could be on one line
    MsgBox("You must select a quantity", , "Quantity")
  Else                                   'all 3 things selected
    MsgBox("All 3 things have been selected!", , "Cutlery")
  End If
End Sub
```

Note two things about this code:

- In previous programs we gave the MsgBox function only a message to display. You can also give it several other optional arguments or parameters One of these, used in the examples here, is a title (e.g. "Brand"). As this is the second optional parameter, and we are not supplying the first optional one, you must indicate this by having the two commas and nothing between them. If you did question 3 in the *Take it from here...* section in Chapter 4 you may have discovered this yourself.

- The **ElseIf**s have several conditions to test and only if they are all true should the message be displayed. Therefore **And**s are needed. The conditions have been written on separate lines here because they will not all fit on one line in this book. Recall that you use the underscore character (_) to join lines in Visual Basic code, and that there must be at least one space before it.

4. Run the program and try out the four routes through the code. First click the Price button without selecting anything, then click it after selecting just a brand, a brand and an item, and then all three things. Question 2 on this program asks you to calculate the price.

end of Program 6.2

Nested If structures

A **nested If** is an alternative to using multiple AND conditions. Using our earlier example of the nightclub we could write:

```
If Age >= 18 Then                                'aged 18 or over
   If Gender = "F" Then                          'and female?
      lblOutput.Text = "Allow into nightclub"
   Else                                          'all other people
      lblOutput.Text = "Do not allow into nightclub"
   End If
End If
```

A nested **If Then...Else** could be used for the earlier exam mark example The original **ElseIf** has been split over two lines and has become a nested **If** instead.

```
If Mark >= 60 Then                               'mark 60 or more
    MsgBox("Merit")
Else
   If Mark >= 40 Then                            'mark 40-59
      MsgBox("Pass")
   Else                                          'mark under 40
      MsgBox("A mark of " & Mark & " is a Fail")
   End If
End If
```

The common feature of both these examples is the pair of **End If**s to match the two earlier **If**s. It's for you to decide whether to use nested **If**s in your code. Again readability should probably be the deciding factor.

Complex multiple conditions

When you are coding a large program you might have to use quite complex multiple boolean conditions made up of a mixture of ANDs and ORs. In Chapter 3 you saw that arithmetic operators have an order of precedence. So do logical operators – AND is done before OR. Program 6.3 illustrates how you must take great care in writing more complex multiple conditions.

PROGRAM 6.3   *Rent a property*

Specification   Illustrate the order of precedence of the AND and OR logical operators

Look at figure 6.4 showing the program in action. A customer wants to rent a holiday property which has 4 or more bedrooms, and it must be a cottage or a detached house. The Correct and Incorrect buttons have correctly and incorrectly written code to output a message to rent the selected property or not. A detached 5-bedroom property has been selected, Correct clicked and the appropriate message **Rent it** displayed.

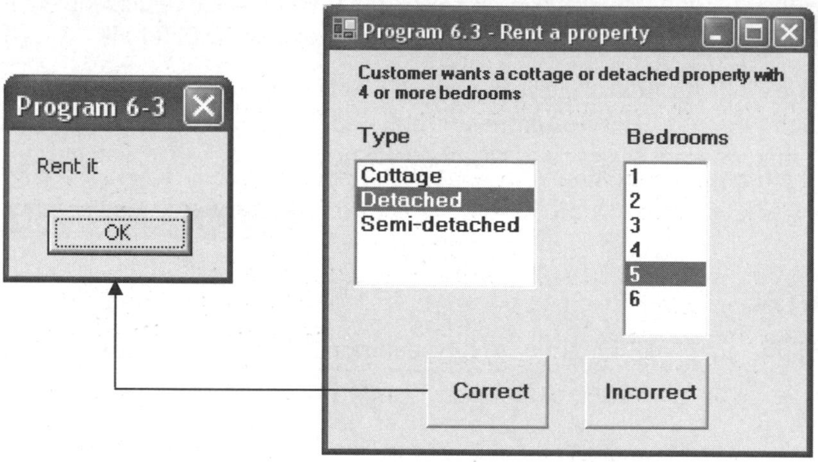

Figure 6.4: Program 6.3

1. Open a new project and place three labels, two list boxes and two buttons on the form. Set the Text properties of the labels and buttons to those shown in figure 6.4

2. Name the list boxes **lstTypes** and **lstBedrooms** and add the items shown in figure 6.4 using their Items property. Name the buttons **btnCorrect** and **btnIncorrect**.

3. Below *Windows Form Designer generated code* declare two global variables:

```
Dim PropType As String      'stores selected item from Type list box
Dim Bedrooms As Integer     'stores selected item from Bedrooms list box
```

4. In human terms we could express the customer's wish as *a cottage or a detached property and it must have 4 or more bedrooms*. If we translate this as it stands into a multiple condition with one *or* and one *and* it would be wrong. So in the Click event procedure for btnIncorrect enter the incorrect code as follows:

```
Private Sub btnIncorrect_Click(...) Handles btnIncorrect.Click
  PropType = lstTypes.Text
  Bedrooms = lstBedrooms.Text
  If (PropType = "Cottage") Or (PropType = "Detached") _
           And (Bedrooms >= 4) Then
    MsgBox("Rent it")
  Else
    MsgBox("Don't rent it")
  End If
End Sub
```

5. Run the program. Select a 4-bedroomed cottage and the correct *Rent it* message appears. Selecting a cottage with 5 or 6 bedrooms or a detached property with 4 or more bedrooms also produces the correct message. But try selecting a 1, 2 or 3-bedroomed cottage. This is not what the customer wants but the message still says *Rent it*.

Try to follow through the logic below if you select **Cottage** and **1**. The multiple condition becomes

(PropType = "Cottage") **Or** (PropType = "Detached") **And** (Bedrooms >= 4)

      True   **OR**   False   **AND**   False

AND has precedence over OR, so doing AND first produces

      True   **OR**   False

This evaluates to True, and so the incorrect message *Rent it* is displayed.

6. One way to correct the multiple condition is to write the condition *Bedrooms >= 4* for both Cottage and Detached. In the Click event procedure for btnCorrect enter the correct coding as follows:

```
Private Sub btnCorrect_Click(...) Handles btnCorrect.Click
  PropType = lstTypes.Text
  Bedrooms = lstBedrooms.Text
  If (PropType = "Cottage") And (Bedrooms >= 4) _
                Or (PropType = "Detached") And (Bedrooms >= 4) Then
    MsgBox("Rent it")
  Else
    MsgBox("Don't rent it")
  End If
End Sub
```

7. Run the program and check that you are only told to rent the property if it has 4 or more bedrooms and it is either a cottage or detached.

Again follow the logic through carefully. If you select **Cottage** and **1** again from the list boxes the multiple condition becomes

(PropType = "Cottage") **And** (Bedrooms >= 4) **Or** (PropType = "Detached") **And** (Bedrooms >= 4)

   True   **AND**   False   **OR**   False   **AND**   False

Since ANDs have precedence over ORs these are done first, which produces

      False   **OR**   False

Finally the OR produces False, and the correct message *Don't rent it* is displayed.

end of Program 6.3

Select Case

In the examples so far the largest number of routes through the **If** structure has been four. If you have more than this the **Select Case** structure is probably a better alternative.

Suppose you wished to output the name of the month corresponding to a number from 1 to 12 input by the user. If this value is stored in Month then you would code this as follows:

```
Select Case Month
   Case 1
      MsgBox("January")
   Case 2
      MsgBox("February")
   Case 3
      MsgBox("March")
              'and so on up to.........
   Case 12
      MsgBox("December")
End Select
```

Visual Basic would look for the value of Month in one of the 12 **Cases** and execute the appropriate code. If it cannot find a match, because the user has entered 13 for example, nothing happens. You can cover this situation by adding an optional **Case Else**:

```
   Case 12
      MsgBox("December")
   Case Else
      MsgBox("You did not enter a valid month number")
End Select
```

PROGRAM 6.4   *Wards and Patients*

Specification   Present the user with two list boxes. One of these lists the wards in a hospital. Clicking on one of the wards displays the names of its patients in the other list box.

Figure 6.5 shows the program. Selecting a ward changes the patient list on the right. This is a technique with many applications in computer projects. Examples include courses and students, departments and employees, authors and books and so on.

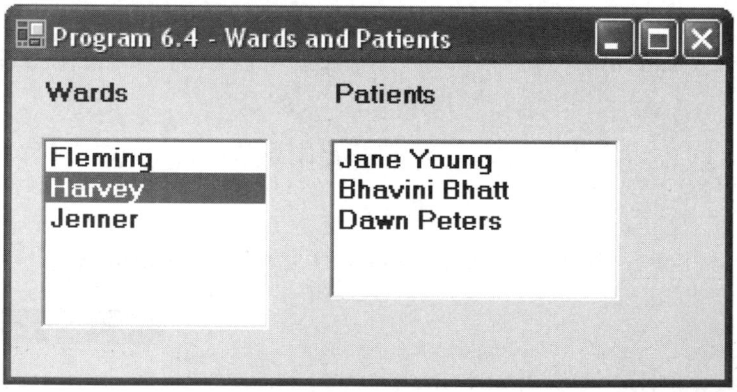

Figure 6.5: Program 6.4

1.   Open a new project. Design the form using figures 6.5 and 6.6. Note that you only have to put items into the Wards list box, not the Patients list box too. These will be coded.

Control	*Property*	*Property setting*
Form	Text	Program 6.4 – Wards and Patients
Label	Text	Wards
Label	Text	Patients
List box	Name Items	lstWards *See the 3 wards listed in figure 6.5*
List box	Name	lstPatients

Figure 6.6: Property settings for the controls in program 6.4

2. Double-click the Wards list box and get the code template for its default event. the SelectedIndexChanged event. Type in the following code:

```
Private Sub lstWards_SelectedIndexChanged(...) _
                              Handles lstWards.SelectedIndexChanged
   Dim Ward As String
   Ward = lstWards.Text          'selected item from wards list box
   Select Case Ward
     Case "Fleming"
        lstPatients.Items.Add("Fred Jones") 'Items.Add method used to
        lstPatients.Items.Add("John Green") 'populate patients list box
        lstPatients.Items.Add("Imran Shah")
     Case "Harvey"
        lstPatients.Items.Add("Jane Young")
        lstPatients.Items.Add("Bhavini Bhatt")
        lstPatients.Items.Add("Dawn Peters")
     Case "Jenner"
        lstPatients.Items.Add("William Black")
        lstPatients.Items.Add("Michael Jones")
        lstPatients.Items.Add("Darren Campbell")
   End Select
End Sub
```

3. Run the program and click on two different wards. After clicking the second ward the list box has patients from both wards. We need to remove the patients from the first ward before the new names are added. Add the following line before *Select Case Ward*:

```
lstPatients.Items.Clear
```

Note that the method of populating the patients list box is not the way you'd do it in a real project. These names would be stored in a file. Files are covered in Chapter 12. With Case "Fleming", for example, the code would read details of those patients in this ward from the file. However you would still need the **Items.Add** method to get them into the list box.

end of Program 6.4

Extensions to Select Case

So far the Case values have all been simple single ones – months (1-12) and ward names. There are several extensions to this. Here are some examples:

A continuous range of values using *To*

```
Select Case Mark
   Case 0 To 39                    'value ranges from 0 to 39
      MsgBox("Fail")
   Case 40 To 59                   'value ranges from 40 to 59
      MsgBox("Pass")
   Case 60 To 100                  'value ranges from 60 to 100
      MsgBox("Merit")
End Select
```

A continuous range of values using *Is*

The code below does the same as the previous example. As relational operators are used the keyword **Is** must follow Case.

```
Select Case Mark
   Case Is < 40                    'value is under 40
      MsgBox("Fail")
   Case Is <= 59                   'value ranges from 40 to 59
      MsgBox("Pass")
   Case Is >= 60                   'value is 60 or over
      MsgBox("Merit")
End Select
```

A non-continuous range of values

```
Select Case Month
   Case 1, 3, 5, 7, 8, 10, 12
      MsgBox("This month has 31 days")
   Case 4, 6, 8, 11
      MsgBox("This month has 30 days")
   Case 2
      MsgBox("This month has 28 or 29 days")
End Select
```

Summary of key concepts

- Visual Basic has two selection constructs - **If** and **Select Case**. Both have several variations.

- With an **If** structure a boolean condition is tested. If it is true the associated code is executed, otherwise control passes to the optional **Else** if there is one.

- No matter how complex a multiple **If** condition is, it must reduce to an overall single true or false.

- Visual Basic .NET supports the following **relational operators**:

=	equal to	<	smaller than
>	greater than	<=	smaller than or equal to
>=	greater than or equal to	<>	not equal to

- Visual Basic .NET's two main **logical operators** are **And** and **Or**. The following rules apply:

  * When you AND two or more conditions each one must be true for the overall condition to be true. If just one of them is false the overall condition is false.

  * When you OR two or more conditions, then if at least one of them is true the overall condition is true. They must all be false for the overall condition to be false.

  * ANDs have precedence over ORs.

Take it from here...

1. Visual Basic .NET has an **IIf** function equivalent to If Then...Else and a **Switch** function equivalent to Select Case. Find out how you might use these functions in code.

2. This chapter covered two logical operators – And and Or. There are several more. Investigate the **Not**, **AndAlso** and **OrElse** logical operators. AndAlso and OrElse are new in Visual Basic. NET.

Questions on the Programs

Program 6.1

*1. When you click to remove the message box, the empty form seems to appear. Add one line of code to stop it appearing.

*2. Extend the code so that a mark of 80 or more gets a Distinction.

Program 6.2

*1. None of the Quantity options are selected by default when the program runs. Suppose that most customers order a quantity of four. Change the program so that this is selected when the program starts.

*2. Although checking the Full Set check box selects the other three check boxes, if you then uncheck one of these three the Full Set check box remains selected. Add code to ensure that the Full Set check box is only selected when the other three are selected.

**3. Add code to the Click event of the Price button to calculate the price of the cutlery using the prices below for a quantity of 1. For a full set and quantity 4 there is a 10% discount, and for a full set and quantity 8 a 20% discount.

	Knife	Fork	Spoon	Full set
Ardennes	£1.50	£1.30	£1.70	£4.50
Jarrier	£1.70	£1.40	£1.90	£5.00
Princeton	£1.95	£1.60	£2.10	£5.55
Regency	£2.20	£1.80	£2.45	£6.45
Tritan	£3.00	£2.50	£3.40	£8.90

Program 6.3

*1. The incorrect code in step 4 can also be corrected by putting a pair of brackets around the multiple OR condition to force the OR to be evaluated before the AND. Try this out.

Program 6.4

*1.   Add two more wards and write code to display three patients in each of them.

**2.   Rewrite the code using the SelectedIndex property of the wards list box rather than the Text property.

End of chapter exercises

*1.   Ask a salesperson to input the total value of their sales this year to the nearest whole pound. If it exceeds £100,000 their bonus is £10,000. If it is from £70,000 to £99,999 the bonus is £7,000 and if it is £50,000 to £69,999 the bonus is £4,000. Sales less than £50,000 receive no bonus. Output the salesperson's bonus.

*2.   A person wishes to attend an overnight conference. They cannot afford to pay more than £40.00 for their hotel, which must be no more than 3 km from the conference hall. Input these two data items and display a message about whether the booking should be made or not.

3.   In Program 3.4 the Quit button had one line of code to exit the program. Replace this with the MsgBox function or the **Message.Show method to ask the user to confirm that they wish to quit. (If you have not done this program just add a Quit button to an empty form.) The message box should look like figure 4.9. Use Help to find out how to program a message box in this way. You will need to use an If statement.

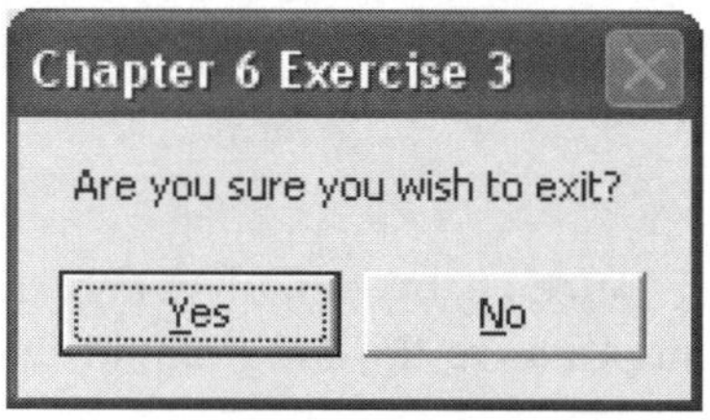

Figure 6.7: Exercise 3

**4.   Write a program that calculates total weekly pay as shown in figure 6.8. The user enters the number of hours worked and selects the hourly rate of pay from a list box. If overtime has been done, the number of hours is also entered. Overtime hours are paid at double rate. A check box handles overtime. Clicking this should make visible the text box (and its label) for inputting the number of overtime hours.

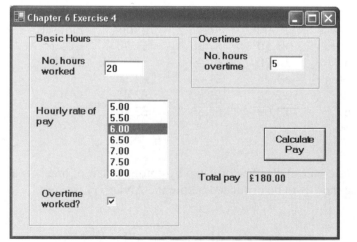

Figure 6.8: Exercise 4

When you have calculated the total pay correctly display a more detailed pay calculation in a message box like that in figure 6.9.

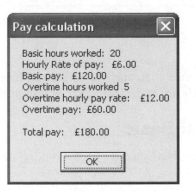

Figure 6.9: Message box output for Exercise 4.

**5.   A sports club has three categories of membership charge. Juniors (aged up to 18) pay £60 per year, Seniors (19-49) pay £120 and Veterans (50 and over) pay £80. Juniors who have been a member for 2 years or more get a £20 reduction. Seniors and Veterans who have been members for 10 years or more get a £30 reduction. Write a program that asks for the member's age and the number of years they have been a member, and outputs their category of membership and how much they must pay. Use input boxes to get the data.

**6.   The Shipshape Packing Company wants a program for their Orders Department to calculate and display the price of an order. The order clerks enter the number of units ordered, whether a customer is a wholesaler or retailer, and whether or not the customer is a special customer. Use a variety of controls for this data entry. The price the customer pays per unit depends on these three things. The prices are as follows:

	Wholesalers		Retailers
No. units	Price per unit (£)	No. units	Price per unit (£)
1-5	50	1 – 3	60
6-10	45	4-8	55
11-20	40	9-15	50
21-50	35	16-40	45
over 50	30	over 40	40

Special customers get a 10% reduction on the prices above.

***7.   Write a program to simulate the changes of a set of traffic lights. Use square labels for the three lights. (If you wish to use circles you will need to find out how to use the System.Drawing.Graphics class. Graphics are not covered in this book.) Set the BackColor property of the top one to red and the other two to white. With each click of a button the traffic lights should change continuously through the sequence: Red, Amber and Red together, Green and finally Amber You may find Exercise 3 in Chapter 1 helpful.

If you get this working now try to meet a different specification. When the button is clicked the traffic lights colour changes should go automatically through the cycle. For this you need to use a Timer control. Set its Interval property to 1000 (i.e. 1000 milliseconds or 1 second).

Chapter 7 – Loops

What is a loop?

A program loop is a section of code that may be repeatedly executed. The loop contains a boolean condition (that evaluates to true or false) to determine when it terminates.

Types of loop in Visual Basic

Visual Basic has seven types of loop, but you only need to understand three of them. These are:

- **For...Next**
- **Do While...Loop**
- **Do...Loop Until**

The code, known as the **loop body**, is inserted in place of the ellipsis (…). Each loop works in a slightly different way and is useful in different circumstances.

For...Next

You use this type of loop when you know exactly how many times the code must be repeated. For example the code below prints the numbers 1 to 10, as shown in figure 7.1. Assume that Number has been declared as an Integer.

```
For Number = 1 To 10
    lstOutput.Items.Add(Number)
Next Number
```

Figure 7.1

The first time the line

```
For Number = 1 To 10
```

is executed the value 1 is stored in Number. The statement in the loop body is then executed and the number 1 is printed. The line

```
Next Number
```

74

indicates the end of the loop and control passes back to the first line. Number is automatically incremented to 2 and the loop body executes again, this time printing 2. This process continues until the loop has been executed exactly 10 times, when control passes to the first statement after the loop.

The general form of a **For…Next** loop is

> **For** *variable identifier = start value* **To** *end value*
> statement(s)
> **Next** *variable identifier*

Note that:

* Start and end values may be integer constants, variables or expressions.
* The variable identifier in the last line of the loop is optional, but it is good practice to include it.

PROGRAM 7.1 *Multiplication table*

Specification Ask the user to enter a number from 2 to 12 and then output the multiplication table for their number. If the user enters 5 then the output is 2 x 5 = 10
3 x 5 = 15
4 x 5 = 20
......and so on up to
12 x 5 = 60

Figure 7.2 shows the program running. Clicking a button displays the multiplication table in a list box.

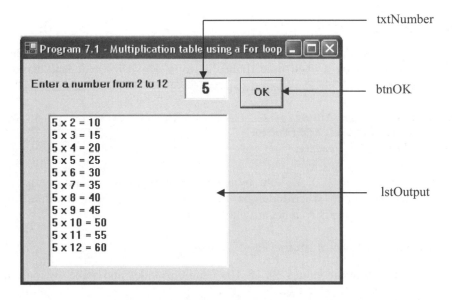

Figure 7.2: Program 7.1

1. Open a new project and build the form using figure 7.2.

2. Double-click the button to bring up its Click event code template and type in the following. Visual Basic will add the word *Next* automatically after you type in *For Index = 2 To 12* and press **Enter**.

```
Private Sub btnOK_Click(...) Handles btnOK.Click
    Dim Number As Integer
    Dim Index As Integer
    Dim Result As Integer
    Number = txtNumber.Text
    For Index = 2 To 12
        Result = Index * Number
        lstOutput.Items.Add(Number & " x " & Index & " = " & Result)
    Next Index
End Sub
```

3. Run the program and if you enter 5 into the text box you should produce the output shown in figure 7.2.

The first line in the loop

```
For Index = 2 To 12
```

stores the value 2 in Index. When Result is calculated by multiplying this by Number (e.g. 2 x 5), the concatenation operator **&** is used three times to output one line in the list box (e.g. 2 x 5 = 10) with

```
lstOutput.Items.Add(Number & " x " & Index & " = " & Result)
```

The line Next Index is then read and control returns to the first line of the loop. When Index has the value 12 the loop runs for the last time.

End of Program 7.1

The Step parameter

In the examples we've looked at so far, the value of the variable which controls whether or not the loop is executed has increased by 1 each time round the loop. However it doesn't have to increase by 1. For example, the code

```
For Index = 1 To 10 Step 2
    lstOutput.Items.Add(Index)
Next Index
```

sets the values of Index to 1, 3, 5, 7 etc. by using the **Step** parameter and giving it a value of 2. The last execution of the loop occurs when Index has the value 9 because the next value, 11, is bigger than the 10 allowed. You can even give Step a negative value. Thus

```
For Index = 20 To 0 Step -5
```

would successively store the values 20, 15, 10, 5 and 0 in Index and make the loop run five times.

A nested *For...Next* loop

A nested loop is when you have one loop inside another. The general structure of a nested **For...Next** loop is:

For.........	*start of outer loop*
For.......	*start of inner loop*
....	*body of inner loop*
Next	*end of inner loop*
Next	*end of outer loop*

Think of the outer loop as a large cog driving a smaller cog which is the inner loop. Every time the larger cog revolves once (one repetition of the outer loop), the inner cog usually revolves more than once. Have a look at the code which follows.

```
For OuterNumber = 1 To 4
  For OuterNumber = 1 To 4                'start of outer loop
    Message = Message & "Outer control variable value is " & _
                                    OuterNumber & vbNewLine
    For InnerNumber = 1 To 2             'start of inner loop
      Message = Message & vbTab & "Inner control variable value is " & _
                                    InnerNumber & vbNewLine
    Next InnerNumber                      'end of inner loop
  Next OuterNumber                        'end of outer loop
  MsgBox(Message, , "Nested For loop")
```

This will produce the output in figure 7.3. The outer loop is run four times, and each time you go round the outer loop the inner loop runs twice.

vbTab produces
this indent

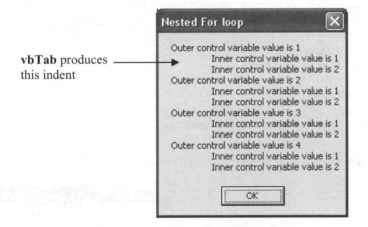

Figure 7.3

PROGRAM 7.2 *Addition Table*

Specification	Write a program to display the sum of row and column numbers

The running program is shown in figure 7.4.

1. Open a new project and double-click on the form to get the form's Load event code template.

2. Declare the following in the form's Load event:

```
Const Max = 5
Dim ColNumber, RowNumber, Sum As Integer
Dim Message As String
```

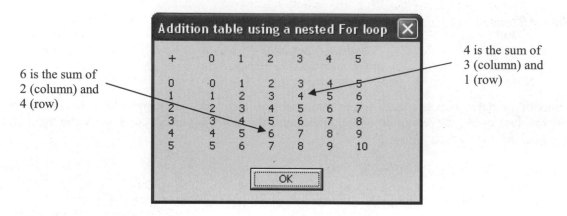

Figure 7.4: Program 7.2

3. Still in the form's Load event, type in the following code to produce the addition table:

```
Message = "+" & Space(11)            'table heading
For ColNumber = 0 To Max             'simple For...Next loop
   Message = Message & ColNumber & Space(8)      'column value and 8 spaces
Next ColNumber
Message = Message & vbNewLine & vbNewLine         'empty line
For RowNumber = 0 To Max             'start of outer loop
   Message = Message & RowNumber & Space(12)      'first number in the row
   For ColNumber = 0 To Max                  'start of inner loop
      Sum = ColNumber + RowNumber
      Message = Message & Sum & Space(8)           'addition of 2 numbers
   Next ColNumber                         'end of inner loop
   Message = Message & vbNewLine                 'new row in table
Next RowNumber                       'end of outer loop
MsgBox(Message, , "Addition table using a nested For loop")
```

4. Run the program and you should get the neat tabular display shown in figure 7.4.

end of Program 7.2

Do While...Loop

The general form of **Do While...Loop** is

> **Do While** *condition* is true
>   statement(s)   = body of loop
> **Loop**

This type of loop executes as long as the boolean condition in the first line of the loop is true, otherwise you skip the loop. Consider the following code:

```
Number = 5
Do While Number <> 10                '<> means not equal to
   1stOutput.Items.Add(Number * Number)
   Number = Number + 1
Loop
```

This will produce the output in figure 7.5.

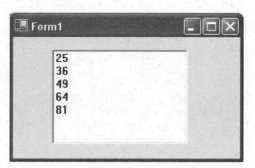

Figure 7.5

Note that:

- If you omitted the line

```
Number = Number + 1
```

the loop would never end, since Number would never equal 10. This is called an **infinite loop**. This is a common mistake made by novice programmers (and sometimes by experienced ones too!). Visual Basic .NET may detect an infinite loop and suspend the program. You would then select **Debug/Stop Debugging** to get out of it.

- If the first line of code was

```
Number = 10
```

then the condition *10 <> 10* would be false, and the loop would not be executed at all. This is one key feature of Do While…Loop which distinguishes it from Do…Loop Until. Do While…Loop can be executed 0 or more times. As you will see Do…Loop Until must be executed at least once.

Loops and event-driven programming

In console applications like those in Chapter 5 repetitive data input, such as a list of names or products, is usually handled by loops. In event-driven programs, such as the Windows applications you have been doing throughout this book, the need for loops for data input is much less. In Program 3.4 for example, you entered a series of exam marks without knowing anything about loops. You simply entered an individual mark in a text box and clicked a button to process it.

Program 7.3 is a console application and uses a loop for data entry. By using input boxes Program 7.4 illustrates the fairly rare need for a loop in an event-driven program requiring repetitive input. As you will see in later chapters, loops in event-driven programs are used more for processing strings, arrays and files.

PROGRAM 7.3   *Driving Test (Console Application)*

Specification	Ask the user to enter "Y", "N" or "Q" (quit) in response to the question "Has the person passed their driving test?" Continue asking this question until the user enters "Q". Output the number and percentage of people who have passed their test.

Figure 7.6 shows the program running.

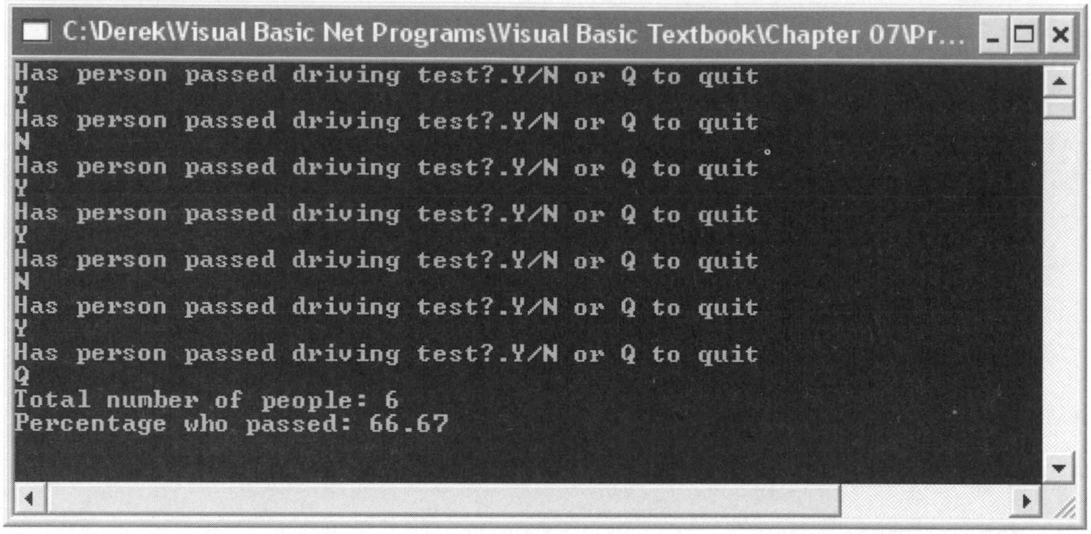

Figure 7.6: Program 7.3

1. Open a new Console Application (see figure 5.3). Recall from Chapter 5 that this type of application has no forms, only code.

2. Write the following code inside the *Main* procedure.

```
Dim TotalNumber, NumberPassed As Integer
Dim Response As String
TotalNumber = 0                      'initialise variables
NumberPassed = 0
Console.WriteLine("Has person passed driving test?.Y/N or Q to quit")
Response = Console.ReadLine()
Do While (Response = "Y") Or (Response = "N")
  TotalNumber = TotalNumber + 1
  If Response = "Y" Then             'person has passed driving test
    NumberPassed = NumberPassed + 1
  End If
  Console.WriteLine("Has person passed driving test?.Y/N or Q to quit")
  Response = Console.ReadLine()
Loop
Console.WriteLine("Total number of people: {0} ", TotalNumber)
Console.WriteLine("Percentage who passed: {0} ", _
          Format(NumberPassed / TotalNumber * 100, "###.00"))
Console.ReadLine()
```

The code to get the input from the user

```
Console.WriteLine("Has person passed driving test?.Y/N or Q to quit")
Response = Console.ReadLine()
```

is written twice, once just before the loop condition is tested and then just before the end of the loop. If the user enters 'Q' the first time they are asked then the loop is not executed at all. If they enter 'Y' or 'N' the loop *is* executed. However if you left out the Console.ReadLine just before the end of the loop you would have an infinite loop because the value of *Response* would never be changed.

2. Run the program and test it by entering several Y's and N's. Note that lower-case 'y' or 'n' is not the same as 'Y' or 'N'. Depending on how you test the code you may get a percentage output of 'NaN'. Question 1 on this program asks you to investigate this.

end of Program 7.3

Do...Loop Until

The general form of this loop is:

> **Do**
>> statement(s)   = body of loop
> **Loop Until** *condition* is true

Since the condition is at the end of the loop the loop body must be executed at least once.

PROGRAM 7.4   *Password Entry*

Specification	Allow the user up to three attempts at entering the password "secret". Inform the user which attempt they are currently on (1, 2 or 3). Inform the user that the password is correct if they get it within the three attempts, otherwise inform them that their password is invalid.

1. Open a new project, drop a button onto the form, set its Name to **btnEnterPassword** and its Text property to **Enter Password**.

2. Double-click the button to bring up the Code window and enter the following code into its Click event procedure:

```
Private Sub btnEnterPassword_Click(...) Handles btnEnterPassword.Click
   Dim Password, InputPassword As String
   Dim Attempt As Integer
   Password = "secret"                          'initialise variables
   Attempt = 0
   Do                                           'start of loop
      Attempt = Attempt + 1
      InputPassword = InputBox("Enter password. This is attempt " & _
                  "number " & Attempt)
   Loop Until (Attempt = 3) Or (InputPassword = Password) 'end of loop
   If InputPassword = Password Then
      MsgBox ("This password is valid")
   Else
      MsgBox ("This password is invalid")
   End If
End Sub
```

The body of the loop asks the user for the password and then adds 1 to the number of attempts the user has had. The condition at the end of the loop is a multiple one:

```
Loop Until (Attempt = 3) Or (InputPassword = Password)
```

The condition is true if either the user has had three attempts or they have entered the correct password. It will also be true if they have entered the correct password at the third attempt since both parts of the multiple condition are true.

3. Run the program to check that it works. Remember that the password is *secret*.

end of Program 7.3

Summary of key concepts

- The general forms of the three loops covered in this chapter are:

  For…Next

  For *variable identifier* = *start value* **To** *end value*
      statement(s)   = body of loop
  Next *variable identifier*

  Do While…Loop

  Do While *condition*
      statement(s)   = body of loop
  Loop

  Do…Loop Until

  Do
      statement(s)   = body of loop
  Loop Until *condition*

- Use a **For…Next** loop when you know how many times the loop must be executed.

- Use **Do While…Loop** if there is the possibility that the loop body should not be executed.

- An **infinite loop** is one that never stops running. The program may just hang. It is caused by not allowing the condition tested in **Do While…Loop** to become false or the condition in **Do…Loop Until** to become true.

Take it from here…

1. It is possible to force a loop to terminate early by using the **Exit** statement. Find out how to exit early from the three types of loop covered in this chapter.

2. The beginning of this chapter said that Visual Basic has seven types of loop, but that you only need to know three of these. Find out about three that were not covered – **Do Until…Loop, Do…Loop While** and **While…End While**. For each of these loops find out how the tested condition works. Also find out whether they must be executed at least once or whether they may be 'skipped' the first time. (The 7th loop is For Each…Next and is for looping through a group of controls.)

Questions on the Programs

Program 7.1

*1. In this program the user is expected to type in a number from 2 to 12. As the code stands they can type any number into txtNumber. Add a loop to ensure that the user enters a value from 2 to 12. You will need to change the way that the user enters the number. Use an input box rather than txtNumber. The input box should appear when the OK button is clicked. Making sure that input data satisfies certain conditions is called **validation**. All you are doing here is validating an inputted number. If the user entered one or more characters by mistake you would get a run-time error.

Program 7.3

*1. If you enter "Q" in response to the first request for input the percentage of people who passed their test is displayed as NaN. Find out what this means. Add code so that a more suitable result is displayed.

*2. Rewrite the program using **Do…Loop Until** instead of Do While…Loop.

End of chapter exercises

For questions 1, 2, 3 and 6 use a console application or a Windows application. If you choose a Windows application use **input boxes** to get data from the user.

*1. Ask the user to input two different numbers. Display all the numbers between the two values they enter. For example if 10 and 20 are entered display the numbers 10, 11, 12 etc. up to 20,

*2. Allow the user to enter as many positive whole numbers as they wish, and to enter 0 to indicate they have finished. Then display the number of even values and number of odd values entered by the user. Use the **Mod** operator to work out whether a number is odd or even.

**3. A disco can hold 500 people. Allow the user to keep entering the number of people in each group as the group comes through the door. Display the running total and how many more people are allowed in before it becomes full. When the running total reaches exactly 500 display a message that the disco is full, or if 500 would be exceeded, a message that the current group of people cannot go in.

4. Use a nested For…Next loop to output the cell references found in the top upper left part of a spreadsheet, within the range A1 to E5, as shown in figure 7.7. You may wish to use two Visual Basic functions, **Asc and **Chr**, to convert characters to their ASCII values and vice-versa.

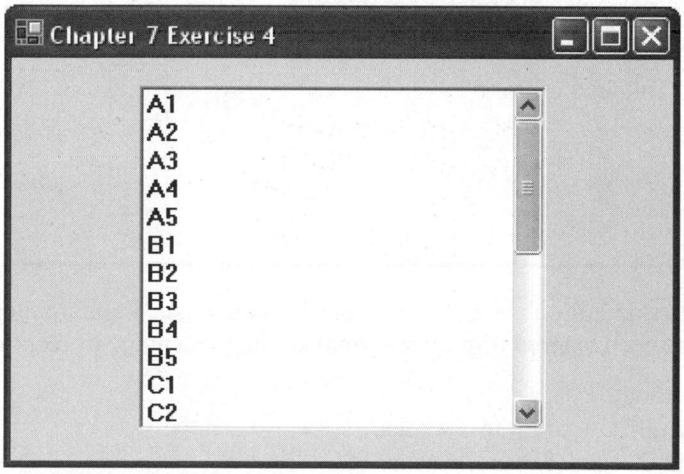

Figure 7.7: Output for Exercise 4

5. Write a program that outputs all the dates in one year in a list box when the user clicks a button. The output is shown in figure 7.8. Use a **For...Next loop to handle the whole year and inside this a **Select Case** to handle each month. You will need to set the MultiColumn property of the list box at design time to allow multiple columns.

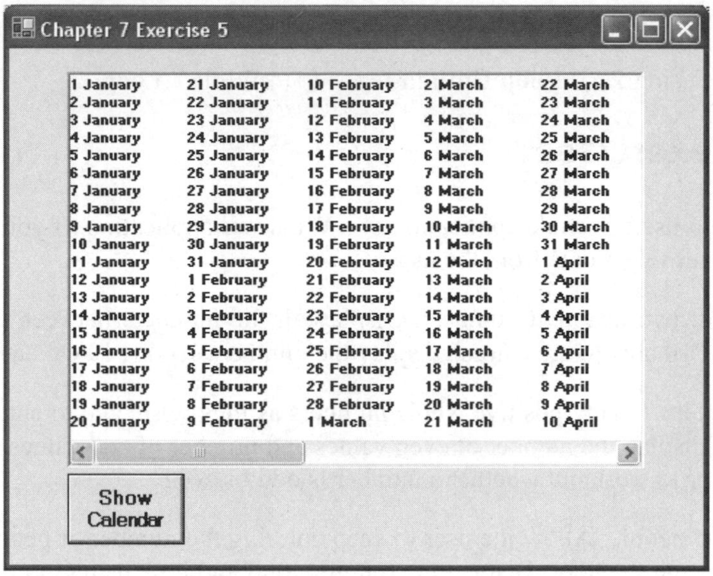

Figure 7.8: Output for exercise 5

***6. People have been surveyed in a shopping centre about the main holiday they had in the past year. They were asked the following questions:

1. Have you had a holiday in the past 12 months?	Yes	☐	No	☐
2. If Yes, was it in Britain or abroad?	GB	☐	Abroad	☐
3. If Yes, how many weeks did it last?	Up to 2 weeks	☐	More than 2	☐

Allow the user to enter data for as many respondents as they wish. Validate the items of data entered. When all the data has been entered display the number and percentage of respondents who

- did not take a holiday.
- took a holiday in Britain of up to 2 weeks.
- took a holiday in Britain of over 2 weeks.
- took a holiday abroad of up to 2 weeks
- took a holiday abroad of over 2 weeks.

Chapter 8 – Handling Strings, Dates and Time

String handing is probably the most common task in programming. Handling dates and time is less common, but when the need arises is very important to understand.

Declaring strings

You have used the two data types for handling strings in several programs – **Char** and the **String** type itself. A Char variable can hold only one character but a String variable can hold up to two billion characters. Earlier versions of Visual Basic had the option of stating how many characters a String variable could hold. The only time you need to do this is when writing String variables to a random access file. Visual Basic .NET has a special way of declaring such a fixed length string (see Chapter 12).

ASCII and Unicode

Earlier versions of Visual Basic allocated one byte of storage for each character in a string using the American Standard Code for Information Interchange (ASCII). Each character was stored as a number from 0 to 255. Visual Basic .NET allocates 2 bytes per character using Unicode, a coding system designed to cover all languages. The first 256 characters of Unicode are the same as the ASCII characters. The following are useful to know:

- Upper-case letters ('A' to 'Z') are stored as numbers 65 to 90.
- Lower-case letters ('a' to 'z') are stored as numbers 97 to 122.
- Numeric digits ('0' to '9') are stored as numbers 48 to 57.
- The space character is number 32.

Processing strings

Using relational operators

The code below outputs two strings, Name1 and Name2, in alphabetical order:

```
If Name1 < Name2 Then            'relational operator < means smaller than
   lblName.Text = Name1 & "   " & Name2
Else                                 'Name2 is alphabetically before Name1
   lblName.Text = Name2 & "   " & Name1
End If
```

Visual Basic does this by comparing the Unicode value of the first character in each string. A lower value indicates that this character comes alphabetically before the other one. If they are the same then the next character in each string is compared and so on. Note that since upper-case letters have lower values than lower-case letters, **Jones** is alphabetically before **brown**.

String methods and functions

Visual Basic has a variety of string **functions**; for example you have used the Len and Format functions in several programs. Visual Basic .NET introduced string **methods** that do the same job as many of these functions, and for most tasks you have the choice of using a function or a method. In this book from now on we will generally use methods. *Take it from here…* lists the equivalent functions and asks you to find out about them.

Searching for a substring using *IndexOf*

The **IndexOf** method returns the position in the main string of the substring being searched for. The code below

```
MainString = "The man looked up and saw the moon"
SearchString = "man"
Position1 = MainString.IndexOf(SearchString)     'use '.' to call a method
Position2 = MainString.IndexOf(SearchString, 2, 4 )
```

stores the value 4 in Position1 since strings are indexed from 0. If the substring is not present the method returns -1. You can pass two further parameters to IndexOf – the index of the character to start searching from and the number of characters to search. Position2 would return -1 because the search starts from the letter 'e' in 'The' and searches this character and three more, i.e. searches 'e ma'.

Extracting substrings using *Substring*

The **Substring** method returns a substring from the main string. Look at the following example:

```
Dim OneCharacter As Char
Dim MainString, Characters As String
MainString = "Keep on looking ahead"
OneCharacter = MainString.Substring(8)    'returns 9th character i.e. 'l'
Characters = MainString.Substring(8, 4)   'Returns 4 characters starting
                                          'at 9th character i.e. 'look'
```

You need to state the position in the main string, and there is the option of specifying how many characters to return (4 in the example above).

You may wish to extract a certain number of characters at the leftmost or rightmost position of a string. To extract a student's ID from the student selected from the list box in figure 8.1 you would write:

```
OneStudent = lstStudents.Text
StudentID = OneStudent.Substring(0, 5)
MsgBox(StudentID, , "Student ID")
```

Figure 8.1

PROGRAM 8.1   *Ensuring a person's name has only one space*

Specification   Ask the user to enter a person's forename followed by their surname into a single text box. Check that only one space character has been used between the names.

1.   Open a new project and design the form using figure 8.2. The message box is displayed through the code.

2.   In the Click event procedure for the button enter the following code:

```
Dim Spaces, Index As Short          'Spaces - counts use of spacebar
Dim Name As String
Dim Character As Char
Name = txtName.Text
Spaces = 0
For Index = 0 To Name.Length - 1 'Length - number of characters in string
   Character = Name.Substring(Index)    'extract one character
   If Character = " " Then              'is this character a space?
     Spaces = Spaces + 1                'if yes, increment Spaces
   End If
Next Index
If Spaces >= 2 Then
  MsgBox("Too many spaces")
End If
```

The **Length** method returns the number of characters in the string. So the For...Next loop must be repeated that number of times in order to process each character. Since characters in a string are numbered from 0 Index must be incremented from 0 to Name.Length – 1.

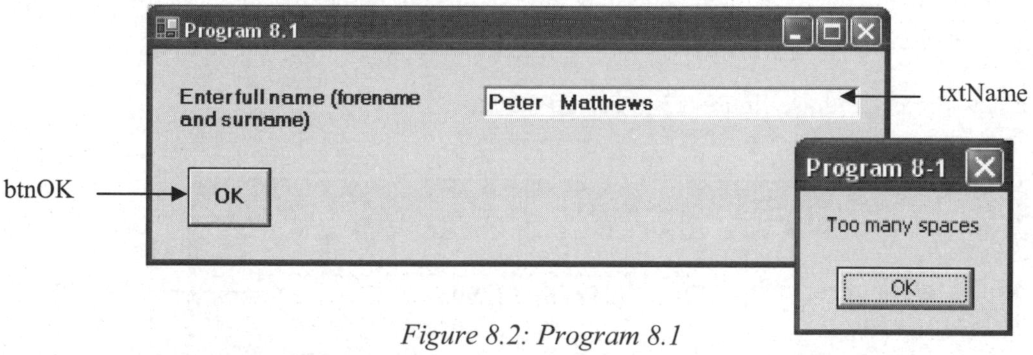

Figure 8.2: Program 8.1

3.   Run the program and test it five times by entering a name with one space between the forename and surname, more than one space between them, no spaces, a space before the forename and between the two parts of the name, and a finally a space after the surname.

end of Program 8.1

Removing spaces with *Trim, TrimStart* and *TrimEnd*

TrimStart removes any leading spaces at the left side of a string. **TrimEnd** does the same thing for trailing spaces on the right side of a string, and **Trim** does the job of both TrimStart and TrimEnd. In program 8.1, where the user is asked to enter a forename and surname with one space between, you could use TrimStart and TrimEnd to remove any accidental spaces before the firstname and after the surname. Thus *Name = Name.TrimStart* would remove any leading spaces. Using Trim would (wrongly) get rid of the space between the two parts of the name also.

Changing case with *ToUpper* and *ToLower*

ToUpper converts all characters in a string into their upper-case equivalents. **ToLower** converts them all into lower-case. If any of the characters are not letters they are ignored. Therefore ToUpper would change "Hello" into "HELLO" and "He**o" into "HE**O". The code below shows a possible use of ToUpper.

```
Dim Reply As String
'user has just entered Y(es) or N(o) into a text box
Reply = txtReply.Text
Reply = Reply.ToUpper        'ensure user reply is upper case
If Reply = "Y" Then
   'do something
End If
```

In this example Reply is a String. If you had declared it as Char you would get a Build error when running the program. To use the ToUpper method with a Char you have to pass the method one parameter – the character itself:

```
Reply = Reply.ToUpper(Reply)
```

PROGRAM 8.2 *Extract the area telephone code*

Specification	A telephone number is input in the form (01442) 12345, where the number in brackets is the area code. The area code may have a varying number of numeric digits. Output the area code without the brackets.

1. Open a new project and use figure 8.3 to design the form.

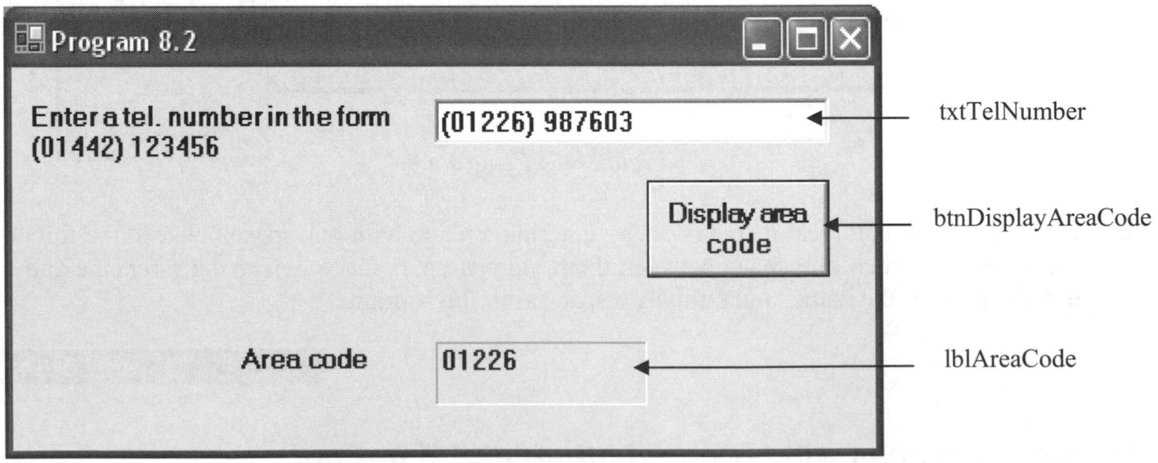

Figure 8.3: Program 8.2

2. Double-click the button and make sure its code is as follows:

```
Private Sub btnDisplayAreaCode_Click(...) Handles btnDisplayAreaCode.Click
  Dim TelNumber, AreaCode As String
  Dim Index As Short
  Dim Character As Char
  AreaCode = ""            'initialise area code to blank
  TelNumber = txtTelNumber.Text
  Index = 0   'set to 0 rather than -1 to skip first bracket of area code
  Do
    Index = Index + 1
    Character = TelNumber.Substring(Index, 1)
    AreaCode = AreaCode & Character 'build up code character by character
  Loop Until Character = ")" 'stop when closing bracket of area code found
  lblAreaCode.Text = AreaCode.Substring(0, AreaCode.Length - 1) 'Remove
                                       'closing bracket from area code
End Sub
```

The first repetition of the loop processes the first digit after the opening bracket because Index has the value 1 (recall that characters in a string are indexed from 0). Each repetition of the loop extracts a character using the **Substring** method and concatenates it to the area code. Because **Do...Loop Until** is used, in which the condition is tested at the end of the loop, the area code will have the closing bracket when the loop finishes. The first line of code after the loop uses **Substring** to remove it.

3. Run the program to check that it works. Try it out with the brackets and then without an opening bracket. Without the bracket the first digit of the code is not displayed. Finally try it without a closing bracket. This will produce a run-time error. Question 2 asks you to investigate these cases.

end of Program 8.2

Handling dates

The **Date** data type is used for dates. It stores a date *and* a time. We saw that with strings you can choose between a method and a function to do most tasks. The Date data type provides a range of methods and properties for handling dates. Some of these have equivalent functions. Sometimes you may need to use a function because there is no equivalent method or property.

There are several ways of storing a value in a Date variable. Three of them are listed below, but note that you can only convert strings to a Date data type if Option Strict is Off.

```
Dim MyDate As Date
MyDate = "16/4/1990"      'must be CDate("16/4/1990") if Option Strict On
MyDate = "16 April 1990"
MyDate = txtDate.Text
```

Today and *Now* functions

The **Today** function simply returns the current date in the format set in Windows Control Panel. The UK format is day/month/year. **Now** returns the current date and time.

Month and *Year* properties

The **Month** property returns an integer representing the month from 1 to 12. **Year** returns an integer representing the year. Thus

```
MyDate = "20 June 1998"
MsgBox(MyDate.Month & " " & MyDate.Year)
```

would display **6 1998**. To display **June 1998** you would need the **MonthName** *function*:

```
MsgBox(MonthName(MyDate.Month) & " " & MyDate.Year)
```

Formatting date output

In Chapter 4 you learned how to format numbers with named and user-defined formats using the **Format** function. You can use this function in a similar way with dates. Figure 8.4 shows the result of running the code below.

```
TheDate = "12/7/2003"
With lstOutput.Items
  .Add("Using named date formats")
  .Add("      Long Date    " & Format(TheDate, "Long Date"))
  .Add("      Medium Date    " & Format(TheDate, "Medium Date"))
  .Add("      Short Date    " & Format(TheDate, "Short Date"))
  .Add("")
  .Add("Using user-defined date formats")
  .Add("      d-M-yy    " & Format(TheDate, "d-M-yy"))
  .Add("      dd/MM/yyyy    " & Format(TheDate, "dd/MM/yyyy"))
  .Add("      dd/MMMM/yyyy    " & Format(TheDate, "dd/MMMM/yyyy"))
  .Add("      MMMM yy    " & Format(TheDate, "MMMM yy"))
  .Add("      dddd dd MMMM yyyy    " & Format(TheDate, "dddd dd MMMM yyyy"))
End With
```

Note that user-defined date formats require the month in upper case since lower-case 'm' means minutes.

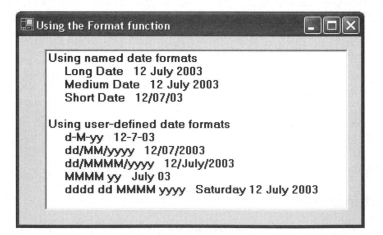

Figure 8.4

PROGRAM 8.3   *College Library issue desk*

Specification	Allow the issue and return of books in a school or college library. Books can be borrowed overnight, for 3 days, 10 days or 1 month. For issuing books the user should select the loan period and the date due back should be displayed in the form *Thursday 30 October 2003*. When a book is returned the user should select its loan period and enter the date due back. The program should display how many days it is overdue and the fine. Fines are 50p, 25p, 10p and 5p per day for overnight, 3-day, 10-day and one month loans respectively.

1. Open a new project and design the form using figure 8.5. Note that group boxes are used for Book issue and Book return.

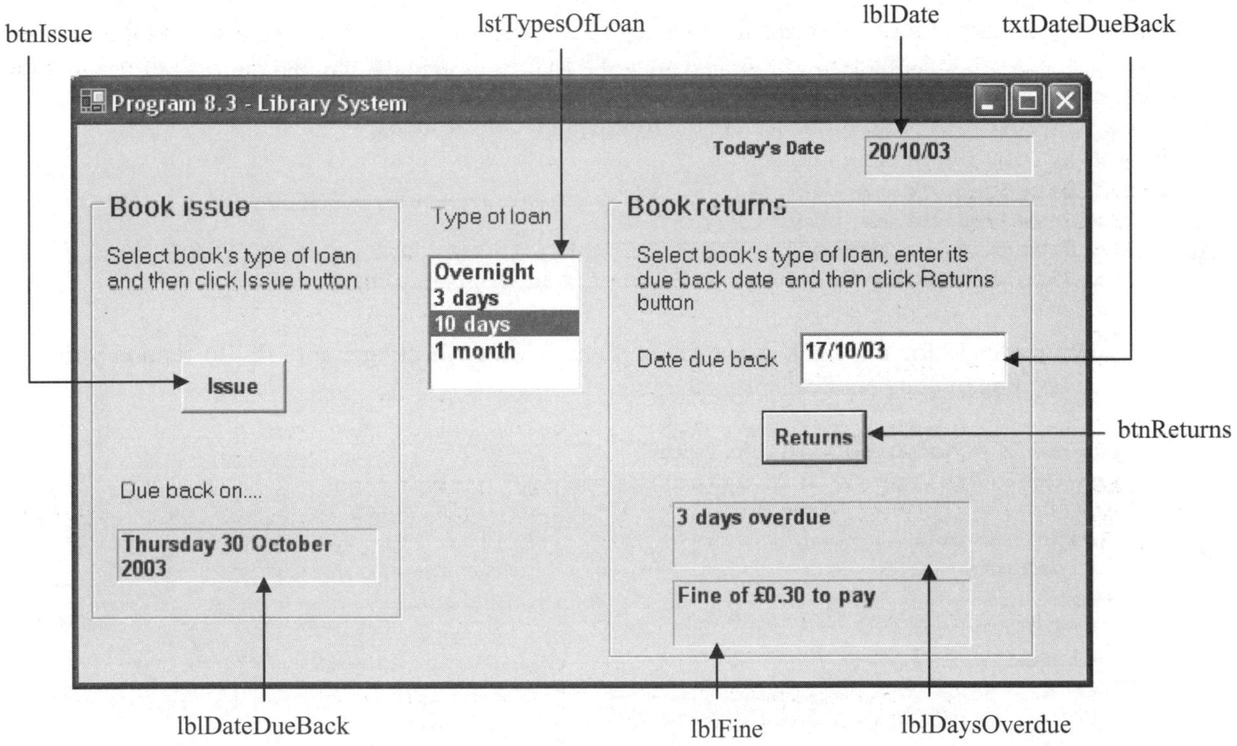

Figure 8.5: Program 8.3

2. Declare a single global variable below *Windows Form Designer generated code*:

```
Dim DaysLoan As Short
```

3. In the form's Load event procedure display the current date with the **Today** function:

```
lblDate.Text = Today
```

4. The code for the Click event of btnIssue converts the length of the loan selected to a number, and adds this to the current date by using the **AddDays** method. This must be passed the number of days to add. The format for displaying the date due back uses the last example in figure 8.4.

```
Private Sub btnIssue_Click(...) Handles btnIssue.Click
  Dim DateDueBack As Date
  Select Case lstTypesOfLoan.SelectedIndex    'index of item from list box
    Case 0
      DaysLoan = 1
    Case 1
      DaysLoan = 3
    Case 2
      DaysLoan = 10
    Case 3
      DaysLoan = 30
  End Select
  DateDueBack = Today.AddDays(DaysLoan)    'AddDays method to add days on
  lblDateDueBack.Text = Format(DateDueBack, "dddd dd MMMM yyyy")
End Sub
```

5. Run the program. Select a loan period and click the Issue button to display the return date.

6. In the Click event of btnReturns declare the following local variables:

```
Dim DateDueBack As Date
Dim DaysOverdue As Short
Dim FineRate As Decimal           '0.50 (50p), 0.25 (25p) etc
Dim Fine As Decimal               'final calculated fine
```

7. Complete the code for the Click event for btnReturns. Look back at figure 4.7 to remind yourself how the last line of code below displays the fine.

```
DateDueBack = txtDateDueBack.Text
Select Case lstTypesOfLoan.SelectedIndex
  Case 0                                'overnight loan
    DaysLoan = 1
    FineRate = 0.5                        'fine is 50p per day
  Case 1                                '3-day loan
    DaysLoan = 3
    FineRate = 0.25                       'fine is 25p per day
  Case 2                                '10-day loan
    DaysLoan = 10
    FineRate = 0.1                        'fine is 10p per day
  Case 3                                '1 month loan (=30 days)
    DaysLoan = 30
    FineRate = 0.05                       'fine is 5p per day
End Select
DaysOverdue = DateDiff("d", DateDueBack, Today)
If DaysOverdue < 0 Then     'If date of return is tomorrow or later
                            'DaysOverdue will have a negative value, so
  DaysOverdue = 0           'set it to 0 as book is not overdue
End If
If DaysOverdue > 0 Then               'is book overdue?
  Fine = FineRate * DaysOverdue
Else
  Fine = 0
End If
lblDaysOverdue.Text = DaysOverdue & " days overdue"
lblFine.Text = "Fine of " & Format(Fine, "Currency") & " to pay"
```

The **DateDiff** function is used to calculate the number of days between two dates. The first parameter is the time interval to be used. In the example here "d" means days. The function subtracts the first date (DateDueBack) from the second date (Today). The result will be positive if the date due back is earlier than the current date, i.e. the book is not overdue.

8. Run the program. Select a loan period, type in a return date earlier than the current date and click the Returns button to display the number of days overdue and the fine.

end of Program 8.3

Handling time

As with strings and dates you can choose between a method and a function to do many tasks. Sometimes a property is appropriate.

TimeString and *TimeOfDay*

TimeString and **TimeOfDay** are both properties. Both return the current time.in the form hh:mm:ss, for example 16:45:32. Assign these to a Date variable or display the time directly in a label through its Text property. You used TimeString in Program 2.3.

Second, Minute and *Hour*

There are **Second**, **Minute** and **Hour** methods and functions. They return an integer in the range 0 to 60 for Second and Minute and 0 to 24 for Hour. For example if the current time is 10:45:12 then

```
MsgBox(Now.Minute)
```

would print 45.

Calculations with time

In step 4 of Program 8.3 we used the AddDays method to add a given number of days to the current date. You cannot use the addition operator (or the subtraction operator) on dates but you can with time calculations.The following examples use the Minute method to calculate the number of minutes between two times. The output is shown in figure 8.6.

```
Dim Time1, Time2, Time3 As Date
Dim MinutesDiff As Integer
Dim Message As String
Time1 = "6:10:30"
Time2 = "6:18:40"
Time3 = "8:30:50"
MinutesDiff = Time2.Minute - Time1.Minute              'ie 18-10
Message = "Minutes difference between " & Time1 & " and " & Time2 & _
          " is   " & MinutesDiff & vbNewLine
MinutesDiff = Time3.Minute - Time1.Minute              'ie 30-18
Message = Message & "Minutes difference between " & Time1 & " and " _
          & Time3 & " is   " & MinutesDiff
MsgBox(Message)
```

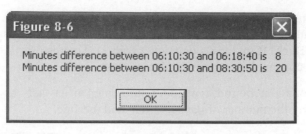

Figure 8.6

The first output in figure 8.6 is correct because the hour (06) is the same, but the second output, with different hours (06 and 08), does not show the correct *total* number of minutes difference. To calculate this you need to use the **Hour** method too. The following code would produce the correct answer of 140:

```
HoursDiff = Time3.Hour - Time1.Hour
MinutesDiff = (HoursDiff * 60) + (Time3.Minute - Time1.Minute)
```

Summary of key concepts

- There are two data types for declaring strings – **String** and **Char**. A Char variable holds one character. The **Date** data type stores a date and a time.

- Use the relational operators (>, < etc.) to compare strings.

- Use the **IndexOf** method to find the position in a string where a substring starts.

- Use the **Substring** method to extract a substring from a string. Use it to process each character of a string in turn.

- The **TrimStart** and **TrimEnd** methods remove leading and trailing spaces from a string. **Trim** removes both leading and trailing spaces.

- The **ToUpper** and **ToLower** methods convert strings to upper and lower case.

- Use the **Today** function to return the current date, **Now** to return the current date and time and **TimeString** or **TimeOfDay** to return the current time.

- Use the **DateDiff** function to find the time interval between two dates.

- Use the **Format** function to format the output of dates and times.

Take it from here...

1. In Program 8.3 you added a given number of days to a date. How would you subtract a given number of days?

2. If you assigned the string "15 Jun 38" to a Date variable would Visual Basic store this as 15/06/1938 or 15/06/2038? Write a piece of code to demonstrate which century would be stored. Use this code to find out which is the boundary two-digit year for storing a date as 20th century or 21st century.

3. Find out about the following string methods – **Compare**, **PadLeft**, **PadRight**, **Remove**, **Replace** and **Insert**.

4. Some string methods have equivalent functions. Find out how to use the equivalent functions for the **IndexOf**, **Substring**, **ToUpper** and **Length** methods.

Questions on the Programs

Program 8.1

*1. The program outputs only one message, if two or more spaces are found. Extend it to output appropriate messages if one or more spaces are found

- before the firstname.
- after the surname.

Program 8.2

*1. Rewrite the code using Do While...Loop instead of Do...Loop Until.

**2. Run the program but do not enter the opening bracket for the area code. Why is the area code displayed without the first digit? Now run the program but do not enter the closing bracket. You will get a run-time error telling you that *Index and length must refer to a location in the string*. What has caused this error? Extend the code so that if one or both of the brackets are not entered an appropriate message is displayed.

Program 8.3

**1. The program uses the Format function to display the full date for the return of issued books. Suppose this function was not available. Write code to display the full date by using the DayOfWeek, Day, Month and Year methods and the Month function. Convert the return value of DayOfWeek into a day (Sunday, Monday etc,) with a Select Case.

End of chapter exercises

*1. Ask the user to enter a string and then display it in reverse using a function called **StrReverse**. For example "Hello there" would be displayed as "ereht olleH". There is a harder way to do this using the **Substring** method. If you use Substring count this as a two-star exercise.

2. Ask the user to enter two dates. Output the number of leap years between both dates as shown in figure 8.7. Use the **IsLeapYear method.

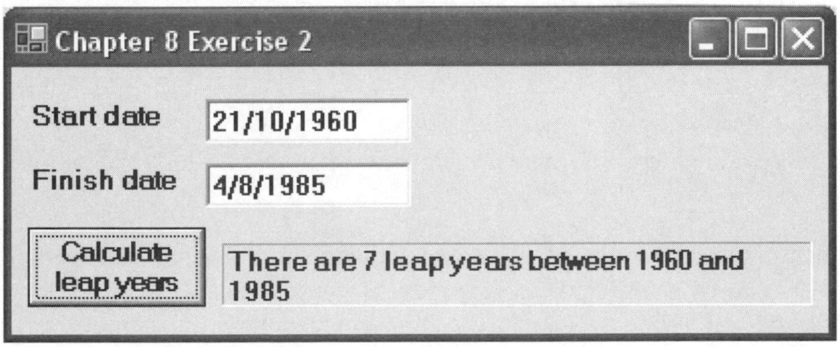

Figure 8.7: Exercise 2

**3. Write a program that reads a string from the user and displays only those words beginning with the letters 'd' or 't'.

**4. Write a program that asks the user to input some text and to indicate which word to search for in the text. Output the number of times this word occurs.

5. Ask the user to enter some text and change it into upper case without using the **ToUpper method (or its equivalent function). You will need to use two functions not covered in the chapter, **Asc** and **Chr**.

***6. A manufacturer of sawn timber sells to a large number of timber yards and DIY shops. Assume the user is processing payments from these customers. Allow the user to input the date an invoice should have been paid by and the total value of the invoice. Calculate how many days late, if any, the payment has been made. If payment has been made 15 or more days before the due date give a 10% discount, otherwise give a 5% discount if it has been paid on time. Output details about whether payment has been made on time, any discount given and the total amount due.

***7. Write a program that counts up and displays how many words the user can type in a minute. The running program can be seen in figure 1.1. Use a Timer control to display how many seconds have elapsed. At the simplest level you could count the number of spaces in the text to calculate the number of words. But for a 3-star exercise you should handle other possibilities. What if two or more spaces are entered by mistake between words? What if the user starts by accidentally pressing the space bar?

Chapter 9 – Procedures

What is a procedure?

A procedure is a separate section of code which performs one or more specific tasks and is identified by having a name.

Types of procedure

Visual Basic .NET has four types of procedure. These are:

- **Event** procedures
- **Sub** procedures
- **Function** procedures
- **Property** procedures

So far you have used only event procedures where code is executed in response to events such as Load, Click and so on. The other three types of procedure are not set off directly by events, but are **called** or executed by code within an event procedure or from within another non-event procedure. Property procedures are used when you adopt an object-oriented approach to programming (see Chapters 17 and 18). Sub and Function procedures are sometimes referred to as **general** procedures and are the subject of this chapter. Figure 9.1 illustrates how procedures may be linked. The Click event procedure calls two general procedures, and one of these, procedure A, in turn calls another general procedure, function C. Note how control returns to the next line of code after the procedure call when the procedure is finished.

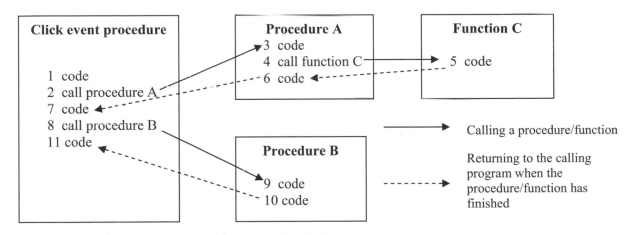

Figure 9.1: An example of how procedures may be linked

Sub and Function procedures

There are two key differences between these types of procedure:

- A **Function** procedure always returns one piece of data to that part of the program which calls it. A **Sub** procedure may return one or more items of data or no data at all. The way in which the two types of procedure return data is different.

- The way in which the procedure is called.

You can really only understand these by doing programs 9.1 and 9.2 (Sub procedures) and 9.3 (Function procedure).

Why use procedures?

Almost all programs you write inevitably use event procedures. You don't *have* to use Sub or Function procedures, but there are several good reasons why you should:

- **Avoid repeating code**. If you have identical code in two or more event procedures you may be able to write it just once in a procedure instead.

- **Make the code more readable**. An event procedure with many lines of code may be easier to understand if some of the code is put into procedures.

- **Help in debugging a program**. Splitting the program up into small logical units will make it easier to trace any errors in the program when it runs. This is called debugging a program.

- **Use a procedure in other programs**. Suppose you had written some code that validated a date. You could use this procedure in any other program that used a similar date.

- **Pass parameters**. All good programmers ought to pass parameters, where appropriate. Only by having procedures can you do this. Parameters are discussed later in this chapter.

What a procedure does is entirely up to you. There are no hard and fast rules, but as a guide use a procedure to carry out one specific task or a small number of related tasks.

PROGRAM 9.1 *Avoid repeating code*

Specification   Illustrate how procedures can make it unnecessary to repeat code in two or more event procedures.

Look back at program 2.4 which coloured a form according to the position of the scroll boxes in three scroll bars (figure 2.13). The code is shown in figure 9.2 – each of the three scroll bars has a single line of identical code for its Scroll event. In this program we will write this code only once, in a Sub procedure.

```
Private Sub hsbRed_Scroll(ByVal sender As System.Object, ByVal e As System.Windows.Forms.Sc
    Me.BackColor = ColorTranslator.FromOle(RGB(hsbRed.Value, hsbGreen.Value, hsbBlue.Value))
End Sub

Private Sub hsbGreen_Scroll(ByVal sender As System.Object, ByVal e As System.Windows.Forms
    Me.BackColor = ColorTranslator.FromOle(RGB(hsbRed.Value, hsbGreen.Value, hsbBlue.Value))
End Sub

Private Sub hsbBlue_Scroll(ByVal sender As System.Object, ByVal e As System.Windows.Forms.S
    Me.BackColor = ColorTranslator.FromOle(RGB(hsbRed.Value, hsbGreen.Value, hsbBlue.Value))
End Sub
```

Figure 9.2

1.   Open a new project. Right-click **Form1.vb** in the Solution Explorer and select **Delete**. Confirm the deletion. Select **File/Add Existing Item**. Select **Form1.vb** from Program 2-4 and click **Open**. A copy of Form1 will be added to the Solution Explorer. (If you did not save Program 2.4 then use the existing form and do steps 1 – 5 from that program now. Then double-click each of the three scroll bars to produce empty code templates for their Scroll events.)

2. Unlike event procedures you must declare a general procedure yourself. Do this after the three Scroll event procedures. Position the cursor between the third End Sub and End Class, press **Enter** for a blank line and declare the procedure **ShowFormColour** as in figure 9.3. Like names of variables and objects Visual Basic does not allow any spaces in a procedure name. Press Enter and an **End Sub** will be added. If you do not include the empty brackets Visual Basic will do this for you.

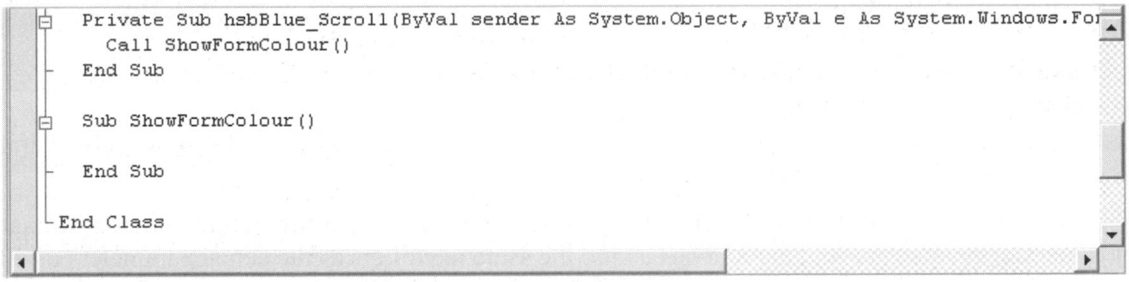

```
Private Sub hsbBlue_Scroll(ByVal sender As System.Object, ByVal e As System.Windows.For
    Call ShowFormColour()
End Sub

Sub ShowFormColour()

End Sub

End Class
```

Figure 9.3.: Declaring the procedure

3. Write a single line of code inside the procedure ShowFormColour. It should be the same as the line inside each of the three Scroll event procedures, as shown in figure 9.2:

```
Me.BackColor = ColorTranslator.FromOle(RGB(hsbRed.Value, _
                              hsbGreen.Value, hsbBlue.Value))
```

4. Delete the single line of code in each of the three Scroll event procedures. If you have not used the form from Program 2.4 then this step is not relevant.

5. Now you have to tell each of the three Scroll event procedures to **call** this Sub procedure. Their code should look as follows:

```
Private Sub hsbRed_Scroll(...) Handles hsbRed.Scroll
  Call ShowFormColour()
End Sub

Private Sub hsbRed_Scroll(...) Handles hsbRed.Scroll
  Call ShowFormColour()
End Sub

Private Sub hsbRed_Scroll(...) Handles hsbRed.Scroll
  Call ShowFormColour()
End Sub
```

The keyword **Call** is optional, but as it makes the code more readable we will use it throughout this book. The empty brackets after the procedure name are not optional. If you do not include them Visual Basic .NET will add them.

6. Run the program to check that it works.

end of Program 9.1

Passing parameters

A **parameter** is a piece of data that is sent to a procedure when it is called and is used by the procedure to help it carry out its task. Not all procedures need parameters; others may need one or more of them.

Actual and Formal parameters

Suppose the user has typed numbers into two text boxes and these are stored in variables FirstNumber and SecondNumber. You could write a procedure, FindSmaller, that works out which of the two numbers is the smallest, and call it with

```
Call FindSmallerNumber(FirstNumber, SecondNumber)
```

FirstNumber and SecondNumber are two parameters which are passed to the procedure. Parameters passed to a procedure are called **actual parameters**.

When you declare the procedure FindSmallerNumber you must declare **formal parameters** to match the actual parameters you are sending it. You can use the same identifiers as the actual parameters or different ones. In this book we will nearly always use different identifiers for the actual and formal parameters. When you declare a formal parameter it is optional whether you declare its data type too. However it makes the code a little easier to understand if you do, so we'll adopt the practice in this book. Thus all of the following procedure declarations are correct:

```
Public Sub FindSmaller(NumberOne As Integer, NumberTwo As Integer) 'use
                    'different identifiers for actual and formal parameters
Public Sub FindSmaller(NumberOne, NumberTwo) 'data types not declared
Public Sub FindSmaller(FirstNumber As Integer, SecondNumber As Integer)
                                                   'use same identifiers
```

Figure 9.4 illustrates the matching of the actual and formal parameters. This example highlights three important rules:

- The number of actual and formal parameters must be the same.
- Parameters are matched according to their position, not according to their names.
- The data types of a matching pair of parameters must be the same.

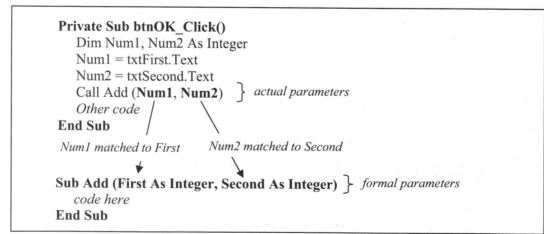

Figure 9.4: Matching actual and formal parameters

Value and Reference parameters

Formal parameters are divided into **value** and **reference parameters.** Reference parameters are used when you need to pass data back from a Sub procedure to the calling program. The code inside procedure FindSmaller will find out which number is the smaller, and since we need to get this information out it must be declared as a reference parameter. The two numbers themselves are not changed in any way, and do not need to be passed out again. Therefore they are **value parameters**. The complete code to call and declare the procedure now becomes:

```
Call FindSmaller(FirstNumber, SecondNumber, SmallerNumber)

Sub FindSmaller(ByVal NumberOne As Integer, _
            ByVal NumberTwo As Integer, ByRef Smaller As Integer)
```

Use the keywords **ByVal** and **ByRef** to declare value and reference parameters. When the procedure has found the smaller number it can be passed back to the calling code through Smaller, and this in turn is matched back onto the actual parameter SmallerNumber. Thus two further rules can be drawn up:

- A reference parameter is used when a piece of data needs to be passed out of the procedure.
- A value parameter is a piece of data used by the procedure. Any changes made to it inside the procedure are not passed back again.

PROGRAM 9.2 *Value and Reference parameters*

Specification   Write a program to illustrate the differences between value and reference parameters.

We'll reuse program 3.4 which calculates the average of a set of exam marks. Let's replace some of the code by two procedures as follows:

- Procedure **ProcessOneNumber**, which will be called from the Click event of the OK button.
- Procedure **CalcMean**, which will be called from the Click event of the Show Mean button.

Because the concepts illustrated by this program are very tricky you may not get an overall view of what is going on as you type small sections of code in the steps below. The complete code for this program can be seen in figure 9.6.

1. Open a new project. Right-click **Form1.vb** in the Solution Explorer and select **Delete**. Confirm the deletion. Select **File/Add Existing Item**. Select **Form1.vb** from Program 3-4 and click **Open**. A copy of Form1 will be added to the Solution Explorer. (If you did not save Program 3.4 then use the existing form and go through steps 1 – 10 from that program now.)

2. Program 3.4 had Option Strict set to On. It does not matter whether it is set to On or Off.

3. Two of the tasks of the Click event of the OK button were to keep running totals of all the marks and of how many exam marks had been entered. Delete the code below which does this:

```
Total = Total + Number
NumberOfMarks = NumberOfMarks + 1
```

We need to send the parameter Number *to* the procedure and to get back the two running totals *from* the procedure. Number should therefore be a value parameter and the other two should be reference parameters. Figure 9.5 shows what is going on. An arrow going into the procedure but without one coming out represents a value parameter. The pair of arrows going into and out of the procedure represent a reference parameter. The identifiers for the outgoing reference parameters are first used in step 5 below.

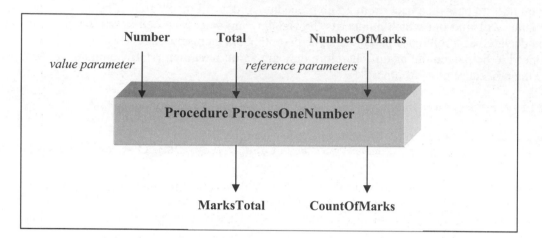

Figure 9.5: Parameters for procedure ProcessOneNumber

4. Replace the code you deleted in step 3 with a call to the procedure:

```
Call ProcessOneNumber(Number, Total, NumberOfMarks)
```

5. Position the cursor between the last End Sub and End Class, press **Enter** for a blank line and write in the procedure declaration. The formal parameters must be listed inside the brackets. Press Enter to get **End Sub**.

```
Sub ProcessOneNumber(ByVal ExamMark As Integer, _
          ByRef MarksTotal As Integer, ByRef CountOfMarks As Integer)
```

6. The code inside this procedure should be the same as the code you deleted in step 3, except that you must use the identifiers of the formal parameters:

```
MarksTotal = MarksTotal + ExamMark
CountOfMarks = CountOfMarks + 1
```

7. Now look at the code in the Click event procedure for the Show Mean button. The code which must be replaced by a procedure call is

```
Mean = Total / NumberOfMarks
```

We need to send two parameters, Total and NumberOfMarks, to be used by the procedure, and to get back from it the calculated mean. These two parameters should be value parameters and the returned mean must be a reference parameter. Figure 9.7 shows this diagrammatically.

8. Replace the line of code in step 7 with

```
Call CalcMean(Total, NumberOfMarks, Mean)
```

```
Form1                          ▼   ▐▌\(Declarations)                              ▼
        Dim Total As Integer           'stores running total of marks
        Dim NumberOfMarks As Integer   'stores number of exam marks entered

   ⊟    Private Sub btnOK_Click(ByVal sender As System.Object, ByVal e As System.Ev
           Dim Number As Integer
           Number = CInt(txtMark.Text)          'read exam mark.Use Cint to convert
           lstMarks.Items.Add(Number)           'copy it to list box
           Call ProcessOneNumber(Number, Total, NumberOfMarks)
           btnShowMean.Enabled = True           'enable the Show Mean button
           txtMark.Text = ""                    'clear out the old exam mark
           txtMark.Focus()                      'place cursor ready for next mark
        End Sub

   ⊟    Private Sub btnShowMean_Click(ByVal sender As System.Object, ByVal e As Sys
           Dim Mean As Double                   'declare local variable
           Call CalcMean(Total, NumberOfMarks, Mean)
           txtMean.Text = CStr(Mean)            'display it
           txtMean.Visible = True               'show text box which displays mean
           lblMean.Visible = True               'and show its label
           txtMark.Enabled = False              'disallow more marks to be entered
           btnOK.Enabled = False                'and disable OK button
        End Sub

   ⊟    Private Sub btnQuit_Click(ByVal sender As System.Object, ByVal e As System.
           Me.Close()
        End Sub

   ⊟    Private Sub txtMark_TextChanged(ByVal sender As Object, ByVal e As System.E
           btnOK.Enabled = True
        End Sub

        Sub ProcessOneNumber(ByVal ExamMark As Integer, _
   ⊟               ByRef MarksTotal As Integer, ByRef CountOfMarks As Integer)
           MarksTotal = MarksTotal + ExamMark
           CountOfMarks = CountOfMarks + 1
        End Sub

        Sub CalcMean(ByVal MarksTotal As Integer, _
   ⊟               ByVal CountOfMarks As Integer, ByRef Average As Single)
           Average = MarksTotal / CountOfMarks
        End Sub
    └─ End Class
```

Figure 9.6: The complete code for Program 9.2

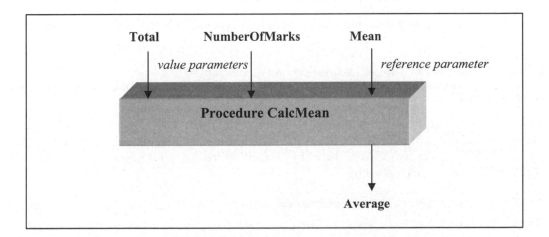

Figure 9.7: Parameters for procedure CalcMean

9. Declare procedure CalcMean below procedure ProcessOneNumber. Press **Enter** to get **End Sub**.

```
Sub CalcMean(ByVal MarksTotal As Integer, _
             ByVal CountOfMarks As Integer, ByRef Average As Single)
```

The parameter Average must be declared as **Single** because this is the data type of its matching actual parameter Mean.

10. Inside this procedure write the code to calculate the mean value:

```
Average = MarksTotal / CountOfMarks
```

11. Run the program.

end of Program 9.2

Practical work on using the correct formal parameters

Visual Basic does not insist that you identify formal parameters as value or reference by using the keywords ByVal and ByRef. If you omit these it treats all parameters as value parameters. However it is good practice to identify the parameter types. The purpose of the steps that follow is to give you a practical demonstration of how things can sometimes go wrong if you don't identify them correctly.

Pass a parameter by reference when it should be by value – no error

1. Open Program 9.2 and change the first parameter, MarksTotal, in procedure CalcMean, from value to reference:

```
Sub CalcMean(ByRef MarksTotal As Integer, _
             ByVal CountOfMarks As Integer, ByRef Average As Single)
```

2. Run the program and everything should work fine. Change the ByRef back to **ByVal**.

Pass a parameter by value when it should be by reference – error!

3. Change the second formal parameter, MarksTotal, in procedure ProcessOneNumber, from reference to value:

```
Sub ProcessOneNumber(ByVal ExamMark As Integer, _
             ByVal MarksTotal As Integer, ByRef CountOfMarks As Integer)
```

4. Run the program. The mean mark will now be displayed as 0. The content of MarksTotal is not passed out of the procedure and therefore is not stored in its matching actual parameter Total. Total stores the value 0 because Visual Basic by default initialises an Integer variable to 0. When procedureCalcMean is then called by

```
Call CalcMean(Total, NumberOfMarks, Mean)
```

a value of 0 is passed into the procedure through Total. This is matched onto CalcMean's formal parameter, MarksTotal, which in turn means that Average is calculated as 0 inside CalcMean. This 0 is passed back to the matching actual parameter Mean.

From steps 1 – 4 two further rules can be stated:

- a parameter declared as reference when it should be declared by value will **not** produce an error
- a parameter declared as value when it should be reference **will** produce an error

5. Change the formal parameter MarksTotal back to **ByRef** and close the program.

Functions

Types of function

A function is a shorter name for a function procedure. Visual Basic has two types of function:

- **Built-in** functions which are supplied as part of the language
- **User-defined** functions which you write yourself

You have used a number of built-in functions in previous programs. Examples include Format, Today and DateDiff, although you have seen that there is an alternative to many built-in functions – use a method. Now you need to learn how to write your own functions.

Calling a function

There are several ways of calling a function. Two important ones are:

- **Assign its return value to a variable**. For example in step 7 of Program 8.3 the number of days a book is overdue was calculated by:

```
DaysOverdue = DateDiff("d", DateDueBack, Today)
```

- **Display its return value directly**. In step 7 of Program 8.3 the number of days a book is overdue could have been displayed directly in the label with:

```
lblDaysOverdue.Text = DateDiff("d", DateDueBack, Today) & " days overdue"
```

PROGRAM 9.3   *Calculating interest*

Specification   Write a function to calculate the amount of interest earned on an investment. The amount invested, the interest rate and the number of years the investment lasts, are to be entered by the user.

If you invested £1000 over 2 years at an interest rate of 10% per year then the interest paid after one year would be £100 (i.e. 10% of £1000). In year 2 you would get 10% of (£1000 + £100), i.e. £110, and so the total interest paid would be £210. In this program a function named **CalculateInterest** will calculate and return this value.

1.   Open a new project and design the form shown in figure 9.8. Name the controls needed in code as **txtAmountInvested, txtInterestRate, txtYears, lblInterest** and **btnCalcInterest**.

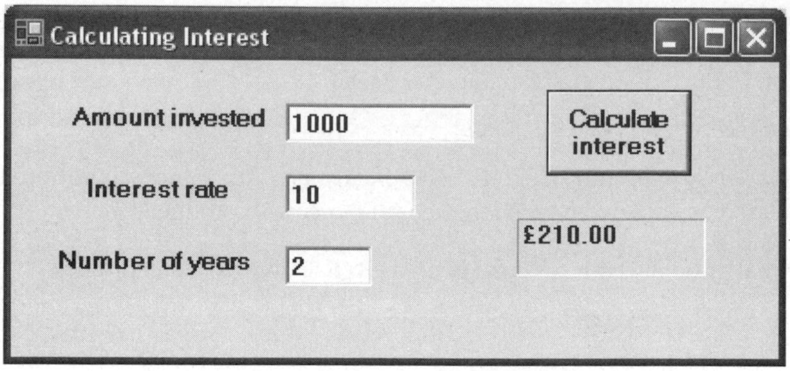

Figure 9.8: Program 9.3

2. Type the following code into the Click event of the button:

```
Private Sub btnCalcInterest_Click(...) Handles btnCalcInterest.Click
   Dim Interest, AmountInvested As Decimal
   Dim RateOfInterest As Single
   Dim Years As Short
   AmountInvested = txtAmountInvested.Text
   RateOfInterest = txtInterestRate.Text
   Years = txtYears.Text
                'call the function and assign its return value to Interest
   Interest = CalculateInterest(AmountInvested, RateOfInterest, Years)
   lblInterest.Text = Format(Interest, "Currency")
End Sub
```

The function CalculateInterest is called as part of an assignment

```
   Interest = CalculateInterest(AmountInvested, RateOfInterest, Years)
```

Three actual parameters are passed, and the data item returned from the function is assigned to the variable Interest.

3. Below the code you wrote in step 2 declare the function CalculateInterest with its three formal parameters. Press **Enter** and **End Function** will be added.

```
Function CalculateInterest(ByVal Principal As Decimal, _
                           ByVal InterestRate As Single, _
                           ByVal NumberYears As Short) As Decimal
End Function
```

Note the following:

- They are all value parameters since they are merely used by the function. Although you *could* use reference parameters in functions to return data as you did with Sub procedures, this would not be considered good programming since the job of a function is really to return one item of data.

- The data type of the piece of data that *is* returned is declared after the last bracket. In this example it is Decimal.

5. Write the code inside the function to calculate the interest:

```
Dim Interest As Decimal
Dim Year As Short
Interest = 0
For Year = 1 To NumberYears
  Interest = Interest + ((Principal + Interest) * InterestRate / 100)
Next Year
Return Interest   'use Return to pass out the function's return value
```

The last line shows one of two ways to return the calculated interest to the calling part of the program. This method is new to Visual Basic .NET. The other way is to assign this data (Interest) to the name of the function (CalculateInterest). This would be written as:

```
CalculateInterest = Interest
```

Note that Interest is of type Decimal because the return data type noted in step 4 is Decimal. (However Visual Basic is not always strict about this, which you will discover by doing question 2 on this program.)

6. Run the program and check that it works by using the sample data in figure 9.6 and other data of your choice.

End of Program 9.3

Form and Standard modules

So far all our general procedures have been written on the single form belonging to a project. There are two other places you could write them:

- On another form in the same project. This is called another **form module**.
- On a **standard module**, which cannot contain controls, only code. This is very similar to a module in a console application (covered in Chapter 5).

In program 9.3 you could have put function CalculateInterest on Form2. To load and reference one form from another you have to declare a variable of the form's type (which is first done in Program 11.1). If this variable is called NextForm then you would call the function by prefixing it with its variable name and a period (**.**) as follows:

```
Interest = NextForm.CalculateInterest(AmountInvested, RateOfInterest, Years)
```

There is a further point to note. You may have noticed that all the event procedure declarations start with the word **Private**. This means they have scope only on the form on which they are declared. You would use **Public** to extend this scope to the other forms in the project. Many of the general procedures in this chapter have not used either of these words although they can be used here too. If you do not use them then Visual Basic assumes the procedure is Public. However if function CalculateInterest had been declared as Private on Form2 then it would not be possible to call it from Form1.

Variables and procedures declared in a **standard module** have scope throughout a project. A standard module is saved as a separate file, to which Visual Basic adds a **vb** extension, and it is displayed in the Solution Explorer. You can then use this standard module in any program you write. Procedures in standard modules are often put together as a **library**. You might write several procedures with a common theme and put them in the same library. An example might be several string-handling routines not provided by the language.

PROGRAM 9.4   *A standard module function*

> **Specification**   Write a function that changes the first letter of a string to upper case. Write it in a standard module and use it in a program.

1. Open a new project and build the form using the running program shown in figure 9.9. Name the controls **btnNewName**, **txtName** and **lblNewName**.

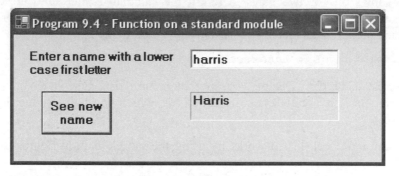

Figure 9.9: Program 9.4

2. Select **Project/Add New Item**, select the **Module** template in the Add New Item dialog box and in the Name box name it **StringLibrary**. Click **Open.** The new module will be added to the Solution Explorer as shown in figure 9.10.

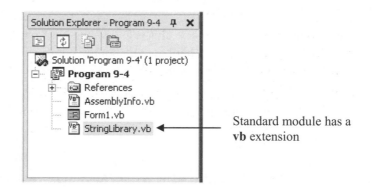

Standard module has a **vb** extension

Figure 9.10: The standard module is added to the project

3. The Code window for this standard module displays the code template using the keywords **Module** and **End Module**. Write the function **UpperCaseFirstLetter** between these keywords:

```
Function UpperCaseFirstLetter(ByVal OldString As String) As String
  Dim FirstLetter As Char
  Dim NewString As String
  FirstLetter = FirstLetter.ToUpper(OldString.Substring(0, 1)) 'Assigns
          'the first letter of OldString to FirstLetter as upper case
  Mid(OldString, 1, 1) = FirstLetter  'Mid statement replaces the first
                'letter of OldString with this upper case letter
  NewString = OldString
  Return NewString
End Function
```

The new thing here is the **Mid** statement. It replaces part of a string with another string. Its second parameter, 1, indicates that the start position for replacing is the first character. Its third parameter, 1 also, indicates that one character should be replaced. Note two things about Mid. First, the string to be changed is indexed from 1 rather than 0 as with the **Substring** method. Second, it is not the same as the Mid *function* which you may have discovered from question 4 of *Take it from here...* in Chapter 8 is an alternative to the Substring method.

4.   In the Click event for the button on Form1 enter the code:

```
Private Sub btnNewName_Click(...) Handles btnNewName.Click
   Dim Name, NewName As String
   Name = txtName.Text
   NewName = UpperCaseFirstLetter(Name)        'call the function
   lblNewName.Text = NewName
End Sub
```

5.   Run the program. Enter a name with a lower-case first letter and click the button.

end of Program 9.4

Summary of key concepts

- **General** procedures are non-event procedures. The two main types are **Sub** and **Function** procedures (functions).

- General procedures are called from within an event procedure or from another general procedure.

- A function may be called in several ways. The commonest is by assigning its return value to a variable. You cannot call Sub procedures in this way. Call them by using the **Call** statement.

- A function always returns one item of data.

- A **parameter** is a piece of data sent to a procedure when it is called. **Actual** parameters are passed to the procedure and matched to the **formal** parameters which are part of the procedure's declaration. The data type of a matching pair of actual and formal parameters must usually be the same.

- Formal parameters are divided into **value** and **reference** parameters. Any changes made to a reference parameter inside the procedure are passed out again. Changes to a value parameter cannot be passed out again.

- You do not have to declare formal parameters as value (**ByVal**) or reference (**ByRef**). If you don't, Visual Basic defaults to value.

- If you pass a parameter by reference when it should be by value no error occurs, but if you pass by value when it should have been by reference, a serious error will occur.

- A **standard module** can only contain code. Its procedures can be used in any programs. Standard modules are sometimes used as **libraries**.

Take it from here...

1.   Two methods of calling a function were covered. You could use a third method – call it in the same way as you call a Sub procedure using the optional keyword Call. Investigate this method by trying it out in code. What do you think happens to the function's return value? What do you think of this method of calling a function?

2. One of the parameter rules is that the number of actual and formal parameters must be the same. Strictly speaking this is not a rule since Visual Basic does allow optional parameters. Find out about these parameters.

Questions on the Programs

Program 9.2

*1. The task of procedure CalcMean is simply to calculate the mean of the exam marks. Extend this to calculate *and display* the mean rather than sending it back to the event procedure to display it. Rewrite the code to handle this new specification.

**2. The chapter points out that parameter passing is not compulsory but that it is considered good programming to do so where appropriate. Rewrite this program so that no parameters are passed to the two procedures, but don't change what the procedures do. To do this some of the variables which would have been passed as parameters must be declared as global, but recall that in Chapter 3 you learned it is poor programming to use global variables when you don't need to. This exercise should show you that parameter passing reduces the number of global variables to a minimum.

Program 9.3

*1. The point was made in step 5 that the variable Interest is declared as Decimal because this is the data type declared as the return data type (in step 4). Experiment by changing the data type of Interest and of the return data type. What can you conclude about how strict Visual Basic is about the data types being the same?

Program 9.4

**1. Change the code in the Click event of btnNewName so that it changes the first letter of each word in the string you enter into the text box. Your code will need to call the function UpperCaseFirstLetter each time a new word is encountered in the string.

**2. Write a second function in module StringLibrary which changes the first letter of every word in a given string into upper case. Name the function UpperCaseFirstLetters. Test it out by calling it from the Click event of the button.

End of chapter exercises

*1. When the user clicks a button on a form display *This is a procedure call* in a message box. The message should be displayed by calling a Sub procedure from the button's Click event.

*2. Ask the user to type a person's age into a text box and then to click a button. Validate that the age lies in the range 18 – 40 by calling a function from the button's Click event. If the age is not valid the Click event procedure should display an appropriate message.

**3. Ask the user to enter two numbers into text boxes as shown in figure 9.11. Clicking the button should call a Sub procedure to swap the numbers, which are then passed back to the calling program. The Click event should then display them in the two labels on the right.

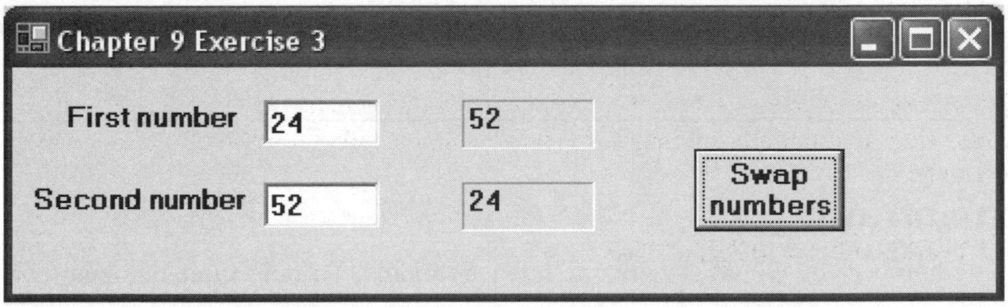

Figure 9.11: Exercise 3

**4. Write a function that is passed two parameters, a string and a character, and returns the number of times that the character is present in the string. Ask the user to enter some text and a search letter in two text boxes, and then to click a button. The button's event procedure should call the function and then the event procedure should output the number of occurrences.

***5. Write a program that processes invoices for a company selling a variety of products. Ask the user to enter the unit cost of the product, how many were sold and the date the invoice had to be paid by. A check box should be used to indicate if the product is VAT rated. When these details have been entered the user should click a button. This event should call two general procedures. The first should calculate and return the basic cost of the invoice, including VAT. The second should reduce this basic cost by 10% if the invoice has been paid on time. The final cost should be displayed by the Click event of the button.

Chapter 10 – Arrays

What is an array?

To store a single number you would declare one Integer variable. To store three numbers you would need three variables:

```
Dim FirstNumber, SecondNumber, ThirdNumber As Integer
```

What about storing hundreds or even thousands of numbers? Clearly things get difficult if not impossible! An **array** is a **data structure** that stores as many items as you require using a single variable. All the items must be the same data type. Thus you can store an array of Integers, an array of Strings and so on. The only way to mix the data types is to store records in the array, but this is the subject of the next chapter.

You have already used the array data structure, probably without realising it. For example in program 2.1 you used the SelectedIndex property of a list box to identify which item in the list box is the currently selected one. Visual Basic numbers the items from 0. So if you had a list box named lstEmployees, Visual Basic .NET stores the 4th item as lstEmployees(3).

How to declare an array

To declare an array that can store 5 whole numbers you would write the following:

```
Dim Numbers(4) As Integer
```

The storage 'slots' in the array are called **subscripts**. In figure 10.1 the variable *Numbers* stores all the data in the array. Numbers(1), for example, refers to the *contents* of subscript 1, i.e. 78, and Numbers(4) to 65.

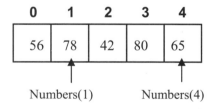

Figure 10.1: An array holding 5 integers

Earlier versions of Visual Basic allowed you to start the indexing of an array from values other than 0 but this is not now supported.

Static and Dynamic arrays

A static array is one whose size is fixed throughout the program. A dynamic array can grow and shrink in size as the program runs. First declare the array without indicating its size by using empty brackets. Then **ReDim** it with the required size at the point in your code where you want it to change. For example:

```
Dim Names() As String        'use empty brackets for first declaration
   'code to do something unrelated to the array goes here
ReDim Names(29) As String        'resize array to store 30 items
   'code to add names to the array goes here
```

If we later ReDim the array again to hold twice as many items, its contents will be lost unless we use the keyword **Preserve**:

```
ReDim Preserve Names(59) As String    'array can now hold 60 items
```

Processing an array

Suppose you have declared an array to hold 40 exam marks as follows:

```
Dim ExamMarks(39) As Integer
```

To store an exam mark in the 4th subscript of the array you could write:

```
Mark = txtExamMark.Text
ExamMarks(3) = Mark
```

Numeric literals, such as 3 in the above example, are not often used to identify a subscript in the array. More often you use a variable. Assuming NumberOfMarks stores how many numbers are in the array, the code below displays the array's contents:

```
For Index = 0 To NumberOfMarks - 1
   lstMarks.Items.Add(ExamMarks(Index))
Next Index
```

PROGRAM 10.1   *Array to hold numbers*

Specification	Allow the user to enter up to 5 numbers and store them in an array. Output an appropriate message if the user attempts to store a 6th number. Allow the user to display the contents of the array at any time, and to enter a number to be searched for in the array. Display the result of this search – whether the number is in the array or not.

1. Open a new project and design the form using figure 10.2. Name the buttons **btnAddToArray**, **btnDisplay** and **btnFindNumber**. Name the text boxes for input and searching **txtNumber** and **txtSearchNumber** respectively, name the list box for output **lstNumbers**, and the label to display the result of the search **lblDisplaySearch**.

2. Declare the array and an index into the array as global variables. These must be globals because they will be used in two event procedures.

```
Dim Numbers(4) As Integer
Dim CurrentIndex As Integer        'currently used subscript of the array
```

3. In the form's Load event procedure initialise CurrentIndex to -1 because, as step 4 shows, the code to add an item to the array starts by adding 1 to its value. The first time this is done we need it incremented to 0, which is the first subscript in the array.

```
   CurrentIndex = -1
```

4. In the Click event for the button to add a number to the array, you need to check if the array is full. If it is not full store the number in Numbers(CurrentIndex), i.e. in the current (free) subscript.

```
Private Sub btnAddToArray_Click(...) Handles btnAddToArray.Click
   Dim Number As Integer
   Number = txtNumber.Text
   If CurrentIndex = 4 Then           'array is full (has 5 numbers in it)
      MsgBox("The array is FULL!")
   Else                               'array not full
      CurrentIndex = CurrentIndex + 1 'Move to next free subscript in array
      Numbers(CurrentIndex) = Number       'and store the number in it
      txtNumber.Text = ""              'Clear text box ready for next number
      txtNumber.Focus                  'and place cursor in it
   End If
End Sub
```

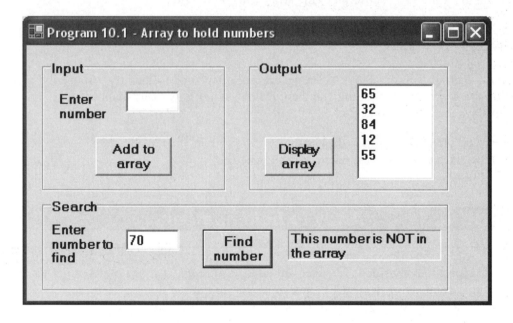

Figure 10.2: Program 10.1 – Five numbers have been stored and a number searched for

5. Because CurrentIndex also stores how many numbers there are in the array, it can be used to control a For…Next loop to display the array's contents. In the Click event of the Display array button, type in:

```
Private Sub btnDisplay_Click(...) Handles btnDisplay.Click
   Dim Index As Integer
   lstNumbers.Items.Clear 'Clear contents of list box or current numbers
                          'in array will be added to list box items
   For Index = 0 To CurrentIndex 'Display each used subscript in array
      lstNumbers.Items.Add(Numbers(Index))        'in the list box
   Next Index
End Sub
```

6. Run the program and check that the storage and display of numbers works.

7. To search the array for the number entered by the user the content of each array subscript must be examined, until either you find what you're looking for, or you reach the last number in the array without finding it. A Boolean value, Found, is initialised to false and switched to True if the number is found. It is used as part of the multiple condition to get out of the loop. The code used here is the standard linear search, and is one that you might find very useful in your project.

```
Private Sub btnFindNumber_Click(...) Handles btnFindNumber.Click
   Dim Index As Integer
   Dim Found As Boolean
   Dim SearchNumber As Integer
   Index = 0
   Found = False      'searching hasn't started yet so Found should be false
   SearchNumber = txtSearchNumber.Text
   Do While (Found = False) And (Index <= CurrentIndex)'One repetition of
                                 'the loop processes one number in the array
     If Numbers(Index) = SearchNumber Then
        Found = True
     Else       'Current subscript does not have number being searched for
        Index = Index + 1     'so go to the next subscript in the array
     End If
   Loop
   If Found Then                           'i.e. if Found = true
     lblDisplaySearch.Text = "This number IS in the array"
   Else
     lblDisplaySearch.Text = "This number is NOT in the array"
   End If
End Sub
```

8. Run the program and test the search code with a number that is present in the array and then with one that is not.

end of Program 10.1

Passing arrays to procedures

Some arrays can be very large. Since an actual parameter passed by value makes a copy of the contents of a parameter and passes this to the procedure, this can use up quite a lot of RAM if the array is very large. A parameter passed by reference sends only its RAM address. Whatever the size of the array, this is simply where its storage in RAM starts from and is a very small overhead. Some languages only let you send arrays by reference. Others, like Visual Basic, allow passing by value as well.

Suppose you have declared an array to hold 40 people's names as follows:

```
Dim Names(39) As String
```

To pass Names by value to a function FindName, which returns True if a particular name is present, you might write:

```
Found = FindName(SearchName, Names) 'actual parameter in function call
...........
Public Function FindName(ByVal WantedName As String, _
                              ByVal NameArray() As String) As Boolean
```

The actual parameter, Names, has no empty brackets but the the formal parameter it is matched to, NameArray, must have them.

PROGRAM 10.2 *Program 10.1 with a function to search the array*

Specification Identical to program 10.1 but use a general procedure to search the array for the required number.

In Program 10.1 several lines of code in the Click event for btnFindNumber carried out the search of the array. This task could have been put into a general procedure. If we take the procedure's job as simply reporting whether or not the number is present, and let the event procedure handle displaying the result of the search, then we can use a function with a Boolean return value.

1. Open a new project. Right-click **Form1.vb** in the Solution Explorer and select **Delete**. Confirm the deletion. Select **File/Add Existing Item**. Select **Form1.vb** from Program 10-1 and click **Open**. A copy of Form1 will be added to the Solution Explorer.

2. We need to change the code in the Click event for btnFindNumber (step 7 of program 10.1). Since its task is now to call the function to search for the required number and to output an appropriate message, any code which contributes to the searching itself can be removed. This means we can remove the variable Index and the loop. The function is passed the number to search for and the array. **Passing the array is actually not necessary since it is a global variable and has scope in the function FindNumber, but it is included here simply to illustrate how to pass an array as a parameter**. The new code should look as follows:

```
Private Sub btnFindNumber_Click(...) Handles btnFindNumber.Click
  Dim Found As Boolean
  Dim SearchNumber As Integer
  SearchNumber = txtSearchNumber.Text
  Found = FindNumber(SearchNumber, Numbers)   'call the function
  If Found Then                    'i.e. if Found = true
    lblDisplaySearch.Text = "This number IS in the array"
  Else
    lblDisplaySearch.Text = "This number is NOT in the array"
  End If
End Sub
```

The return value from the function FindNumber is stored in the Boolean Found and this is used to output the message.

3. Write the function's declaration below the code in step 2.

```
Public Function FindNumber(ByVal WantedNumber As Integer, _
                              ByVal NumberArray() As Integer) As Boolean
```

Both formal parameters can be passed by value because we do not need to change their contents. Since the function must return whether or not the number is present, the return value is declared, outside the parameter brackets, as Boolean.

4. Complete the code to carry out the search and return a true or false value as shown below. The search code is the same as that in program 10.1, except that the formal parameter, WantedNumber, is used.

```
   Dim Index As Integer
   Dim Found As Boolean
   Found = False
   Index = 0
   Do While (Found = False) And (Index <= CurrentIndex)
     If NumberArray(Index) = WantedNumber Then
        Found = True
     Else
        Index = Index + 1
     End If
   Loop
   If Found Then
      Return True     'function's return value is True or False
   Else
      Return False
   End If
End Function
```

5. Run the program and check that the function works when the Find number button is clicked.

end of Program 10.2

Two-dimensional arrays

All the arrays so far have been one-dimensional. Suppose you wished to store a firm's quarterly sales figures for the decade 1990 - 1999. This requires 4 (quarters) x 10 (years) = 40 pieces of data. You could declare a two-dimensional array to hold this data as follows:

```
  Dim SalesFigures(9, 3) As Decimal   '10 rows (years), 4 columns (quarters)
```

After running the following code

```
   SalesFigures(0, 2) = 56800
   SalesFigures(8, 3) = 96400
```

the array would look like the matrix shown in figure 10.3. The years are the rows and the quarters the columns.

You can have arrays with more than two dimensions, but it's unlikely you would ever need to use one. Two-dimensional arrays are useful for storing data for some mathematical problems, but in 'business' type problems they are less useful because all their data items must be of the same data type. An array of records (covered in the next chapter) is often a more convenient data structure.

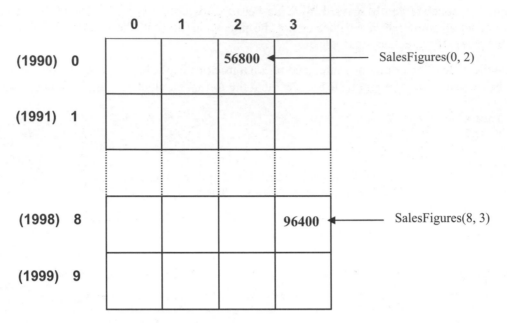

Figure 10.3: A two-dimensional array

Control arrays

A control array is a group of controls which are all of the same type. You can have a control array of text boxes, of buttons and so on. You declare a control array as you would an ordinary array. For example to have an array of 3 text boxes, first declare the array and then populate it with the text boxes:

```
Dim TextBoxArray(2) As TextBox
txtTextBoxArray(0) = txtNumber1
txtTextBoxArray(1) = txtNumber2
txtTextBoxArray(2) = txtNumber3
```

If you then wished to display the numbers 10, 20 and 30 in these text boxes you would write:

```
For Index = 1 To 3
  TextBoxArray(Index - 1).Text = Index * 10
Next Index
```

PROGRAM 10.3   *A control array*

Specification	Represent the 4 tennis courts owned by a small tennis club by numbered labels on a form. They should be coloured green when the program starts. The user should enter a number from 1 to 4 in a text box, and then click a button to change the colour of the corresponding tennis court to red to show that it is in use.

Figure 10.4 shows that court 3 is in use.

1. Open a new project. Build the form using figure 10.4. Name the four tennis court labels **lblCourt1** to **lblCourt4** and set their Text property to **1** to **4** as appropriate. Set their BackColor property to **Green** by clicking the small button in this property, selecting the **Custom** tab and then selecting any green colour. Name the text box **txtNumber** and the button **btnOK**.

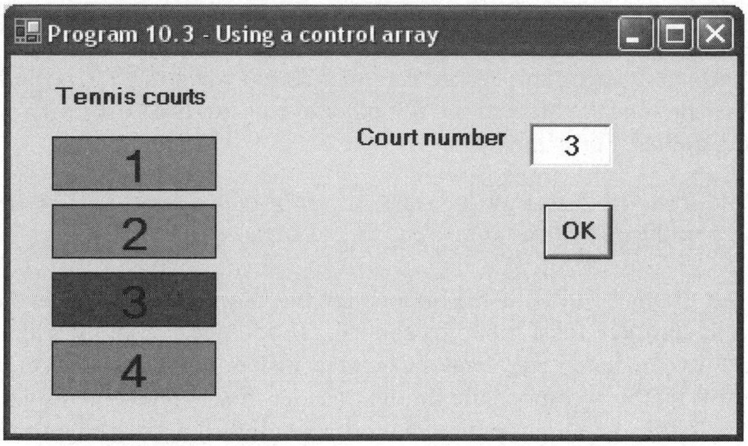

Figure 10.4: Program 10.3 – Tennis court 3 is in use

2. The control array will consist of the four tennis court labels. Declare it as a form variable:

```
Dim lblCourts(3) As Label
```

3. In the form's Load event we need to assign each of the tennis court labels to the control array.

```
lblCourts(0) = lblCourt1
lblCourts(1) = lblCourt2
lblCourts(2) = lblCourt3
lblCourts(3) = lblCourt4
```

4. In the Click event for the **OK** button declare the local variables and store the court number.

```
Private Sub btnOK_Click(...) Handles btnOK.Click
  Dim CourtNumber As String
  Dim Index As Short
  CourtNumber = txtNumber.Text
```

5. We then need to loop through the control array to find the relevant label and colour it red:

```
  For Index = 0 To 3
    If lblCourts(Index).Text = CourtNumber Then
      lblCourts(Index).BackColor = Color.Red
    End If
  Next Index
End Sub
```

6. Run the program. Enter a number from 1 to 4 in the text box and click the button. The corresponding court will be coloured red.

end of Program 10.3

Shared event handler

The code templates provided for every event procedure we have used so far include the keyword *Handles*. A common one has been a button's Click event:

```
Private Sub btnOne_Click(...) Handles btnOne.Click
```

This means that the code in the event procedure can only be run when btnOne is clicked. If we wanted the code to run if two other buttons are clicked (or any other events are fired off), then we would list all these events after the word Handles. For example

```
Private Sub btnOne_Click(ByVal sender As System.Object, ByVal e As _
       System.EventArgs) Handles btnOne.Click, btnTwo.Click, btnThree.Click
```

would execute the code if any of three listed buttons are clicked. The event procedure btnOne_Click has become a **shared event handler** for a group of controls. If you need to know which of the three buttons has fired off the code use the parameter **sender** declared inside the brackets. You can access any of the properties of the control that was responsible through sender. For example, assuming the Text properties of the three buttons are 1, 2 or 3 as appropriate, the following tells you which button has been clicked.

```
MsgBox("You clicked button " & sender.Text)
```

PROGRAM 10.4   *A control array with a shared event handler*

Specification   Like Program 10.3, represent the 4 tennis courts owned by a small tennis club by numbered labels on a form and colour them green when the program starts. The user should enter the name of the player responsible for a court into a text box and then click one of the tennis courts. This should change the tennis court to red to show that it is in use, and display the player's name next to it.

Figure 10.5 shows the program in action. Courts 2 and 3 are in use. The user has just clicked court 3 to colour it red and display the player's name next to it.

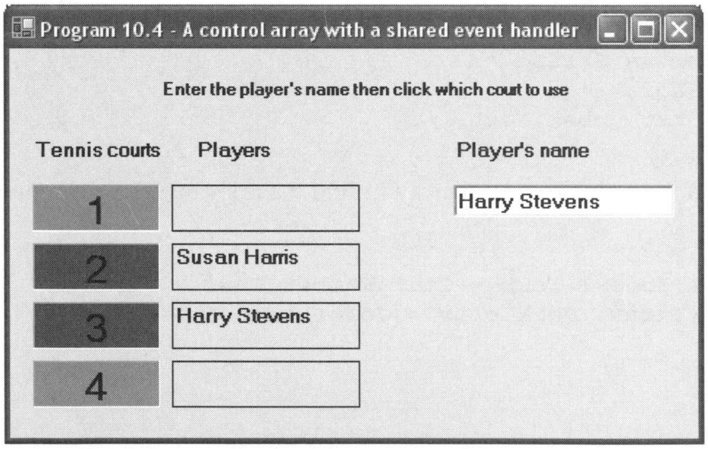

Figure 10.5: Program 10.4

1. Open a new project. Place the title and heading labels and set their Text properties as in figure 10.5. Place the four tennis court labels and name them **lblCourt1**, **lblCourt2**, **lblCourt3** and **lblCourt4**. Do not change any of their other properties.

2. Place the four labels to display the players' names to the right of the tennis court labels. Name them **lblPlayer1**, **lblPlayer2**, **lblPlayer3** and **lblPlayer4**. Do not change any of their other properties.

3. Place a text box and name it **txtPlayer**.

4. Declare the two control arrays as form variables:

```
Dim lblCourts(3) As Label
Dim lblPlayers(3) As Label
```

5. The form's Load event will assign the appropriate labels to the two control arrays. It will also colour the court labels and display the court numbers, and set the Text property of the labels for displaying the players' names to blank. In Program 10.3 we set these properties at design time, but here they are set at run-time by simple For....Next loops.

```
Private Sub Form1_Load(...) Handles MyBase.Load
  Dim Index As Short
  lblCourts(0) = lblCourt1       'assign labels to the courts control array
  lblCourts(1) = lblCourt2
  lblCourts(2) = lblCourt3
  lblCourts(3) = lblCourt4
  For Index = 0 To 3       'NB the Text and BackColor properties could have
    lblCourts(Index).Text = Index + 1            'been set at design time
    lblCourts(Index).BackColor = Color.Green
  Next Index
  lblPlayers(0) = lblPlayer1     'assign labels to the players control array
  lblPlayers(1) = lblPlayer2
  lblPlayers(2) = lblPlayer3
  lblPlayers(3) = lblPlayer4
  For Index = 0 To 3                   'Set the Text of the labels in the
    lblPlayers(Index).Text = ""        'players' control array to blank
  Next Index
End Sub
```

6. Since clicking any of the tennis court labels should fire off the code to change this label's colour and display the player's name next to it, we must make the Click event of one of these labels a shared event handler. Get the Click event code template for lblCourt1 and extend the Handles declaration to include the other three labels. This time the parameters have not been replaced by an ellipsis (**...**) because we will be referring to one of them in the next step.

```
Private Sub lblCourt1_Click(ByVal sender As System.Object, ByVal e As _
                    System.EventArgs) Handles lblCourt1.Click, _
                    lblCourt2.Click, lblCourt3.Click, lblCourt4.Click
```

7. The code in the shared event handler uses the sender parameter to identify which court label has been clicked, and then to colour this court red and display the player's name next to it. Type in the following and then run the program. Enter a player's name and click one of the tennis courts.

```
Dim Name As String
Name = txtPlayer.Text
lblPlayers(sender.Text - 1).Text = Name
lblCourts(sender.Text - 1).BackColor = Color.Red
```

end of Program 10.4

Summary of key concepts

- An **array** can hold any number of items of the same data type.

- Array indexing starts at 0.

- A **static** array cannot change in size at run-time. A **dynamic** array can grow or shrink in size. To change its size redeclare it with the **ReDim** keyword, followed by **Preserve** if you wish to retain the array's contents.

- The storage 'slots' in an array are called **subscripts**. Thus Numbers(5) and Numbers(24) are two subscripts of an array called Numbers. Any array subscript can be read from or written to directly.

- An array passed to a procedure must not include empty brackets. Its matching formal parameter in the procedure declaration must have empty brackets.

- Arrays can have two or more dimensions. A **two-dimensional array** can be viewed as a matrix with rows and columns.

- A **control array** is a group of controls of the same type (labels, text boxes etc.). They share the same name and can be referenced by an index starting at 0.

- A **shared event handler** is an event procedure that can be fired off when any one of two or more events occurs. The **sender** parameter can be used to identify which event triggered the shared event handler.

Take it from here…

1. Find out what the **UBound** function of an array returns. Although the **LBound** function is still supported in Visual Basic .NET it really has no use any more. Why?

2. There is an alternative way of grouping controls as a control array – use a **collection**. Find out about the **Controls collection** and how to build your own **user-defined collection**. Two programs are available from the publisher's web site to help you. **Program 10-3 Controls Collection** meets the specification for Program 10.2 using the Controls collection. **Program 10-4 Own Collection** meets the specification for Program 10.3 with a user-defined collection.

Questions on the Programs

Program 10.1

*1. When a number is added to the array a check is made to see if it is full. Remove this check by commenting out all the code in the If statement body except the four lines which currently belong to Else (and not forgetting the End If too). Run the program and enter 6 numbers. Try to understand the error message you get when you try to store the 6th number.

*2. Allow the user to store more than 5 numbers in the array. Declare it as a dynamic array and increase its size by 1 each time the *Add to Array* button is clicked.

**3. Add buttons to do two things:

- Find and display the highest number in the array. Hint: store the first number in the array into a variable *Highest* and then loop through the rest of the numbers comparing each with the current value of *Highest*. Reset *Highest* as appropriate.

- Calculate and display the mean value of the numbers in the array.

Program 10.2

***1**. If you have done Question 3 for program 10.1, put the code for finding the highest number in the array and for calculating the mean of the numbers in the array, into two general procedures. Call these from the Click event procedures of the buttons. These general procedures can be functions because each of them returns a single value. Their *only* tasks are to return the highest number and calculate the mean. The Click event procedures that call them should display the returned values from the functions.

Program 10.4

*1. Extend the program so that a court in use becomes free again when the user clicks an occupied court. The court should change colour back to green and the player's name next to it should be removed. Note that Visual Basic .NET will not allow you write

```
If lblCourts(Index).BackColor = Color.Green Then
```

You have to use the **ColorTranslator.ToOle** method, which was first covered in Program 2.4.

End of chapter exercises

*1. In the form's Load event fill an array with the numbers 0 to 50, and then copy them from the array into a list box.

*2. Look back at Chapter 3 Exercise 2. At that stage you would have written an event procedure for each of the three radio buttons. Redo this exercise so that the Click event of one of the radio buttons acts as a common event handler.

**3. Write a program to store up to 10 product codes in an array. Product codes have 4 characters (e.g. FD56) and each code must be different from all the other codes. After the user enters a product code check that the code has not been used already, and output an appropriate message if it has. A function should do the checking and the calling program should handle its return value of True or False.

**4. Exercise 3 at the end of Chapter 4 asked you to build a simple calculator. At that stage you would have written separate event procedures for each of the four arithmetic operator buttons. Now group these buttons into a control array and rewrite the program using a single event procedure.

**5. Write a program to help children learn their capital cities. Use two arrays – one for the country names and one for their capitals. Store 6 items in each array (or more if you wish) in the form's Load event procedure, and use two list boxes to display the contents of the arrays when the program starts. The child should select a country from one list box and its corresponding capital from the other. When a button is clicked tell the child if the answer is correct. If the answer is wrong display the correct one.

***6. Figure 10.6 shows the finished program. The user should input the names of up to 10 students and the marks they achieved on each of three exams. Store this data in a two-dimensional array. Because the names must be stored as Strings, the marks must also be of this data type rather than Short or Integer, since all items in an array must be of the same data type. Allow the user to display all the names and marks at any time in a list box. When you have this working extend the program so that the user can select one of the exams and see its average mark. Use radio buttons for selecting the exam.

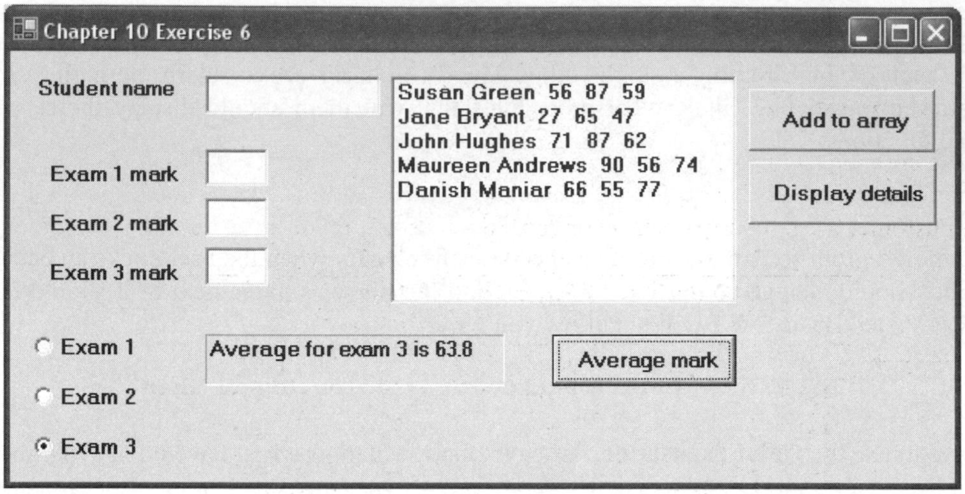

Figure 10.6: Exercise 6

***7.** Write a program to build a more realistic calculator than the one in exercise 4 above, as shown in figure 10.7. Use two control arrays of labels. One of these has the 10 digits plus the decimal point. The other has the 4 arithmetic operators and the '=' sign. The C button clears the display and allows a new calculation to start. The Off button simulates switching the calculator off, i.e. the program closes.

Figure 10.7: The calculator for exercise 7

Chapter 11 – Records

What is a record?

A credit card company holding details about its customers stores many items of data about each one. Four of these items are shown in Figure 11.1. Each item is stored in a column or **field** and all the items for a particular customer are stored in one row or **record**. In Visual Basic a record is called a **structure**.

	Account Number	Surname	Forename	Balance
	4578	Smith	Sally	£10.00
One record ⟶	1208	Jones	John	£20.00
	3217	Cain	Jennifer	£100.00
	4310	Khan	Shazad	£200.00
	5559	White	Peter	£250.00

Figure 11.1: Records or structures

An array of records

You could store the data in figure 11.1 in a two-dimensional array provided that each field is the same data type. This is not always possible and, even if it is, not always desirable. A record allows you to mix data types. If you have many records you can store them in an array; each array subscript has one record. Figure 11.1 shows an array of records, which is really the same as a table in a database.

How to declare an array of records

There are two stages:

- Declare a single record.
- Declare an array of this single record.

To declare a single record to hold the data for one customer in figure 11.1 you would write:

```
Structure CustomerType          'declare data type for one record
   Dim AccountNumber As Integer 'Declare the 4 fields. More
   Dim Surname As String        'readable to declare variables of
   Dim Forename As String       'same data type on separate lines
   Dim Balance As Decimal
End Structure

Dim Customer As CustomerType    'declare variable to hold one record
```

Each field is declared separately, sandwiched between the keywords **Structure** and **End Structure**. The code defines a new data type called CustomerType, similar to the standard data types such as Integer and String. The choice of identifier is yours but it is a good idea to finish it with the word 'Type' so that you can recognise it as a data type in your code. Because you have defined it yourself a Structure declaration is often called a **user-defined** data type. The last line declares a variable, Customer, of data type CustomerType that is capable of storing four items of data.

To store details of 1000 customers you would extend the declaration as follows:

```
Dim Customers(999) As CustomerType
```

Now the variable Customers can store 4 items about 1000 customers, i.e. 4000 items of data.

Processing an array of records

Look carefully at figure 11.2 which shows how to visualise an array of records. The subscripts are numbered along the base and one subscript holds one record, i.e. one customer's details. You can refer to any of the 1000 items of data using the syntax

       Customers(Index).Fieldname

The dot between the bracket and the field name is known as the **field separator**. Thus the data item *Jones* is stored in Customers(1).Surname and the item *112.60* stored in Customers(998).Balance.

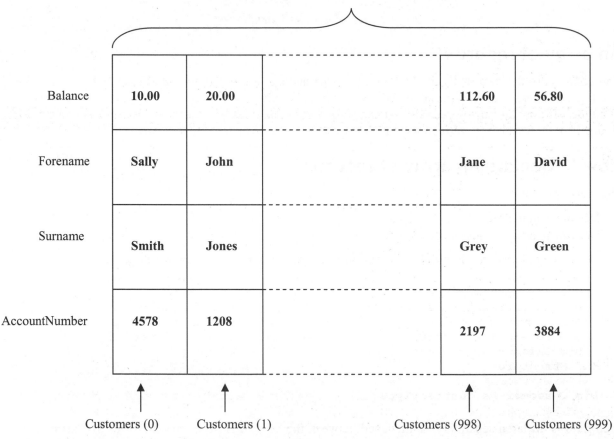

Figure 11.2: An array of records

Think of the syntax as made up of three things that get smaller in size from left to right, as shown in figure 11.3.

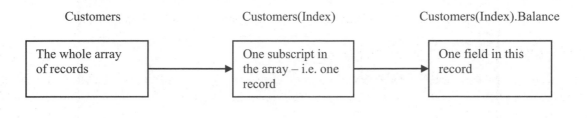

Customers	Customers(Index)	Customers(Index).Balance
The whole array of records	One subscript in the array – i.e. one record	One field in this record

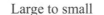

Large to small

Figure 11.3: Different sized parts of an array of records

If you have a text box named txtSurname then you would store what the user types in by writing

```
Customers(Index).Surname = txtSurname.Text
```

If Index currently has the value 59 then the item of data is stored in the 60th record. To output the same piece of data you would write

```
MsgBox(Customers(Index).Surname)
```

PROGRAM 11.1   *Array of records – Football Team Players*

Specification	Write a program to store the following details about players in a football league for one season:
	
	      Name
	      Team
	      Number of games played
	      Number of goals scored
	      Whether ever sent off or not
	
	Store these details in an array of records and display details of one player by using back and forward buttons to navigate through the array. Also allow the user to select a given player and display their details.

The finished program can be seen in figures 11.4 and 11.5. It has two forms, one for entering data and the other for displaying it. In figure 11.4 clicking Add stores the player's details in an array, and clicking New clears the contents of the input controls ready for the next player's details. In figure 11.5 clicking Previous displays the previous player's details (i.e. the previous record in the array), and clicking Next displays the next player's details.

Apart from using an array of records the program uses a standard module, a general procedure with parameter passing (both covered in Chapter 9) and shows how to load one form from another.

Designing the forms

1.   Open a new project and name the form **frmEnterData**.

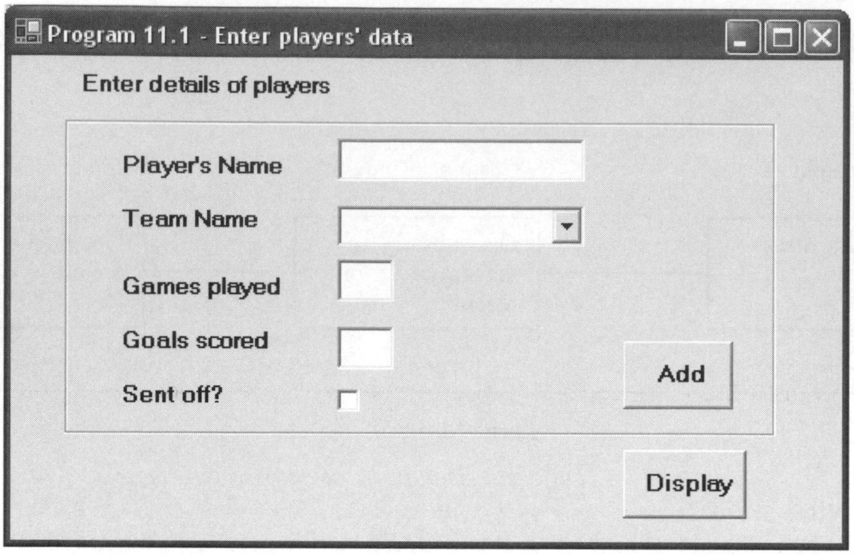

Figure 11.4: Program 11.1 – the opening form

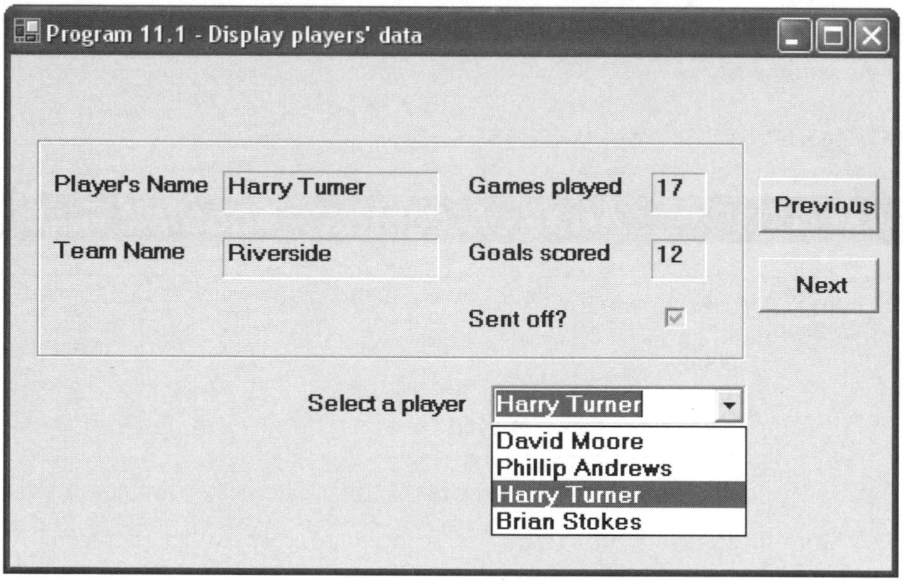

Figure 11.5: Program 11.1 – the second form

2. Design the form using figure 11.4. The controls for entering data are on a group box. The Team Name control is a combo box and the Sent Off control is a check box. Name the data entry controls **txtPlayer**, **cboTeams**, **txtGames**, **txtGoals** and **chkSentOff**. Set the Text property of the combo box to blank and write several team names of your choice into its Items property. You'll need to set the Text property of the check box to blank and use a separate label to position *Sent off?* to its left.

3. Name the buttons **btnAddRecord** and **btnDisplay**.

4. To add the second form select **Project/Add Windows Form**. In the Add New Item dialog box that appears make sure the **Windows Form** template is selected and change its name from Form2 to **frmDisplayData**.

5. The Solution Explorer shows that the file name of this new form is frmDisplayData.vb, but that the first form (that you gave the Visual Basic name frmEnterData) is Form1.vb. Right-click Form1.vb in the Solution Explorer and rename it **frmEnterData.vb** (you must add the .vb extension).

6. Design the form using figure 11.5. The controls for displaying data are on a group box. Name the display controls **lblPlayer**, **lblTeam**, **lblGames**, **lblGoals** and **chkSentOff**. Set the Enabled property of the check box to **False** since it is used for display only. Name the buttons **btnPrevious** and **btnNext**. Name the combo box (for selecting a player) **cboPlayers** and set its Text property to blank.

7. Run the program now. You will get a Build error. Click **No** and in the window below the code the error is explained – *'Sub Main' was not found.....*

When a program runs it must either load a named form or execute the code inside a Sub procedure called Main. A program is set up to run the default form Form1, but as we have renamed this form it reverts to Sub Main. We need to tell Visual Basic that form frmEnterData should be the startup object.

8. You can do this in two ways. One way is to double-click the error message and select frmEnterData from the Startup Object dialog box. The other way is to right-click the program's name in the Solution Explorer, select Properties and then select frmEnterData in the Startup object combo box. Use one of these methods now and then check that the program starts correctly.

Declaring variables

Form variables

9. Declare a form variable in *both* frmEnterData **and** frmDisplayData to index the array. In frmEnterData it keeps track of where in the array to store the next player's details. In frmDisplayData it is for scrolling through the array when clicking the Previous and Next buttons.

```
Dim Index As Integer          'declare this on both forms
```

Standard Module variables

You first used a standard module in Chapter 9. Recall that it can have no controls, only code. Any declarations and general procedures it contains have scope throughout all the forms in a program.

10. Select **Project/Add New Item**, select the **Module** template in the Add New Item dialog box. Leave the default name Module1 and click **Open**.

11. We need a variable to keep track of how many players are stored in the array. Declare it as Public, so both forms can use it, between Module Module1 and End Module.

```
Public NumberOfPlayers As Integer   'number of players stored in array
```

12. Declare a single record or structure, then a Public variable of this type, to store details of 20 players. The record is made up of the five data items (fields) listed in the specification.

```
Structure PlayerType              'data type for one record
  Dim PlayerName As String          'Declare the 5 fields.
  Dim TeamName As String
  Dim Games As Integer
  Dim Goals As Integer
  Dim SentOff As Boolean                    'True if ever sent off
End Structure
Public Players(19) As PlayerType    'stores details of 20 players
```

Entering data

13. When the Add button is clicked we need to store the player's details in the array, increment the number of players stored, and then increment *Index* to point to the next available subscript. Note that the code below does not check whether the array is full.

```
Private Sub btnAddRecord_Click(...) Handles btnAdd.Click
  Players(Index).PlayerName = txtPlayer.Text
  Players(Index).TeamName = cboTeams.Text
  Players(Index).Games = txtGames.Text
  Players(Index).Goals = txtGoals.Text
  Players(Index).SentOff = chkSentOff.Checked   'As SentOff field and
        'check box property both store Booleans, assign one to the other
  NumberOfPlayers = NumberOfPlayers + 1
  Index = Index + 1
```

14. When a player's details are stored we need to set all the fields to blank and position the cursor in the text box ready for the next player's name. The check box can be set to unchecked by default since a player is more likely never to have been sent off (hopefully!).

```
  txtPlayer.Text = ""
  cboTeams.Text = ""
  txtGames.Text = ""
  txtGoals.Text = ""
  chkSentOff.Checked = False              'set check box to unchecked
  txtPlayer.Focus()
End Sub
```

15. Run the program to check that you can store details of players. Nothing visibly will happen when you click the Add button unless you omit to enter the games played or goals scored.

Loading the second form

16. The Display button opens frmDisplayData. You have to use an object-oriented programming concept (covered in Chapter 17) to do this by declaring a frmDisplayData object, then using the **Show** method of this object to load it.

```
Private Sub btnDisplay_Click(...) Handles btnDisplay.Click
  Dim SecondForm As New frmDisplayData()
  SecondForm.Show()
End Sub
```

Displaying data

When frmDisplayData loads there are several things that must happen:

- The combo box must show the players' names;
- Details of the first player in the array should be displayed;
- The Previous button should be disabled because the current record is the first one;
- The Next button should be disabled if the user hasn't entered any data or has entered only one player's details.

17. The code to handle this is:

```
Private Sub frmDisplayData_Load(...) Handles MyBase.Load
  Dim Index As Integer
  btnPrevious.Enabled = False
  If NumberOfPlayers = 0 Then        'no data yet entered
    btnNext.Enabled = False
  ElseIf NumberOfPlayers = 1 Then    'only 1 player stored
    btnNext.Enabled = False
    Call DisplayPlayer(0)            'procedure call with 1 parameter
  Else                               'details of 2 or more players entered
    btnNext.Enabled = True
    Call DisplayPlayer(0)            'procedure call with 1 parameter
  End If
  For Index = 0 To NumberOfPlayers - 1  'Populate combo box with
    cboPlayers.Items.Add(Players(Index).PlayerName)  'players' names
  Next Index
End Sub
```

There is a call to procedure DisplayPlayer, but we haven't written it yet. The parameter 0 that is passed to it will be used by that procedure to display the contents of the array subscript numbered 0, i.e. the first one.

18. When the Previous or Next button is clicked the current subscript of the array must change, and the previous or next player's details displayed by calling procedure DisplayPlayer. If the Previous button is in a disabled state when you click Next, it must be enabled to be able to go back one record.

```
Private Sub btnNext_Click(...) Handles btnNext.Click
  Index = Index + 1
  Call DisplayPlayer(Index)
  btnPrevious.Enabled = True       'ensure user can go back one record
End Sub

Private Sub btnPrevious_Click(...) Handles btnPrevious.Click
  Index = Index - 1
  Call DisplayPlayer(Index)
End Sub
```

Note that there is more that can be done on enabling and disabling the Previous and Next buttons, but this is left for you to do in question 4 on the program later.

The default event of list boxes and combo boxes is **SelectedIndexChanged**. In previous versions of Visual Basic it was the Click event. This event is still available in Visual Basic .NET but it behaves differently. For example it is fired off when you click the combo box button to reveal its contents. What we want here is the default event which is fired off when an item is selected.

19. When the user selects a player's name from the combo box their details should be displayed. We can use the SelectedIndex property of the combo box as an index into the required subscript of the array.

```
Private Sub cboPlayers_SelectedIndexChanged(...) Handles _
                                  cboPlayers.SelectedIndexChanged
  Dim RecordNumber As Integer
  RecordNumber = cboPlayers.SelectedIndex
  Call DisplayPlayer(RecordNumber)
End Sub
```

20. The procedure DisplayPlayer has been called in five places in the code so far. One parameter is passed to it – the subscript in the array to process. Since this parameter is only used and not changed by the procedure, it can be passed by value rather than by reference.

```
Public Sub DisplayPlayer(ByVal Index As Integer)
   With Players(Index)
      lblPlayer.Text = .PlayerName
      lblTeam.Text = .TeamName
      lblGames.Text = .Games
      lblGoals.Text = .Goals
      chkSentOff.Checked = .SentOff
   End With
End Sub
```

Note that the formal parameter here, Index, has the same name as the actual parameter passed to it. This is the only exception in this book to the practice of giving the two matching parameters different names. Index is such a useful term to use!

Note the use of **With…End With** in the code above. You previously used this in Chapter 4 for adding a list of items to a list box (see *The Format* function section). It reduces the amount of code needed. Instead we could have written above:

```
lblPlayer.Text = Players(Index).PlayerName
lblTeam.Text = Players(Index).TeamName
'etc
```

This would require writing *Players(Index)* on each line.

21. Run the program and check that everything works. Recall that the Previous and Next buttons have intentionally not been made to work fully. Question 4 on this program asks you to take this further.

end of Program 11.1

Reflections on program 11.1

If you run program 11.1 a few times you will realise that one drawback is having to enter all the players' details each time. In real-world programs this data would be kept as records on file and read from the file as appropriate. If only one player's details have to be read then a single record variable could be used. If several players' details, or perhaps the whole file, have to be read and copied into RAM then an array of records would be used. Files are studied in the next chapter.

Summary of key concepts

- A record is a data structure in which you can mix data types. It is made up of one or more **fields**.
- To declare a record use **Structure…End Structure**. It is an example of a **user-defined** data type. Declare the type first and then declare a variable of this type.
- To use a variable on all the forms in a program declare it as Public in a standard module.

Questions on the Program

*1. Rewrite the code in the Click event for btnAddRecord using **With…End With**.

*2. Set the Sorted property of the combo box on frmDisplayData to True. Enter several players' names not in alphabetical order. Make a note of the order you entered the names. Try selecting these players from the combo box on frmDisplayData. Can you explain why the wrong player's details are usually displayed? (Change the Sorted property back to False when you've finished.)

*3. Run the program and enter three records. Then click the Next button on the second form three times or more. Nothing appears in the Player's Name, Team Name or Sent Off controls, but the other two controls show 0 values. Explain why. Then keep clicking the Previous button until you get an error message. Can you explain what it is saying?

**4. There is some enabling/disabling of the Previous and Next buttons in the code but it doesn't cover all situations. Extend the code so that the buttons are enabled only when necessary. For example if the array is full the Next button should be disabled, (though in a real program you would either make sure the array is large enough or use a dynamic array).

***5. Extend the program to do the following:

- allow the user to select a team and scroll through only details of players in this team;

- in a list box display the names and teams of all players who have been sent off;

- in a list box display the names and teams of all players who have scored at least a given number of goals. Allow the user to input the number of goals to search on.

End of chapter exercises

*1. Store the following details of a member of a health club in a record – name, weight (in kilograms), height (in metres and centimetres, e.g. 1.86) and age. Have two buttons on the form. Clicking one of them should ask the user for these details by using a series of input boxes. Store the member's details in a single record. Clicking the other should display details of the member in a list box. Note that this question is asking you to process only one record, not an array of records.

**2. A driving instructor books clients for one-hour lessons from 8.00am to 5.00pm. She takes one hour for lunch from 12.00 to 1.00pm. Display the 8 lesson times during one day in a list box. The user should select a lesson from the list box, enter the client's name in a text box, click a check box if this is the client's first lesson, and then click a button to store these three items of data in an array of 8 records. The appropriate lesson in the list box should now include the client's name and whether or not this is their first lesson. Get this extra data from the array of records.

***3. Students on a two-semester course take an exam at the end of each semester. Allow the user to enter student names and their mark (out of 100) in each exam. Store all the data in an array of records. Display:

- the average mark in each exam;
- the name of the student with the highest mark in each exam;
- the names of those students who passed the course. At least 50 marks in both exams are needed for a pass.

Design the form appropriately. Use a general procedure to validate the marks (i.e. to only accept a value from 0 to 100).

Chapter 12 – Files

What is a file?

In all the programs covered so far, any stored data is lost when the program closes, and has to be entered again when the program next runs. For a program like 11.1, where a lot of data might be stored in an array of records, this is clearly a waste of time. The solution is to store the data permanently – in a file.

Types of file in Visual Basic

Visual Basic supports three types of file but you are likely to use only two of these:

- Text files
- Random access files

There are several key differences between these files:

- A text file stores all its data as characters, represented by their ASCII/Unicode codes. For example it would store the number 25 as character 2 (ASCII code 50) and character 5 (ASCII code 53). In binary these two ASCII codes are 0110010 (50) and 0110101 (53). A random access file would store this number differently. Assuming it is stored as a 2-byte Short it would be stored as 0000000000011001.

- A random access file is assumed to store records. In a text file there is no naturally built-in structure to the data since it is simply stored as a sequence of characters.

- You cannot open a text file to be both read from and written to, but you can with a random access file.

- With a random access file you can read and write to any record position within the file. For example you can read the 5th record or overwrite the 8th record. This is also called **direct access**. You cannot directly change the data in a text file. To change some data you would have to read all the data before the data you wish to change and write this to a new file. Then write the changed data to the new file. Finally read all the data after the changed data and write this to the new file too. Because the data must be read from the beginning of the file a text file is often called a **sequential** file.

Getting the file name

When you open a file you must supply its name. Four ways of doing this are:

- Hardcode the full path and file name
- Use the CurDir (Current Directory) function
- Use the OpenFileDialog control
- Use the default bin folder

Hardcode the full path and file name

Assuming Filename has been declared as String you might write:

```
Filename = "C:\My Visual Basic Work\Members.dat"
```

The disadvantage of this method is that the file must be in the folder specified by the path. If you move the file to another folder you have to change the code.

Use the CurDir function

CurDir returns the path to the directory or folder your program is located in. The example below adds the file name to the path.

```
Filename = CurDir() & "\Members.dat"
```

The file must be in the same folder as your program, but this method is more flexible than hardcoding the path and file name since you can move the program and file into any folder and the code will work.

Use the OpenFileDialog control

You have probably used this Windows control many times in various applications such as Word, Excel and of course Visual Basic .NET itself. Program 12.1 shows you how to use it.

Use the default Bin folder

For every program Visual Basic .NET creates a folder named **bin**. If your code uses only the name of the file (rather than the path), it will look inside this folder for it. Programs 12.2 and 12.3 use this method.

PROGRAM 12.1 *Using the OpenFileDiaog control*

Specification   Demonstrate how to use the OpenFileDialog control. Display the selected file name.

The selected filename (including the path) is displayed in a label on the form in figure 12.1.

Figure 12.1: Program 12.1

1.   Open a new project. Design the form using figure 12.1 and name the display label **lblFilename**.

2.   Put an OpenFileDialog control on the form. This is the 37th control in the Toolbox. Like the Timer control it is automatically placed in the pane below the form.

3.   In the form's Load event write code to get a file name and display it.

```
Dim Filename As String
OpenFileDialog1.ShowDialog()          'no need to rename OpenFileDialog1
Filename = OpenFileDialog1.FileName
lblFilename.Text = Filename
```

The **ShowDialog** method will display the same dialog box (window) you get when you select **File/Open** from a Windows application. The FileName property stores the full path and name of the file you select from this dialog box.

4.   Run the program and you'll get the very familiar Open dialog box. Select any file you want, click **Open** and you'll see the path and file name displayed on the form.

It is important to realise that all the ShowDialog method of this control has done is to get the path and file name. **It has not opened the file**. You need to add code to do this (see below).

end of Program 12.1

Processing files

Visual Basic .NET introduced a File System Object model for processing files. However it also supports all the techniques for file-handling in earlier versions of Visual Basic. These earlier techniques are covered in detail in this chapter. The last section of the chapter briefly considers the newer approach.

Text files

Opening

You must always open a file before you can use it. To open a text file use one of the following.

```
FileOpen(1, Filename, OpenMode.Input)    'to read from the file
FileOpen(1, Filename, OpenMode.Output)   'to write to the file
FileOpen(1, Filename, OpenMode.Append)   'to write to the end of the file
```

- The **FileOpen** statement opens a file if it exists. When you open a file to read from it, an error results if it does not exist. When you open a file to write to it, if it doesn't exist FileOpen first creates it and then opens it.

- Filename contains the path and name of the file.

- The **Input**, **Append** and **Output** modes indicate how you wish to read/write. If you open a file for Output, Visual Basic deletes the contents of the file (even if you don't write anything to it). To add data to an existing file you must use Append, which adds the data after the existing data.

- **1** assigns the file the number 1. All files (text or random access) are identified by a number, not by their name. If you have two or more files open at the same time they must have different numbers.

Reading from a file

Visual Basic keeps an imaginary file pointer as it reads through a text file. When the file is opened it points to the first line of a text file. Suppose a file holds a series of whole numbers, one on each line. The following code would display these on a form:

```
Do While Not EOF(1)          'EOF means End Of File.
  Number = LineInput(1)
  lstNumbers.Items.Add(Number)
Loop
```

The **EOF** function returns True when the end of a file has been reached. The While condition uses the **Not** logical operator and is saying *continue until the end of the file is reached*. The **LineInput** statement reads the item of data on the current line in the file and stores it in Number. After reading the single item of data on the line, the file pointer points to the next line.

If a line in a text file contains more than one item of data separated by commas, then you can read each item into separate variables using **Input**. For example the following reads a string and a number:

```
Do While Not EOF(1)
  Input(1, ProductCode)
  Input(1, Quantity)
  lstDisplay.Items.Add(ProductCode & " " & Quantity)
Loop
```

Writing to a file

Use the **Write**, **WriteLine**, **Print** or **PrintLine** statements. Write and Print do not move the file pointer to the next line but WriteLine and PrintLine do include a linefeed. Program 12.2 shows the slight difference in the way Write/WriteLine and Print/PrintLine write to a text file. The code

```
WriteLine(1, Number)
```

writes *Number* to the current file pointer position and positions the file pointer on the next line.

Closing a file

When you have finished using a file always close it. For both text and random access files simply write:

```
FileClose(1)
```

PROGRAM 12.2   *Text file to hold names and ages*

Specification   Allow the user to enter people's names and ages and store these in a text file. Allow the user to display the contents of the file at any time.

Figure 12.2 shows the program after two sets of names and ages have been stored in the file, one set using WriteLine and the other using PrintLine.

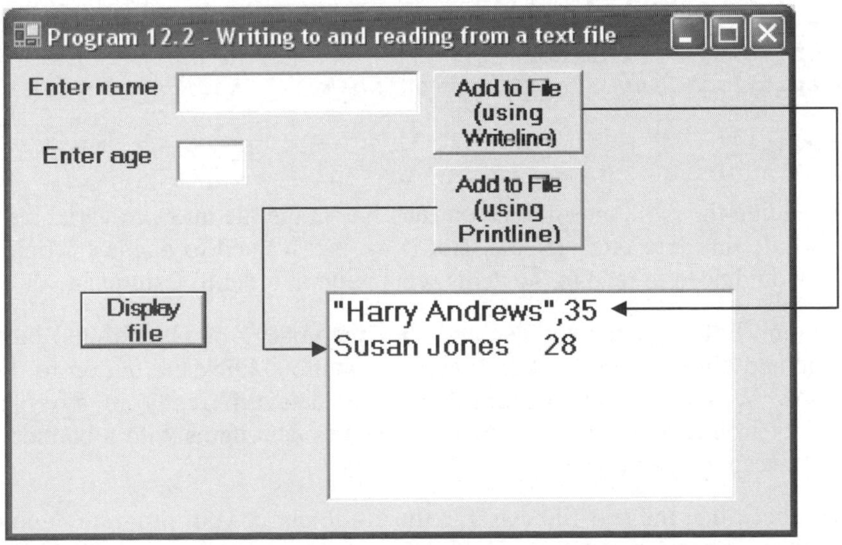

Figure 12.2: Program 12.2 after two names and ages have been stored

1. Open a new project. Build the form using figure 12.2. Name the controls **txtName**, **txtAge**, **btnAddToFileWrite**, **btnAddToFilePrint**, **btnDisplayFile** and **lstDisplayFile**.

2. Declare a global variable to hold the name of the file:

```
Dim Filename As String
```

3. Text files normally have a '.txt' extension, so our file will be called NamesAndAges.txt.

```
Private Sub Form1_Load(...) Handles MyBase.Load
    Filename = "NamesAndAges.txt"   'VB will store file in the bin folder
End Sub
```

4. The code for the Click event of the upper Add button uses WriteLine and so adds a linefeed after writing Name and Age to the file. There are therefore two items of data on one line in the file.

```
Dim Name As String
Dim Age As Integer
Name = txtName.Text
Age = txtAge.Text
FileOpen(1, Filename, OpenMode.Append)
WriteLine(1, Name, Age)
FileClose(1)
txtName.Text = ""
txtAge.Text = ""
txtName.Focus()
```

5. Type in the code for the other Add button but use PrintLine rather than WriteLine.

6. In the Click event of btnDisplayFile write:

```
Dim DataToDisplay As String
FileOpen(1, Filename, OpenMode.Input)
lstDisplayFile.Items.Clear()
Do While Not EOF(1)                        'loop through each line in the file
    DataToDisplay = LineInput(1)           'Read one line
    lstDisplayFile.Items.Add(DataToDisplay)   'and display it
Loop
FileClose(1)
```

Rather than reading the two items of data on each line in the file into two variables, LineInput is used to read the whole line into one variable. But if we had wanted to display people aged over 20 for example, we would need to read in the items separately, in order to test the age data.

7. Run the program. Enter a name and age and click the upper Add (WriteLine) button. Enter another name and age and click the lower Add (PrintLine) button. Click the button to display the file and you'll see how WriteLine and PrintLine store the data differently in the file. WriteLine puts quotation marks around String data items and separates data items with a comma. PrintLine simply puts spaces between the two pieces of data.

8. In Windows, check that the text file exists in the bin folder of your program. You can delete the file from here and run the program again. The FileOpen statements in the two Add button events create an empty file. However if you click the button to display its contents before clicking either of the Add buttons an error results because you are trying to read from a file that does not exist.

end of Program 12.2

Random access files

Declaring records for writing to a file

Because random access files assume you are dealing with records Visual Basic needs to know the record size in bytes. Throughout this book the String data type has been a variable length. When you use it to declare fields in a record that will be written to a file you must state its size, so that the total record size can be calculated. If we stored people's names and ages as in Program 12.1, but in a random access file, we would use the **VBFixedString** attribute to fix the length of the Name field:

```
Structure PersonType
  <VBFixedString(30)> Public Name As String    '30 bytes
  Dim Age As Short                             '2 bytes
End Structure                                  'total record length = 32 bytes
Dim OnePerson As PersonType                    'variable of the defined type
```

Opening and Closing

As with text files use the FileOpen function. It takes 6 parameters, although the fourth and fifth ones are optional (and will not concern us). Indicate these with commas. To open the file *Filename*, which stores the names and ages above, you would write one of the following:

```
FileOpen(1, Filename, OpenMode.Random, , , 32)
FileOpen(1, Filename, OpenMode.Random, , , Len(OnePerson))
```

The first three parameters are the same as those used for opening text files. The last one is the record length which you can write as a number or use the Len function to find the length of the record for you. Len is passed the variable of your defined type, not the defined type itself. Len(PersonType) is wrong.

Close a random access file in the same way as a text file, e.g FileClose(1).

Reading from a file

With a random access file you can only read (or write) one record at a time. You cannot read or write individual fields within a record. Use **FileGet** to read records. To read and display the whole of a random access file you could use a For…Next loop since the number of records can easily be calculated, or Do While…Loop as with the text file example in step 6 of Program 12.2:

```
For Index = 1 To NumberOfRecords
   FileGet(1, OnePerson)      'Note 3rd parameter is optional
   'code to do something with the record read from file
Next Index

Do While Not EOF(1)
   FileGet(1, OnePerson)
   'code to do something with the record read from file
Loop
```

FileGet takes three parameters. The third one is optional and is the record number of the record to be read. Visual Basic numbers the records in a random access file from 1 onwards. In the code above, the file pointer is moved to the next record each time round both loops, so there is no need to state the record number. Visual Basic will process the current record. However to go directly to a particular record you *do* need to state the record number.

Writing to a file

Use **FilePut**. This works in the same way as FileGet to read from a file. The third parameter, the record number, is optional. Without it the record will be written to the current file pointer position. Assuming the number of records in the file is known, to append a record (add it to the end of the file) you would write:

```
FilePut(1, OneProduct, NumberOfRecords + 1)
```

PROGRAM 12.3   *Random access file of Garden Centre products*

Specification   A garden centre stores the following details about each of its 800 products:

- ID
- Description
- Price
- Quantity in stock
- Reorder level (i.e. number to which stock has to fall before it is reordered)

Write a program which stores details of products in a random access file. The number of products in the file should always be displayed. The program should allow the user to search for a product both by record number and by product ID. It should also display the entire contents of the file in a list box in product ID order.

You can see the program in figure 12.3. Since the products were not entered into the file in product ID order, the display in the list box does not reflect their physical order in the file. The details at the bottom left are of record number 3. In a real application you are unlikely to search for a given record number (unless the key field contains values which are the same as the record number values, e.g. membership numbers from 1 upwards). It is included here to illustrate direct access to a given record.

1.   Open a new project and design the form using figures 12.3 and 12.4.

Declaring global variables

2.   First declare a couple of variables for processing the file and for formatting the display of the file's contents in the list box. This format technique was covered in Chapter 4. The fields will be displayed in the order listed in the specification.

```
Dim Filename As String
Dim NumberOfRecords As Short    'no. records currently stored in file
Dim MyFormat As String = "{0, -5}{1, -21}{2, -6}{3, -10}{4, -5}"
```

3.   Declare a data type for the records in the file:

```
Structure ProductType
  Dim ProductID As Short                    '2 bytes
  <VBFixedString(18)> Public Description As String  '18 bytes
  Dim Price As Decimal                      '16 bytes
  Dim QuantityInStock As Short              '2 bytes
  Dim ReorderLevel As Short                 '2 bytes
End Structure                               'total is 40 bytes
```

A variable of type ProductType has *not* been declared here. Since several event procedures will need to use this variable it is much safer to declare it locally when needed.

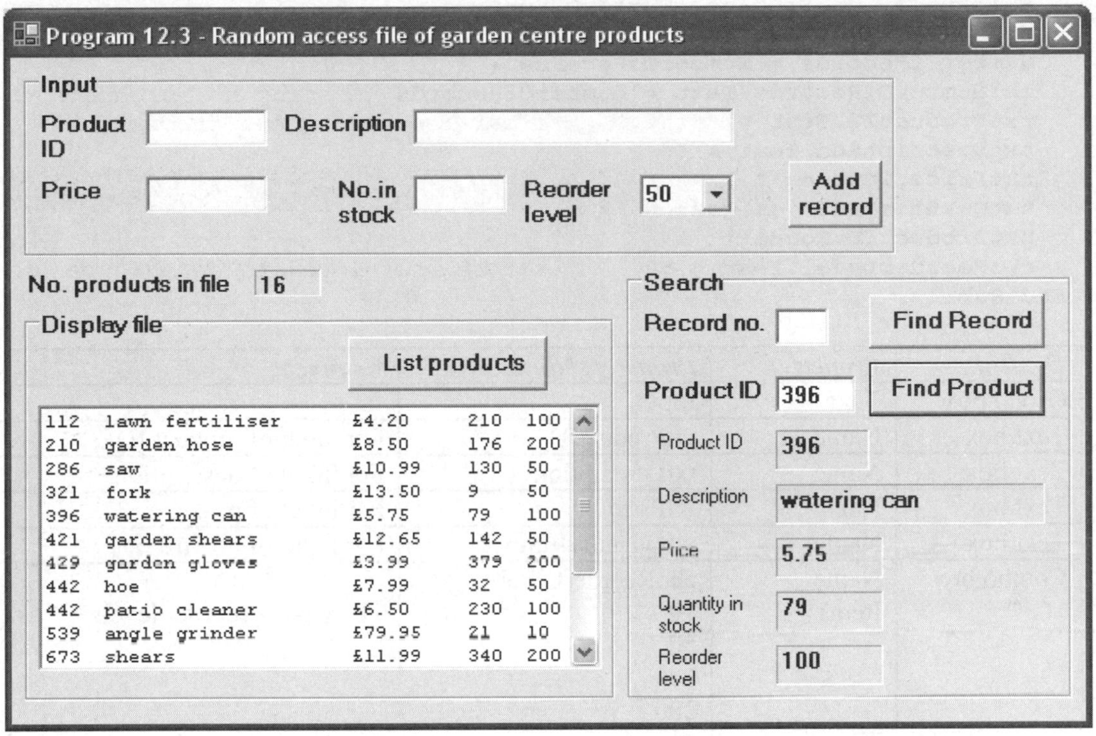

Figure 12.3: Program 12.3

The form's Load event

4. This must store the name of the file and display the number of records currently in it.

```
Dim OneProduct As ProductType
Filename = "Products.dat"               'VB will use the bin folder for file
FileOpen(1, Filename, OpenMode.Random, , , Len(OneProduct))  'open file
NumberOfRecords = LOF(1) / Len(OneProduct)
lblNumberOfRecords.Text = NumberOfRecords
```

There are no rules about naming random access files but in this book the extension 'dat' (for data) will be used. The number of records is calculated by dividing the total size of the file by the size of one record. The function **LOF** (**L**ength **O**f **F**ile) returns the size of an open file.

Adding products to the file

5. Clicking the Add Record button writes the record to the file, updates the number of products in the file, and clears the text boxes ready for the next product:

```
Private Sub btnAddRecord_Click(...) Handles btnAddRecord.Click
  Dim OneProduct As ProductType             'one record
  OneProduct.ProductID = txtProductID.Text 'store data into one record
  OneProduct.Description = txtDescription.Text
  OneProduct.Price = txtPrice.Text
```

```
      OneProduct.QuantityInStock = txtQuantityInStock.Text
      OneProduct.ReorderLevel = cboReorderLevel.Text
      FileOpen(1, Filename, OpenMode.Random, , , Len(OneProduct))  'open file
      FilePut(1, OneProduct, NumberOfRecords + 1) 'write record after current
      FileClose(1)                                                  'record
      NumberOfRecords = NumberOfRecords + 1
      lblNumberOfRecords.Text = NumberOfRecords 'display no. products in file
      txtProductID.Text = ""           'clear input for next product
      txtDescription.Text = ""
      txtPrice.Text = ""
      txtQuantityInStock.Text = ""
      txtProductID.Focus()
      cboReorderLevel.Text = 50        'set reorder level to default value
End Sub
```

Control	Property	Property setting	Comment
Group box	Text	Input	
Text box	Name	txtProductID	For input of product ID
Text box	Name	txtDescription	For input of description
Text box	Name	txtPrice	For input of price
Text box	Name	txtQuantityInStock	For input of no. in stock
Combo box	Name	cboReorderLevel	
	Items	10	There are 4 reorder levels
		50	
		100	
		200	
	Text	50	50 is commonest level, so set as default
Button	Name	btnAddRecord	
	Text	Add Record	
Label	Name	lblNumberOfRecords	Displays no. of records in file
Button	Name	btnDisplayFile	
	Text	List Products	
Group box	Text	Display file	
List box	Name	lstDisplayFile	
	Font	Courier New size 8	Font to keep output in columns
	Sorted	True	Display products in ID order
Group Box	Text	Search	
Button	Name	btnFindRecord	
	Text	Find Record	
Text box	Name	txtSearchRecord	To enter record number to search for
Button	Name	btnFindProduct	
	Text	Find Product	
Text box	Name	txtSearchProduct	To enter product ID to search for
Label	Name	lblProductID	These are the labels in the lower right part
Label	Name	lblDescripton	of the form which display the details of
Label	Name	lblPrice	onr product. (They are not the labels with
Label	Name	lblQuantityInStock	the field names.)
Label	Name	lblReorderLevel	

Figure 12.4: Properties of the controls in Program 12.3

Displaying the file's contents

6. Use a For...Next loop. Each execution of the loop processes one record. The 3rd parameter for FileGet (the record number) is not required since the file pointer will be at the correct record.

```
Private Sub btnListProducts_Click(...) Handles btnListProducts.Click
  Dim Index As Integer
  Dim OneProduct As ProductType          'one record
  lstDisplayFile.Items.Clear()
  FileOpen(1, Filename, OpenMode.Random, , , Len(OneProduct))
  For Index = 1 To NumberOfRecords  'loop through all records in file
    FileGet(1, OneProduct)     'read one record. 3rd parameter not needed
          'use the declared format to display one product in the list box
    lstDisplayFile.Items.Add(String.Format(MyFormat, _
        OneProduct.ProductID, OneProduct.Description, _
        Format(OneProduct.Price, "currency"), _
        OneProduct.QuantityInStock, OneProduct.ReorderLevel))
  Next Index
  FileClose(1)
End Sub
```

Searching the file

The user can search for a given product either by specifying a record number or a product ID. Once the record has been read, the code for displaying its contents is the same for both types of search. Therefore let's write this in our own Sub procedure, DisplayOneProduct (see steps 7 and 9).

7. The code to search for a given product by record number checks that the record number entered by the user is a valid one:

```
Private Sub btnFindRecord_Click(...) Handles btnFindRecord.Click
  Dim RecordNumber As Integer
  Dim OneProduct As ProductType          'one record
  RecordNumber = txtSearchRecord.Text
  If (RecordNumber > 0) And (RecordNumber <= NumberOfRecords) Then
    FileOpen(1, Filename, OpenMode.Random, , , Len(OneProduct))
    FileGet(1, OneProduct, RecordNumber)
    Call DisplayOneProduct(OneProduct)   'pass record as a parameter
    FileClose(1)
  Else
    MsgBox("Invalid record number")
  End If
End Sub
```

8. Finding a product with a given product ID involves a linear search through the file from the first record using Do While...Loop. A Boolean value is switched to True if the record is found and the loop stops. The code checks that the Product ID is a valid one.

```
Private Sub btnFindProduct_Click(...) Handles btnFindProduct.Click
  Dim RecordNumber As Integer
  Dim Found As Boolean
  Dim ProductID As String
  Dim OneProduct As ProductType
  ProductID = txtSearchProduct.Text
  Found = False
```

```
        FileOpen(1, Filename, OpenMode.Random, , , Len(OneProduct))
        Do While (Not EOF(1)) And (Found = False) 'Loop until no more records
                                                   'or record is found

          RecordNumber = RecordNumber + 1
          FileGet(1, OneProduct, RecordNumber)
          If OneProduct.ProductID = ProductID Then     'record found?
            Found = True
          End If
        Loop
        FileClose(1)
        If Found Then
          Call DisplayOneProduct(OneProduct)
        Else
          MsgBox("Invalid Product ID")
        End If
      End Sub
```

9. The general procedure DisplayOneProduct simply displays each field from the record passed to it in the relevant label:

```
    Private Sub DisplayOneProduct(ByVal Product As ProductType)
        lblProductID.Text = Product.ProductID
        lblDescription.Text = Product.Description
        lblPrice.Text = Product.Price
        lblQuantityInStock.Text = Product.QuantityInStock
        lblReorderLevel.Text = Product.ReorderLevel
    End Sub
```

10. Run the program. Enter details of several products, display them and then try looking for a given product by record number and by ID. Enter valid and invalid record numbers and product IDs.

11. After successfully adding records to the file, locate it in the bin folder of your program in Windows. Its size in bytes should be 40 x the number of records it contains.

end of Program 12.3

Using System.IO

All the techniques covered in this chapter have been part of Visual Basic for some time. Visual Basic .NET introduced an alternative way of processing files using the so-called System.IO namespace. To process text files you use the StreamReader class for reading and the StreamWriter class for writing. The amount of understanding needed to use these classes is about the same as that to process text files using the functions covered in this chapter.

To process random access files you use the BinaryReader and BinaryWriter classes. However there is no built-in record structure to random access files when you use these classes. As you have seen, with the older techniques only whole records can be read from or written to random access files. With the newer techniques you have to create the record structure yourself and this means you can read and write individual fields. The whole process is more complicated than the traditional methods.

Summary of key concepts

- The two main types of file are **text** files (**sequential** files) and **random access** files (**direct access** files). Data in text files is stored as a sequence of characters but in random access files it is stored as records.

- If you use only the name of a file in code, and not its path also, Visual Basic .NET uses the **bin** folder for the file.

- In code files are referenced by an integer number, e.g. 1.

- The **FileOpen** and **FileClose** functions open and close a file. A text file can be opened for input or output, but not both at the same time. A random access file *can* be opened for both.

- Use the **LineInput** statement to read one line, and **Input** to read two or more items of data on the same line, from a text file. Use **FileGet** to read from a random access file.

- Use the **Write**, **WriteLine**, **Print** and **PrintLine** statements to write to a text file and **FilePut** to write to a random access file.

Take it from here…

1. In program 12.3 the LOF function is used to find the size of an open file in bytes. Find the name of the function that is used to do the same for a file that is not open.

2. An integer number has been used in programs to identify a file. Visual Basic provides an alternative way by using the **FreeFile** function. Find out how this works.

Questions on the Programs

Program 12.1

*1. The OpenFileDialog control has several useful properties that you can set at design time or in code. Run the program and enter a file name that is not listed. The program will not accept it. Which property must you set so that it will accept it? Which properties must you set so that the Open dialog box displays a directory of your choice and/or files of a particular type (e.g. .txt files)?

Program 12.2

1. Add a button to calculate and display the average age of the people stored in NamesAndAges.txt. Read the name and age for each person into two separate variables and then process the age variable. (Note:** write all the data to the file in the first place with WriteLine, not PrintLine.)

Program 12.3

**1. Add three radio buttons to display in the list box details of those products

- which cost more than a given price – the user enters the search price in a text box;
- whose number in stock exceeds a given value – the user enters this stock value in a text box;
- whose reorder level is the same as or greater than a given level – the user selects this level from a combo box.

**2. Allow the user to change the price of a product by selecting it from the list box. This should present an input box for the new price. The new price should be stored in the file and updated in the list box.

End of chapter exercises

1. Write a program which displays the names of students on a selected degree course by reading from a text file, as shown in figure 12.5. The text file, **DegreeStudents.txt, has the names and course codes for 125 students and can be found on the publisher's web site. The names are unsorted in the file but should be displayed alphabetically in a list box. The course codes are:

COMP	Computing	FRE	French
HIST	History	MA	Mathematics
PHIL	Philosophy		

When you have this working, add a button to create a second file, called DegreeStudentsSorted.txt, with the names in alphabetical order. Do this by copying the contents of the list box to the new file. This new file should contain the names only, not the courses.

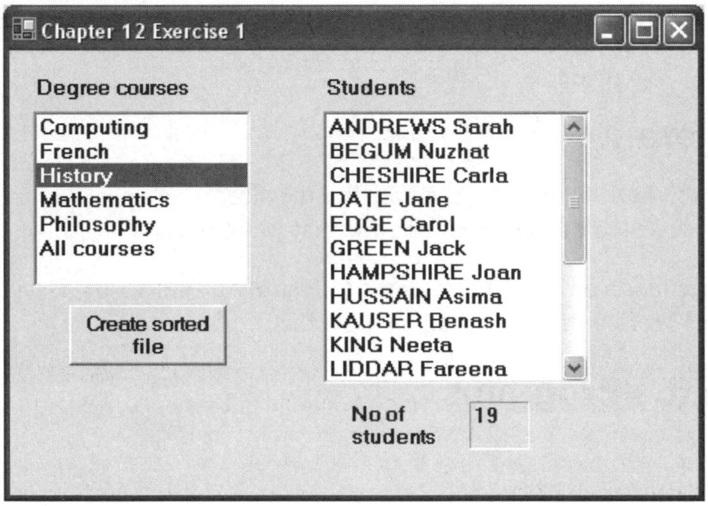

Figure 12.5: Exercise 1: 19 students study History

**2. Programmers working on new business applications sometimes have to convert text files into random access files. Write a program which does this for the file in exercise 1, DegreeStudents.txt. Include a list box to display the contents of the new file. If you allow strings of 20 for the student name field and 4 for the course code field, the total size of the random access file should be 3000 bytes (125 records x 24 bytes).

**3. Write a program that generates a random number from 0 to 100 every second and stores it in a text file, as shown in figure 12.6. (Search Help for the *Rnd* function to find out about producing random numbers.) Clicking the Display File button should display the contents of the file in both a list box and a text box. You have learned how to display data from a text file in a list box. To display the contents in a text box read the entire contents into a single String variable and simply display the contents of this variable at one go. If the variable is *FileContents* then you would write:

```
FileContents = InputString(1, LOF(1))
txtRandomNumbers.Text = FileContents
```

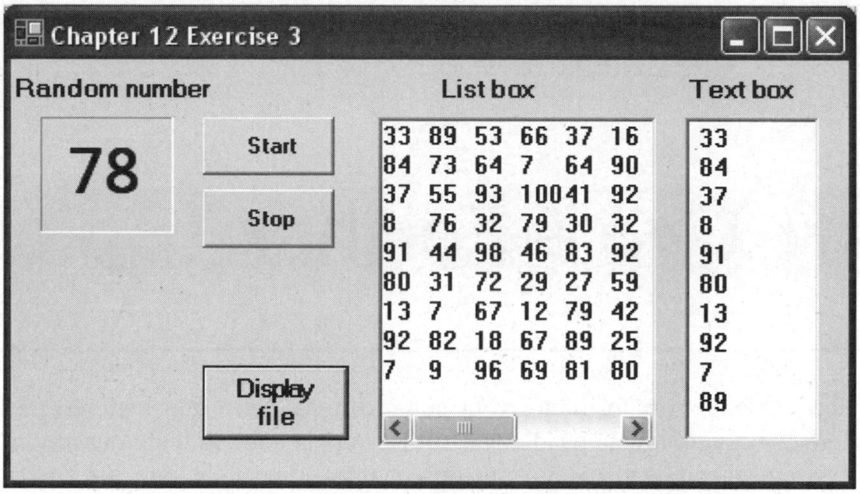

Figure 12.6: Exercise 3

***4.** Write a program to store the following details about second-hand cars for sale:

- registration number
- make (e.g. Ford)
- model
- year of manufacture
- price

Store the details in a random access file and display them in a list box. Do not allow duplicate registration numbers. Allow the user to search for the following (and display the results in the list box):

- a particular car using the registration number to search on – the user should select the registration number from a combo box;
- all cars of a given make and model entered by the user;
- all cars less than a given number of years old – allow the user to enter the number of years.

Part Two – Further Topics

Chapter 13 explains how to **debug** your code to track down any **logic** errors it may contain. It then shows you how to handle **run-time** errors in code so that your program will not crash. You are encouraged to dip into this chapter, especially into the first part on debugging, no later than after reaching Chapter 6.

Chapter 14 teaches you how to **print reports** to files and more importantly to the printer. Visual Basic .NET introduces a totally new way of sending output to the printer.

Chapter 15 explains the ADO .NET model. In particular it shows you how to set up a connection from a Visual Basic program to an Access database, and how to retrieve and display data from its tables. SQL is used at an elementary level to query databases.

Chapter 16 extends the work covered in Chapter 15 by showing you how to update an Access database through Visual Basic.

Chapter 17 introduces you to **OOP** (Object-oriented Programming). First it explains what **classes** and **objects** are, and then it shows you how to create and use your own classes and objects. The chapter concentrates on one of the three main strands of OOP – **data encapsulation**.

Chapter 18 continues from Chapter 17 by looking at the other two main strands of OOP, **inheritance** and **polymorphism**.

Chapter 13 – Debugging and Error Handling

Introduction

A **bug** is some sort of error in the code which can prevent your program from running properly. When you write a substantial program always assume that it contains bugs. When you discover a bug you may or may not know how your code has caused it. **Debugging** is about finding these causes. Visual Basic has a variety of debugging tools, which are discussed in the first part of this chapter. The later part of the chapter looks at how your code might handle run-time errors, for which the normal process of debugging is not relevant.

It makes sense to know about Visual Basic's debugging tools reasonably soon after beginning the language. Handling run-time errors in code is a more advanced topic and probably only one you would consider applying to a program of 'A' level project standard.

Types of error

There are three types of error:

* Syntax error
* Run-time error
* Logic or semantic error

A **syntax error** is a mistake in the grammar of Visual Basic. Examples include misspelling keywords (e.g. Lop rather than Loop), forgetting to write a period (**.**) between a control's name and its property and so on. They are usually simple to fix since the compiler can pick them out for you. A **run-time error** causes the program to stop working. An example was shown in figure 3.5, where trying to store too large a number into a Short variable caused overflow. A **logic error** results from a mistake in the logic of your code. Examples are using the wrong logical operators (AND/OR) in loop conditions or assigning an incorrect value to a variable. It is usually the hardest type of error to track down.

The topic of debugging in this chapter is not concerned with syntax or run-time errors, but with tracking down logic errors. The topic of error handling is concerned with run-time errors so that your program won't crash.

The three program modes

At any time a given program is in one of three modes – **design mode**, **run mode** or **break mode**. Every program you have written has used the design and run modes. If your program produces a run-time error it automatically invokes break mode. Figure 3.5 showed that you can get into this mode by clicking the Break button. You can then hover the cursor over any variable and see its current value. Some of the features covered in the first part of the chapter work only in break mode.

Visual Basic's Debug toolbar and menu

The Debug toolbar and menu are shown in figures 13.1 and 13.2. You'll be using several of these items in this chapter. To get the toolbar select **View/Toolbars/Debug** from the main menu.

Stepping through code

The Debug toolbar has three options, and the Debug menu two of these three options, for stepping through code – executing it one line at a time. The two options they both share are the most useful:

Step Into   Runs the current line of code. If this line calls a general procedure this procedure is entered.

Step Over   Runs the current line, but if this is a general procedure call the procedure is executed without stepping through its code.

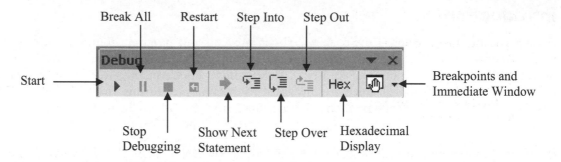

Figure 13.1: The Debug toolbar

Figure 13.2: The Debug menu

Using Breakpoints

A **breakpoint** is a place in the code where the program will temporarily stop. You can set as many of these as you like. When the program stops at a breakpoint you can examine the contents of variables and expressions in the **Watch window** or in the **Immediate window**. Program 13.1 shows how to use the Watch window and Program 13.2 illustrates the Immediate window.

Watches

A **watch** allows you to see the value of a variable or expression as the program runs. As you step through the code this value is displayed in the Watch window. You can only add a watch when the program is in break mode.

PROGRAM 13.1 *Breakpoints, setting Watches and stepping through code*

Specification Demonstrate how to set a breakpoint, set watches on variables and expressions, and how to step through code.

1. Open a new project. Place a list box on the form and name it **lstDisplay.**

2. Type the following into the form's Load event procedure:

```
Dim Number, Counter As Integer
Number = 2
For Counter = 1 To 10
  lstDisplay.Items.Add("2 to the power " & Counter & " is " & Number)
  Number = Number * 2
Next Counter
```

3. Run the program and confirm that it keeps doubling the current number as shown in figure 13.3.

```
Program 13.1 - Stepping through code and setting Watches

2 to the power 1 is 2
2 to the power 2 is 4
2 to the power 3 is 8
2 to the power 4 is 16
2 to the power 5 is 32
2 to the power 6 is 64
2 to the power 7 is 128
2 to the power 8 is 256
2 to the power 9 is 512
2 to the power 10 is 1024
```

Figure 13.3: Output from program 13.1

4. To set a watch on a variable we must be in break mode. One way of getting into this mode is to set a breakpoint somewhere in the program. Click in the Margin Indicator bar to the left of *Number = 2* as shown in figure 13.4. The line of code will be highlighted in brown and a circle will appear next to it in the bar.

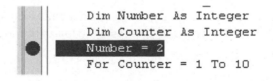

```
Dim Number As Integer
Dim Counter As Integer
Number = 2
For Counter = 1 To 10
```

Figure 13.4: Setting a breakpoint

5. Run the program. Execution will stop at the breakpoint, which will now be highlighted in yellow. To set a watch on the variable Number, highlight it and right-click, and then select **Add Watch**. The Watch window will appear at the bottom of the screen (with the title Watch 1 since you can use up to four Watch windows). The current value of Number is shown as 0 because the breakpoint line of code, which sets it to 2, has not yet been executed.

6. You can also put watches on expressions. In the Watch window add another watch as shown in figure 13.5. Type in **Number > 500** and press Enter. We want to know when Number holds a value greater than 500. At the moment the expression is False.

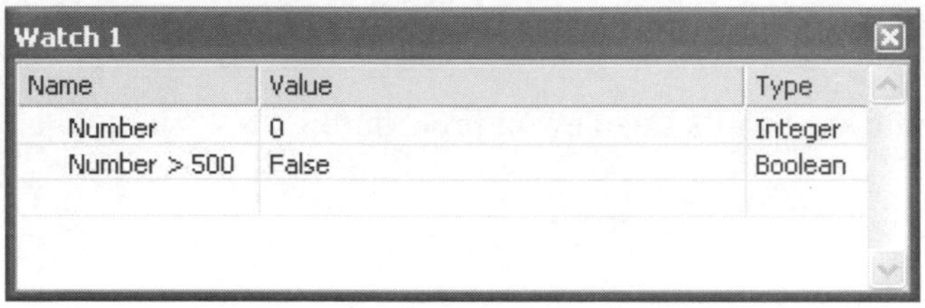

Watch 1			
Name	Value		Type
Number	0		Integer
Number > 500	False		Boolean

Figure 13.5: The Watch window

7. Now we are going to execute the code line by line and see what happens in the Watch window. You can step through the code either by using the F8 key, clicking the Step Into icon on the Debug toolbar, or selecting the Step Into item from the Debug menu. Press the **F8** key once. The start of the For…Next loop is now highlighted and the value of Number is now 2 in the Watch window.

8. Press the **F8** key three more times and the value of Number will be doubled to 4. Keep pressing this key until its value becomes 512. At this point the expression in the Watch window is True.

9. Select **Debug/Stop Debugging** or click **Stop Debugging** on the Debug toolbar to stop the program. Remove the breakpoint by clicking on the circle in the Margin Indicator bar.

End of Program 13.1

The Immediate Window

The Immediate window lets you do a variety of things such as look at and change the contents of variables. As with the Watch window these can only be done in break mode.

PROGRAM 13.2   *The Immediate Window*

Specification	Demonstrate the use of the Immediate Window

This is a simple program that asks the user to enter a product's unit price and the quantity bought. If the total price exceeds £200 there is a 10% discount. It outputs the total price after discount.

1. Open a new project and type the following into the form's Load event procedure:

```
Dim Quantity As Short
Dim Price, Discount, TotalPrice As Decimal
Price = InputBox("Enter price")
Quantity = InputBox("Enter quantity")
If Price * Quantity > 200 Then
  Discount = Price * Quantity * 0.1          'discount is 10%
End If
TotalPrice = Price * Quantity - Discount
MsgBox("Total price is " & Format(TotalPrice, "Currency"))
```

2. Run the program to check that it works.

3. Comment out the two lines that use input boxes to get the data from the user. Place a breakpoint on the line with the If condition.

4. Run the program so that it stops at the breakpoint. Select **Debug/Windows/Immediate** from the main menu to get the Immediate window. (Note that it is actually called the Command window. The Command window can open in two modes, Immediate and Command itself. We will only be looking at the Immediate mode.)

5. In the Immediate window set the values of Price and Quantity as shown in figure 13.6. Press **Enter** after each line.

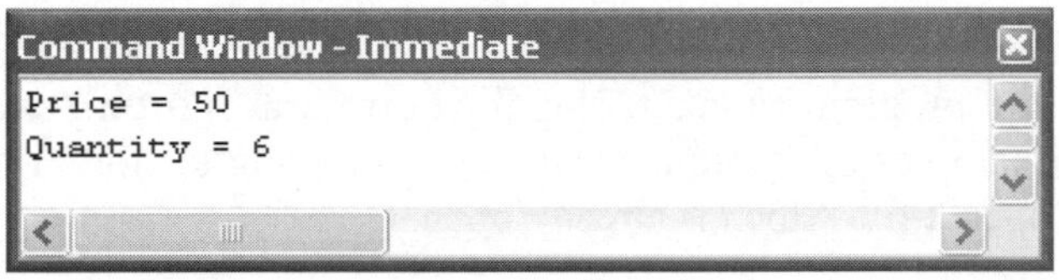

Figure 13.6: The Immediate window

6. Press the **F8** key twice to step through the code to the end of the If statement. In the Immediate window display the value of the variable *Discount* by typing in **?Discount** and pressing **Enter**. The result is shown in figure 13.7. The discount is 30 (10% of 50 x 6). The D after the 30 indicates that the decimal numbering system is used.

Figure 13.7

7. Remove the breakpoint and stop debugging the program (see step 9 of Program 13.1).

end of Program 13.2

The Debug class

Visual Basic .NET supplies the **Debug** class to help you debug a program directly from the code. In Program 13.1 if we had written a **Debug.WriteLine** immediately after the For...Next loop

```
Debug.WriteLine("The finishing value of Number is " & Number)
```

the **Output** window would display the value 2048 (since Number would be doubled from 1024 at the end of the loop but not displayed), as shown in figure 13.8. You will have seen this window many times before when your program has finished running and you are brought back to design mode. If it is not visible you can get it by selecting **View/Other Windows/Output window**.

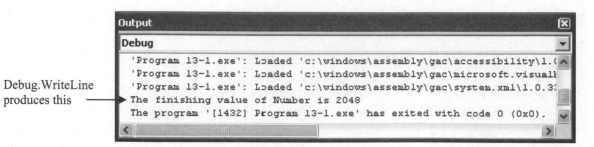

Debug.WriteLine
produces this

Figure 13.8: The Output window

Handling run-time errors with Try…Catch

You have seen that debugging is about tracking down logic errors which will probably produce incorrect results but won't stop the program running. Handling errors at run time which *will* crash the program requires special code. Examples of run-time errors are attempting to store a number that is too big for its data type and trying to open a file which is already open.

The **Try…Catch** statement is used to trap run-time errors. Its general form is:

> **Try**
> > *code that could produce the error*
>
> **Catch**
> > *code to run if a run-time error occurs*
>
> **Finally**
> > *optional code to run whether an error occurs or not*
>
> **End Try**

The Catch part can be divided into a series of **Catch When** statements to identify the particular error that has occurred. Program 13.3 has a single Catch. Program 13.4 extends this Catch by having two Catch Whens to try to pinpoint the type of error more clearly.

PROGRAM 13.3   *Simple Error Handling*

Specification   Ask the user to enter a number into a text box. Write an error routine to handle an invalid number.

1.   Open a new project and construct the form shown in figure 13.9. Name the text box **txtNumber** and the button **btnOK**.

Program 13.3 - Simple error handling

Enter a number

OK

Figure 13.9: Program 13.3

2. In the Click event procedure for the button enter the following code:

```
Private Sub btnOK_Click(...) Handles btnOK.Click
  Dim Number As Short
  Number = txtNumber.Text
End Sub
```

3. Run the program and enter a character instead of a number in the text box. Click the **OK** button and you'll get Visual Basic .NET's default error message window for this type of error, as shown in figure 13.10. (In this example the character 'y' was entered as the number.) Click **Continue**.

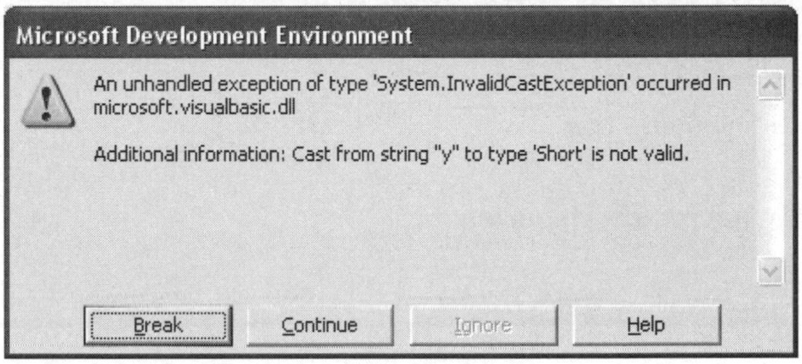

Figure 13.10: Run-time error

4. Run the program again but this time enter a number which is too big to store as a Short – any value over 32767 (see figure 3.1). The run-time error message refers to arithmetic overflow.

5. Use Try...Catch in the button's Click event. The optional **Finally** is included here simply to show you how to use it.

```
Try
  Number = txtNumber.Text
  MsgBox("You entered a valid number")
Catch
  MsgBox("You entered an invalid number")
Finally
  MsgBox("This completes the simple error handling example")
End Try
```

6. Run the program three times to check that the error-handling routine works. First enter a small number and check that the first message appears. Second enter one or more characters, and third enter a number that is too large so that the second message appears.

end of Program 13.3

The Err Object

Program 13.3 displayed a general *invalid number* message for any number that is not valid. It would be better to make your error-handling code appropriate for the type of error that triggers it off. Visual Basic supplies the **Err** object for this. Two of its properties are particulary useful – **Number** and **Description**. All run-time errors are identified by a number and each has a description that explains what it is.

PROGRAM 13.4   *More advanced error handling using the Err object*

> **Specification**   Ask the user to enter numbers into two text boxes. The result of dividing the first number by the second should be displayed. Use the Err object to display different messages for different input errors.

1. Open a new project and design the form using figure 13.11. Name the text boxes **txtFirstNumber** and **txtSecondNumber**, the label for output **lblResult** and the button **btnDivide**.

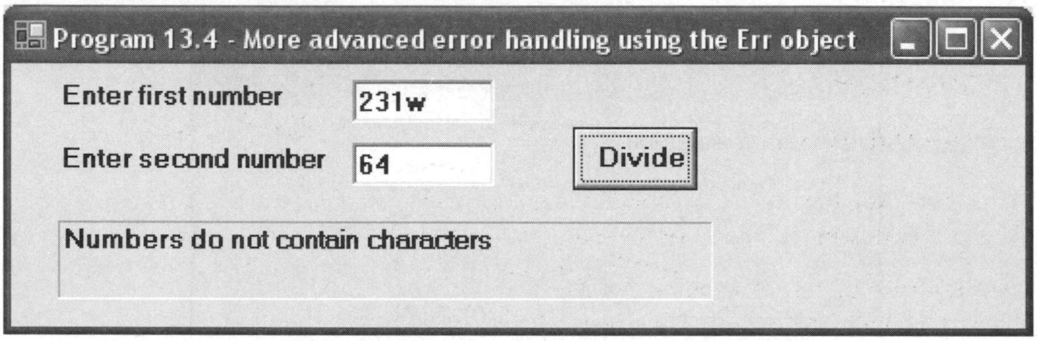

Figure 13.11: Program 13.4

2. The Catch part of the Try…Catch has two Catch Whens to detect when the number contains one or more characters or when it is too large. Each of these situations is detected by using the Number property of the Err object. Type the following code into the Click event of the button:

```
Private Sub btnDivide_Click(...) Handles btnDivide.Click
  Dim FirstNumber, SecondNumber As Short
  Dim Result As Single
  Try
    FirstNumber = txtFirstNumber.Text
    SecondNumber = txtSecondNumber.Text
    Result = FirstNumber / SecondNumber
    lblResult.Text = Result
  Catch When Err.Number = 6
    lblResult.Text = "One or both of the numbers is out of range"
  Catch When Err.Number = 13
    lblResult.Text = "Numbers do not contain characters"
  End Try
End Sub
```

3. Run the program and enter test data to cover the two types of error and to cover acceptable numbers.

end of Program 13.4

Summary of key concepts

- A **bug** is an error in a program. **Debugging** is the process of finding and removing errors.

- The **Debug toolbar** and **Debug menu** provide aids in tracking down **logic** errors.

- To **step** through code is to execute it line by line.

- A **watch** on a variable or expression allows you to see how its value changes during a program. The **Watch Window** displays watches.

- A **breakpoint** is a place in the code where the program temporarily stops.

- **Debug.WriteLine** <variable identifier> in your code displays the contents of a given variable in the **Output Window**.

- The **Try...Catch** statement is used to handle run-time errors.

- The **Err** object's **Number** property can be used to trap different types of error.

Take it from here...

1. Investigate the **QuickWatch** dialog box.

2. The Immediate Window, Watch Window and Output Window were covered in the chapter. Investigate a fourth window used in debugging, the **Locals Window**.

3. Only the **Step Into** option of stepping through a program was used in the chapter. Use any program you have written with one or more general procedures and try out **Step Over**.

4. There is an alternative to using Err.Number to pinpoint the type of error. You could use the **Exception** object. Find out how.

Questions on the Programs

Program 13.4

*1. Error code 13 is used in this program to trap any characters in the number but it will also trap the case where the user forgets to enter a number. Extend the code to display a different message for this situation. Note that this is not asking for another Catch When. Distinguish between numbers with characters and no number entered within the Catch itself.

Chapter 14 – Printing reports

What is a report?

In earlier programs we used a variety of methods to display output. Chapter 4 in particular showed you how to format output in list boxes and message boxes. However you may wish to have a permanent record or **report** of your output. To do this you can print either to a file or to the printer.

Printing to a file

In Chapter 12 you learned how to store data in a text file. Sometimes this might be more appropriate than sending output to the printer. For example if a business wishes to keep a permanent record of its weekly sales these would be stored on file and perhaps printed out when required from Notepad. The disadvantage of using a text file over printing a report directly is that you can do little to format it. Of course you *could* open it in Word or another word processing package and format it there.

The code below stores details of three employees in a text file. It uses PrintLine rather than WriteLine because we don't want quotation marks around the data in the file (see figure 12.2). It also uses the Tab function to position the data in columns. Tab takes one argument – the column (i.e. character) number to move to before the next item is printed. Figure 14.1 shows the resulting contents of the file. The 'J' in John is in column 1 and the 'A' in Andrews in column 12. Although not used below, you could also use the Space function that was first covered in Chapter 4.

```
Dim Filename As String
Filename = "Staff.txt"                'VB will use the bin folder for the file
FileOpen(1, Filename, OpenMode.Output)
PrintLine(1, "List of employees")
PrintLine(1)                                    'to produce a blank line
PrintLine(1, "John", TAB(12), "Andrews", TAB(25), "Senior programmer")
PrintLine(1, "Sarah", TAB(12), "Matthews", TAB(25), "Programmer")
Print(1, "Jane", TAB(12), "Lewes", TAB(25), "Project manager")
FileClose(1)
```

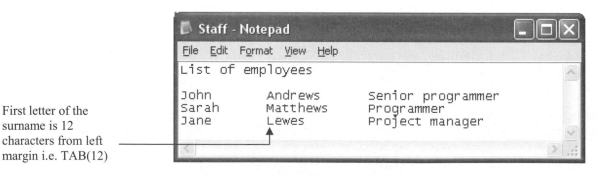

First letter of the surname is 12 characters from left margin i.e. TAB(12)

Figure 14.1: Contents of the text file Staff.txt

Printing to a printer

The techniques for sending data to a printer have completely changed in Visual Basic .NET. You use the **PrintDocument** control and its default event procedure **PrintPage**. The code for printing goes into this event procedure which is fired off by calling the **Print** method of the control. Using the control's default name, PrintDocument1, the code below shows how to send data to the printer by clicking a button, btnPrint.

```
Private Sub btnPrint_Click(...) Handles btnPrint.Click
    PrintDocument1.Print()  'Calls Print method of the PrintDocument
End Sub                  'control - this runs its PrintPage event below

Private Sub PrintDocument1_PrintPage(ByVal sender As System.Object, _
            ByVal e As System.Drawing.Printing.PrintPageEventArgs) _
            Handles PrintDocument1.PrintPage
    'code to do the printing
End Sub
```

The second parameter declared in the PrintPage event procedure is simply named **e**, but it is essential for carrying out the printing. Technically it is an object of class PrintPageEventArgs which itself belongs to the System.Drawing.Printing namespace. The code to do the actual printing uses the **DrawString** method which has the general form shown in figure 14.2.

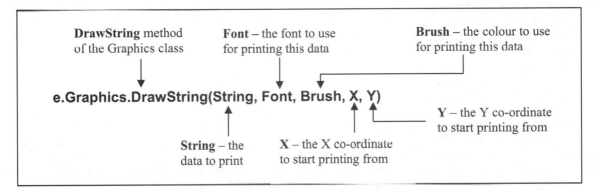

Figure 14.2: General form for printing one line of data

You will see how to use the String, Font and Brush parameters shortly, but to use the X and Y coordinates you must understand what they mean. Any point on a piece of paper is defined by its X and Y coordinates, which are measured in pixels. Figure 14.3 illustrates how these apply to an A4 sheet of paper which is measured by Visual Basic .NET as 827 x 1169 pixels. Note that the coordinates of the central point of the paper can be found using e's **PageBounds** property. PageBounds.Width, for example, gives the number of pixels across the page.

Look back at figure 6.5. Suppose we wished to print a report listing the patients in the ward currently selected. Go carefully through the code on the next page. The DrawString method is called each time one line of text is to be printed. The Y co-ordinate must be increased for each line, and if a given line is to be indented inside the previous line the X co-ordinate must be increased too. The Y co-ordinate is increased in this example by using the **GetHeight** method of the Font object; this returns the number of pixels a line of text in the specified font occupies. Figure 14.4 shows the report in Print Preview, a new and extremely useful feature introduced by Visual Basic .NET.

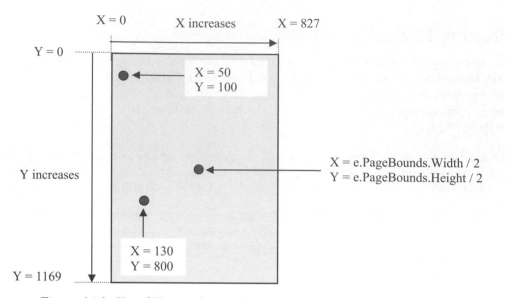

Figure 14.3: X and Y co-ordinates for an A4 sheet of paper

```
Dim Ward, Patient As String
Dim X, Y As Integer              'X and Y co-ordinates
Dim FontHeight As Integer        'height of one line of text in a given font
Dim Index As Integer
Dim MyFont As New Font("Courier New", 12, FontStyle.Regular) 'Set font
FontHeight = MyFont.GetHeight(e.Graphics)'and find its height for 1 line
X = 50                           'start location for printing is near top left
Y = 50
Ward = lstWards.Text
e.Graphics.DrawString(Ward & " Ward", MyFont, Brushes.Black, X, Y) 'Print
                                                  'one line of text
Y = Y + FontHeight                       'reset Y for next line of printing
e.Graphics.DrawString("", MyFont, Brushes.Black, X, Y) 'print blank line
Y = Y + FontHeight
X = 100        'reset X so that patients' names are indented inside title
For Index = 0 To lstPatients.Items.Count - 1
  Patient = lstPatients.Items(Index)
  e.Graphics.DrawString(Patient, MyFont, Brushes.Black, X, Y)'One patient
  Y = Y + FontHeight                     'reset Y for printing next patient
Next Index
```

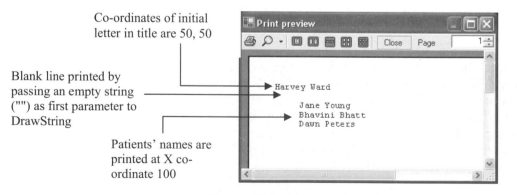

Figure 14.4: Print Preview of the report

PROGRAM 14.1 *Printing reports on sales staff*

Specification Use an existing text file that holds, for each salesperson, their name, the region they work in and the annual value of their sales. Print and Print Preview two reports. One should output the details by salesperson and the other should group these details by region.

This program uses the text file **Sales.txt** which you can get from the publisher's web site. If you cannot download it you can create the file in Notepad in a few minutes (see step 3). Figures 14.7 and 14.8 show the two reports.

1. Open a new project and build the form as shown in figure 14.5.

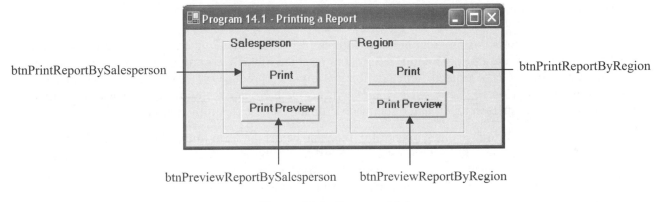

btnPrintReportBySalesperson

btnPrintReportByRegion

btnPreviewReportBySalesperson

btnPreviewReportByRegion

Figure 14.5: Program14.1

2. Place two **PrintDocument** controls and two **PrintPreviewDialog** controls on the form. They will show in the pane below the form. Do not rename them.

3. Place the file **Sales.txt** inside the bin folder for this program. Its contents are shown in figure 14.6. (If you cannot download it you create it now in Notepad.) The numbers refer to the value of sales in thousands of pounds. Thus the first value represents £250,000.

```
Sales - Notepad
File  Edit  Format  View  Help
Jim Smith, North, 250
John James, South, 460
Sarah Hardcastle, South, 320
Tariq Mahmood, East, 578
Eileen Mason, West, 273
Jane Kennedy, West, 140
Frank Delaney, North, 230
Hiten Patel, East, 466
David Lee, West, 663
Harry Marples, South, 111
Robert Thorne, East, 723
Marie Green, North, 563
Ronald Andrews, South, 444
June Whittle, East, 812
Shelina Begum, North, 510
John Endquist, West, 294
```

Figure 14.6: Contents of Sales.txt

3.   Declare a global variable to hold the file name and assign it a value in the form's Load event:

```
Dim Filename As String

Private Sub Form1_Load(...) Handles MyBase.Load
   Filename = "Sales.txt"
End Sub
```

4.   When the Print button is clicked to print the report by salesperson the Print method of one of the PrintDocument controls should be fired off.

```
Private Sub btnPrintReportBySalesperson_Click(...) _
                              Handles btnPrintReportBySalesperson.Click
   PrintDocument1.Print()
End Sub
```

Look ahead at the reports this program producs (figures 14.7. and 14.8). To get the column effect you can use the technique in Program 4.2 to define a format or reset the X and Y co-ordinates each time an item of data on a given line is to be printed. When defining a format to produce columns you must use an even-spaced font such as Courier New, but any font will do for the other method. We will use the format technique for the salesperson report and reset the co-ordinates for the report by region.

5.   Double-click the PrintDocument1 control in the pane below the form to bring up its PrintPage event procedure. This event will be fired off when the Print button is clicked because the line of code in step 4 calls its Print method. The Print method 'knows' to use its PrintPage event procedure. In this procedure declare the variables, initialise the starting X and Y co-ordinates and find the height of one line of the font:

```
Private Sub PrintDocument1_PrintPage(ByVal sender As System.Object, _
           ByVal e As System.Drawing.Printing.PrintPageEventArgs) _
                                Handles PrintDocument1.PrintPage
   Dim MyFont As New Font("Courier New", 12, FontStyle.Regular)
   Dim MyFormat As String = "{0, -20}{1, -10}{2, -12}" '3 column format
   Dim Name, Region, LineToPrint As String
   Dim X, Y, Amount, FontHeight As Integer
   X = 50                       'set co-ordinates of first thing to print
   Y = 50
   FontHeight = MyFont.GetHeight(e.Graphics)'height of 1 line of font used
```

6.   The code inside the PrintPage event to carry out the printing is:

```
                                            'print report title
   e.Graphics.DrawString("Report on annual sales made by sales staff", _
                              MyFont, Brushes.Black, X, Y)
   Y = Y + FontHeight              'reset Y for next line of printing
   e.Graphics.DrawString("", MyFont, Brushes.Black, X, Y) 'blank line
   Y = Y + FontHeight
   LineToPrint = String.Format(MyFormat, "Salesperson","Region", "Amount"
   e.Graphics.DrawString(LineToPrint, MyFont, Brushes.Black, X, Y)
   Y = Y + FontHeight
   e.Graphics.DrawString("", MyFont, Brushes.Black, X, Y) 'blank line
   FileOpen(1, Filename, OpenMode.Input)
   Do While Not EOF(1)
```

```
    Input(1, Name)
    Input(1, Region)
    Input(1, Amount)
    Y = Y + FontHeight          'reset Y for printing next salesperson
    LineToPrint = String.Format(MyFormat, Name, Region, Format(Amount * _
                                       1000, "£#,##0"))
                                  'print details of one salesperson
      e.Graphics.DrawString(LineToPrint, MyFont, Brushes.Black, X, Y)
  Loop
  FileClose(1)
```

7. Run the program and click the Print button for the report by salesperson. The printed report should look like that in figure 14.7 (which shows it in print preview).

8. To preview the report you need to set the **Document** property of one of the PrintPreviewDialog controls to a PrintDocument control. Since we have used PrintDocument1 we will assign this to PrintPreviewDialog1. To display the Print Preview dialog box you must call its **ShowDialog** method. This is the same method you used in Chapter 12 for displaying an OpenFileDialog control.

```
Private Sub btnPreviewReportBySalesperson(...) Handles _
                                  btnPreviewReportBySalesperson.Click
  PrintPreviewDialog1.Document = PrintDocument1    'Assign a document to
                                                   'Print Preview control
  PrintPreviewDialog1.ShowDialog()   'display the Print Preview dialog box
End Sub
```

```
┌─────────────────────────────────────────────────────────┐
│ ▣ Print preview                              [_][□][X]    │
├─────────────────────────────────────────────────────────┤
│ 🖶 🔍 ▾ │ ▣ ▦ ▦ ▦ ▦ │ Close        Page      1⬍          │
├─────────────────────────────────────────────────────────┤
│                                                           │
│    Report on annual sales made by sales staff             │
│                                                           │
│    Salesperson        Region    Amount                    │
│                                                           │
│    Jim Smith          North     £250,000                  │
│    John James         South     £460,000                  │
│    Sarah Hardcastle   South     £320,000                  │
│    Tariq Mahmood      East      £578,000                  │
│    Eileen Mason       West      £273,000                  │
│    Jane Kennedy       West      £140,000                  │
│    Frank Delaney      North     £230,000                  │
│    Hiten Patel        East      £466,000                  │
│    David Lee          West      £663,000                  │
│    Harry Marples      South     £111,000                  │
│    Robert Thorne      East      £723,000                  │
│    Marie Green        North     £563,000                  │
│    Ronald Andrews     South     £444,000                  │
│    June Whittle       East      £812,000                  │
│    Shelina Begum      North     £510,000                  │
│    John Endquist      West      £294,000                  │
└─────────────────────────────────────────────────────────┘
```

Figure 14.7: Report on sales by salesperson

9. Now for the second report which you can see in figure 14.8. When the Print button is clicked the Print method of PrintDocument2 should be fired off, so repeat step 4 now for this button.

10. Double-click the PrintDocument2 control to get its PrintPage event procedure. Figure 14.9 shows that the report title has a larger point size (15) than the rest of the report (size 12) and is bold and underlined. We therefore need to declare two fonts. Note the use of the **Or** operator to make the MyTitleFont both bold and underlined.

```
Private Sub PrintDocument2_PrintPage(...) Handles PrintDocument2.PrintPage
  Dim MyFont As New Font("Arial", 12, FontStyle.Regular)
  Dim MyTitleFont As New Font("Arial", 15, FontStyle.Bold. Or _
                           FontStyle.Underline) 'use Or to extend font
  Dim Name, Region, RegionGroup As String
  Dim X, Y, RegionNumber, Amount, FontHeight As Integer
  X = 50
  Y = 50
  FontHeight = MyFont.GetHeight(e.Graphics)
  e.Graphics.DrawString("Report on annual sales made by sales staff", _
           MyTitleFont, Brushes.Black, X, Y)        'print report title
  Y = Y + FontHeight
  e.Graphics.DrawString("", MyFont, Brushes.Black, X, Y) 'print blank line
  Y = Y + FontHeight
  For RegionNumber = 1 To 4            'loop 4 times - once per sales region
    Select Case RegionNumber
      Case 1
        RegionGroup = "East"
      Case 2
        RegionGroup = "North"
      Case 3
        RegionGroup = "South"
      Case 4
        RegionGroup = "West"
    End Select
    e.Graphics.DrawString(RegionGroup, MyFont, Brushes.Black, X, Y) 'Print
    Y = Y + FontHeight                                  'group header
    FileOpen(1, Filename, OpenMode.Input)
    Do While Not EOF(1)                         'go through whole file
      Input(1, Name)
      Input(1, Region)
      Input(1, Amount)
      If Region = RegionGroup Then           'is region the required one?
        X = 150                  'if yes then indent names of salespersons
        e.Graphics.DrawString(Name, MyFont, Brushes.Black, X, Y)
        X = X + 300                    'print amounts in another column
        e.Graphics.DrawString(Format(Amount * 1000, "£#,##0"), MyFont, _
                                    Brushes.Black, X, Y)
        Y = Y + FontHeight
      End If
    Loop
    FileClose(1)
    X = 50              'align next group header with the report title
    Y = Y + FontHeight
    e.Graphics.DrawString("", MyFont, Brushes.Black, X, Y) 'Blank line at
  Next RegionNumber                               'end of each region
End Sub
```

There are two main points to note about the code:

- The column effect is produced by increasing the value of the X co-ordinate as one line is printed. The **DrawString** method is called each time the salesperson's name and amount are printed on the same line. With the format method on the other report all the data to print on one line was stored in a variable, LineToPrint, and this was the first parameter sent to DrawString.

- The sales region names make up what is called a **group header**. To process one sales region each line in the file must be read to see if its sales region matches the one being processed. To get the file pointer back to the start of the file ready for the next sales region you have to close the file and open it again. This explains why the FileOpen and FileClose statements are *inside* the For…Next loop. If we had been using a random access file we would only need to open and close it once, and reposition the file pointer with FileGet as required.

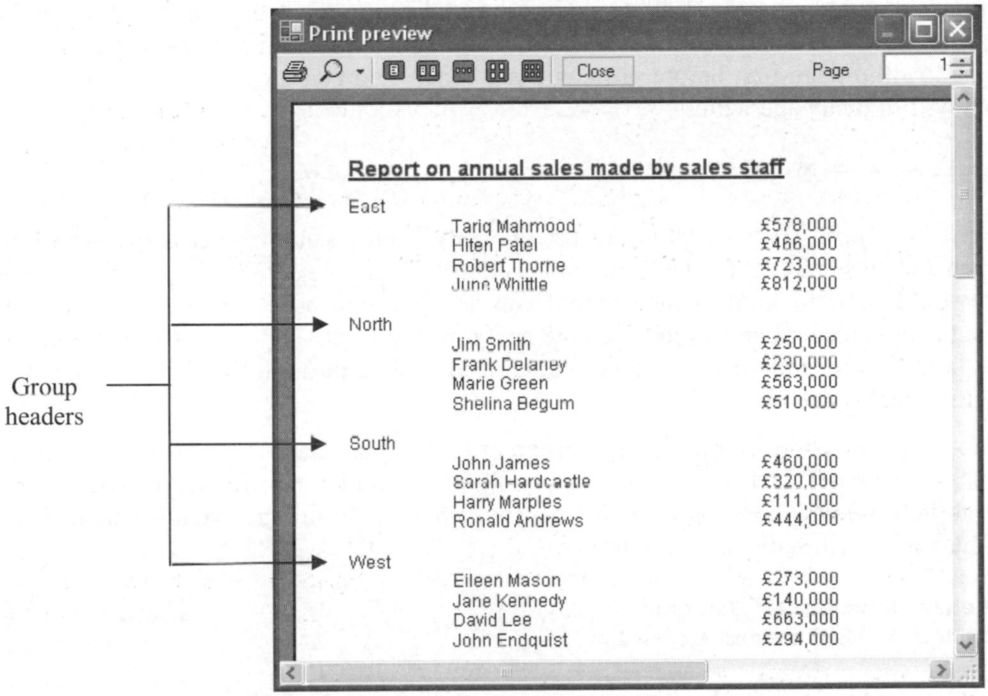

Figure 14.8: Report on sales by region

11. To preview this report repeat step 8 for the other Print Preview button and use PrintPreviewDialog2.

12. Run the program and check that the report is printed correctly.

end of Program 14.1

Printing multiple pages

The data in the file used for Program 14.1 can easily be printed on one page. If there had been about 50 or more salespeople in the file then more than one page would have been needed. Unfortunately Visual Basic .NET does not just carry on printing to the next page. A PrintDocument control's default event procedure is called PrintPage for a good reason. It assembles all the data that can fit on one page and then sends it to the printer. Any extra data that cannot fit on the page is discarded.

To print multiple pages you have to call the PrintPage event procedure for each page to be printed. This is done by setting the **HasMorePages** property of the 'e' parameter to True in the PrintPage event itself. By default it is False. When it is False the program will cease printing.

For some applicatons all you have to do is keep a running count of how many lines on a particular page have been printed, and when this equals the number you require indicate that a new page is needed by setting HasMorePages to True:

```
If LinesOnPage < LinesRequired Then
  e.HasMorePages = False
Else              'required no of lines printed so ask for a new page
  e.HasMorePages = True
End If
```

The number of lines required on a page will depend on the application. To print a list of customers' names 30 to a page is straightforward enough (assuming the font can fit in this number of lines on a page). But what if you wish to fill a page first before printing a new one? You could calculate the number of lines that a given font will fit on a page with:

```
LinesRequired = e.MarginBounds.Height / MyFont.Height
```

Suppose you wished to print some or all the records directly from a random access file. The PrintPage event would open and close the file (just as it did in Program 14.1 for a text file). To use this line counting technique you would need to know which record was the last one processed before a new page is required, so that the next record can be processed the next time the PrintPage event is called. But with text files, which do not support random access, you would need to read through the file from the start each time the PrintPage event is called.

Let's see how to print the report by region from Program 14.1 so that each region is on a separate page. To make things easier assume that the list of salespeople in any region can fit on one page. We would need a variable to indicate which region is to be processed when the PrintPage event is called. This could be a form variable, or a local Static one as follows:

```
Static RegionNumber As Integer
RegionNumber = RegionNumber + 1
```

The For…Next loop in the original code (see step 10 in Program 14.1) loops through all four regions. We need to remove the loop otherwise each new page will start printing the first region again. However the Select Case must be kept so the current page knows which region to process. The last part of the code should check to see if a new page is needed:

```
If RegionNumber = 4 Then
  e.HasMorePages = False
Else
  e.HasMorePages = True
End If
```

Summary of key concepts

• Use a **PrintDocument** control to print a report. Put the code to do the printing in its default **PrintPage** event procedure.

- Use the **PrintPreviewDialog** control to preview a report. Assign it the document to print (a PrintDocument control) and then call its **ShowDialog** method to do the previewing.

- The PrintPage event can only print one page. The event must be called each time a new page is needed. Do this by setting **e.HasMorePages** to True.

Take it from here...

1. Only one PrintDocument event, PrintPage, was covered. Investigate the **BeginPrint** and **EndPrint** events.

Questions on Program 14.1

*1. Add a report footer to display the total sales on both reports.

*2. The code to print a blank line is repeated several times in the program. Write a Sub procedure to do this.

**3. Underline the column headings in the report by salesperson. (Note only underline the headings, not the spaces between the headings too.)

**4. Extend the report by region to include:

- A group footer (i.e. at the end of each sales region) to show the total value of the sales for that region.
- Print each region on a separate page and number the pages.

***5. Extend the report by salesperson to include:

- The total value of all sales.
- The average value of all sales.
- A 4th column indicating how much the salesperson's value of sales exceeds or is below the average, expressed as a percentage.
- Print details of 6 salespeople per page.

End of chapter exercises

*1. Write a program to accept student names and their exam mark (0-100) from the user and store these in an array. Then send a report to the printer showing the names of those who passed the exam. Assume a mark of 50 or more is a pass.

2. Use the random access file **GardenCentreProducts.dat from the web site. It was produced by running program 12.3 and contains details of 16 products. (If you completed this program you may wish to use your own file.) You will need to look at step 3 in program 12.3 to see how the record for one product is declared. Produce the following reports:

(a) The report shown in figure 14.9. The products are listed in file order. The font used in figure 14.9 is Courier New point 11.

(b) A report displaying the same information as figure 14.9 but grouped according to the price of the products. Use 3 groups – under £10.00, £10.00 to £49.99 and £50.00 and over.

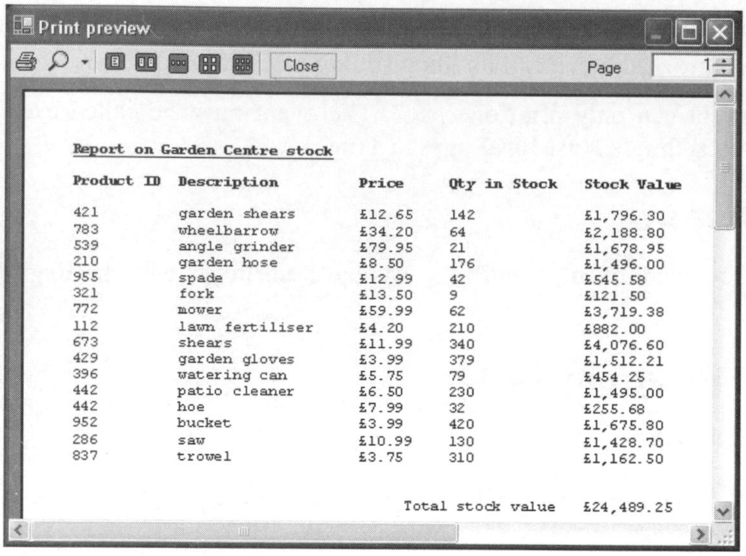

Report on Garden Centre stock

Product ID	Description	Price	Qty in Stock	Stock Value
421	garden shears	£12.65	142	£1,796.30
783	wheelbarrow	£34.20	64	£2,188.80
539	angle grinder	£79.95	21	£1,678.95
210	garden hose	£8.50	176	£1,496.00
955	spade	£12.99	42	£545.58
321	fork	£13.50	9	£121.50
772	mower	£59.99	62	£3,719.38
112	lawn fertiliser	£4.20	210	£882.00
673	shears	£11.99	340	£4,076.60
429	garden gloves	£3.99	379	£1,512.21
396	watering can	£5.75	79	£454.25
442	patio cleaner	£6.50	230	£1,495.00
442	hoe	£7.99	32	£255.68
952	bucket	£3.99	420	£1,675.80
286	saw	£10.99	130	£1,428.70
837	trowel	£3.75	310	£1,162.50
			Total stock value	£24,489.25

Figure 14.9: The report for exercise 2(a)

***3. You may have done exercise 1 at the end of Chapter 12 and used the text file DegreeStudents.txt, which stores the name and main subject for 125 degree students. Use a similar file, **DegreeStudents2.txt** that stores the same data plus the gender (M or F) of each student. The file can be downloaded from the publisher's web site.

(a) Produce a printed report from this file that is grouped on the course as shown in figure 14.10. Print each course on a new page and include the page number and the total number of students on each course. The title should also be on each page. The fonts used are Courier New Bold point 14 for the title and group headers and Courier New point 11 for the student names. The names are printed differently from the way they are stored in the file.

(b) Produce a report which prints the students on each course as in (a) but which also groups on gender *within* each course. Separate totals of the number of male and of female students on each course should be shown, as well as the total number of students on each course. The total number of male and of female students and the total number of students on all courses should be displayed at the end of the report.

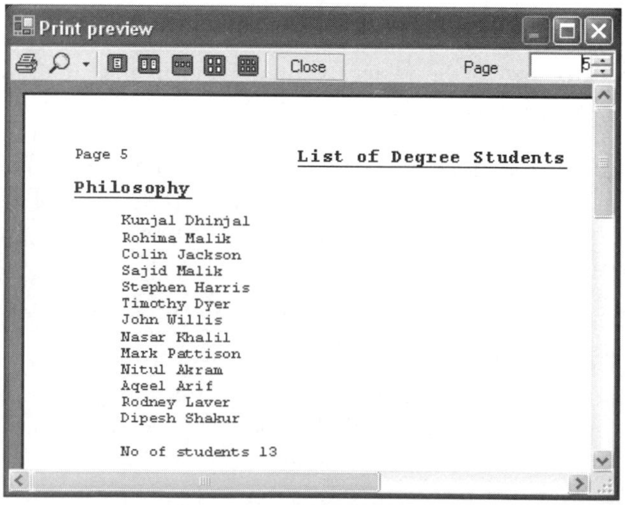

Page 5 **List of Degree Students**

Philosophy

Kunjal Dhinjal
Rohima Malik
Colin Jackson
Sajid Malik
Stephen Harris
Timothy Dyer
John Willis
Nasar Khalil
Mark Pattison
Nitul Akram
Aqeel Arif
Rodney Laver
Dipesh Shakur

No of students 13

Figure 14.10: Report for exercise 3(a) (last page shown)

Chapter 15 – Databases:
Retrieving Data

Introduction

This chapter and Chapter 16 explain how to build a Visual Basic front end to interact with an Access database. In this chapter you will learn how to retrieve data from a database and display it on a Visual Basic form. In the next chapter you will learn how to change data in the Access database through the form. The chapters assume you understand basic database theory and have some experience of Access. In particular they assume you know the following:

- The concept of storing data in tables and the terms **field** and **record**
- How and why tables are linked
- Queries on single or linked tables

Random access files or a database?

In Chapter 12 you learned that random access files store records. They are therefore very similar to a database table, so which should you use? Some Visual Basic textbooks dismiss random access files altogether and say that interacting with a database is the modern way of doing things. If you're studying 'A' level Computing traditional file-handling is still firmly entrenched, and you are expected to know about it.

The ADO .NET model

ADO stands for **A**ctive **D**ata **O**bjects. ADO .NET is at the heart of Microsoft's standard for data access and storage. A complete understanding of ADO .NET is far beyond the purpose of the two chapters on databases, but you will learn how to use its essential features. The main ADO .NET objects used in this chapter are as follows:

Connection   To connect to a database

Command   To provide commands to execute against a database

DataAdapter   To retrieve data from a database

DataSet   To store a copy of the data extracted from a database

DataTable   To store a table, with rows and columns

Figure 15.1 shows the main steps used in the programs in Chapters 15 and 16 to retrieve data from a database and display it on a form. The terms in bold are the names of the Toolbox controls. First you must set up a connection to the database. The data adapter holds the retrieved data. As you will see in Program 15.1 you can provide a command to execute against the database, and therefore extract the exact data you require, through the DataAdapter control. Program 15.2 creates these controls (objects) through code instead, and then you need an **OleDbCommand** control/object to provide the command. This is not shown in figure 15.1.

To get the data from a data adapter onto a Visual Basic form you need to use a suitable data container. Chapters 15 and 16 use datasets and data tables. From here you can display the data in a data grid or other bound controls such as text boxes.

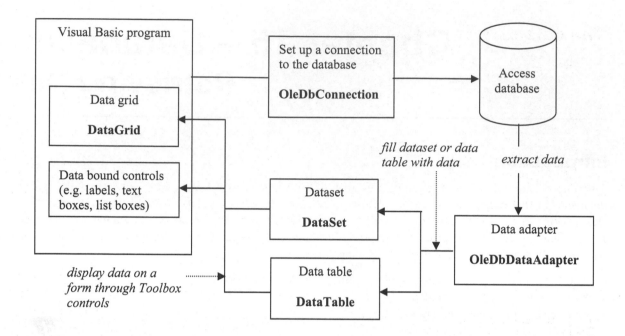

Figure 15.1: Retrieving and displaying data from an Access database (OleDbCommand not included)

Querying a database using SQL

Querying a database involves extracting all or part of its data. There are two ways you can query a database from a Visual Basic .NET program:

- run a query which you have saved as part of the Access database
- run SQL code

SQL stands for **S**tructured **Q**uery **L**anguage and is the world's premier language for creating and querying databases. All good databases support it. It isn't the purpose of this chapter to teach you SQL but a little explanation is needed if you are to understand how to retrieve data from a database, particularly the stage involving the DataAdapter. A typical SQL query has the form

SELECT *field names*
FROM *table(s)*
WHERE *specify search condition*

For example

SELECT * FROM Employees WHERE [Days Absence] >= 10

extracts data from all the fields (indicated by the '*') in the Employees table where the value in the Days Absence field is 10 or more. If a field name has spaces you must use square brackets. In Visual Basic code the SQL statement can be written on one line or over several and double quotation marks must be put around it. Upper-case letters for SELECT etc. are not compulsory but it is common practice to use them.

A good way to learn SQL is to build queries in Access using its QBE grid and then look at the SQL code which Access produces. When you save a query Access actually saves the SQL code. Like Access Visual Basic's DataAdapter provides a QBE grid and the equivalent SQL code which you can use as a learning tool.

The database programs in this book

The six programs in Chapters 15 and 16 use three Access databases and the End of Chapter exercises use a further two. These can be downloaded from the publisher's web site. It would be a good idea to store all five databases in their own folder before starting the practical work. The table below shows where these databases are used.

Access database	15.1	15.2	15.3	15.4	16.1	16.2	Chap 15 Exercises	Chap 16 Exercises
HolidayHomes	×		×		×		×	
ALevels						×		
Vocational Students							×	×
Repayments								×
Hospital		×		×				×

Before using a particular database you should have a look at it in Access to get to know its contents.

PROGRAM 15.1   *Displaying data from a table in a DataGrid control*

Specification   Display all the data from a database table in a DataGrid control. Use as little code as possible.

This uses the **HolidayHomes** database and displays the contents of its single table, **Properties**. Holiday Homes is a small business which rents properties in the west of England. Figure 15.2 shows the program. All the details of each of the 25 properties are displayed in a the DataGrid control. The People field refers to the maximum number of people allowed to occupy the property. The Pets field indicates whether or not pets are allowed to stay.

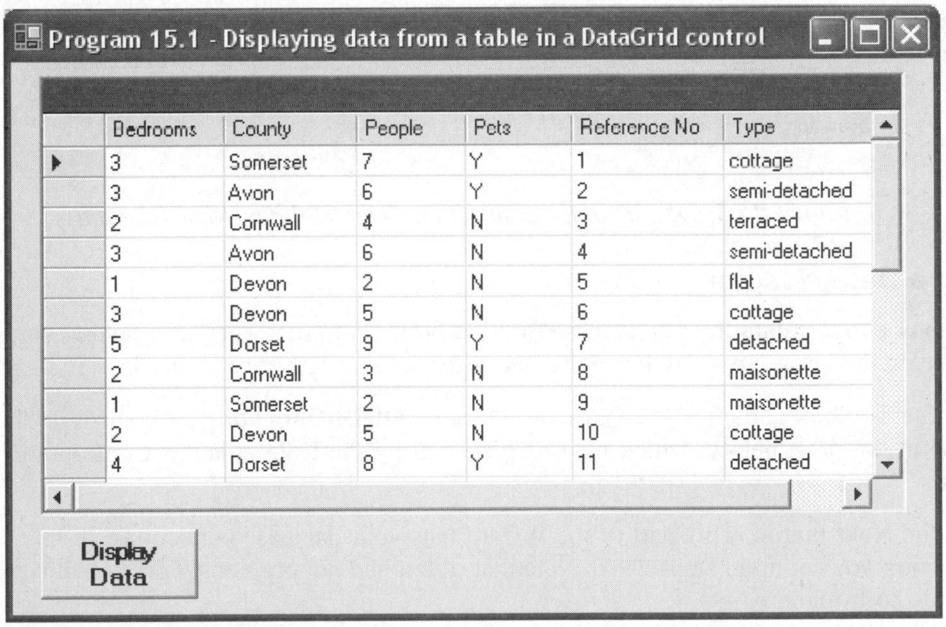

Figure 15.2: Program 15.1

Connecting to the database

1. Open a new project. Select **View/Server Explorer** from the menu to get the Server Explorer window. Apart from letting your program connect to a database, Server Explorer lets you view the structure of tables.

2. Click the **Connect To Database** button at the top of the Server Explorer (the third button from the left) to bring up the Data Link Properties dialog box.

3. Click the **Provider** tab and then select **Microsoft Jet 4.0 OLE DB Provider**. A provider knows how to connect to a database and extract data from it. The Microsoft Jet 4.0 OLE DB Provider is for connecting to Access databases.

4. Click **Next** and then click the ellipsis button to the right of the text box asking you to select a database name. Select the **HolidayHomes** database from wherever you have stored it.

5. Back on the **Connection** tab click the **Test Connection** button. A message box will tell you if a successful connection to HolidayHomes has been made. Click **OK**.

6. The connection is now complete. In the Server Explorer click the plus signs (+) to show details of the the data connection you have just made, as shown in figure 15.3. You can see the single table and the two views or queries. Double-click on **Properties**, **qryDetachedProperties** and **qryPetsAllowed** in turn and you will see the whole table, the 5 detached properties and the 11 properties which allow pets respectively.

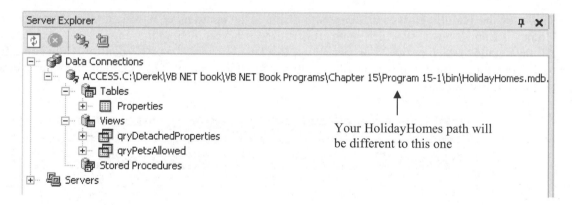

Figure 15.3: Details of the connection to the HolidayHomes database

Creating a Data Adapter

A data adapter extracts data from a database for your program to use. There are several ways of creating a data adapter. In this program we will use the Data Adapter Configuration Wizard.

7. Open the Toolbox and click the **Data** tab. Place an **OleDbDataAdapter** control on the form. It will appear in the pane below, which may be obscured by the Data Adapter Configuration Wizard that appears.

8. Click the **Next** button. This part of the Wizard lists your database conections, in this case the single connection you set up in steps 2 – 6. Note that if you had not previously created this connection, you could do so from here.

9. Click the **Next** button and you are asked to choose how the data adapter should access the database. Only the first option, **Use SQL statements**, is available.

10. Click **Next**. Here you can type in SQL code, or use a similar QBE technique to that in Access, for producing queries. Click **Query Builder** and then the **Add** button to add the single Properties table to the Query Builder. Click **Close**.

11. The specification for this program states that all the data from the Properties table should be displayed. Our SQL query must do this. Click ***(All columns)** in the Properties table and you should get the display shown in figure 15.4. Then click **OK**.

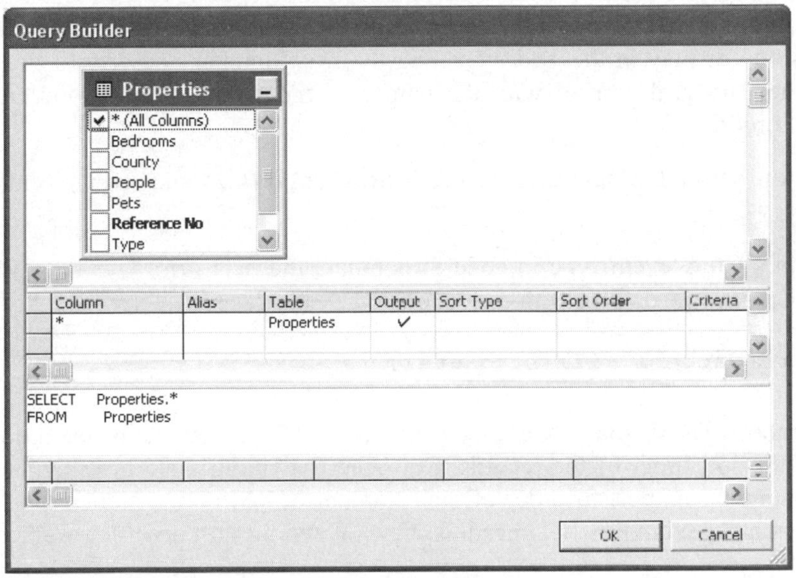

Figure 15.4: Building the SQL query

12. Click **Next** and then on the View Wizard Results form click **Finish**. There will be two controls in the pane below the form — one for the database connection (OleDbConnection1) and the other for the data adapter (OleDbDataAdapter1). If you need to change the SQL query contained in the data adapter you can right-click OleDbDataAdapter1 and select Configure Data Adapter to bring up the Wizard.

Creating a DataSet

A DataSet holds a copy of all the data extracted by the SQL query in the data adapter. If you modify the data in the DataSet the original data is unchanged unless you write code to update these changes. In this program we are using a DataSet only to display data. Chapter 16 shows how to update the data.

13. Make sure the form is selected and then select **Data/Generate Dataset** from the menu. This brings up the Generate Dataset dialog box.

14. Make sure the **New** radio button is selected. Note that the default name is DataSet1 and that the Properties table is checked for inclusion in the dataset. Click **OK**.

15. The dataset appears in the pane below the form as DataSet11 (not DataSet1). Notice also that the Solution Explorer now contains a file called DataSet1.xsd. This holds details of the tables, fields, data types and other details of the database schema in the dataset. You can double-click it to see this information.

Using the DataGrid control

A DataGrid control can be used to display the contents of a dataset. You need to set its **DataSource** property and, depending what you have set this property to, you may need to set its **DataMember** property too. The DataSource property contains the name of the dataset that will be displayed in the data grid. The DataMember property contains a reference to the data in this dataset that will be displayed. In this example we only need to set the DataSource property.

16. Click the **Windows Forms** tab in the Toolbox and drag a **DataGrid** control onto the form so that it occupies much of the upper area as in figure 15.2.

17. Select the data grid and in its DataSource property click the small button, then select **DataSet11.Properties**. (If you had selected DataSet11 instead you would need to indicate which part of the dataset to display in the grid by setting the DataMember property to **Properties**.) A grid will appear in the data grid control with the names of the fields in the Properties table. They are in alphabetical order.

18. Place a button below the data grid. Name it **btnDisplayData** and set its Text property to **Display Data**.

19. In the button's Click event type in code to populate the data grid. Use the **Fill** method of the data adapter to populate the dataset with data extracted by the data adapter.

```
OleDbDataAdapter1.Fill(DataSet11)
```

20. Run the program. The display should look like figure 15.2. You can resize the width of the columns and change the sort order of the records. Click the **Bedrooms** field heading and the records will be sorted in ascending numerical order of their number of bedrooms. Notice the tiny upward-pointing triangle now displayed in this field heading. Click it and the sort order is reversed.

end of Program 15.1

PROGRAM 15.2 *Displaying data from a table and a query in a DataGrid control*

Specification	Display all the data from a database table and an Access query in a DataGrid control. Do not use any Data controls from the Toolbox. Instead use code only. Use a DataTable to populate the data grid.

This program uses the **Hospital** database. This has two linked tables, **Wards** and **Patients**, and two queries. One of the queries, **qryPatients** is used in this program. The query extracts data from both tables. Figure 15.5 shows the program. The contents of the Wards table, the Patients table and the query qryPatients are displayed by clicking the left, central and right buttons respectively. A DataTable is used to populate the data grid with the two tables and a DataSet is used for the query. In Program 15.1 we used three Data controls from the Toolbox. **In this program we will not use controls; everything will be coded**.

1. Open a new project and then copy the Hospital database into the bin folder of the project. When you write code to set up the database connection, Visual Basic .NET assumes the database is in the bin folder if you only code the file name (which we will do) rather than the full path.

2. Place the data grid and the three buttons on the form. Name the data grid **grdHospital** and the buttons **btnWards**, **btnPatients** and **btnPatientsAndWards** as appropriate. Set the buttons' Text properties as in figure 15.5. Add the labels beneath the buttons and set their Text properties.

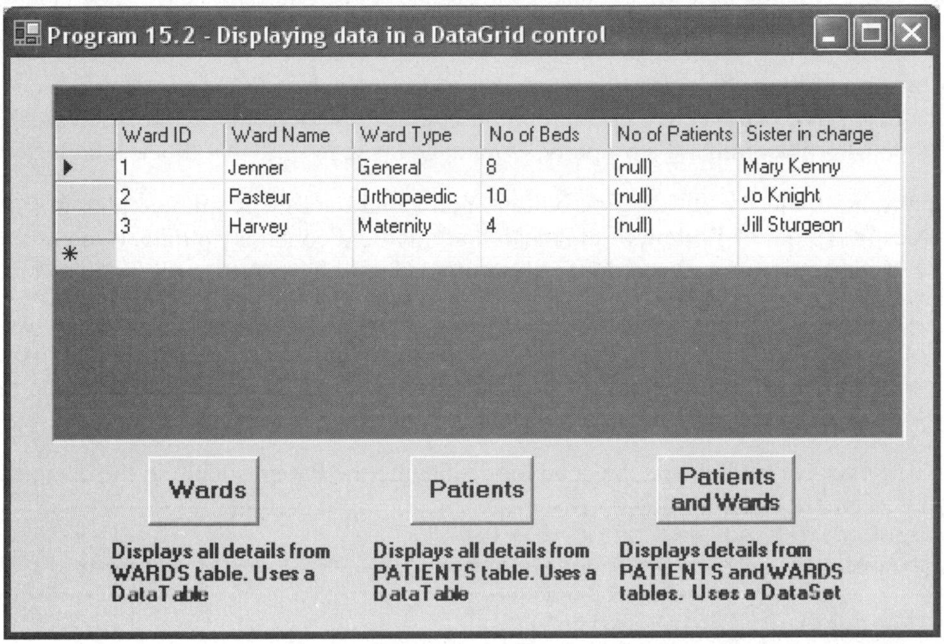

Figure 15.5: Program 15.2 – The Wards button has been clicked to display the Wards table

3. At the top of the code window before *Public Class Form1* import the namespace which has information about the various Data controls.

```
Imports System.Data.OleDb
```

4. Declare form variables to handle the database connection and retrieval of data from it. If the namespace had not been imported in step 1 you would need to prefix each of the Data objects (OleDbConnection etc.) with OleDb followed by a period (.).

```
Dim dbConnection As OleDbConnection
Dim dbCommand As OleDbCommand
Dim dbDataAdapter As OleDbDataAdapter
Dim ConnectString As String = "Provider = Microsoft.Jet.OLEDB.4.0;" & _
  "Data Source = Hospital.mdb" 'Hospital database must be in bin folder
    'for this string to work. Equivalent to steps 3 and 4 in Program 15.1
Dim dtHospital As DataTable
```

5. In the Click event of btnWards the complete code for displaying the Wards table in the data grid is:

```
dbConnection = New OleDbConnection(ConnectString) 'Set up the
                                                  'connection to the database
dbDataAdapter = New OleDbDataAdapter()
dtHospital = New DataTable()
dbCommand = New OleDbCommand("Wards")             'Command object given
dbCommand.CommandType = CommandType.TableDirect   'the Wards table
```

```
dbDataAdapter.SelectCommand = dbCommand  'Data adapter set to Wards
dbDataAdapter.SelectCommand.Connection = dbConnection
dbConnection.Open()            'open the database connection
dbDataAdapter.Fill(dtHospital) 'populate data table from data adapter
grdHospital.DataSource = dtHospital 'populate data grid from data table
dbConnection.Close()           'close the database connection
```

The Command object (dbCommand) represents a string (such as SQL) or a stored procedure name (a table or query) that can be executed through a connection. Here the string is "Wards" and the next line of code uses dbCommand's property, CommandType, to state that this is a table.

6. Run the program and try out the first button. You should get the display shown in figure 15.5. The Null values in the **No of Patients** field mean that this field contains no data. (One of the exercises at the end of Chapter 16 asks you to update this automatically from data in the Patients table.)

You could use the code in steps 4 and 5 above as a template for displaying the data from any table in a data grid. All the stages in figure 15.1 are covered. It is possible to leave out the code above which sets up the database connection and start with the data adapter. This object is capable of setting up the connection itself. We will write this shorter version for displaying data from the Patients table.

7. In the Click event of btnPatients the code for displaying the Patients table in the data grid is:

```
Dim dtHospital As New DataTable()
dbDataAdapter = New OleDbDataAdapter("SELECT * FROM Patients", _
             ConnectString)
dbDataAdapter.Fill(dtHospital)
grdHospital.DataSource = dtHospital
```

The second line initialises the data adapter with the SQL string *Select * From Patients* which will extract all the data from the table using the connection string declared in step 4 earlier. This is sufficient to establish a database conection and populate the data adapter. Don't think that because a connection was set up in the first button's Click event that the program still knows about it. You will not find it in the Server Explorer. That connection existed only during btnWard's Click event.

8. Run the program. You should get the display shown in figure 15.6.

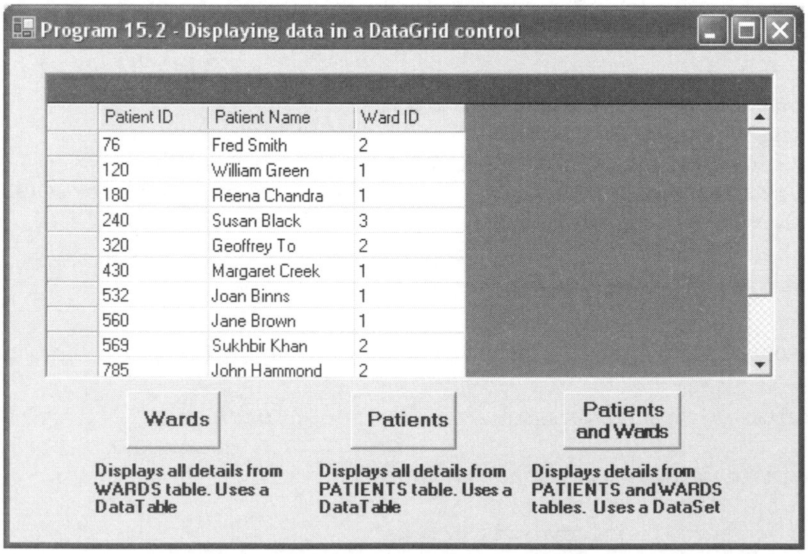

Figure 15.6: Program 15.2 – The Patients button has been clicked to display the Patients table

The third button will display data from the query qryPatients. This time we will use a DataSet object rather than a DataTable, although visually there is no difference because both populate the data grid.

9. The code for the Click event of btnPatientsAndWards is:

```
Dim dsPatients As New DataSet()
dbConnection = New OleDbConnection(ConnectString)
dbDataAdapter = New OleDbDataAdapter()
dbCommand = New OleDbCommand()
dbCommand.CommandText = "qryPatients"    'A query is an example of a
dbCommand.CommandType = CommandType.StoredProcedure 'stored procedure
dbDataAdapter.SelectCommand = dbCommand
dbDataAdapter.SelectCommand.Connection = dbConnection
dbConnection.Open()
dbDataAdapter.Fill(dsPatients, "qryPatients")
grdHospital.DataSource = dsPatients
grdHospital.DataMember = "qryPatients"
dbConnection.Close()
```

This code is very similar to that in step 5, but there are two differences to note:

- Because we have used a dataset rather than a data table the data grid's DataMember property has to be set (to qryPatients). If you had done this in step 5 a run-time error would result.

- The Command object, dbCommand, is set to qryPatients using its CommandText property. Actually we could have written this in the same way as in step 5 as follows:

```
dbCommand = New OleDbCommand("qryPatients")
```

10. Run the program and try out the third button. You should get the display shown in figure 15.7. The query takes data from both tables.

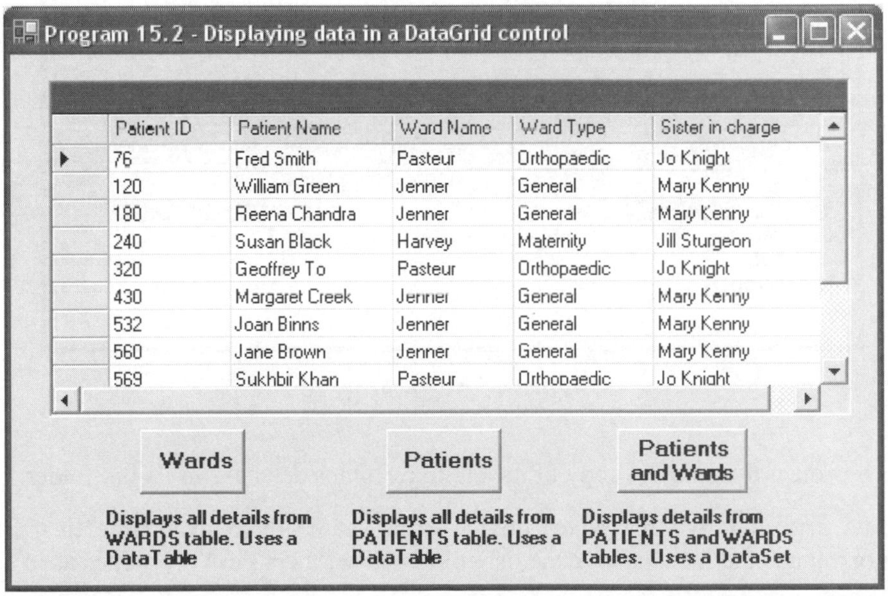

Figure 15.7: Program 15.2: The Patients and Wards button has been clicked

end of Program 15.2

PROGRAM 15.3 *Displaying data through SQL queries in a DataGrid control*

Specification   Demonstrate how to query a database through SQL code

This program uses the **HolidayHomes** database. We will use the three Data controls we had in Program 15.1 – OleDbConnection, OleDbDataAdapter and a DataSet control – although we will configure them using a different technique to that in Program 15.1. We will also use an OleDbCommand control.

Figure 15.8 shows the program. It displays details of all 25 properties on loading. The user can then search on county or number of bedrooms by selecting from two list boxes. In figure 15.8 the user has just chosen to view the properties in Cornwall. Note that the selection from the other list box works independently of the county selected. For example if the user selects 2 from this list box all two-bedroomed properties are displayed, not just those in Cornwall.

We will use different techniques for coding the SelectedIndexChanged events of the list boxes. To search on county we will create new Data objects in code as they are required, just as in Program 15.2. A DataTable will populate the data grid. To search on bedrooms we will reuse the four Data controls from the Toolbox in code. These include a DataSet control to populate the data grid.

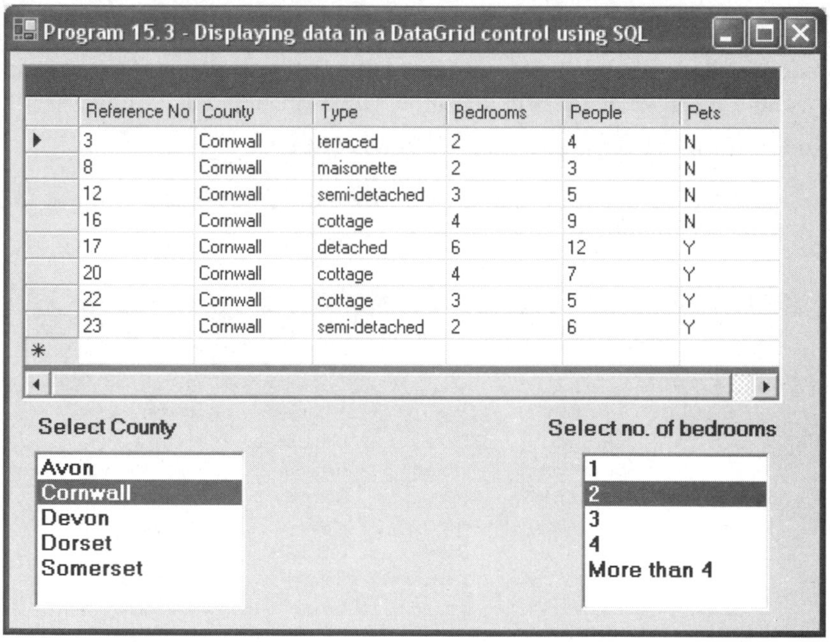

Figure 15.8: Program 15.3

1. Open a new project then store a copy of the HolidayHomes database in its bin folder.

2. Place a data grid and two list boxes on the form. Name them **grdProperties**, **lstCounties** and **lstBedrooms**. Place the labels above the list boxes and set their **Text** properties as in figure 15.8.

3. Enter the items displayed in the two list boxes in figure 15.8 into the list boxes' **Items** property.

4. At the top of the code window before *Public Class Form1* import the namespace which has information about the various Data objects:

```
Imports System.Data.OleDb
```

5. Open the Server Explorer by selecting **View/Server Explorer**. If you did at least the early part of Program 15.1 you should see the connection to the HolidayHomes database you created at that time (see figure 15.3). If this connection is not listed repeat steps 2 – 5 of that program, but connect to the HolidayHomes database in the bin folder of the the current program. If you do have a connection to the database listed in the Server Explorer you can use this connection for displaying the whole table when the program loads. Our later code will connect to the file in the bin folder.

6. In Program 15.1 we had to create the SQL code for the data adapter to be able to extract the whole table (steps 7 – 12). When a connection is listed in the Server Explorer there is a quicker method. Make sure your connection is displayed as in figure 15.3, click the small icon to the left of Tables and drag it onto the form. This will place OleDbConnection and OleDbDataAdapter controls on the pane area.

7. The OleDbDataAdapter control is already prepared for use. To show this, right-click it and select **Configure Data Adapter**. The Data Adapter Configuration Wizard starts. Click **Next** on this and the next two Wizard forms and you will see the SQL code to extract all the records. Click **Cancel**.

8. Make sure the form is selected and then select **Data/Generate Dataset** from the menu. This brings up the Generate Dataset dialog box. There is no need to change anything. Click **OK**. A DataSet control appears in the pane area with the name DataSet11.

9. Drag an OleDbCommand control from the Toolbox to the form and it will appear in the pane area.

10. Click the small button in the DataSource property of the data grid, then select **DataSet1.Properties**. A grid will appear in the data grid control with the names of the fields in the Properties table.

11. In the form's **Load** event type code to fill the dataset.

```
OleDbDataAdapter1.Fill(DataSet11)
```

12. Double-click the counties list box to bring up its default code template and type in code to display only those properties in the county selected. The coded database connection below will only work if HolidayHomes is in the bin folder. The SQL SELECT statement is split over two lines. You can write it on one line, but if you do split it make sure it is split exactly as below otherwise a compiler error may result. It looks messy, with double quotation marks enclosing single ones, but this is how you must write it.

```
Private Sub lstCounties_SelectedIndexChanged(...) Handles _
                            lstCounties.SelectedIndexChanged
'Uses new Data objects for each query
Dim County, SQLString As String
Dim dtProperties As New DataTable() 'DataTable will populate data grid
Dim dbDataAdapter As OleDbDataAdapter
Dim ConnectString As String = "Provider = Microsoft.Jet.OLEDB.4.0;" & _
                            "Data Source = HolidayHomes.mdb"
County = lstCounties.Text
SQLString = "SELECT * FROM Properties WHERE County = " & "'" _
      & County & "'" & "" '2 egs here of a single quote inside double
dbDataAdapter = New OleDbDataAdapter(SQLString, ConnectString) 'quotes
dbDataAdapter.Fill(dtProperties)
grdProperties.DataSource = dtProperties
End Sub
```

If you do not understand the SQL code above, imagine Avon has been selected. The SQL boils down to:

```
"SELECT * FROM Properties WHERE County = 'Avon'"
```

13. Run the program. The data grid should have all 25 records. Clicking each of the counties in the list box should display those in the selected county. Notice that the order of the fields is not alphabetical by field name as it was when the whole table was displayed. It is the same order as in the Access database.

14. We will use a different technique for displaying properties with a selected number of bedrooms. The code below reuses the four Data controls in the form's pane rather than creating new ones for each query. As before, if you split the SQL statement make sure you do so exactly as shown. Its syntax is easier than for the county example because the variable NumBedrooms is not a String and therefore does not need single quotation marks.

```
Private Sub lstBedrooms_SelectedIndexChanged(...) Handles _
                                    lstBedrooms.SelectedIndexChanged
'Uses existing Data controls for each query. A DataSet populates the
'data grid
  Dim NumBedrooms As Short
  Dim SQLString As String
  Dim ConnectString As String = "Provider = Microsoft.Jet.OLEDB.4.0;" & _
                  "Data Source = HolidayHomes.mdb"
  If lstBedrooms.Text = "More than 4" Then
    SQLString = "SELECT * From Properties WHERE Bedrooms > 4"
  Else
    NumBedrooms = lstBedrooms.Text
    SQLString = "SELECT * FROM Properties WHERE Bedrooms = " _
                                  & NumBedrooms & ""
  End If
  OleDbDataAdapter1.SelectCommand = OleDbCommand1
  OleDbDataAdapter1.SelectCommand.Connection = OleDbConnection1
  OleDbDataAdapter1.SelectCommand.CommandText = SQLString
  OleDbDataAdapter1.Fill(DataSet11)
  grdProperties.DataSource = DataSet11
  grdProperties.DataMember = "Properties"
End Sub
```

15. Before running the program comment out the single line in the form's Load event so that the data grid is empty when the program loads. Now select **1** bedroom from the list box. You should see two records in the data grid. Now select **4** bedrooms. The four properties with 4 bedrooms are displayed but so too are the two properties with 1 bedroom. After selecting all the items in turn from the list box the 25 records will be displayed. There is a problem!

The cause is simple – since we are reusing the DataSet for each query new records are being added to it, but the old ones are not being removed. This did not happen with the counties list box because each query created a new DataTable. The next step puts things right.

16. Immediately after **End If** clear out the contents of the DataSet object with

```
DataSet11.Clear()
```

17. Remove the comment from the line in the form's Load event and run the program. Properties meeting the selected number of bedrooms should now be displayed correctly. Note, however, that the

field order is back to alphabetic because we are reusing the Toolbox controls which display them in this order when the program loads. In a real project you would need to have a consistent display.

end of Program 15.3

Displaying data in text boxes and list boxes

So far the only control we have used to display data from a database is a DataGrid. This is usually fine for displaying a lot of records, but you may wish to display only one record and perhaps allow the user to scroll through and view one record at a time. Text boxes or labels would be suitable controls to display the data, one text box or label for each field.

Controls used in this way are said to **bind** to the data source. You need to set their **DataBindings** property, which can be done through the Properties Window or through code. In code the syntax for binding a control is:

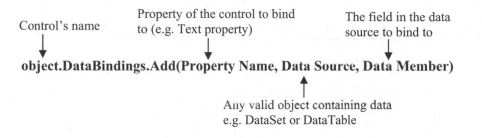

Each form has a **BindingContext** object which looks after all the bindings on a form. This has many properties, but a particularly useful one is **Position** which you can use to display any particular record.

You can also use list boxes and combo boxes to display data. For example you might wish to use one of these controls to display primary key items, such as student or customer IDs, from a table. The user would select an item and details of that record could be displayed in the bound text boxes.

PROGRAM 15.4   *Displaying one record through bound text boxes*

Specification	Display one record from a table/query in a series of text boxes. Scroll through the records by clicking forward and backward buttons. Display the primary key values in a list box; selecting one of these values should display details of that record in the bound text boxes.

Figure 15.9 shows the program. It displays data from the **Hospital** database, which you used in Program 15.2. The user has selected a patient ID from the list box and some of that patient's details are displayed. You can scroll through the patients by clicking the Previous or Next buttons.

The Patient ID and Patient Name data comes from the Patients table and the Ward Name and Ward Type data comes from the Wards table. We will populate a DataSet using an SQL query on these two tables. The four text boxes will be bound to this DataSet. We could bind the list box to the DataSet to display the patient IDs, but for contrast we will use a DataTable.

1.   Open a new project. In Program 15.2 you copied the Hospital database into the program's bin folder. You can either use the database file stored there or copy it to the bin folder of Program 15.4.

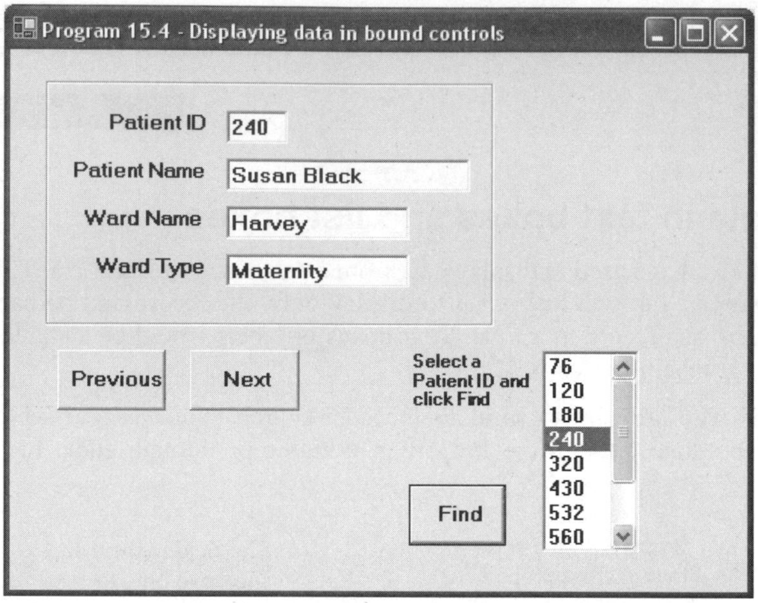

Figure 15.9: Program 15.4.

2. Open the Server Explorer (**View/Server Explorer**). If you have a connection to the Hospital database that you wish to use go to step 3 now. If you want to establish a connection click the **Connect to Database** button at the top of the Server Explorer. Click the **Provider** tab in the Data Link Properties dialog box and then select **Microsoft Jet 4.0 OLE DB Provider**. Click **Next** and then click the ellipsis button to the right of the text box asking you to select a database name. Select the **Hospital** database from wherever you have stored the copy you wish to connect to. Back on the **Connection** tab click **Test Connection** to check that a connecton has been made. Click **OK**.

3. Click the **Data** tab in the Toolbox and drag an OleDbDataAdapter to the form. In the Data Adapter Configuration Wizard click the **Next** button. Make sure the connection to the Hospital database is selected on the next form (or click the **New Connection** button and select it). Click **Next** on this and the next form and then click **Query Builder**.

4. Add both the Patients and Wards tables to the Query Builder. We need to build a query that will extract the Patient ID and Patient Name from the Patients table and the Ward Name and Ward Type from the Wards table. Click on these fields so that your Query Builder looks like that in figure 15.10. Note that the SQL code includes the words INNER JOIN to indicate the link between the two tables.

5. Click **OK** and then **Next**. You will get a form called View Wizard Results. Click **Finish**.

6. Select the form and select **Data/Generate Dataset** (or right-click the OleDbDataAdapter1 control in the pane and select Generate Dataset). Click the **New** radio button and change the default name to **dsPatientsAndWards**. You should now have three controls in the pane area – a connection, a data adapter and a dataset.

7. Build the form using figure 15.9. Name the text boxes **txtPatientID**, **txtPatientName**, **txtWardName** and **txtWardType**, the three buttons **btnPrevious**, **btnNext** and **btnFind**, and the list box **lstPatientIDs**.

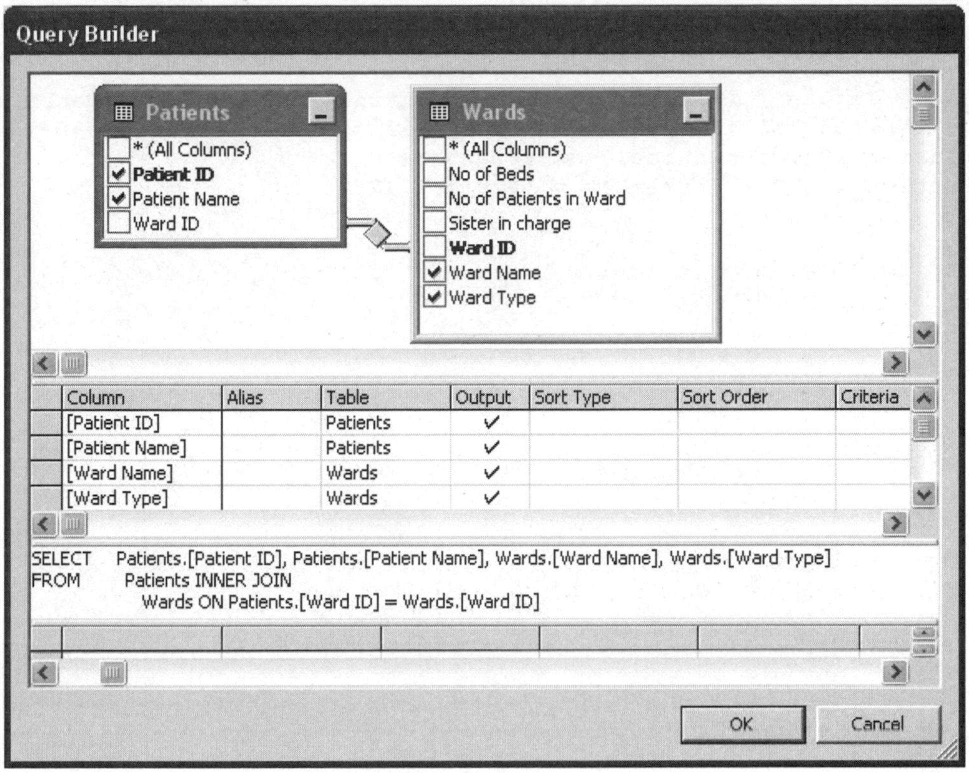

Figure 15.10: The Query Builder

We need to bind the four text boxes to fields in the dataset. We will bind those displaying the patient ID and name through the Properties Window (steps 8 and 9), and those displaying the ward name and type through code (step 10) to demonstrate the two methods.

8. Find the **DataBindings** property of txtPatientID and click the small + to its left. Click the button in the Text row that is revealed. Click + next to DataSet11 and then + next to Patients. This lists all the fields in the dataset (which includes Ward ID even though we did not ask for it in step 4, because this forms the link field) as shown in figure 15.11. Note that the name used for the 'container' of these fields is Patients. Don't confuse it with the Patients table: when we built the query in steps 4 and 5 this is the name Visual Basic decided on. Select **PatientID** to bind the text box to this field.

9. Repeat step 8 for txtPatientName and select the **Patient Name** field.

10. In the form's **Load** event write code to fill the dataset from the data adapter and then to bind the two text boxes displaying details about the wards to the Ward Name and Ward Type fields in the dataset.

```
OleDbDataAdapter1.Fill(DsPatientsAndWards1)
txtWardName.DataBindings.Add("Text", DsPatientsAndWards1, _
                            "Patients.Ward Name")
txtWardType.DataBindings.Add("Text", DsPatientsAndWards1,
                            "Patients.Ward Type")
```

11. Still in the form's Load event declare a DataTable (before the code in step 10) and use it to populate the list box with patient IDs. You must set the list box's **DataSource** property to the data table and **DataMember** property to the field to display. The latter is necessary even though the SQL string passed to the data adapter extracts only one field.

```
Dim dtPatientIDs As New DataTable()

Dim daPatientIDs As New OleDbDataAdapter _
               ("Select [Patient ID] From Patients", ConnectString)
daPatientIDs.Fill(dtPatientIDs)          'fill data table from data adapter
lstPatientIDs.DataSource = dtPatientIDs
lstPatientIDs.DisplayMember = "Patient ID"
```

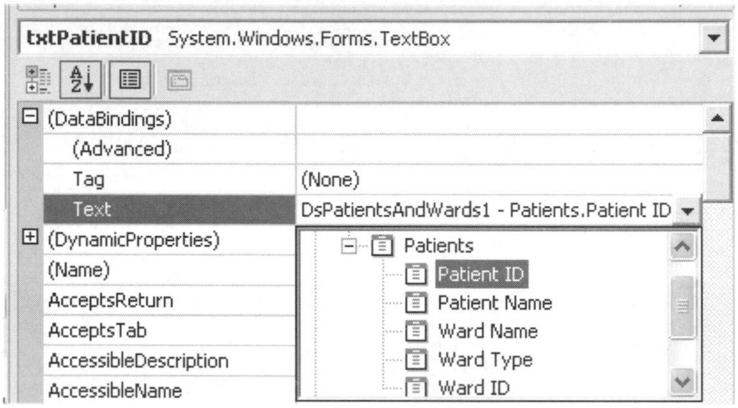

Figure 15.11: Setting the DataBindings property

12. Run the program and you should see the first record displayed in the text boxes and the patient IDs in the list box. Check the contents of this record from the first row in the data grid in figure 15.7.

13. To scroll to the previous record, decrement the **Position** property of the **BindingContext** object of the form. This object must be passed the dataset and the table/query which holds the data to be displayed. Visual Basic numbers the records in table/query from 0 (unlike record numbering in a file which starts at 1).

```
Private Sub btnPrevious_Click(...) Handles btnPrevious.Click
  BindingContext(DsPatientsAndWards1, "Patients").Position = _
      BindingContext(DsPatientsAndWards1, "Patients").Position - 1
End Sub
```

Note that you could write the shorthand method for incrementing/decrementing a value which was first introduced in step 8 of Program 4.1:

```
  BindingContext(DsPatientsAndWards1, "Patients").Position -=1
```

14. To move to the previous record simply increment the **Position** property by 1. Use the shorthand method in step 13 if you prefer (in this case +=1).

```
Private Sub btnNext_Click(...) Handles btnNext.Click
  BindingContext(DsPatientsAndWards1, "Patients").Position = _
      BindingContext(DsPatientsAndWards1, "Patients").Position + 1
End Sub
```

15. When the user selects a patient ID from the list box, use the control's **SelectedIndex** property to match onto the **Position** property of the **BindingContext** object.

```
Private Sub btnFind_Click(...) Handles btnFind.Click
  Dim Index As Short
  Index = lstPatientIDs.SelectedIndex
  BindingContext(DsPatientsAndWards1, "Patients").Position = Index
End Sub
```

16. Run the program and scroll through the records. Note that if you attempt to scroll before the first record or after the last record Visual Basic makes sure nothing happens. If this had been an array or a random access file you would get a run-time error. Select a patient ID from the list box and click **Find** to display this patient's details.

end of Program 15.4

Summary of key concepts

- Four Data controls are provided for processing an Access database – an **OleDbConnection**, **OleDbCommand**, **OleDbDataAdapter** and **OleDataSet**. These controls allow a connection to a database to be established and specified data to be extracted.

- Data extracted from a database via the DataAdapter can be stored in a **DataSet** or a **DataTable**. Use the **Fill** property of the DataAdapter.

- Use a **DataGrid** to display multiple records from a table or query. To display a single record you can use text boxes or labels by setting their **DataBindings** property.

- You can query an Access database either by using a query stored in the database itself or by **SQL** code sent from a Visual Basic program.

- The **Position** property of the form's **DataBindings** object can be used to go to any record in a DataSet.

Take it from here...

1. The only Data control which can be used with an Access database, and which was not used in this chapter, is the **DataView** control. Find out how to use it.

2. Visual Basic supplies the **Data Form Wizard** to help you build forms that can display data from a database (and to update the database, though this is the subject of the next chapter). To get the Wizard select **File/Add New Item** from the menu and select the **Data Form Wizard** template. Find out what the Wizard can do.

Questions on the Programs

Program 15.1

*1. Change a property of the data grid control so that the records are displayed in alternating white and light blue colours.

185

Program 15.3

*1.   Add three buttons to the form. One of these should display the whole table in the data grid. The other two should run the two queries stored in the Holiday Homes database – qryDetachedProperties (which finds all the detached properties) and qryPetsAllowed (which finds those properties allowing pets).

*2.   Add a third list box so that you can display properties of a selected type (detached, cottage etc.).

**3.   The two list boxes, and the third one if you've done question 2 above, work independently of each other. Now try to get the original two working together so that a query might be *find all 4-bedroom properties in Cornwall*. You will need to write slightly more complex SQL code than in the examples in the program. If you cannot write the SQL directly, do the query in Access, look at the code produced and adapt it for your program.

Program 15.4

*1.   Add buttons to display the first and last records in the dataset.

*2.   Add a label to display the record number of the current record being displayed. For example if the third record is displayed this label should say *record 3 of 11*. The total number of records can be found from a property of the BindingContext object.

End of chapter exercises

To do these exercises you need the two Access databases you used in the programs in this chapter and one new database from the web site. The new one is **Vocational Students.mdb**. It has two linked tables (and one query to be used in the next chapter). The Students table has details of 126 vocational students. The Portfolio Grade field holds the overall grade for the coursework (D = distinction, M = merit, P = pass, X = not passed). Students have to pass a given number of module tests. How many they have passed is stored in the Students table but how many they must pass in total is in the Courses table.

*1.   Design a form to display data from the Students table in the Vocational Students database, as shown in figure 15.12. Null data displays mean that no data is stored. (The Final grade field has no data in it; Chapter 16 has an exercise to calculate these grades and update the table.)

	Course Code	Final Grade	Left	Portfolio Grade	Sex	Student Name	Student ID	Tests Passed
▶	HSC-I	(null)	(null)	P	F	BEGUM, Husna	AFG5540	3
	ICT-I	(null)	(null)	X	M	TRELORNE, Peter	AFG8673	4
	BS-A	(null)	(null)	P	F	KAUSER, Benash	AFG9427	0
	ICT-I	(null)	(null)	M	F	ANDREWS, Petra	AFG9845	4
	BS-A	(null)	(null)	P	M	ALI, Bilal	CGR2189	7
	BS-A	(null)	(null)	D	F	WALLACE, Amy	CGR2286	7
	ICT-A	(null)	(null)	M	F	DHINJAL, Kunjal	CGR3384	7
	ICT-A	(null)	(null)	P	F	MALIK, Rohima	CGR4329	7
	ICT-A	(null)	(null)	D	M	JACKSON, Colin	CGR4396	7
	ICT-I	(null)	(null)	X	F	KAUSER, Shasta	CGR5521	1
	ICT-A	(null)	(null)	P	M	MALIK, Sajid	CGR9981	7

Figure 15.12: Program for exercise 1

2. Build a program to practise querying the Holiday Homes database using SQL. Figure 15.13 shows an example. You write SQL in the text box and then click the **Search button. Those records from the Properties table in the database matching the SQL query are displayed. In figure 15.13 the SQL query is searching for cottages in Cornwall.

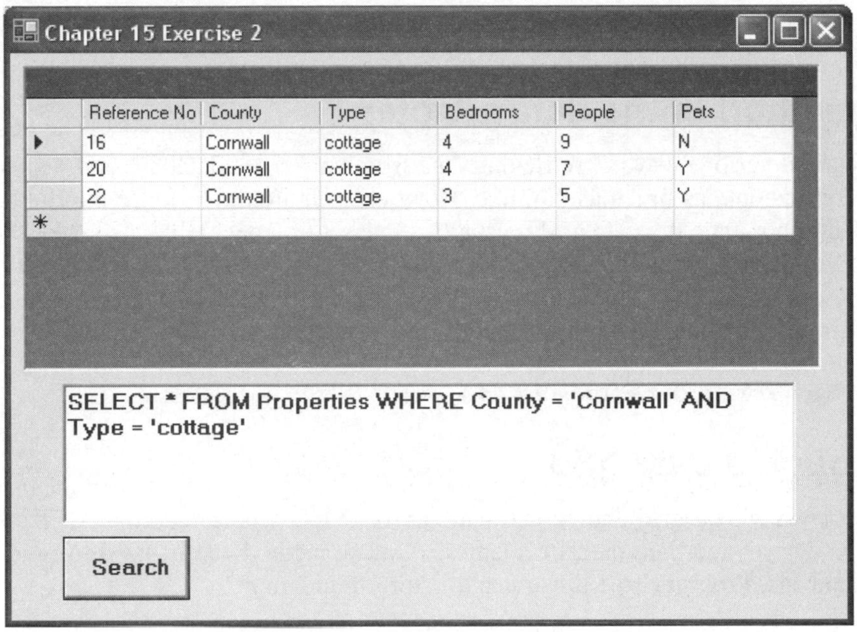

Figure 15.13: Exercise 2

There is one very annoying feature here. If there is a syntax error in your SQL code a run-time error is produced. When you run the program again you have to type in the SQL again. Chapter 13 explained how to handle run-time errors using Try…Catch. Structure your code as follows:

```
Try
    'code which may generate the run-time error goes here, i.e. it
    'includes the SQL string
Catch
    MsgBox("Invalid SQL syntax")
End Try
```

**3. Develop your form in question 1 above to allow the user to query the Students table. Display:

- Students on a given course (selected by the user).
- Students who have a particular portfolio grade (selected by the user).

How you design the interface is up to you. If you use list boxes as in program 15.3 you will have to write SQL statements. You may wish to design the query in Access and then adapt the SQL code Access produces. Instead you could build separate queries in Access for each possible selection made by the user, and then just use the query names in your code. However this is a long-winded method and should only be done if all else fails.

Chapter 16 – Databases: Updating Data

The Update method of the data adapter

In Chapter 15 you learned various ways of retrieving data from an Access database and displaying it on a form. You can modify this data as much as you like. However you are only modifying the data contents of the object you used to populate the data grid – usually a dataset or a data table. To make these changes in the database itself you have to send the modified dataset or data table back to the database by using the **Update** method of the data adapter. For example if you used a data adapter and a dataset from the Toolbox and kept their default names, you would write:

```
OleDbDataAdapter1.Update(Dataset11)
```

Updating through a data grid

You can edit any items in a data grid and or you can add or delete whole records. All the changes are updated at once in the dataset and then the data adapter's Update method can be used to send the new set of data back to the database. Program 16.1 illustrates this sort of updating.

PROGRAM 16.1 *Updating a database through a DataGrid*

Specification   Illustrate how to update a database table by modifying the data in a data grid.

This program is similar to Program 15.1 but with the addition of the updating. Look back at figure 15.2. We will display the data from the single Properties table in the Holiday Homes database in the Form's Load event, rather than by clicking a button as in Program 15.2. Instead we will use the button for updating the database.

1. Open a new project and store a copy of **HolidayHomes.mdb** in its bin folder (or if you do not wish to take up extra storage space you can make a connection to wherever else you have stored this database in step 2).

2. Drag an OleDbDataAdapter control onto the form. Click **Next** in the Data Adapter Configuration Wizard. If you wish to use an existing connection to the Holiday Homes database select it from the combo box. If you have stored it in the bin folder click **New Connection**, then click the **Provider** tab. Select **Microsoft Jet 4.0 OLE DB Provider**. Click **Next** and then click the ellipsis button to select the database. Back on the **Connection** tab click the **Test Connection** button to check that a connection has been made. Click **OK**.

3. Click **Next** on the next two Wizard forms and then click **Query Builder**. Click **Add** to add the Properties table to the Query Builder and then **Close**. Click ***(All columns)** so that the display looks like that in figure 15.4. Click **OK,** and then **Next** and **Finish** to complete the Wizard.

4. There will now be OleDbConnection and OleDbDataAdapter controls in the pane area. Right-click the data adapter control and select **Generate Dataset**. Make sure the **New** radio button is selected.

Note that the single Properties table is checked for inclusion in the dataset. Click **OK**. A DataSet control named DataSet11 will be added to the pane area.

5. Click the **Windows Form** tab in the Toolbox and drag a **DataGrid** control onto the form. Set its **DataSource** property to **DataSet11.Properties**.

6. In the form's **Load** event use the data adapter's **Fill** method to populate the dataset:

```
OleDbDataAdapter1.Fill(DataSet11)
```

7. Add a button to the form. Name it **btnSave** and set its **Text** property to **Save Changes**. In its **Click** event use the **Update** method of the data adapter to update the Holiday Homes database with any changes that are made to the displayed data.

```
OleDbDataAdapter1.Update(DataSet11)
```

8. Run the program. The 25 records from the Properties table should be displayed as in figure 15.2. Change any item of data in the first record. As soon as you change it a small pencil icon appears in the row header to the left. Click the **Save Changes** button: this should update the database. Open it in Access and check that the change has been made.

9. You can also add and delete whole records. Make a note of the contents of the first record, then select the whole record by clicking its grey row header and press **Delete**. Click **Save Changes** and then check that it has gone from the database. In your Visual Basic program scroll to the last record and click inside the extra row with the asterisk. A series of Nulls appears. Type in the details of the record you just deleted and then click Save Changes. Check that the record is back in the database. Close the program and run it again. The record you added, with Reference No 1, is displayed as the last record. Although Access displays it as the first record because Reference No is the primary key, a dataset displayed in a data grid displays them in the order they were stored in the database. You can make this record appear first by clicking the **Reference No** field header to sort the records.

end of Program 16.1

'Batch' updating

Sometimes you may wish to update the database in a way that does not involve the user modifying a data grid or individual records in text boxes. For example consider a credit card company. Each day large numbers of payments are entered into the database through a Visual Basic program. Each customer's account may be updated immediately or in a 'batch' update at the end of the day. Program 16.2 illustrates the batch update process.

PROGRAM 16.2   *Batch updating*

Specification   Illustrate how to batch update a database table.

This program uses the Access database **ALevels.mdb** which you may already have stored from the publisher's web site. It has two tables, **Candidates** and **Exam Results**, linked on the Candidate ID field. These are shown in figure 16.1. The Exam Results table contains the grades that the candidates achieved on each of their A levels. Grades A to E are pass grades and grade U is a fail. The Number Passed field is empty; the purpose of this program is to update it. For example Susan Smith has passed three subjects and so 3 should be stored in this field for her.

Candidates

Candidate ID	Name	Number Passed
12345	Susan Smith	
33366	Tamir Khan	
54445	Jenny Green	
888111	Bhavini Bhatt	
98765	John Jones	

Exam Results

Candidate ID	Exam	Result
12345	Maths	B
12345	Physics	C
12345	Chemistry	A
33366	Maths	D
33366	Biology	U
33366	English	C
54445	Geography	U
54445	History	U
54445	English	B
88811	History	C
88811	French	A
88811	German	C
98765	Chemistry	E
98765	Biology	U
98765	Computing	D

Figure 16.1: The two tables in the ALevels database

Figure 16.2 shows the program. The **Calculate Passes** button calculates and displays the number of passes for each candidate and updates the database. **Reset Passes** sets the values in this field back to null and updates the database by setting the field items to blank.

The program will use Data controls from the Toolbox rather than creating and setting the properties of these objects in code. We will keep the default names. There will be one database connection (OleDbConnection1) and two data adapters (OleDbDataAdapter1 and OleDbDataAdapter2), one for each table. Although we could put the data from both data adapters into one dataset we will have two, again one for each table, DataSet1 and DataSet2. In code these are then referred to as DataSet11 and Dataset21.

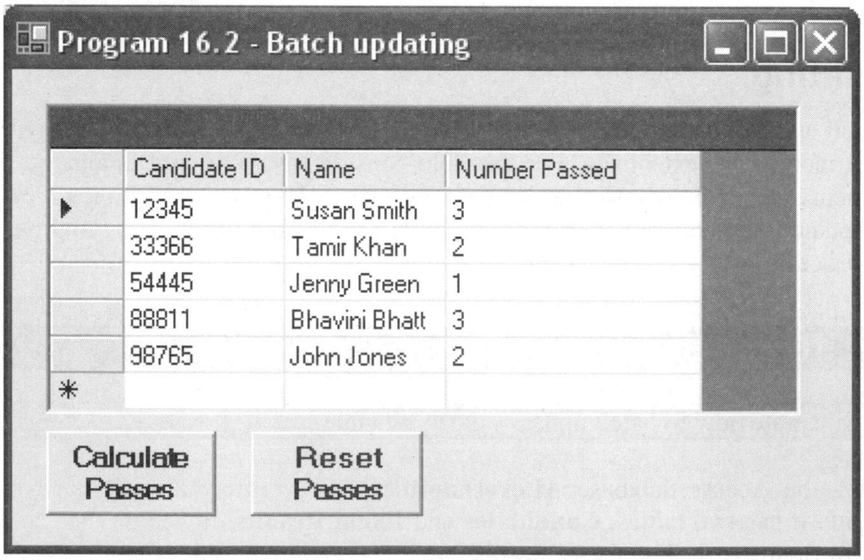

Figure 16.2: Program 16.2

1. Open a new project and store a copy of **ALevels.mdb** in its bin folder.

2. Drag an **OleDbDataAdapter** control onto the form. Click **Next** in the Data Adapter Configuration Wizard. Click **New Connection**, then click the **Provider** tab. Select **Microsoft Jet 4.0 OLE DB Provider**. Click **Next** and then click the ellipsis button to select the database. Back on the **Connection** tab click the **Test Connection** button to check that a connection has been made, then click **OK**.

3. Click **Next** on the next two Wizard forms and then click **Query Builder**. Click **Add** to add the Candidates table to the Query Builder and then **Close**. Click ***(All columns)** so that all the fields are extracted. Click **OK,** and then **Next** and **Finish** to complete the Wizard.

4. There will now be OleDbConnection and OleDbDataAdapter controls in the pane area. Right-click the data adapter control and select **Generate Dataset**. Make sure the **New** radio button is selected. Note that the Candidates table is checked for inclusion in the dataset. Click **OK**. A DataSet control named DataSet11 will be added to the pane area.

5. Repeat step 2 but use the connection to the database you set up during step 2. Repeat steps 3 – 4 to create a data adapter and a dataset for the Exam Results table. On the View Wizard Results form will be a couple of warning results with small yellow triangles (because this table is on the many side of a one-to-many link). These can safely be ignored.

6. Drag a **DataGrid** onto the form and set its **DataSource** property to **DataSet11.Candidates**.

7. In the form's **Load** event use DataAdapter1's **Fill** method to populate DataSet1 with the Candidates table

```
OleDbDataAdapter1.Fill(DataSet11)
```

8. Run the program to check that the Candidates table is displayed.

9. Put two buttons on the form and name them **btnCalculatePasses** and **btnResetPasses**. Set their **Text** properties as shown in figure 16.2.

Before writing code to calculate how many passes each student has gained, you must be clear about the main steps involved. First we need to look at the initial record in the Candidates table, containing Candidate ID 12345, and then go through all the records in the Exam Results table trying to find a match on this ID. If a match is found then look at the exam grade and increase a count of some sort if it is an E or better. The first three records in the Exam Results table have a matching candidate ID. Then go to the next record in the Candidates table and repeat the process of looking through all the records in the other table for matches. The overall structure is an outer loop (one repetition processing one record in the Candidates table) driving an inner loop (one repetition processing one record in the ExamResults table).

There are several objects we could use to calculate and update the number of passes. Let's use two data tables, one for each Access table.

10. Declare the two data tables as form variables:

```
Dim dtCandidates As New DataTable()
Dim dtExamResults As New DataTable()
```

11. The code to calculate the number of passes does three main things – puts data in the two data tables, calculates the number of passes (which are then automatically displayed in the data grid), and updates the database.

```
Private Sub btnCalculatePasses_Click(...) Handles _
                                       btnCalculatePasses.Click
  Dim CandidatesIndex, ExamResultsIndex, Count As Short
  Dim CandidateID As String
  dtCandidates = DataSet11.Tables(0)                 'Put data in the two
  OleDbDataAdapter2.Fill(dtExamResults)              'data tables
                                   'outer loop processes one candidate
  For CandidatesIndex = 0 To dtCandidates.Rows.Count - 1
    Count = 0
    CandidateID = dtCandidates.Rows(CandidatesIndex)(0)  'Get candidate
              'ID from data table using index for its row and column
                     'inner loop goes once through Exam Results table
    For ExamResultsIndex = 0 To dtExamResults.Rows.Count - 1
      If (CandidateID = dtExamResults.Rows(ExamResultsIndex)(0)) And _
             (dtExamResults.Rows(ExamResultsIndex)(2) <= "E") Then
        Count = Count + 1
      End If
    Next ExamResultsIndex
    dtCandidates.Rows(CandidatesIndex)(2) = Count    'Update data table
                                       'Column 2 is Number Passed
  Next CandidatesIndex
  OleDbDataAdapter1.Update(DataSet11)                'update database
End Sub
```

The code uses the Fill method which you are familiar with by now to populate the exam results data table. We could have used this for the other data table, but for contrast a different technique is used above:

```
dtCandidates = DataSet11.Tables(0)
```

A dataset's tables are indexed from 0 and so Tables(0) refers to the first table in the dataset. Actually this dataset only has one table anyway, but we *could* have used one dataset for both tables.

You can reference any item in a data table by indexing its row and column. Numbering starts at 0. So the line coded above

```
CandidateID = dtCandidates.Rows(CandidatesIndex)(0)
```

finds the candidate ID in a variable row but in column 0. Column 0 is the Candidate ID column. You can write the column name (inside quotation marks) instead of the index if you prefer.

12. To reset the number of passes to null, loop through the candidates data table and set column 2 (Number Passed) of each row:

```
Private Sub btnResetPasses_Click(...) Handles btnResetPasses.Click
  Dim Index As Short
  dtCandidates = DataSet11.Tables(0)
  For Index = 0 To dtCandidates.Rows.Count - 1
    dtCandidates.Rows(Index)(2) = DBNull.Value
  Next Index
  OleDbDataAdapter1.Update(DataSet11)                'update database
End Sub
```

13. Run the program. Click the **Calculate Passes** button and the numbers in figure 16.2 should be displayed. Check that the table in Access has been updated. Click **Reset Passes** and check that the field is now empty again in Access.

end of Program 16.2

Updating records through text boxes

Program 15.4 displayed one record at a time in a series of text boxes. You can add and delete records using the form's BindingContext object that you met in this program. If the dataset contains a table, Customers, then to add a new record to the table use the object's **AddNew** method as follows:

```
BindingContext(DataSet11,"Customers").AddNew()
```

This would clear out the text boxes and allow you to type in the new details. To delete a record use the object's **RemoveAt** method. This needs to know the record number to delete which is provided by the Position property:

```
BindingContext(DataSet11,"Customers").RemoveAt _
          (BindingContext(DataSet11,"Customers").Position)
```

Both these methods operate on the dataset. To update the database itself use the **Update** method as in Programs 16.1 and 16.2:

```
OleDbDataAdapter1.Update(DataSet11)
```

Summary of key concepts

- Use the **Update** method of the data adapter to update a database.

- You can edit, add and delete records in a database directly through a data grid. To add records through bound text boxes use the **AddNew** method of the form's **BindingContext** object. To delete a record use this object's **RemoveAt** method.

- You can go through a table record by record, updating where needed, by using the **Rows** property of a data table or dataset.

Take it from here...

1. Find out about the **EndCurrentEdit** and **CancelCurrentEdit** methods of the BindingContext object and how you might use them when adding and deleting records through bound text boxes.

2. Find out how to use a **recordset** to perform a batch update like that in Program 16.2.

Questions on the Programs
Program 16.2

*2. Add controls to display the total number of 'A' level passes and the average number of passes per student.

**3. Add a list box with the names of the 'A' level subjects. Then loop through the ExamResults data table to display in a message box the number of students who have passed the subject selected from this list box.

End of chapter exercises

These exercises require the Hospital database that you used in two Chapter 15 Programs, the Vocational Students database that was used in the exercises at the end of Chapter 15, and a new database **Repayments.mdb**. This has two tables. The Customers table has a field storing how much each customer owes the company. The other table, Cheques Received, lists payments which have been made.

**1. Use the Repayments database. Write a program that updates the *Balance* field in the Customers table from the data in the *Amount* field of the *Cheques Received* table. Display the updated results. (The database has a form from which you can reset the original balance values. This uses Access Basic code.)

2. Use the **Hospital database. Write a program that calculates the number of patients in each ward and updates the *No of Patients in Ward* field. Display the updated results.

***3. Design a form to display records from the Patients table of the **Hospital** database in text boxes as you did for displaying records from a query in Program 15.4. Have Previous and Next buttons to navigate through the records. Then use the AddNew and RemoveAt methods to add and delete records to the table. When this is working extend the program to check that the ward is not full before calling the AddNew method. Display an appropriate message if the ward is full. (The *No of Beds* field in the Wards table stores how many beds are in each ward.)

***4. In the Students table of the **Vocational Students** database the Final Grade field is blank. Write a program that updates this field with an appropriate grade (D, M, P or X). You need to know the following:

- If a student has not passed the required number of tests then the final grade is X, no matter what their portfolio grade is.

- If a student has passed the required number of tests their portfolio grade becomes their final grade.

Note that students with no portfolio grade shown have left the course. No final grade should be filled in for these students.

The database has a single query which will reset the Final Grade field to blanks for your convenience.

Chapter 17 – OOP: Classes and Objects

Introduction

OOP stands for **Object-oriented** Programming, which offers a different way of designing and coding programs to the traditional **structured** programming used throughout nearly all of this book It has been around for some time, but is still often looked on as something new. Some languages are written so that you have to use OOP principles throughout. Other languages, such as Visual Basic .NET, support OOP but it is up to the programmer whether to adopt OOP or keep to the more traditional approach.

There are three main OOP concepts that you should understand. These are:

- Data encapsulation
- Inheritance
- Polymorphism

Data encapsulation is covered in this chapter. Inheritance and polymorphism are covered in Chapter 18.

Built-in classes and objects

The starting point in OOP is an understanding of the terms **class** and **object**. Whenever you use a control from the Toolbox you make use of a class and an object. You already know that controls are considered to be objects, and that they have **properties** you can set at design or run time, and **methods** you can call at run time only. Take the list box for example. Figure 17.1 shows a list box on a form. When you set one of its properties some code gets to work behind the scenes and stores the current setting of the property.

A list box also has a number of methods – something that the object can do. You have used the most useful of the list box methods, **Items.Add**, many times already. When you write a line such as:

```
lstCourses.Items.Add(CourseName)
```

some built-in code is fired off to add another item to the list box. Technically you have just called a method belonging to the object lstCourses.

All list boxes belong to a particular class and we create an **instance** of this class when we place a list box on a form. In figure 17.1 the word *ListBox* is the class from which all individual *list boxes* are made. When you create an instance of a class you are creating an **object**. The two terms mean the same thing. On a form you create an object simply by clicking and dragging the appropriate tool from the Toolbox.

Sometimes you have to create an object in code in order to do something. A good example is step 16 in Program 11.1 which opens a second form by clicking a button on the first form. The code was

```
Dim SecondForm As New frmDisplayData()
SecondForm.Show()
```

The keyword **New** creates a frmDisplayData object and its **Show** method is called to display it.

Whatever means you use to create an object, it is given all the properties and methods of its class. When you use one of the methods, the code which is fired off is hidden. You can use the method but are not allowed to see how it works. If you adopt a full OOP approach to your programming you create your own classes and objects. For these *you* have to write the code that will assign property values and carry out the methods.

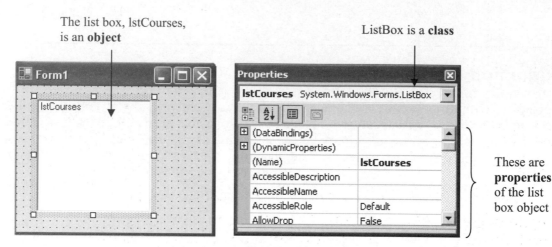

Figure 17.1: ListBox class and list box object

Your own classes and objects

Imagine you are a teacher at secondary school and have organised a skiing trip for 40 pupils. You wish to write a Visual Basic program using OOP techniques to process the payments the pupils make towards the trip. Suppose they make an initial deposit payment of a minimum of £20.00 and then pay by instalments whenever they can.

Working out the properties and methods on paper

You wish to store the following details about each pupil:

- Name
- Deposit
- Total amount paid
- Number of payments (excluding deposit)

These four items are the properties of the class. Assume that you do not wish to store details of the payments themselves, but just use each payment to recalculate the total amount paid and number of payments.

The methods are the actions which send data to the object or retrieve data from the object. Assume we need six actions:

- Store the pupil's name
- Store the deposit
- Send a payment (to recalculate the total amount paid and the number of payments)
- Retrieve the pupil's name
- Retrieve the total amount paid
- Retrieve the number of payments

You may find figure 17.2, which shows the program in action, useful as we go through how to build and use a class and object. You can download the program, **OOP Ski Trip**, from the publisher's web site.

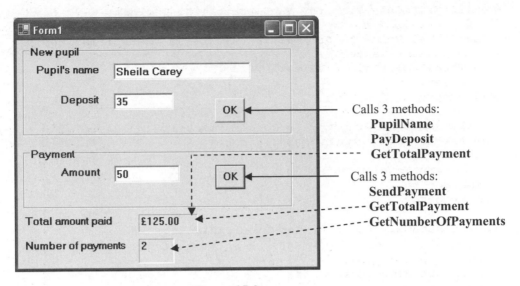

Figure 17.2

Creating the class and object

The class is declared in a separate class module, which like an ordinary module can only contain code. Each of the four properties is declared as Private or Public. As you will see shortly Private declarations are nearly always needed.

```
Public Class Pupil
   Private Name As String
   Private Deposit As Decimal
   Private TotalAmountPaid As Decimal
   Private NumberOfPayments As Short
End Class
```

Properties can be assigned values and their values retrieved through **Property methods**. These are the same as procedures. There are three types of Property method, which allow you to:

- write to and read from the object
- only write to the object
- only read from the object

Look back at the six methods/actions listed on the previous page. Storing and retrieving a pupil's name involves reading from and writing to the object. We only need to store the deposit, not retrieve it, so this involves a write only. The total amount paid and the number of payments are retrieved only and so involve only reads. The keywords for write and read are **Get** and **Set** respectively and so the code for assigning and retrieving property values is:

```
Public Property PupilName() As String
'Stores pupil name and retrieves it
  Get
    Return Name
  End Get
  Set(ByVal Value As String) 'Value is pupil name passed to this method
    Name = Value
  End Set
End Property
```

```
Public WriteOnly Property PayDeposit() As Decimal
'Assigns values to Deposit and TotalAmountPaid properties
  Set(ByVal Value As Decimal)      'Value is the initial deposit
    Deposit = Value
    TotalAmountPaid = Value
  End Set
End Property

Public ReadOnly Property GetTotalPayment()
'Retrieves total amount paid so far
  Get
    Return TotalAmountPaid
  End Get
End Property

Public ReadOnly Property GetNumberOfPayments()
'Retrieves number of payments made (NB excludes initial deposit)
  Get
    Return NumberOfPayments
  End Get
End Property
```

Note the following:

- The name of a Property method must not be the same as the name of a property.

- Property methods that include a Set (write) declare the data type of the item of data passed to the method after the empty brackets.

- Property method PupilName could have been split into two Property methods – a write only and a read only method.

The third action listed earlier, to send a payment, recalculates the TotalAmountPaid and NumberOfPayments properties. This could be handled using a write only Property method but you do not have to use property methods. Instead you can use a Sub method (procedure), as follows:

```
Public Sub SendPayment(ByVal Payment As Decimal)
  TotalAmountPaid = TotalAmountPaid + Payment
  NumberOfPayments = NumberOfPayments + 1
End Sub
```

If your class needs to do some processing that does not involve changing the value of any properties then you would have to use a Sub or Function method.

When the upper OK button in figure 17.2 is clicked, an object of class Pupil is created and then the two methods of the new object, PupilName and PayDeposit, are called. Visual Basic .NET provides a **constructor** method, called **New**, which is called automatically when an object is created. You can initialise any of the properties through this method. As an alternative to the PupilName and PayDeposit methods you could write code inside the New method:

```
Public Sub New(ByVal PupilName As String, ByVal DownPayment As Decimal)
  Name = PupilName
  Deposit = DownPayment
  TotalAmountPaid = DownPayment
End Sub
```

However, since the PupilName method included a Get you would need to code a read only property method to retrieve the pupil's name.

Before you can use a class you must declare an object of that class. This is not done on the class module but on a form.

```
Dim OnePupil As New Pupil()
```

If you had decided to use the New method to initialise some of the properties, as described above, you would pass the data as parameters inside the brackets.

Using the class and object

The Click event of the upper OK button should call the PupilName and PayDeposit property methods to assign values to the Name and Deposit properties. To call a write method, or the write part of a read and write method, use the object's name, followed by a period (.) and then the method name. Assign the value to send to the method in the way you assign a value to any variable. The GetTotalPayment method involves a read. Its return value can be displayed directly in the label.

```
Private Sub btnNewPupil_Click(...) Handles btnNewPupil.Click
    OnePupil.PupilName = txtName.Text
    OnePupil.PayDeposit = txtDeposit.Text
    lblTotalAmount.Text = Format(OnePupil.GetTotalPayment, "Currency")
End Sub
```

The lower OK button calls the SendPayment method and passes it the amount paid. The return values from the GetTotalPayment and GetNumberOfPayments methods are displayed directly in the labels.

```
Private Sub btnProcessPayment_Click(...) Handles btnProcessPayment.Click
    Dim Payment As Decimal
    Payment = txtPayment.Text
    OnePupil.SendPayment(Payment)
    lblTotalAmount.Text = Format(OnePupil.GetTotalPayment, "Currency")
    lblNumPayments.Text = OnePupil.GetNumberOfPayments
End Sub
```

Reflections

The properties were declared as Private rather than Public. This means that they can be accessed only through the object's methods. If you had tried to access a property directly, for example with

```
OnePupil.Name = "Peter Matthews"
```

then an error would result. Such **data hiding** is technically called **data encapsulation** and is a fundamental feature of OOP.

The methods were all declared as Public because these need to be accessed by code on the form. Sometimes, though, you may write a method whose task is an internal one of use only to the object itself. The outside world never needs to know about it and so it can be declared as Private.

One of the six actions/methods listed earlier was not used – reading the pupil's name. In the simple program above you do not need it, but a real program would need to store details of 40 students (on a file of course). Retrieving details of a particular student is likely to be an important process. The question of handling many objects of the same class, or in this case storing an array of students in one object, is covered after Program 17.1.

PROGRAM 17.1   *A Bank Account Class*

> **Specification**   Ask the user for the following details of a new bank account – account number, customer's name and balance. The customer may deposit some money when opening a new account and so this is the opening balance. Then allow the customer to deposit and withdraw money. The user should enter the amount of money for each of these transactions and the current balance should always be displayed.

Figure 17.3 shows the program. The customer started the account with £250.00. A small number of deposits and withdrawals have been made. The last transaction was a withdrawal of £24.50.

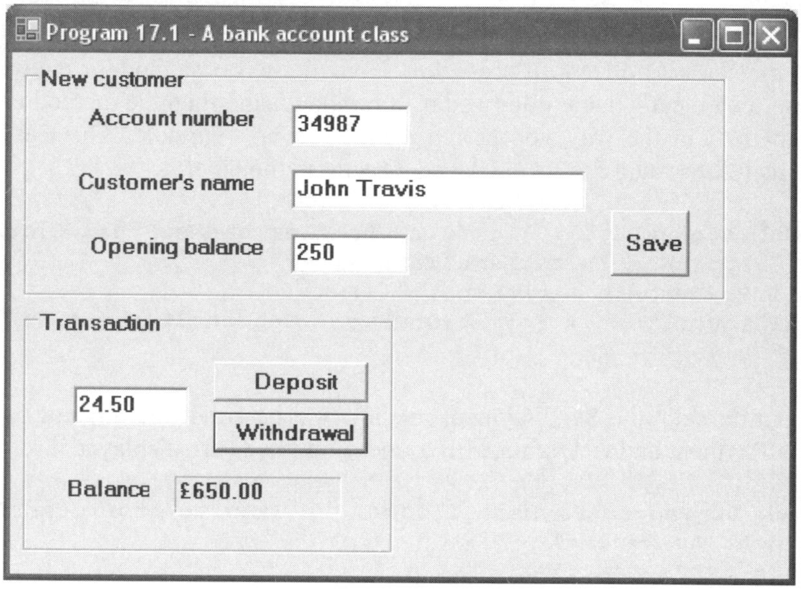

Figure 17.3: Program 17.1

Working out the properties and methods on paper

We need to store three things about each customer. These are the class's properties:

- Account number
- Name
- Balance

We need methods to handle the following:

- Store the account number
- Store the customer's name
- Store the opening balance
- Retrieve the balance
- Make a deposit
- Make a withdrawal

The first four can be done through Property methods. A read and write method can handle the balance and write only methods can handle the account number and customer name. Sub methods will be used for making deposits and withdrawals.

Building the form, the class and the object

1. Open a new project. Build the form using figure 17.3. Name the three input text boxes **txtAccountNumber**, **txtCustomerName** and **txtOpeningBalance**. Name the Save button **btnOpenAccount**, the transaction buttons **btnDeposit** and **btnWithdrawal**. Name the label for displaying the current balance **lblCurrentBalance**.

2. Select **File/Add new item** and select the **Class** template in the Add New Item dialog box. Change its name to **BankAccount.vb** and click **Open**. The class module will be listed in the Solution Explorer.

3. In the Code window of this class module declare class BankAccount and its three properties:

```
Public Class BankAccount
  Private AccountNumber, Name As String
  Private Balance As Decimal
```

4. When you press Enter after the opening line of the write only Property method to store an account number, Visual Basic .NET provides all the other lines except the one to assign the account number.

```
Public WriteOnly Property CustomerAccountNumber() As String
  Set(ByVal Value As String)
    AccountNumber = Value
  End Set
End Property
```

5. The write only property method to store the customer name is very similar:

```
Public WriteOnly Property CustomerName() As String
  Set(ByVal Value As String)
    Name = Value
  End Set
End Property
```

6. The read and write property handles storing the opening balance and retrieving the current balance:

```
Public Property CustomerBalance() As Decimal
  Get
    Return Balance
  End Get
  Set(ByVal Value As Decimal)
    Balance = Value
  End Set
End Property
```

7. The Sub method for deposits simply adds the amount paid in to the balance. The Sub method for withdrawals subtracts the amount withdrawn from the balance.

```
Public Sub Deposit(ByVal Amount As Decimal)
  Balance = Balance + Amount
End Sub

Public Sub Withdrawal(ByVal Amount As Decimal)
  Balance = Balance - Amount
End Sub
```

8. On the form (i.e. not on the class module), declare an object of class BankAccount:

```
Dim OneAccount As New BankAccount()
```

Using the class and object

9. When you click the **Save** button we must send the account number, customer name and opening balance to the appropriate method.

```
Private Sub btnOpenAccount_Click(...) Handles btnOpenAccount.Click
    Dim AccountNumber, Name As String
    Dim Balance As Decimal
    AccountNumber = txtAccountNumber.Text
    Name = txtCustomerName.Text
    Balance = txtOpeningBalance.Text
    OneAccount.CustomerAccountNumber = AccountNumber   'Calls to the 3
    OneAccount.CustomerName = Name                'write and read/write
    OneAccount.CustomerBalance = Balance          'methods of the object
    lblCurrentBalance.Text = Format(OneAccount.CustomerBalance, "Currency")
End Sub
```

The last line above, to display the current balance, *could* have taken the opening balance from the text box rather than call (the Get part of) the CustomerBalance method.

10. The two transaction buttons on the form call the Deposit and Withdrawal Sub methods to recalculate the balance, and display this new balance by calling the CustomerBalance method.

```
Private Sub btnDeposit_Click(...) Handles btnDeposit.Click
    Dim Amount As Decimal
    Amount = txtAmount.Text
    OneAccount.Deposit(Amount)
    lblCurrentBalance.Text = Format(OneAccount.CustomerBalance, "Currency")
End Sub

Private Sub btnWithdrawal_Click(...) Handles btnWithdrawal.Click
    Dim Amount As Decimal
    Amount = txtAmount.Text
    OneAccount.Withdrawal(Amount)
    lblCurrentBalance.Text = Format(OneAccount.CustomerBalance, "Currency")
End Sub
```

11. Run the program and check that you can open an account and deposit and withdraw money.

end of Program 17.1

Why not use records?

Class BankAccount has three properties – account number, customer name and balance. Why not let the calling program store these in a record and send this to the class rather than having a series of Property methods? A single method could unwrap the record and assign the separate pieces of data to the class's properties. Retrieving the data could be done in a similar way – let a class method put the property values into a record and send this off to the calling program. In Program 17.1 we only wished to retrieve the customer balance, so a record would be pointless, but the principle seems sound. All this would appear to make even more sense if you were sending ten or twenty items of data rather than just the three in Program 17.1.

Unfortunately Visual Basic .NET will not allow this! Suppose you had declared the three properties of class BankAccount as a record in the following way:

```
Private Structure Account
   AccountNumber, Name As String
   Balance As Decimal
End Structure
```

You might then code the declaration part of a Property method as

```
Public Property CustAccount() As Account
```

However the compiler will tell you that you *cannot expose a Private type outside of the Public class 'BankAccount'*. Since OneAccount is a Private type this is saying that you cannot use a record.

If you can't use a record perhaps you can send and retrieve more than one item of data using a single Property method? The answer is again no. Consider the code that sent the account number to the Property method CustomerAccountNumber:

```
OneAccount.CustomerAccountNumber = AccountNumber
```

To send more than one item of data you would need more than one variable on the right side of the '=' and this is not possible. In a similar way, when calling a read only Property method you cannot have more than one variable on the left of the '='.

Many Property methods or an alternative?

It seems from the previous section that if you have several properties then you need the same number of Property methods if you wish to write to and read from all these properties. Actually you do not *have* to use Property methods at all. For example in Program 17.1 you could use a Sub procedure and pass all the items to it at once. In the code below OpenAccount is the method that handles the account number, name and opening balance together.

```
Public Sub OpenAccount(ByVal CustAccNo As String, ByVal CustName As _
                String, ByVal CustBalance As Decimal)
   AccountNumber = CustAccNo
   Name = CustName
   Balance = CustBalance
End Sub


   'Call OpenAccount in Click event of btnOpenAccount
   OneAccount.OpenAccount(AccountNumber, Name, Balance)
```

You may feel that using a procedure like this is preferable to three Property methods. An advantage of the Property methods is that the code is possibly more readable.

Processing many bank accounts

Program 17.1 only processes a single account. To process many accounts you could do one of two things:

- Declare an array of bank account objects and process the array.
- Redefine the class so that it contains an array of records. Use a single object as before, but now the object has the array of records to hold all the account details. One object stores all the bank accounts.

Use an array of objects

In step 8 of Program 17.1 you would replace the single object *OneAccount* by declaring:

```
Dim Accounts (99) As BankAccount        'declares 100 objects
```

Then you have to initialise all members of the array. In the form's Load event you would write:

```
For Index = 0 To 99
   Accounts(Index) = New BankAccount()
Next Index
```

Note that Visual Basic .NET will *not* allow you to do all the above at one go with

```
Dim Accounts (99) As New BankAccount()
```

The 3 lines of code in step 9 which store the values entered by the user into the single (bank account) object must be replaced by

```
Accounts(1).CustomerAccountNumber = AccountNumber
Accounts(1).CustomerName = Name
Accounts(1).CustomerBalance = Balance
```

This would store details in the first object in the array. In practice you would use a variable to identify the object rather than a fixed value like 1.

Redefine the class to include an array of records

You would replace the declaration in step 3 with:

```
Private Structure BankAccount
   AccountNumber, Name As String
   Balance As Decimal
End Structure
Private Accounts (99) As BankAccount        'stores 100 accounts
```

You would still use the declaration in step 8 to create the single object needed. The code on the form would not need to be changed at all, although you would probably wish to change the object's name from OneAccount to Accounts. However the code in the class methods would need to be extended so that the appropriate bank account is processed. For example the Property method to store an account number could search *Accounts* for the first 'empty' record. An alternative way might be to declare another property of the class to store the number of accounts, and use this to go directly to the first empty record.

Summary of key concepts

- The main unit of OOP in Visual Basic .NET is the **class**. **Objects** (instances) are created from a class.

- A class, and therefore objects belonging to that class, has **properties** and **methods**. A property is a static feature of an object and a method is an action that can be done on an object.

- If the properties of a class are declared as Private they can be written to and read from only using the class's methods. This is called **data encapsulation**.

- Methods can either be **Property** methods or **Sub/Function** methods. Property methods are used for writing to and reading from properties. A Property method uses **Get** for reading and **Let** for writing.

Take it from here...

1. Use the Object Browser, by selecting **View/Other Windows/Object Browser** from the menu, to look at the class you created in Program 17.1.

2. All the parameters passed to the class methods in this chapter are value (ByVal) parameters. Think carefully about whether it would be acceptable to pass a reference (ByRef) parameter, recalling that you normally use this if your intention is to change the parameter's contents and pass this change back to the calling program.

3. The chapter refers to the New method of an object, which is automatically called when an object is first created and allows you to initialise properties at this time. Find out about the method that is automatically called just before an object is destroyed.

Questions on Program 17.1

Program 18.1 in the next chapter uses Program 17.1 to illustrate inheritance. If you do any of the questions below make a copy of the program to work on.

*1. At present the only property that can be retrieved is the customer's balance. Rewrite the Property methods for class BankAccount to retrieve the account number and the customer's name. When the Save button is clicked to process a transaction, retrieve all three properties and in lblCurrentBalance display a message that reads something like "John Travis, account number 34987, current balance is £650.00". Don't cheat here. You *could* retrieve the account number and name data directly from the text boxes!

**2. Extend class BankAccount to store the customer's overdraft limit. This is the amount the balance is allowed to fall to without penalty (e.g. -£500.00). Name this property Overdaft. Extend the form so that the overdraft limit can be entered for a new account. If processing a withdrawal means that this limit is exceeded, a message box should display something like *Withdrawal denied. Overdraft limit is £500.00.* In this situation do not allow the withdrawal.

***3. The program can only store and manipulate the account of one customer. Extend it so that up to 10 customer accounts can be handled by using one of the two approaches outlined in the section *Processing many bank accounts*. Extend the program by allowing the user to search for a particular customer on their account number. Output the details of this customer if the account is found, or the message *Account number invalid* if it is not found.

End of chapter exercises

**1. Declare a class, Golfer, to store and retrieve three pieces of data about a golfer – their name, gender and handicap. (The handicap for males is from 0 to 28 and for females is 0 to 36. The lower the number the better the player.) Store the golfer's details and display them using Property methods. When you have this working allow the user to increase or decrease the handicap by any amount using only the Property methods you have already written.

**2.   Rewrite Program 3.4, which calculates the mean value of a series of exam marks, using OOP techniques. Read the program specification carefully before drawing up a list of properties and methods.

**3.   Students on a course take three module exams. They can have two attempts at each exam and the best result counts. Declare a class, Student, that stores the student's ID, name and the three exam marks (out of 100). If the mark for a given module is the student's second attempt at that module, store the second attempt mark, otherwise keep the first mark. The calling program should output how many modules the student passed along the lines of *John Jones, ID 3465, passed 2 modules*. A mark of 50 or more is a pass. Calculating the number of passes should be one of the class's methods.

**4.   Extend exercise 3 to handle more than one student. The message should relate to a student selected by the user. Also list the names of those students who passed a particular module selected by the user, and list those students who passed all three modules.

***5.   Part 3 of this book has a detailed sample project which keeps track of the use of the tables in a snooker club. Although OOP techniques are not used in this project, for this exercise create a class, Table, with the following properties:

- table number
- start time of game (stored in the form hh:mm, e.g. 14:20)
- whether or not the table is occupied

Between them the methods should:

- initialise a table
- start a game
- finish a game
- find out whether or not the table is occupied

You *could* determine whether a table is occupied by seeing whether there is a start time stored but you are asked to use the third property listed above. Use the New method to assign the table number and set the table's start time to an empty string. The method to start a game should set the start time and indicate that the table is occupied. The method to finish a game should set the start time to an empty string and indicate that the table is not occupied.

Write a program that uses this class to keep track of which tables are in use. The visual interface is left up to you to design, but you don't need to have more than 5 or 6 tables. You may find Programs 10.3 and 10.4 help you with the interface.

Chapter 18 – OOP: Inheritance and Polymorphism

Chapter 17 introduced you to classes and objects. You learned about data encapsulation, one of three major concepts in OOP. The other two major concepts, **inheritance** and **polymorphism** are covered in this chapter.

Inheritance

Inheritance is when one class inherits all the properties and methods of another class. The class which inherits is the **child** class and the class from which it inherits is the **parent** class. The child class can use all of its parent's properties and methods as well as any of its own. If the child class in turn is used as a parent, its child will inherit two 'generations' of properties and methods.

Figure 18.1 shows an inheritance diagram. Child1 and Child2 inherit the same properties and methods from Parent1. In the example they both have two new properties, D and E. Grandchild1 inherits properties A, B, C from Parent1 and D, E from Child1. Grandchild1 is not allowed to inherit from Child2 as well as Child1. Only one parent is allowed.

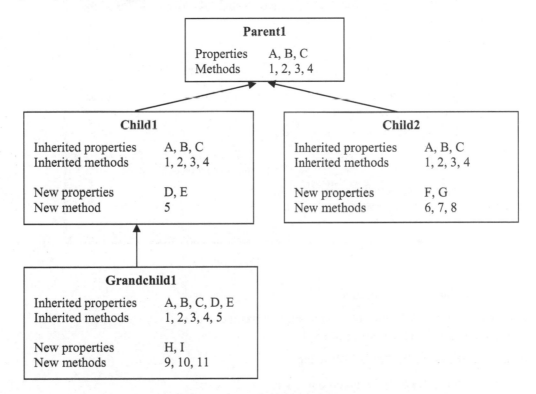

Figure 18.1: An inheritance diagram

To indicate that a child class inherits a parent class use the keyword **Inherits** followed by the parent class name. For example using the classes in figure 18.1 you would write:

```
Class Child1
  Inherits Parent1
  'Declare properties D, E here
  'Write method 5 here
End Class

Class Grandchild1
  Inherits Child1
  'Declare properties H, I here
  'Write methods 9, 10, 11 here
End Class
```

PROGRAM 18.1   *Inheritance – a student bank account class*

Specification	Extend Program 17.1 to process student customers only. Create a student bank account class that inherits the BankAccount class used in that program. In addition students can take out a special loan of up to £2,000. The new class must handle the loan. Display a message in a list box about whether the student has taken out a loan and, if they have, how much the loan is.

Figure 18.2 shows the program. It is similar to figure 17.3 but with a few extra controls.

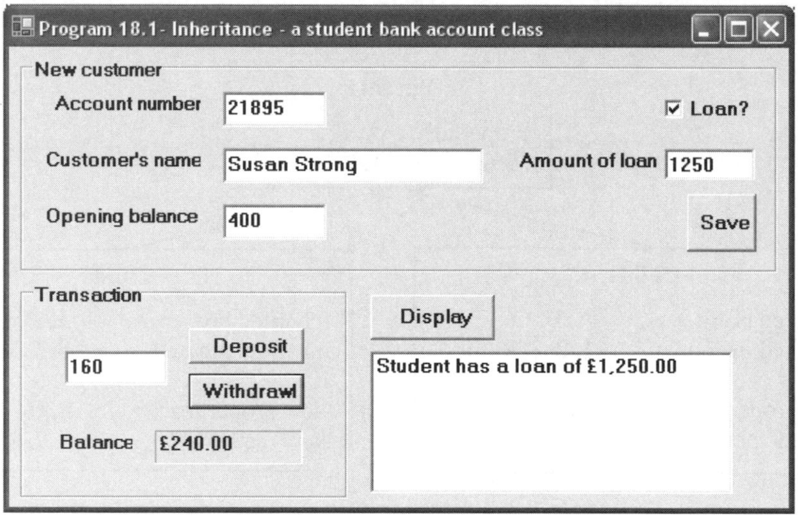

Figure 18.2: Program 18.1

The new class will have two properties:

- HasLoan   Whether or not the student has taken out a loan
- LoanAmount   The amount of the loan

We need new methods to handle the following:

- Store whether a loan has been taken out
- Store the amount of the loan
- Retrieve whether a loan has been taken out
- Retrieve the amount of the loan

Since there is a read and write operation on each of the two properties we can use a Property method with Get and Set for each one.

1. Open a new project. Right-click **Form1.vb** in the Solution Explorer and select **Delete** to delete the form. Select **File/Add Existing Item** and select **Form1.vb** from Program 17.1. Select **File/Add Existing Item** again and select **BankAccount.vb** from Program 17.1 (the class module).

2. Extend the form to look like figure 18.2. Name the two extra controls for the loan in the upper right part of the form **chkLoan** and **txtLoan**, the Display button **btnDisplay** and the list box **lstDisplay**.

Visual Basic .NET allows any number of classes to be declared on a single class module (unlike previous versions which allowed only one). However it is sensible practice to put classes which are not closely related in separate modules. It is a debatable point whether parent and child classes are necessarily closely related! In this example we will separate them and so have two class modules.

3. Select **File/Add New Item** and select the **Class** template. Name it **StudentBankAccount.vb** and click **Open**.

4. In this new class module declare class StudentBankAccount and its two properties. Also declare that it should inherit the BankAccount class.

```
Public Class StudentBankAccount
   Inherits BankAccount
   Private HasLoan As Boolean
   Private LoanAmount As Decimal
```

5. Write the Property method for storing and retrieving the amount of the loan.

```
Public Property StudentLoan() As Decimal
   Get
      Return LoanAmount
   End Get
   Set(ByVal Value As Decimal)
      LoanAmount = Value
   End Set
End Property
```

6. Write the Property method for storing and retrieving whether or not a loan has been taken out.

```
Public Property LoanTaken() As Boolean
   Get
      Return HasLoan
   End Get
   Set(ByVal Value As Boolean)
      HasLoan = Value
   End Set
End Property
```

7. Declare an object of class StudentBankAccount. Since you are reusing the form from Program 17.1 replace the object declaration already here.

```
Dim OneAccount As New StudentBankAccount()
```

8. Extend the code in the Click event of the Save button to handle the loan requirements. The asterisked lines below are the new ones.

```
     Private Sub btnOpenAccount_Click(...) Handles btnOpenAccount.Click
       Dim AccountNumber, Name As String
       Dim Balance As Decimal
 *     Dim Loan As Decimal
       AccountNumber = txtAccountNumber.Text
       Name = txtCustomerName.Text
       Balance = txtOpeningBalance.Text
       OneAccount.CustomerAccountNumber = AccountNumber
       OneAccount.CustomerName = Name
       OneAccount.CustomerBalance = Balance
 *     If chkLoan.Checked = True Then        'Does student require a loan?
 *       Loan = txtLoan.Text                 'If yes then call the new
 *       OneAccount.LoanTaken = True         'class's two methods
 *       OneAccount.StudentLoan = Loan
 *     Else                                  'If no, call LoanTaken method to
 *       OneAccount.LoanTaken = False        'set property HasLoan to False
 *     End If
       lblCurrentBalance.Text = Format(OneAccount.CustomerBalance, "Currency")
     End Sub
```

9. The Display button calls the LoanTaken method to output the appropriate message. It returns True if the student has a loan or False if they do not have one. If the return value is True the StudentLoan method is called to return the amount of the loan.

```
     Private Sub btnDisplay_Click(...) Handles btnDisplay.Click
       Dim Loan As Decimal
       lstDisplay.Items.Clear()
       If OneAccount.LoanTaken Then        'This method returns a Boolean
         Loan = OneAccount.StudentLoan
         lstDisplay.Items.Add("Student has a loan of " & Format(Loan, _
                               "Currency"))
       Else
         lstDisplay.Items.Add("Student has not taken out a loan")
       End If
     End Sub
```

10. Run the program and check that the BankAccount class is inherited and that the new loan features work correctly.

end of Program 18.1

Polymorphism

Polymorphism is an extension of inheritance. It is when two classes have a method with the same name but it is coded differently to meet a different specification. You use the keyword **Overridable** in declaring the polymorphic method in the parent class and the keyword **Overrides** in declaring the method in the child class.

In figure 18.1 Child1 inherits method 4 from Parent1. If this is the polymorphic method you would write the code as follows:

```
Class Parent1
  'Declare properties A, B, C here
  'Write methods 1, 2, 3, 4. Method 4 declared as follows:
  Public Overridable Sub Method4
End Class

Class Child1
  Inherits Parent1
  'Declare properties D, E here
  'Write methods 4 and 5 here. Method 4 declared as follows:
  Public Overrides Sub Method4
End Class
```

PROGRAM 18.2 *Polymorphism – student grading system*

Specification Students on a three-module course get a mark out of 100 for each module. The final grade for the course depends on the average mark as follows: A (80-100), B (70-79), C (60-69), D (50-59), E (40-49) and U (0-39). U stands for unclassified and is the only fail grade. A new grading system running parallel with this one has just been introduced. An average mark of 80-100 gets a Distinction, 60-79 a Merit, 40-59 a Pass and 0-39 a Fail. Build a class based on the old grading system to store the student's name and the three module marks. It must calculate the final grade – use a function CalcFinalGrade for this. Build a second class that inherits the first class but redefines the function CalcFinalGrade. Allow the user to select which grading system to use and display the appropriate final grade.

Figure 18.3 shows the program. On the old grading system the student would have achieved a grade C.

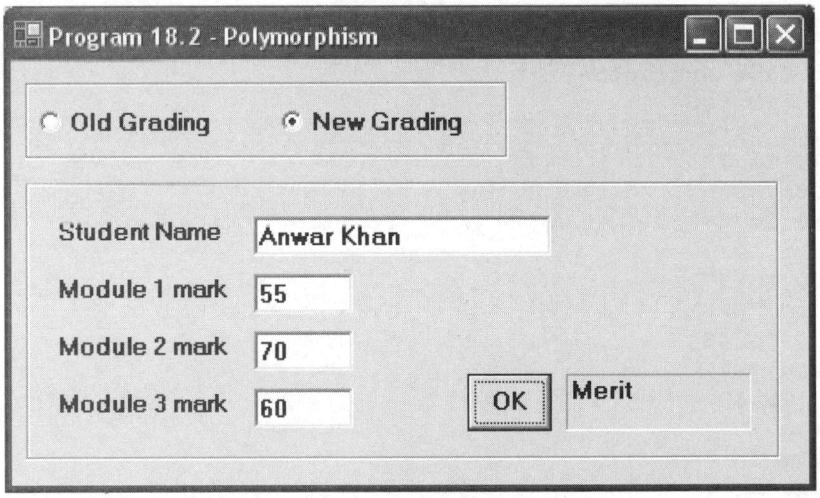

Figure 18.3: Program 18.2

1. Open a new project. Build the form using figure 18.3. Name the radio buttons **radOldGrading** and **radNewGrading**, the four text boxes **txtName**, **txtMark1**, **txtMark2**, **txtMark3**, the button **btnOK** and the label displaying the grade **lblGrade**.

2. Select **File/Add New Item** and select the **Class** template. Do not change the default name. Click **Open**.

3. Declare a class for the old grading system, by replacing the default name for the class by OldGradedStudent. We will use a Property method for storing the student's name, but rather than having three Property methods for storing the marks we will have our own Sub method StoreMarks.

```
Public Class OldGradedStudent
  Private Name As String
  Private Module1Mark, Module2Mark, Module3Mark As Short

  Public WriteOnly Property StudentName()
    Set(ByVal Value)
      Name = Value
    End Set
  End Property

  Public Sub StoreMarks(ByVal Mark1 As Short, ByVal Mark2 As Short, _
                                          ByVal Mark3 As Short)
    Module1Mark = Mark1
    Module2Mark = Mark2
    Module3Mark = Mark3
  End Sub
```

4. The polymorphic function, CalcFinalGrade, has the keyword **Overridable**. Although it returns a single letter, its return data type is String rather than Char. The function that will override this one in the newer class will return Distinction, Merit etc. This return data type must be String. The return data types of the two polymorphic methods must be the same.

```
Public Overridable Function CalcFinalGrade() As String
  Dim AverageMark As Single
  AverageMark = (Module1Mark + Module2Mark + Module3Mark) / 3
  Select Case AverageMark
  Case 80 To 100
    Return "A"
  Case 70 To 79
    Return "B"
  Case 60 To 69
    Return "C"
  Case 50 To 59
    Return "D"
  Case 40 To 49
    Return "E"
  Case 0 To 39
    Return "U"
  End Select
End Function
```

5. Declare and define the new grading class, NewGradedStudent, in the same class module as class OldGradedStudent. Apart from inheriting the old class we only have to redeclare and define the polymorphic function CalcFinalGrade. This uses **MyBase** to refer back to its parent class.

```
Public Class NewGradedStudent
  Inherits OldGradedStudent

  Overrides Function CalcFinalGrade() As String
    Dim FinalGrade As Char
    FinalGrade = MyBase.CalcFinalGrade
    If FinalGrade = "A" Then
      Return "Distinction"
    ElseIf (FinalGrade = "B") Or (FinalGrade = "C") Then
      Return "Merit"
    ElseIf (FinalGrade = "D") Or (FinalGrade = "E") Then
      Return "Pass"
    Else
      Return "Fail"
    End If
  End Function
End Class
```

6. On the form declare an object of each class and use the appropriate one depending on which radio button is selected.

```
Dim OneOldGradedStudent As New OldGradedStudent()
Dim OneNewGradedStudent As New NewGradedStudent()

Private Sub btnOK_Click(...) Handles btnOK.Click
  Dim Name As String
  Dim Mark1, Mark2, Mark3 As Short
  Name = txtName.Text
  Mark1 = txtMark1.Text
  Mark2 = txtMark2.Text
  Mark3 = txtMark3.Text
  If radOldGrading.Checked = True Then
    OneOldGradedStudent.StudentName = Name
    OneOldGradedStudent.StoreMarks(Mark1, Mark2, Mark3)
    lblGrade.Text = OneOldGradedStudent.CalcFinalGrade
  Else
    OneNewGradedStudent.StudentName = Name
    OneNewGradedStudent.StoreMarks(Mark1, Mark2, Mark3)
    lblGrade.Text = OneNewGradedStudent.CalcFinalGrade
  End If
End Sub
```

7. Run the program. Select the **Old Grading** radio button, enter the data and click **OK**. A letter grade should be displayed. Select the **New Grading** radio button, click **OK** again and this grade should be converted to the new descriptive grade.

end of Program 18.2

Summary of key concepts

- **Inheritance** is when one class (the child class) inherits all the properties and methods from another class (the parent class). A child class can only inherit from one parent class.

- A child class can have properties and methods of its own which are not inherited.

- **Polymorphism** is when two classes have a method with the same name but it is coded differently to meet a different specification. One class inherits the other: a polymorphic method is declared **Overridable** in the parent class and the child class uses **Overrides** in declaring the method.

Take it from here...

1. Find out what the keyword **MustOverride** means.

End of chapter exercises

For the two exercises below use the Ski Trip example covered in Chapter 17. You can either build it yourself from Chapter 17 or download it from the publisher's web site. Exercise 1 covers inheritance and must be done before exercise 2, which covers polymorphism.

**1. Suppose it is now required to store the date and amount of each payment the pupil makes. Declare a class, NewPupil, that inherits Class Pupil but meets the new specification by having an array of records to store these dates and amounts. This array constitutes one property of NewPupil. Add a method that returns this array. Add a button to the form that displays the contents of this array.

**2. The Sub method SendPayment of Class Pupil recalculates the two properties TotalAmountPaid and NumberOfPayments. In Class NewPupil make this a polymorphic method that recalculates these properties by using the amounts stored in the array property you have added in exercise 1. Note that this exercise is simply to practise polymorphism, and is a contrived one for two reasons. The new way of recalculating the properties is more complex than the old way, and the end result of the new way is the same as the old. In a real program you would leave the old approach alone!

Part Three – The Project

Module 6 of the AQA Board 'A' level Computing is a project worth 40% of the A2 part of the couse. Part Three takes you through the analysis and design stages of a sample project and then shows you how to code the design. The purpose of this section on coding is to demonstrate how Visual Basic .NET can be used to produce a solution. Those parts of module 6 which are independent of the language used are not covered. These include testing and the user manual. The exception is a short section on appraising the project.

Chapter 19 briefly reviews how the marks are allocated for the project. It then introduces the sample project – Smiley's Snooker club – and runs through the first stage, **Analysis.** This is about finding out what the user requires the solution to do.

Chapter 20 covers part of the **Design** stage. It shows you how to design the layout of the **forms** and **reports** to meet Smiley's requirements. It then explains how to design the various **files** needed and how to process them. Finally there is a review of the **data validation** needed for all the data input by the user.

Chapter 21 continues with the **Design** stage. It lists all the tasks that must be done by the various events that will occur when the forms designed in Chapter 20 are used. Some of these tasks are put into Sub and Function procedures. At design time it is possible to list these and decide on the parameters they will need. Techniques for documenting these general procedures, including **module structure charts**, are explained.

Chapter 22 – 25 take you through the complete **coding**. Each chapter deals with a clearly-defined part of the user requirements.

Chapter 26 covers the final section of the project, **Appraisal**. In particular the question of how the Smiley's project could be improved is discussed in some detail.

Chapter 19 – Introduction and Analysis

Requirements of an 'A' level project

The requirements of the 'A' level Computing project vary from board to board but for this part of the book we'll use the AQA syllabus. Module 6 of the syllabus requires candidates to "*demonstrate skills of practical application and problem solving, as well as the techniques of documentation and system testing. The system developed by the candidate should allow interaction with the user, storage and manipulation of data, and output of results.*" It is expected that the end-user should be a real person or group of people.

The AQA mark scheme for candidates who use a standalone programming language like Visual Basic to carry out their project (rather than a package with programming facilities such as Access), is shown in Appendix B. The project is divided into the following sections:

	Marks
Analysis	12
Design	12
Technical Solution	12
System Testing	6
System Maintenance	6
User Manual	6
Appraisal	3
Quality of Communication	3

Total 60

Analysis

This stage should report on what the user wants the computerised solution to do. You should draw up a list of general and specific objectives of your solution, identify possible methods of meeting them, and justify the method they have chosen.

Design

Design covers several important topics. These include:

- what the interface will look like – use of various controls and so on;
- the files needed – their structure, organisation and processing;
- how the data will be validated;
- the procedures needed.

Quite clearly you cannot draw up a complete design unless you know Visual Basic reasonably well. Design is covered in Chapters 20 and 21.

Technical Solution

This is your Visual Basic program and is covered in Chapters 22 – 25.

System testing

Testing is evidence that the system you have implemented really does work. The evidence should normally be hard copy (printouts). You should first draw up a test plan and then carry out each test carefully. This is not covered in the sample project.

System Maintenance

This should include the following:

- A printout of your program code with suitable comments within the code itself or with handwritten annotations about how the code works. Using the commenting facility of Visual Basic is more sensible.

- A list showing all the variables and procedures you have used.

- Some sample algorithms using a recognised method of presentation.

The first of these is fully covered in the sample project. The second is partly covered in Chapter 21.

User Manual

This is a guide for the user, several pages in length, that explains how to use your system. It should include screen displays, refer to error messages which may crop up and how to recover from these errors. This is not covered in the sample project.

Appraisal

How well have the objectives listed in the Analysis been met? Feedback from the user would be very useful here. Are there any improvements you could make, either to the way you have coded your solution or in extensions to the program sometime in the future? This is covered in Chapter 26.

Quality of Communication

How well written and clearly set out is your report?

The mark scheme suggests that only 12 of the 60 marks come from coding, but the importance of coding is much greater than this. Many of the marks for system maintenance, testing and even the user manual can only be earned if your coding has been done reasonably well in the first place. You can't test what you haven't coded for example!

In Part Three of this book you will be shown how to design and code a full project of 'A' level standard. The Analysis stage will not be covered in great detail, but we do need to cover enough in order to know what to design and code.

Introducing the sample project – Smiley's Snooker Club

The project is based on a snooker club called Smiley's Snooker. It is a private club with 20 snooker tables and about 400 members. 300 of these are Seniors (over 18 years of age) and 100 are Juniors. The club is open from 10.00 am to 10.00 pm each day. There is no booking system at present. Members just turn up and ask to play. The part of the business that Smiley's has asked you to computerise is handling the allocation of tables and to keep a record of the membership of the club. These aspects will now be looked at in more detail in the Analysis stage which follows.

The Analysis stage

The Analysis stage covers your early discussions with Smiley's when you would make a careful study of how the present manual system works. You would try to find out in as much detail as possible just what Smiley's wants your computerised solution to do. The discussion below is deliberately too short for a good 'A' level project. For example it does not say much about how the club currently handles its games. However the purpose of the sample project is to concentrate on those aspects which are closely related to your Visual Basic work. It does not try to explain how to conduct a full analysis of an existing system. There is just enough detail in what follows to get on with the next stage, the design.

The initial findings

On your first visit to Smiley's you have gathered a range of details about how the club works and which part of it you need to computerise. The following is a summary of your findings.

It was mentioned above that Smiley's has 20 snooker tables and that there is no booking system at present. They do not wish to have a booking system and want your computerised solution to simply make the allocation of tables and calculating the cost of games much easier than it is at present.

A member may bring along one guest to play snooker. At present the charge to play is 4p a minute if a senior member is playing with a guest or another member (senior or junior) and 3p a minute if two juniors or a junior plus guest are playing. If two members play a game then one of them is responsible for the payment. If a member plays with a guest then this member is responsible for the payment. If a senior and junior member play then details of the senior member should be recorded as payment is based on this category of membership. When members come to play they should show their membership card. However, sometimes they forget so the system should be able to retrieve a particular membership number by the member's name.

Smiley's wants to be able to see on screen at any time which tables are free and which have games going on. For those tables with games going on, the times that the games started should be displayed. When a new game starts the system should display the membership number, the table number and the time the game started for the receptionist. When a game finishes the table number, membership number, category of membership, finish time, the length of playing time in hours and minutes and the cost should be displayed. A record of each completed game, containing the table number, details of how long the game took and the cost, should be kept. At the end of each day Smiley's wants a printed report showing the usage of each table. It should show the total length of time each table has been used that day, how many games have been played on it and the amount of income it has made. The overall income for the day is also required.

Smiley's wants to keep a record of all its members and so be able to add new members and delete others. The club requires, at any time, a printed list of their members. This should list the names alphabetically, the category of membership, the total number of senior and junior members and the overall total number of members.

Membership numbers have the format LLDDDD where L is an upper-case letter and D a numeric digit from 0 to 9. The two upper-case letters represent the member's first name and surname. No-one seems to know why there are four digits but Smiley's wishes to keep this format. Tables are numbered from 1 to 20.

Reflections

You have studied your initial findings at home and several questions spring to mind that you'd like to ask Smiley's about. These questions are:

1. *The costs per minute should be stored in a file, so when they inevitably go up will Smiley's know how to change them if they are stored in a text file?*

   The alternative to storing the costs per minute in a file is to code them into your program. But when the costs change Smiley's would require a programmer to change them. This would be good for you since they may need to pay you, but it would be more reasonable to allow Smiley's to change the prices themselves without getting involved in code. If the costs are stored in a text file Smiley's can change them in a simple text file editor, such as Notepad or WordPad that comes with Windows, or you can let this to be done through one of the forms in your program.

2. *Smiley's has said that it wants a printed report at the end of each day showing details of the usage of each table. Will Smiley's want to produce this report at other times of the day, sometimes at the end of the morning for example?*

   If Smiley's only wants to produce the report at the end of the day then you can delete the file that stores the data for this report immediately after the report is printed. The next day the file should start afresh again with no data in it. However if Smiley's wish to produce the report more than once in a day then you must not delete its contents.

3. *Smiley's closes at 10.00pm. Is this likely to be extended in the future so that games could finish after midnight?*

   You need to know this because even at this early stage you are thinking about how to calculate the cost of a game. It will be calculated by multiplying the number of minutes the game lasts by the rate per minute, and in turn the number of minutes will be calculated by doing some arithmetic on the start and finish times of the game. If games finish after midnight this will probably affect the way this arithmetic is done.

Second visit

The answers to the questions have been cleared up.

1. Smiley's does not want to change the contents of the file directly. You know their fears are exaggerated, but they are rather afraid of doing something wrong. They would prefer your program to handle this.

2. Yes, on reflection they would like to produce the daily usage report at any time during the day.

3. No, it is most unlikely that the closing time will be extended.

Final thoughts on the Analysis stage

The analysis stage is worth 12 marks and must be more thorough than the outline given here for Smiley's Snooker to earn them. For example it is very likely that the club would want more from the computerised solution to the membership part of the system than just adding and deleting members. The problem is that a few more requests from the user will generate a project that is just too big if implemented fully. In the analysis you should discuss all the needs of the user but make it clear, if these are too wide, where you are drawing the boundary for your computerised solution.

Chapter 20 – Design: Forms, Reports, Files and Data Validation

What is design?

Design is all about preparing the groundwork so that during the next stage, coding, the only major decisions that have to be made are about the coding itself. If an experienced Visual Basic programmer could take your design and get on with building the program without having to come back to you about non-coding issues, then you have probably done a good design. But since you are both designer and programmer it can be very tempting to start coding before a sound design is in place. But resist it if you can! It will pay off in the end.

Design covers quite a range of topics although some of these will be much more important than others in your project. For Smiley's Snooker we will concentrate on the big topics which have a bearing on how the program is coded. We'll cover the following in the order listed:

- form design
- design of printed reports
- file design – structure, organisation and processing
- data validation
- design of the overall modular structure

The hardest of these is designing the modular structure and is discussed in the next chapter.

Designing the forms

You should produce paper designs of all the forms in your project, drawn by hand or by using a software package. For Smiley's Snooker we will have four forms as outlined in figure 20.1.

General name	Purpose
Main form	Displays the 20 snooker tables and their state of play. Prints a report on daily usage of tables. Allows the other 3 forms to be loaded
Game form	Input/output appropriate data when a game either starts or finishes. Calculates the cost of a finished game. Stores details of games on file.
Members form	Allows new members to be added and others to be deleted. Displays full list of members. Prints a membership report.
Utilities form	Creates lost or missing files. Backs up files. Changes price of snooker game.

Figure 20.1: The project's forms

Main form

Figure 20.2 shows a sketch of the design of the main form.

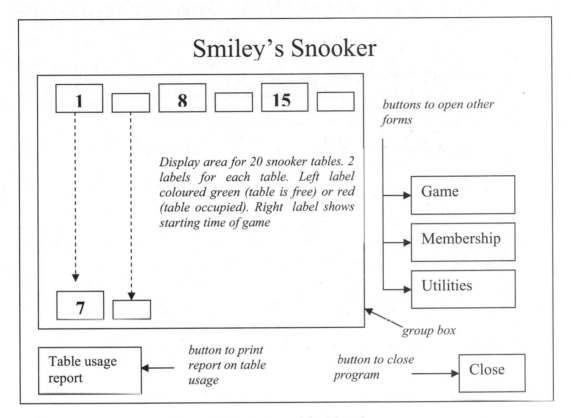

Figure 20.2: Design of the Main form

Game form

Figures 20.3 and 20.4 show sketches of this form. Depending on which radio button is clicked, Start Game or Finish Game, a different set of controls is made visible. When the form first loads, by clicking the Game button on the Main form, the controls for starting a game will be visible.

Starting a game

The following will happen:

- The receptionist enters the person's membership number.

- The member's name and their category of membership will automatically appear. The receptionist confirms these details with the player.

- The combo box will display the numbers of all those tables which are available for play. When the receptionist selects a table number the current time is taken from the system clock and displayed in the Start Time control. The receptionist will confirm with the member the starting time of the game for payment calculations.

- Clicking the Start Game button stores details of the game on a file and clears all the text boxes. It also changes the table's colour from green to red on the Main form and displays the starting time next to it.

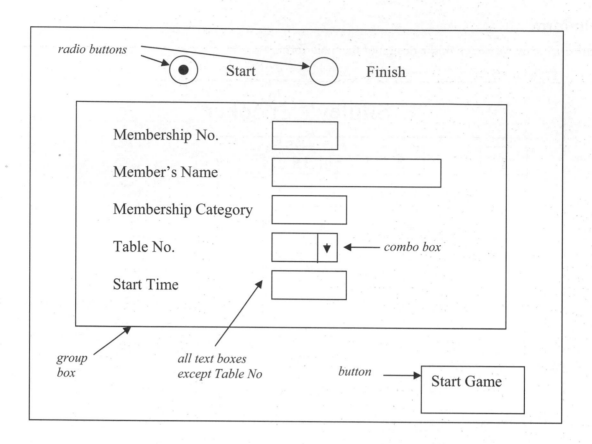

Figure 20.3: Design of the Game form – Starting a game

Finishing a game

The following will happen:

- The receptionist will ask the player which table they have been using and selects this from the tables currently in use that are displayed in the combo box.

- Selecting a table number triggers the display of data in all the other controls.

- The finishing time of the game is taken from the system clock and the playing time and cost of the game calculated automatically.

- Clicking the Finish Game button stores details of the completed game on file and clears all the text boxes. It also changes the table's colour back to green and removes the start time next to it on the Main form.

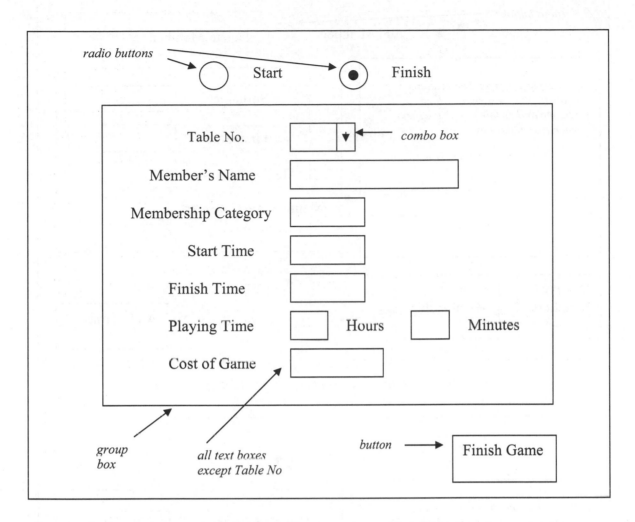

Figure 20.4: Design of the Game form – Finishing a game

Members form

Figures 20.5 and 20.6 show sketches of the form. Depending on which radio button is clicked, Add Member or Delete Member, a different set of controls is made visible. When the form first loads, the controls for adding a member will be available.

Adding a member

The receptionist enters a new membership number, the member's name and category of membership and then clicks the Add Member button. The details are added to a file.

Deleting a member

The receptionist enters a membership number and clicks the Delete Member button. The member is deleted from a file.

The list box displays details of each member. These details can be printed out.

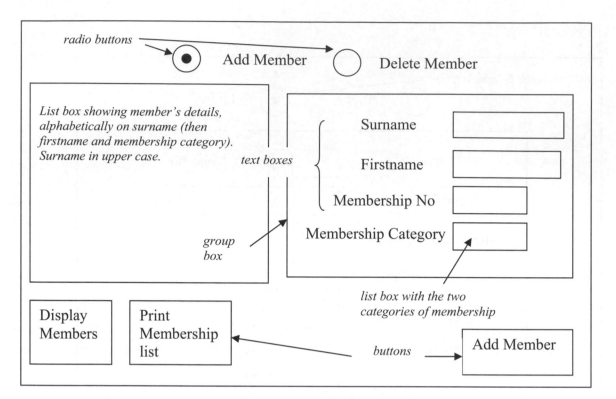

Figure 20.5: Design of the Members form – Adding a member

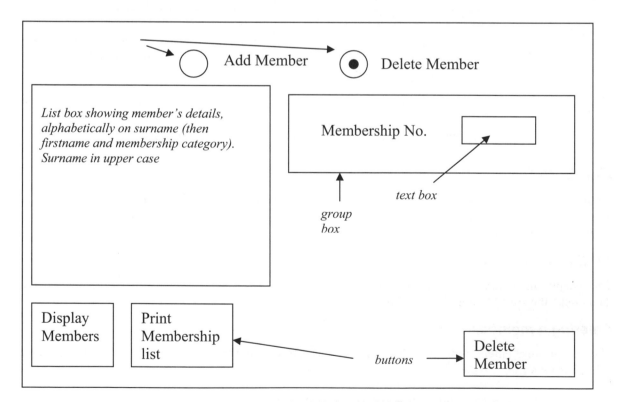

Figure 20.6: Design of the Members form – Deleting a member

Utilities form

Figure 20.7 shows a sketch of the form. The controls for entering new payment rates for a game are only made visible if the user clicks the appropriate radio button.

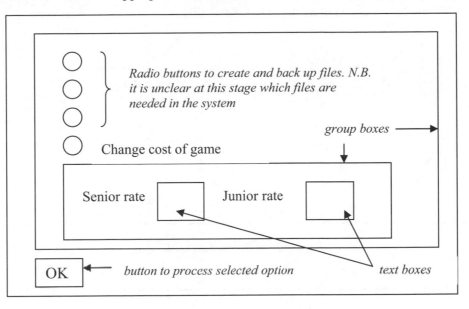

Figure 20.7: Design of the Utilities form

Printed reports

Our Analysis found that Smiley's wants two printed reports:

- At any time during the day, but most likely at the end of the day, a report showing the usage of each table. This includes the total length of time the table has been in use, how many games were played on the table and how much income the table made. The overall income for the day is also required.

- An alphabetical list of members showing their name and category of membership, the total number of senior and junior members and the overall total.

In your project you should draw sketch designs of all your reports. Figures 20.8 and 20.9 show these for the two reports requested by Smiley's.

Files

For each of the files your project uses you should state:

- its name
- its organisation (text file or random access file)
- its record structure (random access files) or "structure" of its data if it is a text file. If it is a random access file state the size of one record.
- the likely size of the file when in use
- how the file is processed – how data is added, deleted and changed
- what it is used for

Four files are needed for Smiley's Snooker. Three of these will store records and therefore be random access files (for which we'll use a '.dat' extension in the file name) and one is a text file ('.txt' extension).

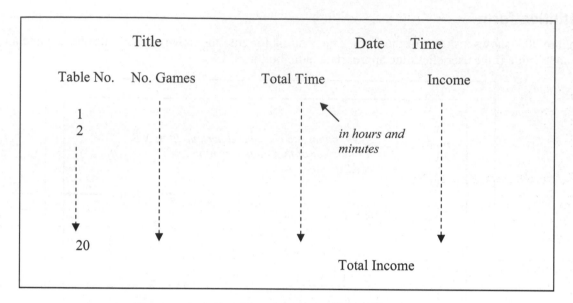

Figure 20.8: Report on table usage

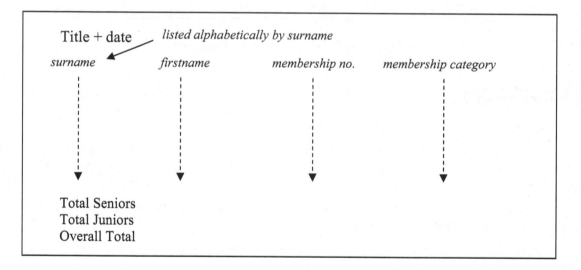

Figure 20.9: Report on membership

CurrentGames.dat   Stores details of the status of each table (in use or not) and the membership number of the player responsible for the game. Note that the data in this file *could* be stored only in RAM, but if the user accidentally closed the program these details would be lost.

FinishedGames.dat   Stores details of games that have finished. It will be used for printing the report Smiley's wants on table usage. Smiley's does not require any details about which members used the tables in this report so these can be omitted. We do need to store details of the length of each game because the report only needs to show the total amount of time each table has been used. A good rule in file design is not to store data that can be calculated from existing data. If there was a single cost rate at Smiley's, rather than senior and junior rates, we would not need to store how much each game cost because we would only have to multiply the rate by the number of minutes the game takes. Because there are different rates we must either store the cost of the game or the membership category of the member in charge of the game. Let's store the cost.

Costs.txt Stores the senior and junior rates as pence per minute.

Members.dat Stores details of each member – membership number, name and category of membership. As explained below it also has a flagged field to indicate if the member has been deleted.

CurrentGames.dat file

External file name	CurrentGames.dat		General name Current Games	
Description	Stores details of the current status of each table - if in use details of the game played on it			
Used for	Colouring the tables on the Main form green or red when the form loads Retrieving details of game when processing a finished game			
Organisation	Random access			
Processing	File is created with all records initialised to appropriate values. TableID values correspond to record numbers and are used for direct access			
Record structure				
Field name	Field description		Data type (and length)	No. bytes
TableD	Table number (1 to 20)		Short	2
MemberID	Membership ID (2 letters + 4 numeric digits)		String(6)	6
StartTime	If table has a game, time game started		Date	8
Occupied	Whether table has a game. Stores Y or N		Char	2
Record size	18 bytes			
Typical size of file	File always has 20 records (1 per table) – size is 360 bytes			

FinishedGames.dat file

External file name	FinishedGames.dat		General name Finished Games	
Description	Stores details of all completed games for the current day			
Used for	Producing the printed report on daily table usage			
Organisation	Random access			
Processing	New records appended. No deletions/changes to data required. Linear searching of file to produce printed report on daily table usage.			
Record structure				
Field name	Field description		Data type (and length)	No. bytes
TableID	Table number (1 to 20)		Short	2
StartTime	Time game started		Date	8
FinishTime	Time game finished		Date	8
Cost	Cost of game		Decimal	16
Record size	34 bytes			
Typical size of file	1 record for each completed game. Assuming all tables are used all day (12 hours) and that a game averages 1 hour, 12 x 20 records stored – maximum total size 8160 bytes			

Costs.txt file

External file name	Costs.txt	General name	Costs
Description	Stores the senior and junior rates per minute for a game		
Used for	Calculating cost of a finished game		
Organisation	Text file		
Structure of data	Only 1 line containing the two rates (e.g. 4, 3.5 etc)		
Typical size of file	A few bytes		

Members.dat file

Recall from the Analysis section that the only things Smiley's needs to store about a member is their membership number, name and category of membership. At this point, though, we have to consider how we will add and delete members from the file since this will affect how we design it. Take deleting a member first. Two algorithms you might consider are:

- Copy all the records except the one to delete to a new file, delete the old file and rename the new one with the same name as the old one. This **physically** deletes the record.

- Delete the record in the existing file **logically** by flagging one of its fields to indicate the record has been deleted. The record is still there physically.

If your own project has a file which will grow very large and contain many deletions, the first option might be the best since the file will not use a lot of wasted space storing deleted records. On the other hand how long would it take to carry out a deletion? If you need on-line processing and deletions are very frequent this method might be counterproductive. If you use batch processing you could flag the record for deletion and carry out all the deletions once every so often.

For Smiley's Snooker there's nothing to choose between the two algorithms. Let's use the second one, which means that we need a field to flag whether the record has been deleted. It will hold a single character Y or N.

To add a new record to the Members file we could simply append it (add it after the last record in the file). But let's keep the file as physically small as possible and overwrite the first record that has been flagged as deleted.

External file name	Members.dat	General name	Members
Description	Stores details of all current members		
Used for	Displaying data on Game form when a new game starts or a game finishes. Displaying list of members in Members form. Producing printed list of members		
Organisation	Random access		
Processing	Records are logically deleted. Linear search made to find first logically deleted record when adding a new member – if none found record is appended.		
Record structure			
Field name	**Field description**	**Data type (and length)**	**No. bytes**
MemberID	Membership ID (2 letters + 4 numeric digits)	String (6)	6
Surname	Member's surname	String (15)	15
Firstname	Member's firstname	String (15)	15
Category	Category of membership – S (senior) or J (Junior)	Char	2
Deleted	Has this member been deleted? Stores Y or N	Char	2
Record size	40 bytes		
Typical size of file	1 record for each member. With 400 members = 16,000 bytes		

Data validation

Data input by the user may not be entered correctly. Any check to ensure that it is acceptable is called data validation. At the design stage of your project you are expected to list the validation checks you would like to build into your system. A word of warning here though; at design time you may think of plenty of checks but eventually find that the proportion of your code given over to validation is too high. In some projects to carry out very thorough validation could take up to half your code. By all means do it thoroughly at design time but be prepared not to implement all of it. You could refer to any uncoded validation in the Appraisal section of your project.

Figure 20.10 lists all the validation in Smiley's Snooker that will be coded in the chapters which follow. As we have no Visual Basic names for the controls yet, the identifiers below refer to those shown in the form design sketches earlier.

Control	*Form*	*Validation check*
Membership No, (Adding a member)	Members	• Length 6 characters • Not already used for another member. This means that the MemberID field in the Members.dat file is a primary key field (i.e. a field that cannot contain duplicate values)
Membership No. (Deleting a member)	Members	• Must not be blank
Surname	Members	• Must not be blank
Firstname	Members	• Must not be blank
Membership Category	Members (list box)	• Must be Senior or Junior
Senior (rate per game)	Utilities	• Must be a number
Junior (rate per game)	Utilities	• Must be a number
Membership No. (start a game)	Game	• Must not be blank • Membership number must exist (on Members file). This is a **file lookup check**, and since the membership number will be stored on the Finished Games file, it is also an example of **referential integrity**.
Table No. (start a game)	Game (combo box)	• Must be the number of a table available for play. • A value must be selected from the combo box
Table No. (finish a game)	Game (combo box)	• Must be the number of a table currently in use • A value must be selected from the combo box

Figure 20.10: Summary of validation checks

Entering the membership number of a new member lends itself to further validation. Since membership numbers consist of two characters followed by four digits you could check for this. This is briefly taken up in Chapter 26 which looks at how the project might be improved.

Visual Basic makes validating some data very easy by the use of list or combo boxes. In the three validation checks listed above that involve these controls, the user is forced to select a correct item of data. However you could still check that they have made a selection in the first place.

Chapter 21 – Design and System Maintenance: Modular Structure

Modular structure

The term 'modular structure' refers to the way in which the whole program is broken up into procedures and functions. Compared to a non-visual language, Visual Basic makes things a little easier by having event procedures. You have no choice but to structure your program using these event procedures. However you do have the choice about writing your own general procedures. A full-sized project ought to have general procedures for many reasons. Chapter 9 briefly described some of these.

Deciding on the general procedures you need at the design stage is not easy. You need to carefully work out what you want to happen when an event is triggered. If a particular task must happen that is not directly related to the event itself, then you should probably put it into a general procedure. If it needs particular items of data to do this task pass these as parameters. For example when the receptionist enters a player's membership number to start a new game and then tabs out of this control, the event procedure itself (the Leave event) can check if the user has entered a valid membership number. But checking that the valid membership number actually exists in the Members file can be done by a general procedure since this is a task one step removed from the event.

Event procedures

It's useful first to identify all the event procedures in your program, as shown in Figure 21.1. The asterisked tasks are those that will be assigned to general procedures.

Event	Control	Processing
Main form – buttons		
Click	Close	Closes program
Click	Game	Displays/loads Game form
Click	Membership	Displays/loads Members form
Click	Utilities	Displays/loads Utilities form
Click	Table Usage Report	* Prints report on table usage * Deletes Finished Games file (if user requests this)
Main form – other		
Load	n/a	Colours tables red or green according to whether or not they are in use, and displays starting time of game next to red ones.
Game form – Starting a game		
Load		* Populates combo box (tables available for play)
Checked Changed	Start radio button	Makes input controls for finishing a game invisible. Makes those for starting a game visible Changes text of button to 'Start Game'
Leave	Membership No. text box	* Displays member's name and category of membership
SelectedIndex Changed	Combo box	* Converts starting time of game to hours/minutes only Displays this starting time

Click	Start Game button	* Stores record of game in Current Games file * Changes table's colour to red and displays starting time next to it on the Main form * Populates combo box (with available table numbers)
Game form – Finishing a game		
Checked Changed	Finish radio button	Makes input controls for starting a game invisible. Makes those for finishing a game visible. Changes text of button to 'Finish Game' * Populates combo box (with occupied table numbers)
SelectedIndex Changed	Combo box	* Retrieves record of game from Current Games file * Retrieves player's details from Members file * Calculates playing time in hours and minutes * Calculates cost of game * Converts starting and finishing times of game to hours/minutes Displays start and finish time and cost of completed game
Click	Finish Game button	* Retrieves details of game from Current Games file * Updates record of finished table in Current Games file (sets Occupied field to 'N') * Changes colour of table to green and removes starting time * Stores record of finished game in Finished Games file * Populates combo box (with occupied table numbers)
Members form – Adding a member		
Checked Changed	Add radio button	Makes input control for deleting a member invisible. Makes controls for adding a member visible Changes text of button to 'Add Member'
Click	Add Member button	* Checks that membership number has not been used before * Stores new member's details in Members file
Members form – Deleting a member		
Checked Changed	Delete radio button	Makes input controls for adding a member invisible. Makes control for deleting a member visible Changes text of button to 'Delete Member'
Click	Delete Member button	* Deletes member from Members file
Members form – other buttons		
Click	Display Members	Displays details of all current members in list box
Click	Print Membership List	Prints report on current membership
Utilities form		
Checked Changed	Change Price of Game radio button	Displays controls for entering new senior and junior rates
Click	OK button	* Backs up Current Games and Finished Games files * Backs up Members file * Creates Current Games file * Stores new rates in Costs file

Figure 21.1: The tasks of the event procedures

General procedures

Ideally at design time you should be able to state the following for each general procedure that you intend to write:

- its name
- the type of general procedure – a Sub procedure or a Function procedure
- exactly what it does
- parameters – their data types and whether they are passed by value or by reference
- if a function, its return value
- where it is called from

This is a tall order for inexperienced programmers, and it is very likely that many of these items will be decided as you code. Some students doing the project will not have understood parameter passing and will therefore have to miss this part out. Your program can work perfectly without parameters, but the overhead is more global variables, the likelihood of more errors, and the perception by your assessor that the program is not quite as good as it could be.

One of the main stages of an 'A' level Computing project noted in Chapter 19 was Systems Maintenance. This covers three things – a code listing (with plenty of comments), samples of algorithms, and an overall system design including the modular design. Although the list of features about each procedure noted above should ideally be worked out at design time, realistically you won't draw these up completely until writing up the system maintenance. So the title of this chapter covers takes in two stages of the project. If you change any of the design time decisions when you code, these should be documented as part of the system maintenance.

Let's take some of the event procedures listed in figure 21.1, which call one or more general procedures, and see how to draw up a modular structure.

Game form's Load event, Finish radio button CheckedChanged event and Start/Finish Game button's Click event

Because the controls for starting a game will be visible when the form loads, the Load event should list the free tables in the combo box. When the user clicks the radio button for finishing a game the occupied tables should be listed. Both these tasks are similar and can be done by the same general procedure. No parameters are needed and nothing is returned so it can be a Sub procedure. We will name it **ListTables**.

A useful way of documenting a general procedure is shown in figure 21.2. You should do this for each of the general procedures in your own project. Figure 21.2 shows that ListTables does not need any parameters, but you might be thinking that it needs to know whether a game has just started or finished. It does, and the text of the button on the form, which shows 'Start Game' or 'Finish Game', can be used for this (figures 20.3 and 20.4).

Name	ListTables
Type	Sub Procedure
Parameters/ReturnValue	None
Called from	Load event, Finish radio button CheckedChanged event and Start/Finish Game button's Click event on the Game form.
Purpose	If starting a game, populates the 'start' combo box with table numbers that are free. If finishing a game, populates the 'finish' combo box with table numbers that are occupied.

Figure 21.2: Documenting the general procedure ListTables

Leave event of Membership No. text box

This event is triggered when the user leaves the text box to select a table from the combo box. Figure 21.1 shows that the Leave event of the membership number text box (for starting a game) should display the name and category of membership of the player whose membership number has just been entered. As it is possible that the membership number does not exist, we could consider breaking the task into two sub-tasks, each in its own procedure:

- check to see if the membership number exists
- retrieve the record from the Members file

The second sub-task will only be done if the first sub-task reports that the number does exist. Since the 'parent' Leave event calls these procedures, the question is how the first sub-task reports back that the membership number exists or not. A function is an appropriate type of procedure and a Boolean return value looks promising. But if the number does exist, the next sub-task needs to know which record number in the file to go to. It could search the file for the membership number, but this has already been done by the first sub-task. A good solution is to make the return value of the first sub-task the record number in the file if the membership number is there, and another integer value if the number does not exist. A value of 0 will do (since record numbers begin at 1).

Figure 21.3 uses a **module structure chart** to show the modular structure of this part of the program. An arrow going into a general procedure represents a value parameter and a return arrow represents a reference parameter (for a Sub procedure) or a return value (for a Function procedure).

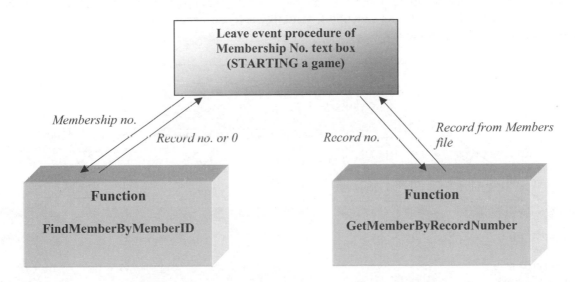

Figure 21.3: Modular structure chart for the Leave event of the membership no. text box (for starting a game)

Selecting from the combo box (starting a game) to display start time

The start time of a game is taken from the system clock and this includes seconds as well as hours and minutes. The receptionist does not need the seconds part displayed so we will have a function, **ShortenTime**, that is sent a time and returns only the hours and minutes part. Figure 21.4 shows its documentation. Note that other events also call it, and that an identifier for the parameter, *FullTime*, has been used to make the description of the purpose easier to write.

Name	ShortenTime
Type	Function
Parameters/ReturnValue	String value parameter (FullTime) – a time Returns String
Called from	Combo box SelectedIndexChanged event (both for starting and finishing a game) Main form's Load event
Purpose	Strips off the seconds part of FullTime and returns the hours and minutes part

Figure 21.4: Documentation of function ShortenTime

Selecting from the combo box for finishing a game

Each of the five asterisked tasks in figure 21.1 for the SelectedIndexChanged event procedure can be put into a general procedure. The last one, to convert the starting and finishing times to hours and minutes only, has already been designed – ShortenTime above.

Each of the general procedures can be written as a function since they all return one item of data. Figure 21.5 shows the details. The first function, to retrieve a particular table's details from the Current Games file, needs to be passed the table number. The second function, to retrieve a particular member's details from the Members file, needs to be passed a membership number. Function **NumberOfMinutes** needs to be passed the start and finish times of a game in order to calculate how many minutes the game took. Finally, to calculate the cost of a game requires the number of minutes it took (which has just been returned from NumberOfMinutes) and the category of membership. You'll see in Chapter 25 that the senior and junior rates, which this function **CalculateCost** also needs, will be global variables, and are therefore not passed as parameters.

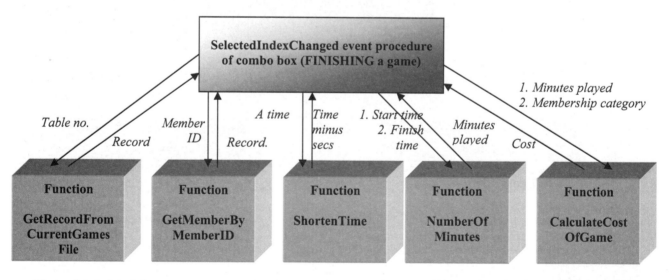

Figure 21.5: Modular structure chart for the SelectedIndexChanged event of combo box for finishing a game

Clicking the Start Game button for a new game

Figure 21.1 lists three tasks that must be done when processing a new game. These are:

- store details of the new game in the Current Games file
- change the table's colour to red and display the starting time
- repopulate the combo box so that the newly-used table is not listed

Figure 21.6 shows the modular structure chart for these tasks. No data needs to be returned to the calling event procedure and so Sub procedures are used. We saw earlier that ListTables does not need to be passed any parameters (figure 21.2) and so the line connecting it to its parent event procedure in figure 21.6 does not have an arrow. Note that **UpdateTableDisplay** in turn needs to call ShortenTime. This is so it can display the start time of the new game on the Main form.

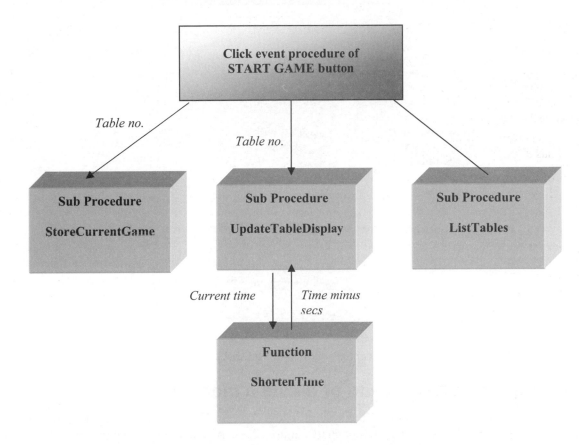

Figure 21.6: Modular structure chart for the Click event of the Start Game button

Clicking the Finish Game button for a finished game

Figure 21.1 lists five tasks that must be done when the user clicks the button to process a finished game:

- retrieve details of the game that has finished from the Current Games file
- update the record of this table in the Current Games file so that its Occupied field stores 'N'
- change the colour of the table to green and remove the starting time
- store details of the finished game in the Finished Games file
- repopulate the combo box with tables that are in use

Figure 21.7 shows the modular structure for these tasks. We have already designed procedures to handle the first and third tasks. Since **ResetGameInCurrentGamesFile** simply overwrites the occupied field with 'N', it only needs the table number. Procedure **StoreGameInFinishedGamesFile** needs the table number and the start time. The start time will have been retrieved in the record returned from **GetRecordFromCurrentGamesFile**.

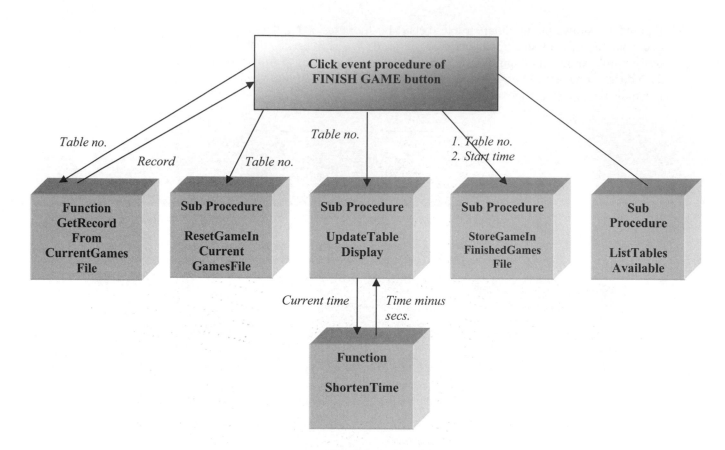

Figure 21.7: Modular structure chart for the Click event of Finish Game button

Clicking the button to add or delete a member

The modular structure for this part of the system is less complex than for processing a game and we can put everything into one modular structure chart (figure 21.8). When adding a member we need to check that the new membership number does not already exist (unlikely but possible). This task is assigned to the function **CheckDuplicateMemberID**. It returns a Boolean value to indicate whether or not the membership number already exists.

Procedure **AddMember** actually writes the new record to the Members file, but recall from Chapter 20 that we decided to find the first logically deleted member (the Deleted field contains 'Y') and overwrite this record with the new one. The task of locating this deleted member is assigned to function **FindDeletedMember**. If there is a deleted one it returns the record number; if there isn't one it returns 0. It is the job of AddMember to handle the 0 if this is returned.

Only one general procedure, **DeleteMember**, is used to process a deleted member. It is passed a membership number and searches the Members file for this number. If it finds the number it logically deletes the member and returns True. If it doesn't find the number the return value is False, and no changes are made to the file. Note that we could have had a separate function to check if the membership number exists in the file and given DeleteMember the single task of deleting the appropriate record. Instead we have packed two closely related tasks into DeleteMember.

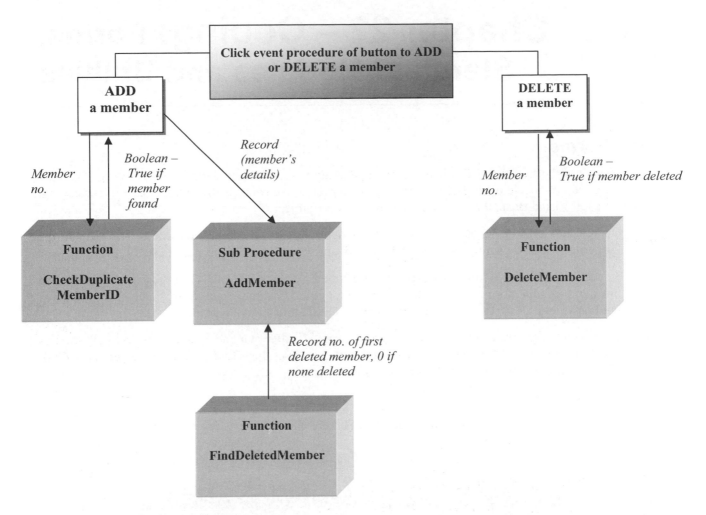

Figure 21.8: Modular structure chart for the Click event of the button to add or delete a member

Complete modular structure

There are several other tasks assigned to general procedures in figure 21.1 that we haven't covered above. These are called from the Click events of buttons on the Main form to print the table usage report or on the Utilities form to carry out the task selected by the user. None of them needs parameters and none return any data, so they must all be Sub procedures.

Final thoughts

It's worth repeating the point that all the details about the modular structure of your project *can* be done at the design stage. It's quite a skill getting everything worked out before you start to code and quite understandable that inexperienced programmers will shuffle between design and coding. Nevertheless it's worth spending some time trying to sort out the modular structure before coding as it will really help you with this later stage of the project.

Chapter 22 – Coding: Forms, Standard Modules and Utilities

The Forms

The designs of the four forms in Chapter 20 can be used directly to build them in Visual Basic. The only things we did not decide on at design time were the names of the controls that will be used in our coding. First let's tell Visual Basic that we want four forms in our project.

1. Open a new project. In the Solution Explorer right-click Form1.vb and rename it **Main.vb**. In the Properties window change its Name to **frmMain** and set its Text property to blank.

2. Select **Project/Add Windows Form**. In the Name box change Form1.vb to **Game.vb**. This is the file name for the form. Click **Open**. In the Properties Window change its Name from Game to **frmGame** and set its Text to **Smiley's Snooker – Start and Finish a game**.

3. Get two more forms. In their Name box name them **Members.vb** and **Utilities.vb**. In the Properties Window name them **frmMembers** and **frmUtilities** and set their Text to **Smiley's Snooker – Club Membership** and **Smiley's Snooker – Utilities**.

The Main form

Figure 22.1 shows the form in use. Tables 5, 6 and 10 have games being played on them. The BorderStyle property of the labels to display the starting times of games in play has been set to Fixed3D simply so that they can be seen in the figure. The default value, None, might be a better choice in the project itself.

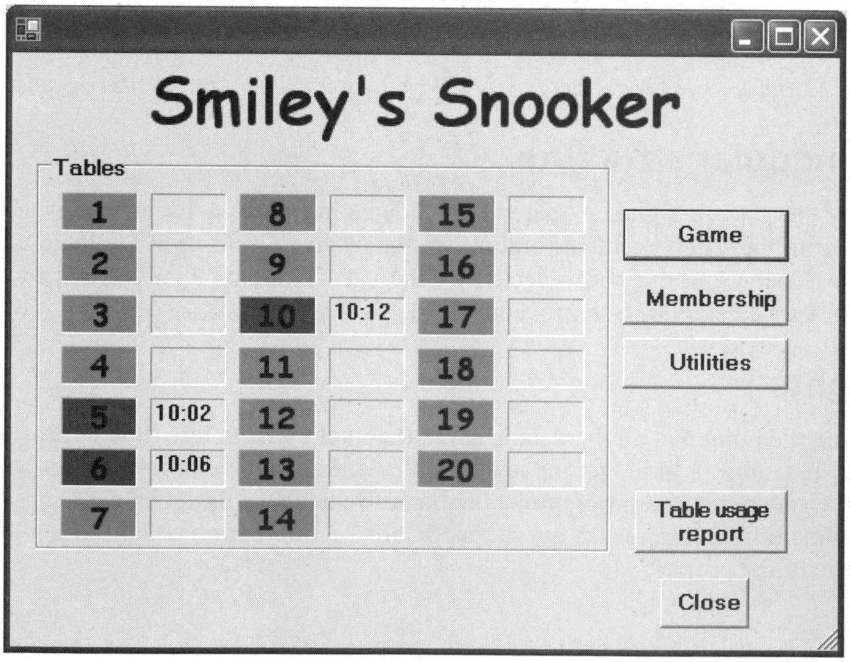

Figure 22.1: The Main form

1. On frmMain place a label for the title and set its Text property to **Smiley's Snooker**. The font in figure 22.1 is **30 pt bold Comic Sans MS**, but use whichever font you feel is appropriate.

2. Place a group box to contain the tables. Set its Text to **Tables**.

3. Place a label in the top left of the group box for table 1. Name it **lblTable1**. Set its Text property to **1** to indicate table number 1.

4. Now add 19 more labels (numbered 2 to 20 in figure 22.1). Name them **lblTable2** to **lblTable20** and set their Text property as **2** to **20** as appropriate.

5. Press the **Shift** key and select all 20 labels. Change their BorderStyle property to **Fixed3D**. Set their BackColor property to **Lime** by clicking the small button in this property, selecting the **Custom** tab and then selecting the third green colour from the top.

6. Set the Font property of these labels to one of your choice. Figure 22.1 uses **14 pt bold Comic Sans MS**. Set the TextAlign property to **MiddleCenter**.

7. Now for the labels to display the starting times of games being played. Place a label to the right of the table 1 label. Name it **lblStartTime1**. Set its Text property to blank. You may wish to set its BorderStyle property to Fixed3D to be able to see exactly where it is on the form. You can change it back to None later. Accept the default Font but set it to **bold**.

8. Place 19 more labels next to the tables. Name these **lblStartTime2** to **lblStartTime20**. Set the BorderStyle as in step 7.

9. Place the 5 buttons shown in figure 22.1 on the form. Set their properties as shown in figure 22.2.

Name	Text
btnGame	Game
btnMembership	Membership
btnUtilities	Utilities
btnPrintReport	Table usage report
btnClose	Close

Figure 22.2: Properties of the buttons on the Main form

10. If you have set the BorderStyle of the lblStartTime1 to lblStartTime20 to Fixed3D Single (steps 7 - 8), change it back to **None**.

11. The code for all the buttons except the Table usage report button is simple. The first three load a form. This technique was covered in step 16 of Program 11.1. That example used the Show method. Here we are using the **ShowDialog** method, which means that the user will not be able to get back to the Main form unless they first close the form they are on.

```
Private Sub btnGame_Click(...) Handles btnGame.Click
    Dim GameForm As New frmGame()          'declare a frmGame object
    GameForm.ShowDialog()                  'display the form
End Sub

Private Sub btnMembership_Click(...) Handles btnMembership.Click
    Dim MembershipForm As New frmMembers()
    MembershipForm.ShowDialog()
End Sub
```

```
Private Sub btnUtilities_Click(...) Handles btnUtilities.Click
  Dim UtilitiesForm As New frmUtilities()
  UtilitiesForm.ShowDialog()
End Sub


Private Sub btnClose_Click(...) Handles btnClose.Click
  Me.Close()                          'Me refers to the current form
End Sub
```

12. Because we have renamed the form we need to tell Visual Basic .NET that it should run this renamed form. (Steps 7 and 8 in Program 11.1 explained why.) In the Solution Explorer right-click the program's name **Smiley's Snooker** and select **Properties**. In the Startup object combo box select **frmMain** and click **OK**. Now run the program. Check that the tables are numbered correctly and are (lime) green in colour. Also check that you can navigate to the other three forms and that the Close button works. You could experiment by using the Show method for one of the forms, instead of ShowDialog, and seeing how it behaves differently.

The Game form

Figures 22.3 and 22.4 show the finished form based on the sketches in figures 20.3 and 20.4. Since several of the controls are duplicated on the two group boxes their names will end with Start or Finish as appropriate. Thus txtMemberIDStart refers to the membership number text box in figure 22.3 and txtMemberIDFinish to the membership number text box in figure 22.4.

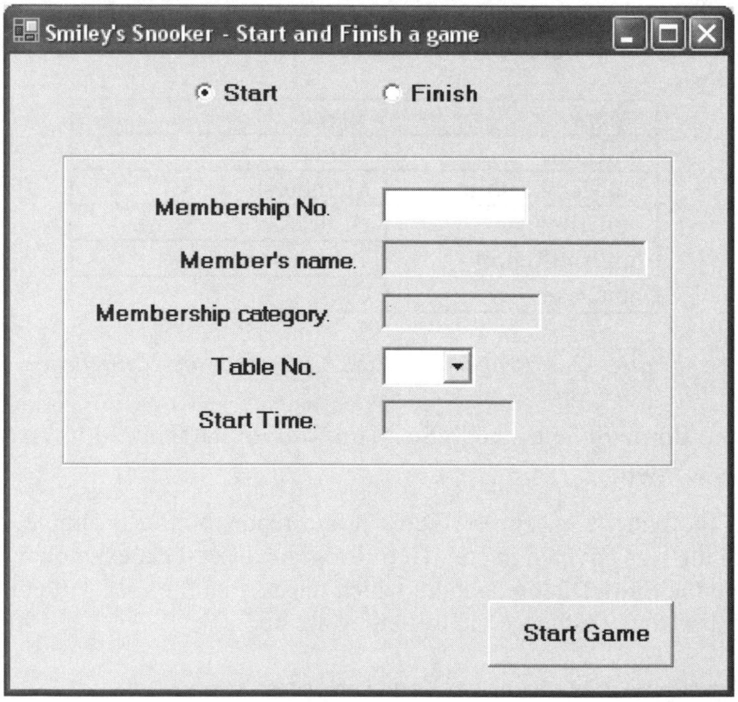

Figure 22.3: frmGame when the Start radio button is selected

1. Place the two radio buttons, name them **radStart** and **radFinish** and set their Text property to **Start** and **Finish**. Set the Checked property of radStart to **True** so that it is selected by default when the form loads.

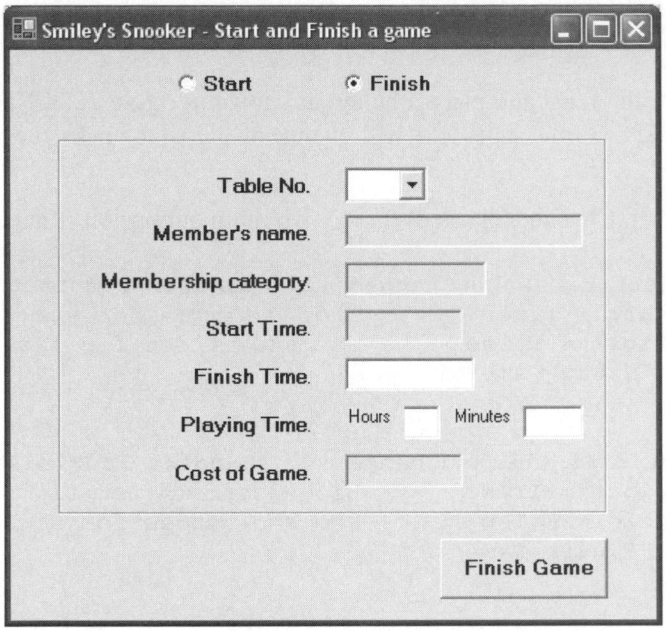

Figure 22.4: frmGame when the Finish radio button is selected

2. Place a group box below the radio buttons. Name it **grpStart** and set its **Text** property to blank.

3. Put the 5 labels shown in figure 22.3 on the group box and set their Text properties

4. Position the 4 text boxes and the combo box shown in figure 22.3. Set their Text property to blank and name them **txtMemberIDStart, txtMemberNameStart, txtCategoryStart, txtStartTimeStart** and **cboTableNumbersStart.**

5. Set the **DropDownStyle** property of the combo box to **DropdownList**. In a true combo box (with the default DropDownStyle of Dropdown) the user can either select an item or enter one that is not listed in the edit box at the top of the control. In our project the user must only select a table from those listed, which the DropdownList type enforces.

6. The text boxes that display the member's name, category of membership and starting time of game should be read-only, so set their Enabled property to **False**.

When the Finish radio button is clicked the controls for finishing a game must replace those for starting a game. We will put them on a group box below the one you have just built and then move this second group box over the first one so that the top left co-ordinates of both group boxes are the same.

7. Position another group box below grpStart. You will need to increase the form's height to fit it in. Name it **grpFinish** and set its Text property to blank.

8. Put the 9 labels shown in figure 22.4 on the group box and set their Text properties.

9. Place the combo box and the 7 text boxes. (4 of these text boxes are disabled in figure 22.4 and resemble labels.) Set their Text properties to blank and name them **cboTableNumbersFinish, txtMemberNameFinish, txtCategoryFinish, txtStartTimeFinish txtFinishTime, txtHours, txtMinutes** and **txtCost.**

10. Set the **DropDownStyle** property of the combo box to **DropdownList** as explained in step 5.

11.   To position grpFinish exactly over grpStart set its Location property values to the same as those of grpStart.

12.   Reduce the height of the form and place a button as shown in figure 22.3. Name it **btnOK** and set its Text property to **Start Game**. This text will change if the user clicks the radio button to finish a game.

13.   Code the default event, CheckedChanged, for the two radio buttons on frmGame as follows:

```
Private Sub radStart_CheckedChanged(...) Handles radStart.CheckedChanged
   grpStart.Visible = True        'Hide controls for starting a game
   grpFinish.Visible = False      'and show those for finishing one
   btnOK.Text = "Start Game"
End Sub

Private Sub radFinish_CheckedChanged(...)Handles radFinish.CheckedChanged
   grpFinish.Visible = True       'Hide controls for finishing a game
   grpStart.Visible = False       'and show those for starting one
   btnOK.Text = "Finish Game"
End Sub
```

14.   Run the program and test that the radio buttons make a different set of controls visible.

The Members form

We designed this form in figures 20.5 and 20.6. Figures 22.5 and 22.6 show the form in use when the Display Members button has been clicked. Making the group box visible and invisible works in the same way as the Start/Finish button on frmGame.

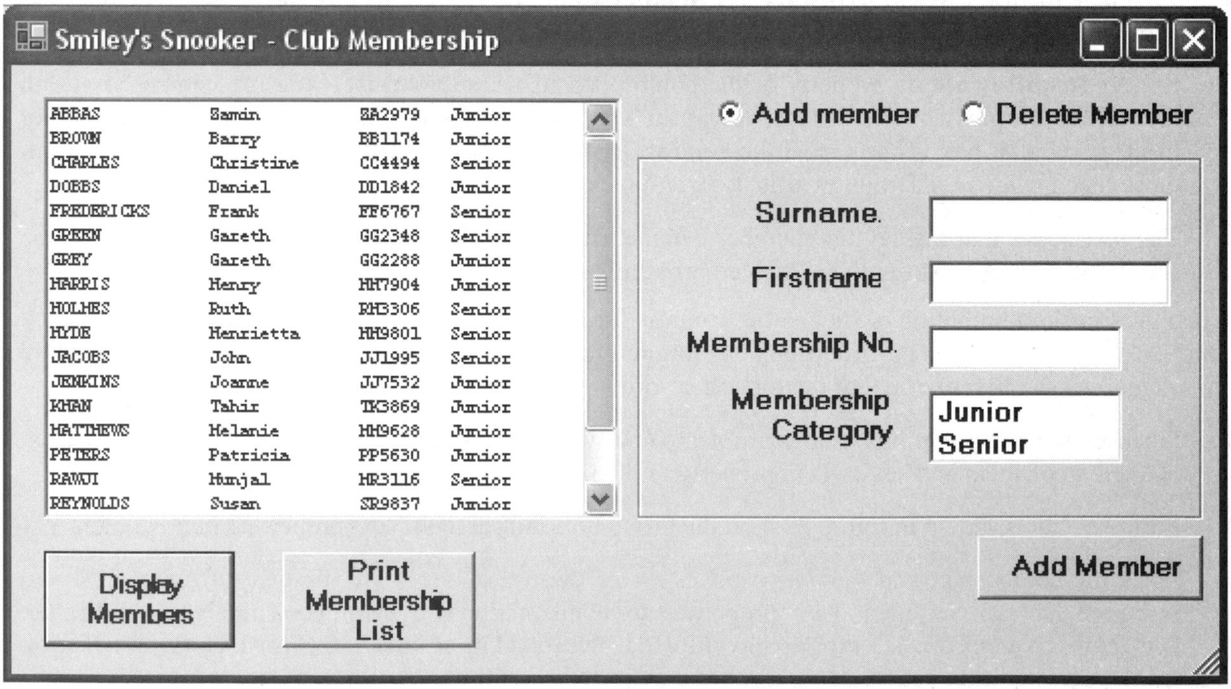

Figure 22.5: frmMembers when the Add Member radio button is selected

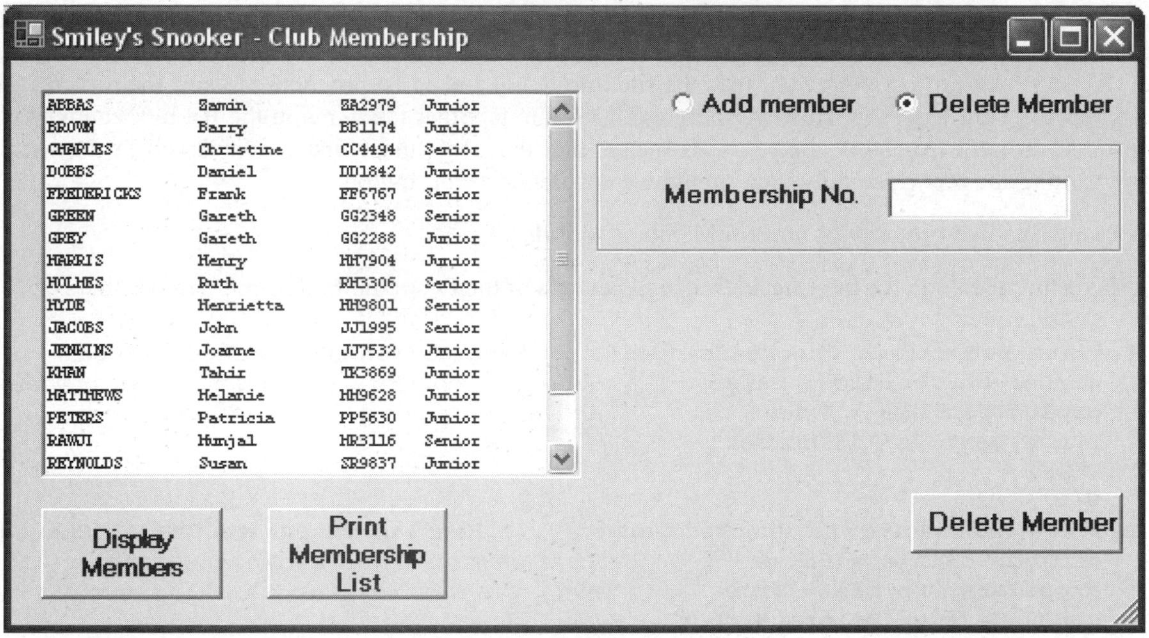

Figure 22.6: frmMembers when the Delete Member radio button is selected

1. On frmMembers place the two radio buttons near the top. Name them **radAdd** and **radDelete** and set their Text property to **Add Member** and **Delete Member**. Set the Checked property of radAdd to **True** since we want this option selected by default when the form loads.

2. Place a group box below the radio buttons. Name it **grpAdd** and set its Text property to blank.

3. Put the 4 labels shown in figure 22.5 onto the group box and set their Text property.

4. Position the 3 text boxes and the list box. Set their Text property to blank and name them **txtSurname**, **txtFirstname**, **txtMemberIDAdd** and **lstCategory**.

5. Add the two items **Junior** and **Senior** to the Items property of the list box.

6. Position another group box below grpAdd. Name it **grpDelete** and set its Text property to blank.

7. Put the label and text box shown in figure 22.6 on the group box. Name the text box **txtMemberIDDelete**.

8. Set the Location property of this group box to the same values as grpAdd. This will position their top edges in the same place.

9. Place a button below the bottom right of grpAdd. Name it **btnOK** and set its Text property to **Add Member**. This text will change if the user selects the radio button to delete a member.

10. Position the large list box on the left and name it **lstMembers**. Since it must display members alphabetically by surname, set its Sorted property to **True**.

11. Since we want the member details displayed in columns we need an even-spaced font. Change the Font property of the list box to **Courier New**.

12. Place two buttons below the list box. Name them **btnDisplayMembers** and **btnPrintMembers** and set their Text property to **Display Members** and **Print Membership List**.

We need to disable the button to print the report because of the method we'll use later to print the membership list. The report must list members by surname but the records in the file will not be in this order. In your own project you *could* read the file into RAM and call a procedure to sort the records. This would impress your assessor! However here we'll use the fact that the items in the list box can be sorted and printed directly from this control. This means that the items must first be displayed in the list box before printing the report, so only then should we enable the report button.

13.   Set the Enabled property of btnPrintMembers to **False**.

14.   Make sure the code for the CheckedChanged events of the two radio buttons on frmMembers is:

```
Private Sub radAdd_CheckedChanged(...) Handles radAdd.CheckedChanged
   grpDelete.Visible = False      'Hide the control for deleting a member
   grpAdd.Visible = True          'and show controls for adding one
   btnOK.Text = "Add Member"
End Sub


Private Sub radDelete_CheckedChanged(...) Handles radDelete.CheckedChanged
   grpAdd.Visible = False         'Hide controls for adding new member
   grpDelete.Visible = True       'and show control for deleting one
   btnOK.Text = "Delete Member"
End Sub
```

15.   Run the program and test that the radio buttons make a different set of controls visible.

The Utilities form

This is based on the sketch in figure 20.7 and is shown in figure 22.7. When the option to change the price of a game is selected the Senior and Junior controls and the short help instruction are made visible.

1.   On frmUtilities place the large group box. Leave its default name but set its Text property to blank.

2.   Put the 4 radio buttons on the group box and set their Text properties. From top to bottom name them **radBackup1**, **radBackup2**, **radCreateFile** and **radChangeCost**.

3.   Place the smaller group box within the larger one, below the last radio button. Name it **grpCosts**. Set its Text property to blank and its Visible property to **False**.

4.   Place labels and text boxes for the two rates on grpCosts as shown in figure 22.7. Name the text boxes **txtSeniorRate** and **txtJuniorRate**. Place a label to the right of the group box. Name it **lblHelp** and set its Text property as the instruction to the user shown in figure 22.7.

5.   When the user clicks the 4th radio button the controls for the new costs should be made visible. If the user then clicks another radio button they should be removed. The code in the CheckedChanged event for radChangeCost to do this is:

```
Private Sub radChangeCost_CheckedChanged(...) Handles _
                                    radChangeCost.CheckedChanged
   grpCosts.Visible = Not grpCosts.Visible
End Sub
```

6.   Place a button below the larger group box. Name it **btnOK** and set its Text property to **OK**.

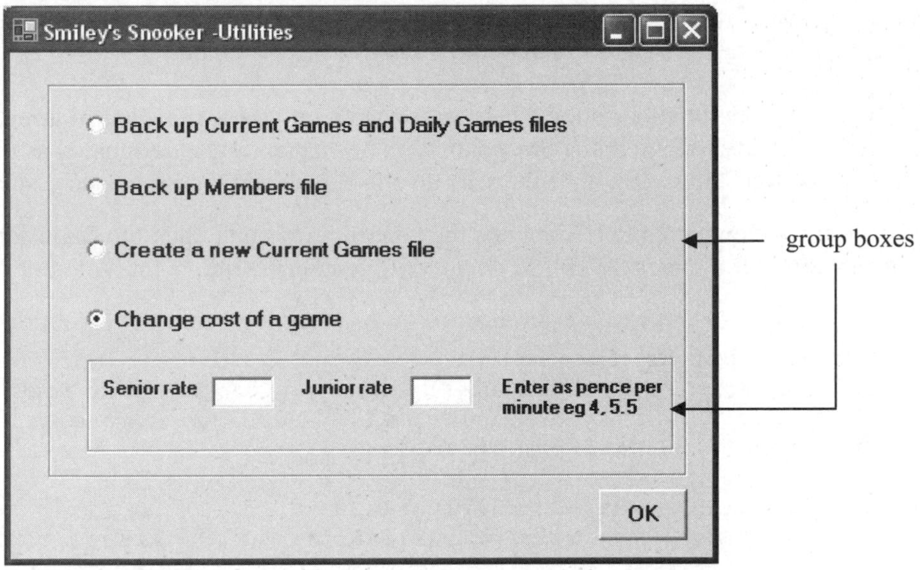

Figure 22.7: frmUtilities when the radio button to change the cost of a game is selected

7. Run the program and test that clicking the last radio button on frmUtilities displays the cost controls. Then click any of the other radio buttons to remove them.

Standard modules

Recall that a standard module cannot contain any controls, only code. For Smiley's Snooker we will use standard modules to cover the following:

- Create two control arrays, one each for the 20 labels on the Main form to indicate the tables and the 20 labels to display the start times of the games. You named these lblTable1 to lblTable20 and lblStartTime1 to lblStartTime20.

- Declare a constant to hold the number of tables (20). This will be used in several loops to process all the tables.

- Declare user-defined data types for processing records in the Current Games, Finished Games and Members files. These will be used by all the forms.

- To calculate the cost of a game you need to multiply the number of minutes the game lasts by the cost per minute. We decided on function NumberOfMinutes in Chapter 21 (see figure 21.5). It is passed two time values and returns the number of minutes difference between them.

- When displaying the start and finish times the receptionist would be put off by having the seconds shown. We decided on function ShortenTime in Chapter 21 (figures 21.4 to 21.6). It is passed a time value and returns the hours and minutes part.

The two functions referred to above are used only on the Game form and so *could* be written there. But in your own project it is a good idea to put functions like these, which might be used in other programs dealing with time, into a standard module.

Declarations and control arrays

1. Select **Project/Add New Item**. Select the **Module** icon and name it **modDeclarations.vb**.

2. Declare the two control arrays after Module modDeclarations in the module's Code window:

```
Public lblTables(19), lblStartTimes(19) As Label
```

We will put the code to allocate the labels on frmMain into these two control arrays into a Sub procedure called Main. You may recall that a procedure with this name can be designated as the start up object when a program first runs. Since it will be the start up object it should therefore also display frmMain.

3. Write the following code to populate the control arrays and open the Main form. In each of the two places where the code says *and so on up to....* you must write 17 lines of code.

```
Sub Main()
  Dim MainForm As New frmMain()           'declare a frmMain object
  Dim GameForm As New frmGame()           'declare a frmGame object
  lblTables(0) = MainForm.lblTable1     'populate control array of tables
  lblTables(1) = MainForm.lblTable2
  ............     'and so on up to
  lblTables(19) = MainForm.lblTable20
  lblStartTimes(0) = MainForm.lblStartTime1   'Populate control array of
                                              'start times
  lblStartTimes(1) = MainForm.lblStartTime2
  ............     'and so on up to
  lblStartTimes(19) = MainForm.lblStartTime20
  MainForm.ShowDialog()                   'display Main form
End Sub
```

4. Declare a constant to store the number of tables and then the three user-defined types for storing records. Recall from Chapter 12 that when writing a record to a random access file you must declare the length of any String fields. Use **<VBFixedString>** for this.

```
Public Const MaxTables = 20          'Smiley's has 20 tables

Structure GameType      'data type for a record to store one current game
  <VBFixedString(6)> Public MemberID As String    '6 bytes
  Dim TableID As Short                '2 bytes
  Dim StartTime As Date               '8 bytes
  Dim Occupied As Char                '2 bytes
End Structure                         'one record is 18 bytes

Structure GameFinishedType   'data type for record for a finished game
  Dim TableID As Short                '2 bytes
  Dim StartTime As Date               '8 bytes
  Dim FinishTime As Date              '8 bytes
  Dim Cost As Decimal                 '16 bytes
End Structure                         'one record is 34 bytes

Structure MemberType          'data type for a record to store one member
  <VBFixedString(6)> Public MemberID As String       '6 bytes
  <VBFixedString(15)> Public Surname As String       '15 bytes
  <VBFixedString(15)> Public Firstname As String     '15 bytes
  Dim Category As Char                '2 bytes
  Dim Deleted As Char                 '2 bytes
End Structure                         'one record is 40 bytes
```

5. To check that Sub Main is the first thing that runs when the program starts, make it the startup object. Look back at step 12 in *The Main Form* section of this chapter to see how to do this. When the program runs the Main form will load from Sub Main.

Library of time functions

6. Add a second module to the project. Name it **modTimeFunctions**.

7. Write code for the function to calculate the number of minutes between two time values. It uses the two built-in time functions Hour and Minute. Chapter 8 has a similar example to this.

```
Public Function NumberOfMinutes(ByVal Time1 As Date, ByVal Time2 As _
                                              Date) As Integer
'Returns the number of minutes difference between Time1 and Time2
'Time1 must be a later time than Time2
   Dim HoursDiff As Integer
   Dim MinutesDiff As Integer
   HoursDiff = Time1.Hour - Time2.Hour
   MinutesDiff = Time1.Minute - Time2.Minute
   Return (HoursDiff * 60) + MinutesDiff
End Function
```

8. A quick way to check that this works is to write the following at the end of Sub Main in module modDeclarations. Then run the program, click the Close button on the Main form and the message should display 130 (i.e. the number of minutes difference between the two times).

```
MsgBox(NumberOfMinutes("12:30:30", "10:20:55"))
```

9. The code for the function to display a time minus the seconds uses the Substring method which was covered in Chapter 8.

```
Public Function ShortenTime(ByVal FullTime As String) As String
'Removes the seconds from a time value and returns the hours and minutes
'FullTime is a string in the format 19:42:54 or 19.42.54
   Return FullTime.Substring(0, 5)
End Function
```

10. Check this works by replacing the line of code in step 8 with the one below which should display 12.34. Remove this message box line of code when you have checked that ShortenTime works.

```
MsgBox(ShortenTime("12:34:56"))
```

Utilities

Figures 20.7 and 22.7 show the four utilities we need to code. The user selects one of the radio buttons and then clicks **OK**. Figure 21.1 suggested that each of these utilities would be coded in a separate procedure. Each of them is called from the Click event of the OK button.

1. On the Utilities form the Click event for btnOK finds out which radio button has been selected and then calls the relevant procedure. The procedures will be coded in steps 2 – 4.

```
Private Sub btnOK_Click(...) Handles btnOK.Click
'Finds out which option has been selected and calls relevant procedure
  If radBackup1.Checked = True Then
    Call BackupGamesFiles()
  ElseIf radBackup2.Checked = True Then
    Call BackupMembersFile()
  ElseIf radCreateFile.Checked = True Then
    Call CreateCurrentGamesFile()
  ElseIf radChangeCost.Checked = True Then
    Call ChangeCostOfGame()
  End If
End Sub
```

2. The code for the **BackupGamesFiles** Sub procedure uses the **FileCopy** statement to copy the two games files to the root directory of a floppy disk. It assumes the files to be copied are in the bin folder of the project.

```
Public Sub BackupGamesFiles()
  Dim Source1, Source2, Destination1, Destination2 As String
  Source1 = "CurrentGames.dat"          'file must be in bin folder
  Destination1 = "a:\CurrentGames.dat"
  FileCopy(Source1, Destination1)
  Source2 = "FinishedGames.dat"            'file must be in bin folder
  Destination2 = "a:\FinishedGames.dat"
  FileCopy(Source2, Destination2)
End Sub
```

3. The procedure to make a backup of the Members file is the same as the previous one:

```
Public Sub BackupMembersFile()
  Dim Source, Destination As String
  Source = "Members.dat"                  'file must be in bin folder
  Destination = "a:\Members.dat"
  FileCopy(Source, Destination)
End Sub
```

4. To create the Current Games file requires a For…Next loop. Each repetition writes one record to the file with details of one table:

```
Public Sub CreateCurrentGamesFile()
'Creates Current Games file with one record for each table
  Dim OneGame As GameType
  Dim TableNumber As Short
  FileOpen(1, "CurrentGames.dat", OpenMode.Random, , , Len(OneGame))
  For TableNumber = 1 To MaxTables       'loop 20 times, once for each table
    OneGame.MemberID = ""                'set member ID to blank
    OneGame.TableID = TableNumber        'assign a number from 1 to 20
    OneGame.Occupied = "N"               'set to not occupied
    FilePut(1, OneGame, TableNumber)     'write record to file
  Next TableNumber
  FileClose(1)
End Sub
```

5. To change the cost of a game simply requires writing the two new values to the **Costs.txt** file. Recall that this is a text file consisting of one line only – the senior and junior rates in pence per minute.

```
Public Sub ChangeCostOfGame()
'Stores new senior and junior rates in Costs file
  Dim JuniorCost, SeniorCost As String
  SeniorCost = txtSeniorRate.Text       'get the two new rates from user
  JuniorCost = txtJuniorRate.Text
  If (Not IsNumeric(SeniorCost)) Or (Not IsNumeric(JuniorCost)) Then
    MsgBox("One or both of the rates are not numbers. Please re-enter")
  Else
    FileOpen(1, "Costs.txt", OpenMode.Output)
    Print(1, SeniorCost, JuniorCost)  'write new rates to the file
    FileClose(1)
  End If
End Sub
```

One of the data validation checks we decided on at design time was that valid numbers are entered for the new costs (see figure 20.10). In the code above, the **IsNumeric** function returns True if its parameter forms a valid number. The expression **Not IsNumeric** therefore means *does not form a valid number*.

6. The Utilities are now ready for trying out. To test the two backup options you need any three files with the names (and extensions) used in the code above in the bin folder of Smileys Snooker, and a floppy disk. To check that the Current Games file has been created go to Windows and look for **CurrentGames.dat**. It should be 360 bytes in size (20 records x 18 bytes per record). To check that the costs of a game have been stored, look for **Costs.txt** in the bin folder and open it in Notepad or WordPad. When you run the code for changing the costs Visual Basic will create the file if it doesn't exist.

Chapter 23 – Coding: Membership

Adding a new member

The sequence of events when the user clicks the button on the Members form to add a new member is:

- A validation check is made that the membership number has 6 characters.
- A check is made that the membership number has not already been used by calling function CheckDuplicateMember.
- A check is made that the user has entered data in the surname, firstname and category controls.
- If the above three checks are satisfied the procedure AddMember is called.
- Procedure AddMember calls the function FindDeletedMember to get the record number of the first logically deleted record in the Members file.
- AddMember stores the record in the first logically deleted record space if there is one, otherwise it appends the record to the file.

First let's write the code for the general procedures. Look back at figure 21.8 to remind yourself of the modular structure for adding a member. We decided on three general procedures.

Function CheckDuplicateMemberID

1. This function needs to be passed one parameter – the membership number to search for in the file. As this is not changed inside the function it can be passed by value.

```
Private Function CheckDuplicateMemberID(ByVal MemberID As String) As _
                                                    Boolean
'Returns True if MemberID has already been used as a membership number,
'otherwise returns False
   Dim Found As Boolean
   Dim OneMember As MemberType                       'one record
   Found = False
   FileOpen(1, "Members.dat", OpenMode.Random, , , Len(OneMember))
   Do While (Not EOF(1)) And (Found = False) 'Keep looping until a
     'a duplicate ID has been found or the end of file reached
     FileGet(1, OneMember)          '3rd parameter, record number, not needed
     If (MemberID = OneMember.MemberID) AND (OneMember.Deleted = "N") Then
                                          'member ID used before?
       Found = True
     End If
   Loop
   FileClose(1)
   Return Found                       'return True or False from function
End Function
```

Function FindDeletedMember

2. This function does not need any parameters. Recall that Visual Basic .NET numbers the records in a random access file from 1. The function returns the number of the first record with a 'Y' in its Deleted field., or returns 0 if it can't find a deleted record. Type in the following code:

```
Private Function FindDeletedMember() As Integer
```

```
'Finds the first record in Members file that is logically deleted
'A logically deleted record has the Deleted field set to Y
'Returns the record number of the first deleted record, or returns 0 if
'there are none
  Dim Found As Boolean
  Dim RecordNumber As Short
  Dim OneMember As MemberType
  Found = False
  FileOpen(1, "Members.dat", OpenMode.Random, , , Len(OneMember))
  Do While (Not EOF(1)) And (Found = False)
    RecordNumber = RecordNumber + 1   'identify current record number
    FileGet(1, OneMember)             'read record from file
    If OneMember.Deleted = "Y" Then   'is record logically deleted?
      Found = True
    End If
  Loop
  FileClose(1)
  If Found Then             'There IS a deleted record so
    Return RecordNumber     'return its number
  Else
    Return 0                'return 0 if no deleted record in file
  End If
End Function
```

Sub Procedure AddMember

3. This procedure is passed a record to add to the Members file. It first calls FindDeletedMember to see if there is an existing record it can use. If there is it uses the record number returned from FindDeletedMember to write the new record to this space. If there is no deleted record, because FindDeletedMember returned a 0, it appends the new record. The code is:

```
Private Sub AddMember(ByRef OneMember As MemberType)
'Stores record in Members file. Calls FindDeletedMember function to get
'first logically deleted record in the file and uses this space for the
'new record.If no such record it appends new record
  Dim NumberOfRecords, DeletedRecordNumber As Short
  Dim sender As System.Object  'sender and e must be sent as parameters
  Dim e As System.EventArgs    'to btnDisplayMembers_Click
  DeletedRecordNumber = FindDeletedMember()
  FileOpen(1, "Members.dat", OpenMode.Random, , , Len(OneMember))
  If DeletedRecordNumber <> 0 Then  'There IS a deleted record to use so
    FilePut(1, OneMember, DeletedRecordNumber)'store record in this space
  Else                              'No deleted records so calculate no. of
    NumberOfRecords = LOF(1) / Len(OneMember)    'records in file and
    FilePut(1, OneMember, NumberOfRecords + 1)   'append new record
  End If
  FileClose(1)
  Call btnDisplayMembers_Click(sender, e)  'so new member is in list box
End Sub
```

The LOF (**L**ength **O**f **F**ile) function was covered in step 4 of program 12.3. The last line of code is an example of calling an *event* procedure from code. You haven't written the Click event for btnDisplayMember yet but its task will be to display all the members' details in the list box. Calling it here will have the effect of adding the new member to the list box. Button Click events expect two parameters (which in most programs in this book have been replaced with **. . .**). These are declared in the code above.

Deleting a member

This is more straightforward than adding a member. Only one procedure is needed, DeleteMember.

Function DeleteMember

1. This function must be passed a membership number. It searches the file for the record with this membership number, and if it is found checks whether this member has already been logically deleted. (This is unlikely but possible - the receptionist would have accidentally just entered the membership number of a member who has left the club, but their record space in the file has not yet been used for a new member.)   As with procedure AddMember above, a call is made to btnOK_Click, but this time in order to remove the member. The call has to be done before using the Return keyword because the function finishes when it returns a value using Return.

```
Private Function DeleteMember(ByVal MemberID As String) As Boolean
'Logically deletes record with membership no. MemberID from Members
'file by setting its Deleted field to Y. Returns True if deletion
'is successful, otherwise returns False
  Dim OneMember As MemberType
  Dim RecordNumber As Short
  Dim Found As Boolean
  Dim sender As System.Object
  Dim e As System.EventArgs
  RecordNumber = 0
  Found = False
  FileOpen(1, "Members.dat", OpenMode.Random, , , Len(OneMember))
  Do While (Not EOF(1)) And (Not Found)
    RecordNumber = RecordNumber + 1
    FileGet(1, OneMember)                      'read one record from file
    If OneMember.MemberID = MemberID Then      'is this the required record?
      If OneMember.Deleted = "Y" Then          'has this member been deleted?
        MsgBox("This member does not exist")
      Else
        OneMember.Deleted = "Y"
        Found = True
      End If
    End If
  Loop
  FilePut(1, OneMember, RecordNumber)          'write record to file
  FileClose(1)
  Call btnDisplayMembers_Click(sender, e)      'remove member from list box
  If Not Found Then                            'no record in file to delete
    Return False
  Else                                         'a record HAS been deleted
    Return True
  End If
End Function
```

Calling the adding and deleting procedures

Now that the general procedures are in place we need to write code for the Click event of btnOK, the button that actually fires everything off. First, though, we need to decide which radio button the user has selected, Add or Delete. One way of doing this is to look at the current text of btnOK. When we built the Members form in the last chapter, in step 14 we set the text to *Add Member* or *Delete Member* according to which radio button was selected.

1. The code for the Click event of btnOK is quite long, so take it slowly and read the comments carefully. The If statement is nested to four levels, largely to validate and check that a membership number entered for a new member is not in current use. When you type in the code below don't split the MsgBox parts over two lines as you are liable to make errors. (They are split here to fit on the page.) The only new things in the code below are to do with the MsgBox function. The example which asks the user to confirm a deletion includes the parameter **vbYesNo**. The *Take it from here...* section in Chapter 4 invited you to investigate the parameters you can pass MsgBox. The parameter vbYesNo means that Yes and No buttons will be placed in the message box. The function returns the value 6 if the user clicks Yes (and 7 for No).

```
Private Sub btnOK_Click(...) Handles btnOK.Click
'Processes either adding or deleting a member
  Dim MemberID As String
  Dim MemberDeleted As Boolean       'return value from DeleteMember
  Dim Duplicate As Boolean  'True if membership number already in use
  Dim Response As Short  'reply when asked to confirm impending deletion
  Dim OneMember As MemberType
  If btnOK.Text = "Add Member" Then                    'add a member
    If txtMemberIDAdd.Text.Length = 6 Then   'a 6-character ID entered
      MemberID = txtMemberIDAdd.Text
      Duplicate = CheckDuplicateMemberID(MemberID)    'Is membership
                                       'number already in use?
    If Not Duplicate Then     'membership number is not in use
      'member's details have been entered on form so use them
      If (txtSurname.Text <> "") And (txtFirstname.Text <> "") And _
            (lstCategory.Text <> "") Then
        OneMember.MemberID = txtMemberIDAdd.Text        'Collect details
                                               'into one record

        OneMember.Surname = txtSurname.Text
        OneMember.Firstname = txtFirstname.Text
        If lstCategory.Text = "Senior" Then
          OneMember.Category = "S"
        Else
          OneMember.Category = "J"
        End If
        OneMember.Deleted = "N"
        Call AddMember(OneMember)        'add new member to file
        txtMemberIDAdd.Text = ""         'clear member details on form
        txtSurname.Text = ""
        txtFirstname.Text = ""
      Else
        MsgBox("You have not filled in all details of the member")
      End If
    Else                    'user has entered a duplicate membership number
      MsgBox("Membership No. " & MemberID & _
                            " has been used. Enter a different one")
      txtMemberIDAdd.Focus()
    End If
  Else                        'not enough characters typed in for membership no.
    MsgBox("You must enter a membership number with 6 characters")
    txtMemberIDAdd.Focus()
  End If
```

```
    Else 'Else part of (If btnOK.Text = "Add Member") ie delete a member
      MemberID = txtMemberIDDelete.Text
      If MemberID = "" Then     'user has not entered a membership number
        MsgBox("You haven't entered a membership number")
      Else
        Response = MsgBox("Confirm you want to delete this member?", _
                                         vbYesNo)
        If Response = 6 Then           'user DOES wish to delete
          MemberDeleted = DeleteMember(MemberID) 'True if deletion a success
          txtMemberIDDelete.Text = ""
          If Not MemberDeleted Then            'deletion not successful
            MsgBox("Member not deleted. Membership number " _
                                       & MemberID & "does not exist")
          End If
        End If
      End If     'end of (If MemberID = "")
    End If   'end of (If btnOK.Text = "Add Member")
End Sub
```

2. Run the program and try adding and deleting members. You will need to comment out the line in each of the AddMember and DeleteMember functions which calls the Click event of btnDisplayMembers because you haven't written this procedure yet. You can only check that members have been added by noting that Members.dat has been created, and that for every record you add it should grow in size by 40 bytes. Since deleting a member does not physically delete a record the file size won't change. You'll have to wait for the next section to prove to yourself that this part works.

Displaying members in the list box

Figures 22.5 and 22.6 show how members' details are displayed in the list box. Clicking the Display Members button will loop through all the records in the Members file. If the record is not logically deleted, because the Deleted field stores 'N', the surname and first name are concatenated. The surname is changed into upper case by using the ToUpper method. Chapter 4 showed you how to define a format to use for displaying data in columns in a list box. But we do not need to do this here, because all the fields in one record in the Members file that are directly displayed in the list box are fixed length strings.

1. Copy the code below for the Click event of btnDisplayMembers.

```
Private Sub btnDisplayMembers_Click(...) Handles btnDisplayMembers.Click
'Displays full name, membership no, and category of membership
'of all members in list box
  Dim FullName, Category, MemberID As String
  Dim OneMember As MemberType
  lstMembers.Items.Clear()
  FileOpen(1, "Members.dat", OpenMode.Random, , , Len(OneMember))
  Do While Not EOF(1)
    FileGet(1, OneMember)        'read one record from Members file
    If OneMember.Deleted = "N" Then   'member has not been deleted
      FullName = OneMember.Surname.ToUpper & " " & OneMember.Firstname
      MemberID = OneMember.MemberID
      If OneMember.Category = "S" Then      'S or J stored on file - change
                                            'to Senior or Junior
        Category = "Senior"
      Else
        Category = "Junior"
```

```
        End If
        lstMembers.Items.Add(FullName & MemberID & "    " & Category)
      End If
  Loop
  FileClose(1)
  btnPrintMembers.Enabled = True    'Can print report only after list
          'box displays members' details since report takes details from
          'list box rather than the file
End Sub
```

2. Remove the commenting out of the calls to btnDisplayMembers_Click you added in the previous step 2 and run the program. Check that the list box displays only those members who have not been deleted. Because the Sorted property is True you can't visually see that a new member physically occupies the space of the first deleted one in the file. Experiment by changing the property to False, delete the first member and then add a member. It should be the first one displayed in the list box.

Printing the membership report

Clicking the Print Members button prints the report on the current members. We designed this in figure 20.9. A print preview of the last page of the report can be seen in figure 23.1. Since the members are listed alphabetically by surname we can simply use the contents of the list box, although this means that the width used for one member's details on the report is determined by the spacing used in this control. If you took the details from the Members file instead you would have more control over the spacing of the output. However the members would not be sorted. (In your own project always take every opportunity to demonstrate the use of advanced techniques, and here is a good one. You *could* copy the Members file into an array of records and write code to sort it on the surname field. Then print from this sorted array.)

1. Place a PrintDocument control on the form. It will locate itself in the pane below the form.

2. In the Click event of btnPrintMembers call the Print method of this control:

```
    PrintDocument1.Print()
```

3. Double-click the PrintDocument control to bring up its default PrintPage event template. The code counts the number of lines printed on the current page. If this reaches the number of lines that can fit on the page it asks for another page by setting e.HasMorePages to True. The object e is one of the parameters sent to PrintPage when it is called (but replaced below by **...** in the procedure declaration). When a new page is printed we must remember where the last member on the previous page is located in the list box, so that printing can start from the next one. *MembersPrinted* holds this index value. It is a Static variable because it must retain its value between calls to PrintPage. There are two calls to procedure PrintBlankLine which you will code in step 4.

```
Private Sub PrintDocument1_PrintPage(...)Handles PrintDocument1.PrintPage
'Prints a list of all current members and totals of senior and junior
'members. 'Data is taken from the list box showing members' details
    Static NumberSeniors, NumberJuniors As Short    'Running totals
    Static MembersPrinted As Short  'running total of no.of members printed
    Dim LinesPrinted As Short 'total no. of lines printed on current page
    Dim LinesRequired As Short   'no. of lines that can fit on one page
    Dim FontHeight As Short      'height of 1 line of font used
    Dim Category, OneMemberDetails As String
    Dim MyFont As New Font("Courier New", 11, FontStyle.Bold)
    Dim MyTitleFont As New Font("Courier New", 13, FontStyle.Bold Or _
```

```
                                                    FontStyle.Underline)
    Dim X, Y As Short                'co-ordinates for printing
    Dim FooterPrinted As Boolean 'True when footer (2 totals) are printed
    FontHeight = MyFont.GetHeight(e.Graphics)
    LinesRequired = e.MarginBounds.Height / FontHeight
    X = 50                    'print title from near top left corner of page
    Y = 50
    e.Graphics.DrawString("Smiley's Snooker. List of current members on " _
         & Format(Today, "Long Date"), MyTitleFont, Brushes.Black, X, Y)
    Call PrintBlankLine(X, Y, FontHeight, MyFont, e)
    LinesPrinted = 2          '2 lines needed for title and blank line
    Do While (LinesPrinted < LinesRequired) And (MembersPrinted <= _
                            lstMembers.Items.Count - 1)
      OneMemberDetails = lstMembers.Items(MembersPrinted)
      e.Graphics.DrawString(OneMemberDetails, MyFont, Brushes.Black, X, Y)
      LinesPrinted = LinesPrinted + 1
      MembersPrinted = MembersPrinted + 1
      If OneMemberDetails.IndexOf("Senior") <> -1 Then 'IndexOf returns -1
                                      'if search string is not present
        NumberSeniors = NumberSeniors + 1
      Else
        NumberJuniors = NumberJuniors + 1
      End If
      Y = Y + FontHeight
    Loop
    If MembersPrinted = lstMembers.Items.Count Then    'all members printed?
      Call PrintBlankLine(X, Y, FontHeight, MyFont, e)
      e.Graphics.DrawString("Number of Juniors: " & NumberJuniors, _
                            MyFont, Brushes.Black, X, Y)
      Y = Y + FontHeight
      e.Graphics.DrawString("Number of Seniors: " & NumberSeniors, _
                            MyFont, Brushes.Black, X, Y)
      FooterPrinted = True
    End If      'stop printing if no more lines left to print
    If (LinesPrinted < LinesRequired) Or (FooterPrinted) Then      'Stop
      'printing if no more lines left or totals have been printed
      e.HasMorePages = False
      MembersPrinted = 0        'Must reset these to 0 in case user clicks
      NumberSeniors = 0         'print button a 2nd or subsequent time
      NumberJuniors = 0
    Else          'another page needed if there is still data to print
      e.HasMorePages = True
    End If
End Sub
```

4. As we will use Sub procedure PrintBlankLine for the other report in this project, write it in module modDeclarations. It will print a blank line for any given font. Note that the Y coordinate parameter is ByRef since its new value must be passed back to the calling program.

```
Public Sub PrintBlankLine(ByVal XCoord As Short, ByRef YCoord As _
      Short, ByVal OneLineHeight As Short, ByVal FontToUse As Font, _
      ByVal e As System.Drawing.Printing.PrintPageEventArgs)
   YCoord = YCoord + OneLineHeight
   e.Graphics.DrawString("", FontToUse, Brushes.Black, XCoord, YCoord)
   YCoord = YCoord + OneLineHeight
End Sub
```

5. To check that the printing works you may wish to use a PrintPreviewDialog control to preview it rather than actually print the report. (See steps 2 and 8 in Program 14.1 on how to do this.) However, unless you have 50 or so members in the file you will not be able to check that the multi-page part of the code works. To check this set the number of lines that can fit onto one page to a small enough number so that more than one page will be needed. For example the file used to produce figure 23.1 has 20 members and *LinesRequired* is set to 12. This prints 10 members per page since *LinesPrinted* is set to 2 after printing the title, leaving $12 - 2 = 10$ lines of member details per page. So you would write

```
LinesRequired = 10
```

rather than

```
LinesRequired = e.MarginBounds.Height / FontHeight
```

6. The code is now complete but you may wish for a fuller understanding of how part of it works. Experiment by commenting out the three lines in the last If statement which set *MembersPrinted*, *NumSeniors* and *NumJuniors* to 0. Print or print preview the report twice in sucession. On the second occasion only the two totals, and no members' details, will be printed because the second condition in the Do While loop (*MembersPrinted <= lstMembers.Items.Count – 1*) is false. Printing of the members is done inside this loop but the totals are printed after it. Because the correct totals are printed on the 2nd and subsequent clicks of the print button, you might be thinking that there is no need to reset *NumSeniors* and *NumJuniors* to 0. Keep these two lines commented out but remove the comment from the line that sets *MembersPrinted* to 0. Run the program and print the report twice. Apart from printing only the totals, the second report's totals have doubled (and a 3rd printing would multiply the totals by 3 and so on). Remove any commenting when you have finished.

```
Smiley's Snooker. List of current members on 12 October 2003

JACOBS        John        JJ1995    Senior
JENKINS       Joanne      JJ7532    Junior
KHAN          Tahir       TK3869    Junior
MATTHEWS      Melanie     MM9628    Junior
PETERS        Patricia    PP5630    Junior
RAWJI         Munjal      MR3116    Senior
REYNOLDS      Susan       SR9837    Junior
TANG          David       DT1842    Junior
WHITE         William     WW7831    Senior
WINTERS       Anne        AW9703    Senior


Number of Juniors: 11
Number of Seniors: 9
```

Figure 23.1: The last page of the members' report

Chapter 24 – Coding: Starting a Game

Displaying a member's details automatically

The first thing the receptionist does onscreen when handling a new game is to get to the Game form where the controls for starting a new game will be displayed. You have already coded this navigation in Chapter 22. Then she enters the player's membership number and tabs out of this control or clicks the combo box of available tables so that this member's name and category of membership are displayed. The Leave event of the control in which the membership number is entered will handle this.

As with the last chapter let's start with the general procedures and work back to the event procedure that calls them. For automatically displaying a member's details our design identified two general procedures – FindMemberByMemberID and GetMemberByRecordNumber (see figure 21.3).

Function FindMemberByMemberID

This is passed a membership number and uses it to search the Members file for a match. If a match is found it passes back the record number in the file; if not it passes back 0.

1. The function has one formal parameter, MemberID, which it uses to search the Members file.

```
Private Function FindMemberByMemberID(ByVal MemberID As String) _
                                                As Integer
'searches Members file for membership number MemberID. Returns
'the file record number if this ID exists, otherwise returns 0
  Dim RecordNumber As Short
  Dim OneMember As MemberType
  Dim Found As Boolean
  RecordNumber = 0
  Found = False
  FileOpen(1, "Members.dat", OpenMode.Random, , , Len(OneMember))
  Do While (Not EOF(1)) And (Found = False)
    RecordNumber = RecordNumber + 1
    FileGet(1, OneMember)           'read one record from Members file
    If OneMember.MemberID = MemberID Then    'Is its member ID the one
                                             'we are looking for?

      Found = True
    End If
  Loop
  FileClose(1)
  If Found Then                     'Membership no. MemberID does exist
    Return RecordNumber             'so return its record no.
  Else
    Return 0                        'or return 0 if it does not exist
  End If
End Sub
```

Function GetMemberByRecordNumber

The record number that is passed back by FindMemberByMemberID can in turn be passed into GetMemberByRecordNumber to retrieve the record. This is the first time in this book we have gone straight to any particular record in a file, and to do so the FileGet function will need this third parameter.

2. The parameter RecordNumber is not changed in any way and so can be passed by value. In the code below the data type of the returned value, MemberType, was declared in module modDeclarations, and can store a record for one member.

```
Private Function GetMemberByRecordNumber(ByVal RecordNumber As Integer) _
                                         As MemberType
'returns record from Members.dat file at RecordNumber position
  Dim OneMember As MemberType
  FileOpen(1, "Members.dat", OpenMode.Random, , , Len(OneMember))
  FileGet(1, OneMember, RecordNumber)
  FileClose(1)
  Return OneMember
End Function
```

The Leave event procedure for txtMemberIDStart

Now that the two general procedures are in place we can look at the event that calls them.

3. The code for the Leave event is shown below. The only validation done on the membership number is that it is not empty. We don't really need any more ambitious validation since the call to FindMemberByMemberID will report whether the membership number exists. Recall that it returns 0 if the membership number does not exist, or the record number in the file if it does exist. If the membership number is found this record is retrieved from the file as the return value of the function GetMemberByRecordNumber (see figure 21.3). This is then used to display the member's name and category of membership.

```
Private Sub txtMemberIDStart_Leave(...) Handles txtMemberIDStart.Leave
'Calls FindMemberByMemberID to check that membership number entered when
'starting a game exists. If it does exist then calls
'GetMemberByRecordNumber to retrieve record and displays member's name
'and category of membership
  Dim MemberID As String
  Dim RecordNumber As Short
  Dim OneMember As MemberType
  MemberID = txtMemberIDStart.Text
  If MemberID <> "" Then        'something entered into member ID control?
    RecordNumber = FindMemberByMemberID(MemberID)
    If RecordNumber = 0 Then            'membership number does not exist
      MsgBox("Membership Number " & MemberID & " does not exist")
      txtMemberIDStart.Focus()
    Else                               'membership number does exist
      OneMember = GetMemberByRecordNumber(RecordNumber) 'retrieve record
      txtMemberNameStart.Text = OneMember.Firstname.TrimEnd _
                              & " " & OneMember.Surname.ToUpper
      If OneMember.Category = "S" Then
        txtCategoryStart.Text = "Senior"
      Else
        txtCategoryStart.Text = "Junior"
      End If
```

```
        End If            'end of (RecordNumber = 0)
    Else                  'a membership ID has not been entered
      MsgBox("You must enter the member's ID")
      txtMemberIDStart.Focus()
    End If            'end of (If MemberID <> "")
End Sub
```

4. Run the program and try out what you've coded. Enter one membership number you know exists and one that does not. You must tab out from the membership number text box or click the combo box for the member's name and category to be displayed.

Populating the combo box with available tables

In our design we decided to have one Sub procedure, ListTables, for populating the combo boxes with the appropriate table numbers when starting or finishing a game (see figure 21.2). This procedure is called by the form's Load event (to display the tables available for play, since the Start group box is visible when the form loads), and when the radio button to finish a game is clicked (to display the occupied tables).

1. The procedure uses the Text property of the button on the form to determine whether the user wishes to start or finish a game, in the same way as we used this property to decide on whether adding or deleting a member had been chosen on frmMembers. Enter the code below:

```
Private Sub ListTables()
'Populates combo boxes of table numbers with appropriate table numbers
'If starting a game then only green tables are listed. If finishing then
'only red tables are listed
  Dim Index As Short
  If btnOK.Text = "Start Game" Then         'a new game
    cboTableNumbersStart.Items.Clear()
    For Index = 0 To MaxTables - 1          'check each table on Main form
                                'MaxTables is declared on modDeclarations
    If ColorTranslator.ToOle(lblTables(Index).BackColor) = _
          ColorTranslator.ToOle(Color.Lime) Then 'is the table lime?
      cboTableNumbersStart.Items.Add(Index + 1)'if yes,display its number
    End If
  Next Index
  Else                                       'a finished game
    'to be coded later
  End If
End Sub
```

When you built the Main form in Chapter 22 you set the BackColor property of the labels that represent the snooker tables to lime (see step 5). If you have not set the colour correctly the code above will not work. Note that Visual Basic .NET will not allow

```
      If lblTables(Index).BackColor = Color.Lime Then
```

You have to use the **ColorTranslator.ToOle** method, which was first covered in Program 2.4.

2. Since ListTables will be called from the Game form's Load event write the following line of code in this event procedure:

```
  Call ListTables()
```

Displaying the start time of a new game

After the receptionist has entered a player's membership number and their name and category of membership have been displayed, she must select an available table from the combo box. When a table has been selected the starting time of the game will be displayed as hours and minutes (since seconds would probably be annoying to her and not necessary in calculating the cost of a game). The receptionist can inform the player when the cost of the game will be calculated from. For this we need the SelectedIndexChanged event of the combo box that displays the tables available for use.

1. This event procedure calls the function ShortenTime you wrote in the standard module modTimeFunctions (step 9 under Standard Modules in Chapter 22). You pass a time in the form hh:mm:ss and it returns the hours and minutes part only.

```
Private Sub cboTableNumbersStart_SelectedIndexChanged(...) Handles _
                            cboTableNumbersStart.SelectedIndexChanged
'Displays starting time of a new game
  Dim StartTime As String
  StartTime = ShortenTime(TimeOfDay)
  txtStartTimeStart.Text = StartTime
End Sub
```

Processing a new game

When the receptionist clicks the Start/Finish Game button, details of the new game should be stored in the Current Games file, and the table on the Main form changed to red with the game's starting time displayed next to it. Our design settled on two new Sub procedures to handle this processing, StoreCurrentGame and UpdateTableDisplay, and two we've already coded, ListTables and ShortenTime (figure 21.6).

Sub procedure StoreCurrentGame

1. This procedure is passed a table number which the user will have selected from the combo box. It's quite a simple one – wrap the details up in one record and send it off to the file. The FilePut statement is passed the parameter TableNumber, to position the file pointer at the required position and then to write the record to the file at this position.

```
Private Sub StoreCurrentGame(ByVal TableNumber As Short)
'Stores details of one game in CurrentGames.dat file
  Dim OneGame As GameType
          'get details of game from form's controls and store in a record
  OneGame.MemberID = txtMemberIDStart.Text
  OneGame.TableID = TableNumber
  OneGame.StartTime = TimeOfDay
  OneGame.Occupied = "Y"
  FileOpen(1, "CurrentGames.dat", OpenMode.Random, , , Len(OneGame))
          'write record to file
  FilePut(1, OneGame, TableNumber)'write direct to required part of file
  FileClose(1)
End Sub
```

There's one minor thing to point out in the code above. Note that the starting time is taken from the system clock, not from the text box displaying the start time. Recall that the text box did not display the seconds. In practice there could be a slight discrepancy between the two, but only if the receptionist for some reason took some time over clicking the Start Game button after entering details of the game. This might be something to talk over with Smiley's. Customers might complain if they are charged for time wasted at the reception desk!

Sub procedure UpdateTableDisplay

2. This procedure is used to change the colour of the table on which a new game has just started to red, and of a table that has just had a finished game to lime green. The code for the finished game will be dealt with later. A call is made to the ShortenTime function in the standard module modTimeFunctions to display the starting time (minus the seconds).

```
Private Sub UpdateTableDisplay(ByVal TableNumber As Short)
'If a new game then changes table TableNumber from lime to red and
'displays start time of game. If a finished game then changes table from
'red to lime and removes starting time
  If btnOK.Text = "Start Game" Then                  'a new game?
    lblTables(TableNumber - 1).BackColor = Color.Red
    lblStartTimes(TableNumber - 1).Text = ShortenTime(TimeOfDay)
    txtMemberIDStart.Text = ""        'clear text boxes for next game
    txtMemberNameStart.Text = ""
    txtCategoryStart.Text = ""
    txtStartTimeStart.Text = ""
  Else                                               'a finished game
    'to be coded later……….
  End If
End Sub
```

Click event of Start Game button (btnOK)

The receptionist will click the Start Game button to complete the processing of a new game. The modular structure (figure 21.6) showed that three Sub procedures are called, to store a record in the Current Games file, to update the table display by colouring the table red and to repopulate the combo box of tables.

1. Before calling the first two of these three Sub procedures we have to check that the user is starting a game, rather than finishing one, by using the button's text. We must further check that a membership ID has been entered and that a table has been selected from the combo box

```
Private Sub btnOK_Click(...) Handles btnOK.Click
  Dim Table As Short
  If btnOK.Text = "Start Game" Then                  'a new game?
    If txtMemberIDStart.Text <> "" Then            'member ID entered?
      If cboTableNumbersStart.Text <> "" Then       'table selected?
        Table = cboTableNumbersStart.Text          'store table to play on
        Call StoreCurrentGame(Table)        'to store details of game on file
        Call UpdateTableDisplay(Table)             'to colour table red
      Else
        MsgBox("You have not selected a table number")
    Else
      MsgBox("You have not entered a member ID")
    End If
  Else                                               'a finished game
    'to be coded later….
  End If
  Call ListTables()            'to repopulate combo box with table numbers
End Sub
```

ListTables, to repopulate the combo box, is called whether a new game or a finished game is being processed, and so is outside the main If statement. This procedure is shown in both figures 21.6 and 21.7, but of course is the same procedure call.

2. Everything is now in place for starting a new game. Try it out and check that the tables used are coloured red and the start time is displayed next to them. You can't check that details of a game have been written to the Current Games file by looking at the file size because this never changes from 360 bytes. You can open it up in Notepad or WordPad and see data in the string fields. Figure 24.1 shows the file in Notepad when table 2 has been used by member number FF6767. You may wish to recreate CurrentGames.dat again from the Utilities form as you try the code out.

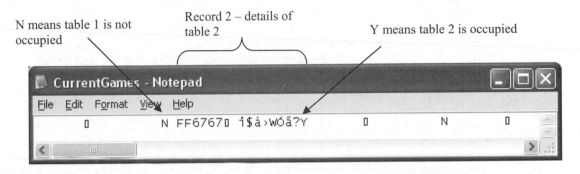

Figure 24.1: CurrentGames file in Notepad after table 2 has been used for a new game

Displaying table information when the program loads

UpdateTableDisplay colours a table red and displays the starting time of its game. But if the receptionist accidentally closes the program this information would not be displayed when the Main form is reloaded. We can write code in its Load event to display the colours of the tables and the starting times of the red tables. Since this needs to use the data in the Current Games file we need to check that this file exists, and if it does not exist tell the user to create it. One reason why it may not exist is that this is the first time Smiley's is using the program. Another reason might be accidental deletion.

1. Step 2 uses the **Exists** method to check whether a file exists. This is a method of class File, which in turn is found in the System.IO namespace (IO stands for **I**nput **O**utput). You have to add the following to the very top of the Main form (above Public Class frmMain):

```
Imports System.IO          'tell VB that you wish to use this namespace
```

2. In the Load event for the Main form enter the following code. It also checks that the Costs.txt file exists.

```
Private Sub frmMain_Load(...) Handles MyBase.Load
'Reads from Current Games file to set table display. Checks that this
'file and file Costs.txt exist
  Dim Index As Short
  Dim OneGame As GameType
  Dim GameForm As New frmGame()
  If Not File.Exists("CurrentGames.dat") And Not _
                              File.Exists("Costs.txt") Then
    MsgBox("2 files missing: CurrentGames.dat. and Costs.txt " & _
                    "Go to the Utilities form to create them")
  Else
```

```
      If Not File.Exists("CurrentGames.dat") Then
        MsgBox("1 file missing: CurrentGames.dat. Go to the Utilities " & _
                                   "form to create it")
      Else
        FileOpen(1, "CurrentGames.dat", OpenMode.Random, , , Len(OneGame))
        For Index = 0 To MaxTables - 1
          FileGet(1, OneGame)
          If OneGame.Occupied = "Y" Then              'table in use?
            lblTables(Index).BackColor = Color.Red  'if yes colour it red
                                             'and display start time of its game
            lblStartTimes(Index).Text = ShortenTime(OneGame.StartTime)
          End If
        Next Index
        FileClose(1)
        If Not File.Exists("Costs.txt") Then
          MsgBox("1 file missing: Costs.txt. Go to the Utilities " & _
                                        "form to create it")

        End If
      End If
    End If
End Sub
```

3. Run the program. Assuming you have one or more games in progress their tables should be coloured red and their start times displayed on the Main form. Try deleting first Costs.txt and then CurrentGames.dat from the bin folder to check that the different messages appear. You can recreate them easily from the Utilities form.

Chapter 25 – Coding: Finishing a Game

When a game has finished the receptionist must get to the Game form and, as the controls for a new game are currently displayed, click the radio button for a finished game. She asks the player which table they used and selects this from the occupied tables displayed in the combo box. All the other details (see figures 20.4 and 22.4) are automatically filled in and she just has to click the Finish Game button. This will write a record of the finished game to the Finished Games file, update the appropriate record in the Current Games file (so that the table is now unoccupied), change the colour of the table to lime and remove the displayed start time on the Main form.

Before the receptionist can select the table from the combo box, however, we have to write code to populate it with the appropriate tables.

Populating the combo box with occupied tables

1. In Chapter 24 we wrote part of the code for populating the combo box with tables available for a new game. In the part of Sub procedure ListTables with the comment *to be coded later* (the Else part of the If statement), insert the following:

```
For Index = 0 To MaxTables - 1          'check each table on Main form
   If ColorTranslator.ToOle(lblTables(Index).BackColor) = _
           ColorTranslator.ToOle(Color.Red) Then   'is the table red?
      cboTableNumbersFinish.Items.Add(Index + 1    'display its number
   End If
Next Index
```

2. In Chapter 24 three events on the Game form called this procedure ListTables – the form's Load event, the CheckedChanged event of the Finish radio button and the Click event of the Start/Finish Game button. When the user clicks the Finish radio button the controls for finishing a game are made visible. One of these, the combo box, must display the occupied tables. So in the CheckedChanged event of radFinish add the line of code:

```
Call ListTables()
```

3. Try out the combo box by entering data for one or more games and then inspecting the list of tables in the combo box for finishing a game. Only the occupied tables should be there.

Selecting a table from the combo box

In our modular structure design (figure 21.5) we identified three main processing stages that occur as soon as a table has been selected from the combo box. The functions ShortenTime and NumberOfMinutes in figure 21.5 play a supporting role.

- Retrieve the record from the Current Games file for the table that has just had the finished game.
- Retrieve the record from the Members file for the member who has just finished playing.
- Calculate the cost of a game.

Retrieving a record from the Current Games file

1. The function GetRecordFromCurrentGamesFile handles this (figure 21.5). It needs to be passed the table number (i.e. the record number) to go to in the file.

```
Private Function GetRecordFromCurrentGamesFile(ByVal TableNumber As _
                                        Short) As GameType
'Returns record of the current game for table TableNumber
  Dim OneGame As GameType
  FileOpen(1, "CurrentGames.dat", OpenMode.Random, , , Len(OneGame))
  FileGet(1, OneGame, TableNumber) 'Go straight to record and retrieve it
  FileClose(1)
  Return OneGame                         'return record from function
End Function
```

Retrieving a record from the Members file

The previous function returns a record from the Current Games file. This record includes the membership number of the player who has finished the game. This can be used to find the member's details from the Members file in order to display them onscreen for the receptionist.

2. The function GetMemberByMemberID (figure 21.5) is passed a membership number. It searches the Members file for the record with this membership number and returns the record.

```
Private Function GetMemberByMemberID(ByVal MemberID As String) _
                                        As MemberType
'returns record from Members.dat file with membership number MemberID
  Dim Found As Boolean
  Dim OneMember As MemberType
  Dim RecordNumber As Short
  Found = False
  FileOpen(1, "Members.dat", OpenMode.Random, , , Len(OneMember))
  Do While Not Found          'loop until record found in file
    FileGet(1, OneMember)
    If OneMember.MemberID = MemberID Then  'Membership no. of record
                                           'same as search membership no?
      Found = True
    End If
  Loop
  FileClose(1)
  Return OneMember                         'return record from function
End Function
```

Just in case you thought the loop above might never stop, think about what switches Found to True. If the membership number passed into the procedure is present in the file, Found is set to True. Actually it *must* be present because it was taken from the record retrieved by GetRecordFromCurrentGamesFile above, and this record in turn was stored in the Current Games file only after getting the player's membership number from the Members file in the first place.

Calculating the cost of a game

To calculate the cost of a game you need to know how long the game lasted and the cost per minute. The cost per minute depends on whether the player is a senior or junior member. Function CalculateCostOfGame (figure 21.5) returns the cost of a game.

3. Two parameters are passed to the function – the number of minutes the game took and the category of membership.

```
Private Function CalculateCostOfGame(ByVal MinutesPlayed As Short, _
                            ByVal Category As String) As Decimal
'Reads the 2 rates from Costs.txt file and calculates cost of one game
  Dim SeniorRate, JuniorRate As Single
  FileOpen(1, "Costs.txt", OpenMode.Input)
  Input(1, SeniorRate)
  Input(1, JuniorRate)
  FileClose(1)
  If Category = "Senior" Then
    Return (SeniorRate * MinutesPlayed) / 100
  Else
    Return (JuniorRate * MinutesPlayed) / 100
  End If
End Function
```

SelectedIndexChanged event procedure of the combo box

Now we need to return to what happens when the receptionist selects a table from the combo box. Apart from calling the three functions you've just coded it has to display several items of data, and then calculate and display how long the game took and how much the game costs.

4. The code is shown below. Two calls are made to ShortenTime in modTimeFunctions to display the start and finish times minus the seconds. The start time is retrieved from the Current Games file. A call is made to the other function in modTimeFunctions, NumberOfMinutes, to calculate the number of minutes the game took. Finally it expresses this in hours and minutes and calculates the cost of the game.

```
Private Sub cboTableNumbersFinish_SelectedIndexChanged(...) Handles _
                        cboTableNumbersFinish.SelectedIndexChanged
'Calls functions to retrieve player's details and table's start time from
'file. Displays these and calls function NumberOfMinutes to calculate
'length of time game took in minutes. Then calcs and displays game time
'in hrs and mins and calls a function to calculate cost of game
  Dim Table, MinutesPlayed, Hours, Minutes As Short
  Dim OneGame As GameType
  Dim OneMember As MemberType
  Dim MembershipNo, Category As String
  Table = cboTableNumbersFinish.Text
  OneGame = GetRecordFromCurrentGamesFile(Table) 'Retrieve details of
                                'game just finished from Current Games file
  MembershipNo = OneGame.MemberID
  OneMember = GetMemberByMemberID(MembershipNo) 'retrieve player's
                                        'details from Members file
  If OneMember.Category = "S" Then
    txtCategoryFinish.Text = "Senior"
  Else
    txtCategoryFinish.Text = "Junior"
  End If
  FinishTime = TimeOfDay
  txtMemberNameFinish.Text = OneMember.Firstname.TrimEnd & "   " & _
                        OneMember.Surname.ToUpper
  txtStartTimeFinish.Text = ShortenTime(OneGame.StartTime)
```

```
    txtFinishTime.Text = ShortenTime (FinishTime)
    MinutesPlayed = NumberOfMinutes(FinishTime, OneGame.StartTime)
    If MinutesPlayed >= 60 Then          'calculate number of hours played
      Hours = MinutesPlayed \ 60         'the '\' calculates an integer result
    Else
      Hours = 0
    End If
    Minutes = MinutesPlayed Mod 60       'calculate number of minutes played
    txtHours.Text = Hours
    txtMinutes.Text = Minutes
    Category = txtCategoryFinish.Text
    CostOfGame = CalculateCostOfGame(MinutesPlayed, Category)'calculate
    txtCost.Text = Format(CostOfGame, "Currency") 'cost and display it
  End Sub
```

Note the use of the two arithmetic operators '\' and Mod to change the length of the game in minutes into hours and minutes. If you don't understand them look back at figure 3.9 to see them in action.

There's one small, but crucial, point to make about the code above. The variables FinishTime and CostOfGame are not declared in the procedure. Let's deal with them separately.

- FinishTime stores the finishing time of the game by using the TimeOfDay property to get the system time. At this point the receptionist has not yet clicked the Finish Game button to finally complete the processing. As you'll see later, this stores the finishing time on file by calling procedure StoreGamesInFinishedGamesFile. There may well be a (small) time delay between clicking the combo box and this Finish Game button, which would mean that the finish time on file (assuming TimeOfDay is used again to get it) would be different from the one used to calculate the cost. This in turn would produce a mismatch between actual income and calculated income on the report Smiley's require on daily table usage. If we could send FinishTime from the event procedure above directly to StoreGameInFinishedGamesFile there would be no problem. Although this is possible it would create other difficulties in our situation. The solution is to declare FinishTime as a form variable so both procedures can use it.

- CostOfGame stores the cost of a game, and this will also be needed later when details of a finished game are stored in the Finished Games file. As with FinishTime we will declare it as a form variable.

5. Declare FinishTime and CostOfGame as form variables:

```
    Dim FinishTime As String      'time at which game finishes
    Dim CostOfGame As Decimal     'cost of one game
```

6. You can now try out the code to see what happens when a table is selected from the combo box. Make sure the Costs.txt file exists with the two rates. You can create it through the Utilities form.

Click event of the Finish Game button (btnOK)

When the receptionist clicks the Finish Game button, the following should happen:

- details of the finished game should be retrieved from the Current Games file
- the table's colour should change to lime green and the start time next to it removed
- the table's record in the Current Games file should be updated to indicate the table is not occupied
- details of the finished game should be stored in the Finished Games file
- the combo box should be repopulated with tables which are available

Our modular structure design allocated each of these to a general procedure (see figure 21.7). You have already written the first and last ones, GetRecordFromCurrentGamesFile and ListTables. The former is called when the receptionist selects a table from the combo box. We *could* have stored the record returned from this function as a form variable in step 4 above so that the Click event of the Finish Game button would not need to call the function again. However it is good practice to reduce global variables to a minimum, so we will call it again in the Click event of the Finish Game button.

Sub procedure ResetGameInCurrentGamesFile

1. This procedure needs to be passed the table number of the finished game. To indicate that the table is free again it changes the Occupied field of this table's record in the Current Games file from Y to N.

```
Private Sub ResetGameInCurrentGamesFile(ByVal TableNumber As Short)
'Updates record in Current Games file for table TableNumber by setting
'occupied field to N
  Dim OneGame As GameType
  FileOpen(1, "CurrentGames.dat", OpenMode.Random, , , Len(OneGame))
  FileGet(1, OneGame, TableNumber)
  OneGame.Occupied = "N"
  FilePut(1, OneGame, TableNumber)
  FileClose(1)
End Sub
```

Complete procedure UpdateTableDisplay

In Chapter 24 you wrote code for procedure UpdateTableDisplay to handle a new game. The table's colour was changed to red and the start time displayed next to it. Now you need to complete the code to handle a finished game.

2. In the commented section *to be coded later* of UpdateTableDisplay add the code below. The first two lines change the table's colour and remove the start time. The rest just clears out the controls on the Game form ready for the next finished game.

```
    lblTables(TableNumber - 1).BackColor = Color.Lime   'change to lime
    lblStartTimes(TableNumber - 1).Text = ""
                                        'clear text boxes
    txtMemberNameFinish.Text = ""
    txtCategoryFinish.Text = ""
    txtStartTimeFinish.Text = ""
    txtFinishTime.Text = ""
    txtHours.Text = ""
    txtMinutes.Text = ""
    txtCost.Text = ""
```

Sub procedure StoreGameInFinishedGamesFile

We haven't used the Finished Games file yet in this project. You declared a data type, FinishedGameType, in modDeclarations in Chapter 22 (step 4 under Standard Modules) for processing its records.

3. The procedure StoreGameInFinishedGamesFile needs to be passed the table number and the time the finished game started. Recall in step 5 above that the finishing time and cost of the game were assigned to form variables so that they could be accessed by this procedure.

```
Private Sub StoreGameInFinishedGamesFile(ByVal TableNumber As Short, _
                                         ByVal StartTime As Date)
'Stores record of finished game in Finished Games file
  Dim NumberOfRecords As Short
  Dim OneFinishedGame As GameFinishedType
  OneFinishedGame.TableID = TableNumber
  OneFinishedGame.StartTime = StartTime
  OneFinishedGame.FinishTime = FinishTime   'Uses two form variables
  OneFinishedGame.Cost = CostOfGame          'assigned values by
                                   'cboTableNumbersFinish_SelectedIndexChanged
  FileOpen(1, "FinishedGames.dat", OpenMode.Random, , , _
                                         Len(OneFinishedGame))
  NumberOfRecords = LOF(1) / Len(OneFinishedGame)
  FilePut(1, OneFinishedGame, NumberOfRecords + 1)
  FileClose(1)
End Sub
```

The LOF (**L**ength **O**f **F**ile) function was covered in step 4 of program 12.2. To append the finished game record to the file we need to position the file pointer just beyond the last record. Dividing the total length of the file in bytes by the length of one record in bytes gives the number of records in the file. FilePut adds 1 to this value to get beyond the last record.

Completing the code for btnOK_Click

The procedures above, to update the finished game's table details in the Current Games file and store details of the finished game in the Finished Games file, are called from btnOK. You've already coded that part dealing with a new game in Chapter 24. Now we must complete the coding for btnOK's Click event.

4. Two more local variables are needed:

```
Dim OneGame As GameType
Dim StartTime As Date
```

5. Add the code below in place of the comment *'to be coded later*. This includes another If statement to ensure something has been selected from the combo box.

```
If cboTableNumbersFinish.Text <> "" Then
   Table = cboTableNumbersFinish.Text
   OneGame = GetRecordFromCurrentGamesFile(Table)
   StartTime = OneGame.StartTime
   Call ResetGameInCurrentGamesFile(Table)
   Call UpdateTableDisplay(Table)
   Call StoreGameInFinishedGamesFile(Table, StartTime)
Else
   MsgBox "You must select a table number"
End If
```

6. Now try out the code for steps 1 to 5 above to process a finished game when the Finish Game button is clicked. When StoreGamesInFinishedGamesFile is run for the first time the file will be created for you by the FileOpen statement. It was different for the Current Games file, where you needed to create the file with 20 records before using it for the first time. You can check that records have been stored in the Finished Games file by looking at its size in Windows; each finished game requires 34 bytes.

Printing the report on table usage

Remind yourself how we designed this by looking back at figure 20.8. Figure 25.1 shows what it will look like in print preview. As it will always have about 25 lines in total we are not concerned with multiple pages. Clicking btnPrintReport on the Main form will produce the report.

```
Print preview                                                    _ □ ×
  🖨 🔎 ▾  ▣ ▦ ▦ ▦ ▦   Close                          Page        1

        Smiley's Snooker. Table use for 12/01/2003 13:08:53

        Table No.    No. Games    Time             Income

        1            2            0 hrs 2 mins     £0.06
        2            0            0 hrs 0 mins     £0.00
        3            0            0 hrs 0 mins     £0.00
        4            0            0 hrs 0 mins     £0.00
        5            0            0 hrs 0 mins     £0.00
        6            1            0 hrs 14 mins    £0.42
        7            0            0 hrs 0 mins     £0.00
        8            2            1 hrs 57 mins    £3.51
        9            1            4 hrs 6 mins     £7.38
        10           1            1 hrs 12 mins    £1.08
        11           0            0 hrs 0 mins     £0.00
        12           0            0 hrs 0 mins     £0.00
        13           0            0 hrs 0 mins     £0.00
        14           0            0 hrs 0 mins     £0.00
        15           0            0 hrs 0 mins     £0.00
        16           0            0 hrs 0 mins     £0.00
        17           1            1 hrs 6 mins     £0.99
        18           0            0 hrs 0 mins     £0.00
        19           1            4 hrs 5 mins     £7.35
        20           0            0 hrs 0 mins     £0.00

                                    Total Income:  £20.79
```

Figure 25.1: Report on table use

1. Place a PrintDocument control on the Main form. It will locate itself in the pane below the form.

2. In the Click event of btnPrintReport call the Print method of this control:

```
PrintDocument1.Print()
```

3. Double-click the PrintDocument control to bring up its default PrintPage event template. First declare the local variables and write code to print the report heading and column headings. The method used to produce columns is to define our own format as covered in Chapter 4. It calls Sub procedure PrintBlankLine in modDeclarations that you wrote when producing the membership report. The Now function used in the report heading returns the time and date.

```
Private Sub PrintDocument1_PrintPage(...) Handles _
                                    PrintDocument1.PrintPage
'Prints a report on table usage. For each table displays number of games,
'total playing time and income. Gives overall total income also
   Dim Index, NumberOfRecords, RecordNumber, Table As Short
   Dim Minutes, Hours As Short
   Dim X, Y As Short
   Dim FontHeight As Short
   Dim OneFinishedGame As GameFinishedType
   Dim GamesForOneTable As Short       'no. games played on a given table
```

```
    Dim TimeForOneTable As Short 'total time in mins a table has been in use
    Dim IncomeForOneTable As Decimal    'total income for given table
    Dim TotalIncome As Decimal      'total income from all tables
    Dim MinutesPlayed As Short      'no. minutes a given game lasted
    Dim MyFont As New Font("Courier New", 11, FontStyle.Bold)
    Dim MyTitleFont As New Font("Courier New", 13, FontStyle.Bold Or _
                                            FontStyle.Underline)
    Dim MyFormat As String = "{0, -15}{1, -15}{2, -25}{3, -15}" '4 columns
    Dim LineToPrint As String
    X = 50
    Y = 50
    FontHeight = MyFont.GetHeight(e.Graphics)
    e.Graphics.DrawString("Smiley's Snooker. Table use for " & _
                Now, MyTitleFont, Brushes.Black, X, Y) 'print title
    Call PrintBlankLine(X, Y, FontHeight, MyFont, e)
    LineToPrint = String.Format(MyFormat, "Table No.", "No. Games", _
                    "Time", "Income")         'print column headings
    e.Graphics.DrawString(LineToPrint, MyFont, Brushes.Black, X, Y)
    Call PrintBlankLine(X, Y, FontHeight, MyFont, e)
```

2. Add the following to the code above to print the details of each table:

```
For Table = 1 To MaxTables              'loop for each table
    FileOpen(1, "FinishedGames.dat", OpenMode.Random, , , _
                                Len(OneFinishedGame))
    NumberOfRecords = LOF(1) / Len(OneFinishedGame)
    GamesForOneTable = 0
    TimeForOneTable = 0
    IncomeForOneTable = 0
    For Index = 1 To NumberOfRecords        'Search whole file for records
                                            'of the current table
        FileGet(1, OneFinishedGame)         'read one record
        If OneFinishedGame.TableID = Table Then    'current table found?
            GamesForOneTable = GamesForOneTable + 1    'one game more
            MinutesPlayed = NumberOfMinutes(OneFinishedGame.FinishTime, _
                                    OneFinishedGame.StartTime)
            TimeForOneTable = TimeForOneTable + MinutesPlayed
            IncomeForOneTable = IncomeForOneTable + OneFinishedGame.Cost
        End If
    Next Index
    TotalIncome = TotalIncome + IncomeForOneTable 'Add table's income
                                            'to running income total
    If TimeForOneTable >= 60 Then           'Calculate hours played on
        Hours = TimeForOneTable \ 60        'current table
    Else
        Hours = 0
    End If
    Minutes = TimeForOneTable Mod 60        'calculate minutes played
    LineToPrint = String.Format(MyFormat, Table, GamesForOneTable, _
                        Hours & " hrs " & Minutes & " mins", _
                        Format(IncomeForOneTable, "Currency"))
    e.Graphics.DrawString(LineToPrint, MyFont, Brushes.Black, X, Y)
    Y = Y + FontHeight
    FileClose(1)
Next Table
```

- The outer loop will be executed 20 times, once for each table. It is essential that the file is opened and closed each time round the loop because you must start at the first record again when the next table is processed. If you opened the file once before the loop and closed it after the loop only table 1's details would be calculated.

- The inner loop is repeated once per record. The start and finish times are sent to the NumberOfMinutes function, and then calculated as hours and minutes.

3. To print the total income at the end of the report is straightforward. However the value of the X co-ordinate, 425, can only be found by trial and error.

```
  Call PrintBlankLine(X, Y, FontHeight, MyFont, e)
   LineToPrint = "Total Income:  " & Format(TotalIncome, "Currency")
   e.Graphics.DrawString(LineToPrint, MyFont, Brushes.Black, 425, Y)
End Sub
```

4. To check that the printing works you may wish to use a PrintPreviewDialog control to preview it rather than actually print the report. (See steps 2 and 8 in Program 14.1 on how to do this.)

Creating a new Finished Games file each day

In our Analysis we learned that Smiley's does not wish to keep permanent records of past games. If the report is printed at the end of the day the Finished Games file should be emptied, but if printed before this time the records should be kept until the report is printed at the end of the day. One way of doing this is to ask the user, when the report is being printed, whether they would like to delete the file.

1. Write a Sub procedure DeleteFinishedGames to delete the file. The next finished game that is processed will create the file again (by the FileOpen statement in StoreGameInFinishedGamesFile).

```
Private Sub DeleteFinishedGamesFile()
'deletes Finished Games file. NB file does not go to Recycle Bin
   Dim Response As Short
   Response = MsgBox("Delete today's games from the file?", vbYesNo)
   If Response = 6 Then              'User replied Yes
     Kill("FinishedGames.dat")      'so delete it
   End If
End Sub
```

2. Finally, call this procedure by inserting the following line just before End Sub in step 3 above.

```
    Call DeleteFinishedGamesFile()
```

Chapter 26 – Appraisal

Chapter 19 listed Appraisal as the last stage of a project. It is worth 3 marks. Appendix B shows that you should cover three things:

- discuss how far your project meets the system objectives listed in the Analysis
- discuss any improvements you could make and indicate how you might make them
- get some feedback from your user on what they think of the solution

Meeting the system objectives

All the objectives referred to in the Analysis have been implemented. In your own project you should briefly go through each one indicating whether or not it has been met. It may be that some of the objectives have only been partly implemented. Point out which parts have and which have not, with a brief explanation for those things not covered.

Improvements

List a few ways you might improve the interface, the efficiency of your coding, the design of your files or whatever, and briefly say how you would do these. The following are some improvements we might make to the sample project.

1. Since the first two characters of membership numbers are supposed to be the initial letters of the member's firstname and surname, these two characters could be automatically displayed in the membership number text box when the user has typed in the new member's name. To do this write code in the Enter event procedure of txtMemberIDAdd. It may be that the code here should simply display these letters and that a function be written to return them to this event procedure code.

2. When the user backs up the files from the Utilities form the code copies them to a floppy disk. It would provide more flexibility if the user could choose the drive and directory. A text box could be made visible in which the path is entered by the user, although this assumes the user will enter a valid path. You might remember that Smiley's is not very good at using a computer. (Recall that they wanted to be able to change the payment rates from inside the program rather than change the contents of the text file directly.) A SaveFileDialog control could be used.

3. The user has to type in a member's ID when entering a game. Although the member's file is searched for this ID and an appropriate message output if it is not found (implying that the user has entered the ID incorrectly), it would be better to let the user select the ID from a combo box. Since this can be populated only with current IDs from the Members file there is no need for any checking. (Actually the checking method was deliberately used to show you how to go about it.)

4. When the user chooses any of the utilities a message to say the action has been successful might be useful. A message box could be used for this.

5. When the user clicks btnOK to process a new game the various controls are cleared ready for the next game. If the player has forgotten which table he has been given, and the receptionist also can't remember, the only way to find out is by looking for the most recent start time displayed on the Main form. This isn't very time-consuming, but it would be a little easier if the table could be spotted at once. Perhaps the most recent start time could be displayed in a colour, or the most recent table number displayed in a separate label.

6. If for some reason the Members and/or Finished Games files are not present in the bin folder the FileOpen statement creates them again when the file needs to be used. It would be better, though, if the user was aware that the file is missing. The **File.Exists** method that was used when the program loads to check if the Current Games and/or Costs files exist, could be used for these files too.

7. A record in the Finished Games file stores the start and finishing times of a game. When the report on table usage is printed these times are passed to the function NumberOfMinutes to calculate how many minutes the game lasted. Strictly this is an example of inefficiency. Why not store the number of minutes in the record instead, since this will have just been calculated before the record of a finished game is written to the file? Of course the amount of time taken to do the calculations again before the report is printed is undetectable (any noticeable time taken is in doing the printing itself) so the inefficiency is really only a theoretical one.

8. Another possible example of inefficiency is storing the membership categories as 'S' and 'J' in the Members file. In several places these codes need to be changed and displayed as full words. The conversion code wouldn't be necessary if the full words were stored on file in the first place (and recall that the user wouldn't be typing them in since they are selected from a list box). An alternative might be to avoid repeating the code and put it into a Sub procedure.

Another area you might wish to refer to, if you haven't used it already in your project, is the use of error-handling code. If your testing has thrown up a number of run-time errors you could briefly point out how in principle to handle these. Chapter 13 covered this topic.

Feedback from the user

Get your user to confirm in writing what they think of your solution. Take care here – assessors are used to candidates writing their own letters, which usually say how wonderful the project is! No-one is expecting your user necessarily to really use your project, though it is very gratifying if they want to. An honest opinion about what they think of your efforts is what is needed.

Appendix A

Summary of the chapter Programs

Prog	Program name	Main new topic(s) covered
1.1	Display your name	Display text in a label
1.2	Change a message	Click buttons
2.1	A list box of countries	List box
2.2	Radio buttons, check boxes and group boxes	Radio button, check box, group box
2.3	Displaying the time	Timer
2.4	Changing a form's colour using scroll bars	Scroll bar, RGB function
3.1	Add two numbers	Variables, addition, input box
3.2	Illustrating global and local scope	Scope of variables
3.3	Using a static variable	Static variables
3.4	Calculating the average exam mark	Initialising variables, Enabling/disabling controls
4.1	Using a label, text box and message box for display	Message box, carriage returns, linefeeds, string concatenation
4.2	Tabular display in a list box	String.format method, Space function
5.1	A simple console application	Console application
6.1	Deciding exam grades	If statement
6.2	Selecting cutlery	Checking if radio buttons and check boxes are selected
6.3	Rent a property	Logical operators AND and OR
6.4	Wards and Patients	Select Case statement
7.1	Multiplication table	For…Next loop
7.2	Addition table	Nested For…Next loop
7.3	Driving test (console application)	Do While…Loop
7.4	Password entry	Do…Loop Until
8.1	Ensuring a person's name has only one space	Length and Substring string methods
8.2	Extract the area telephone code	Building a string by repeated concatenation
8.3	College library issue desk	Processing dates
9.1	Avoid repeating code	Putting repeated code into a Sub procedure
9.2	Value and reference parameters	Passing parameters by value and by reference
9.3	Calculating interest	User-defined function
9.4	A standard module function	Standard module
10.1	Array to hold numbers	One-dimensional array
10.2	Program 10.1 with a function to search array	Passing an array as a parameter to a procedure
10.3	A control array	Control array
10.4	A control array with a shared event handler	Shared event handler
11.1	Array of records – football team players	Record, array of records, 2 forms in project
12.1	Using the OpenFileDialog control	OpenFileDialog control
12.2	Text file to hold names and ages	Reading to/writing from a text file
12.3	Random access file of garden centre products	Reading to/writing from a random access file
13.1	Breakpoints, setting Watches, stepping through code	Breakpoint, Watch, stepping through code
13.2	The Immediate window	Immediate window
13.3	Simple error handling	Try…Catch
13.4	Advanced error handling using the Err object	Err object
14.1	Printing reports on sales staff	PrintDocument and PrintPreviewDialog controls
15.1	Displaying data from a table in a DataGrid control	OleDbConnection, OleDbDataAdapter, OleDbDataSet controls
15.2	Displaying data from a table and a query in a DataGrid control	Creating and using Data controls in code, OleDbCommand and DataTable objects
15.3	Displaying data through SQL queries in a DataGrid	Constructing SQL queries
15.4	Displaying one record through bound text boxes	DataBindings property, BindingContext object
16.1	Updating a database through a DataGrid	Data adapter Update method, updating table through data grid
16.2	Batch updating	Updating all rows in a table through code
17.1	A Bank Account Class	OOP – Classes and Objects
18.1	Inheritance – a student Bank Account class	OOP – inheritance
18.2	Polymorphism – a student grading system	OOP – polymorphism

Appendix B

Assessment criteria for the AQA Examining Board 'A' level Computing project (excluding stages not covered in Part Three)

Analysis			
Marks: 0 – 2	Marks: 3 – 6	Marks: 7 – 9	Marks: 10 – 12
Little or no evidence of any analysis Little or no evidence of investigation of a problem or an appropriate problem selected, that does not produce a useable computer-based solution No measurable system objectives No consideration of user needs	Some analysis but limited in scope and perception Some evidence of investigation of a problem with limited scope resulting in a standard exercise with no external constraints System objectives unclear or implicit Little evidence of consideration of user needs	Evidence of a well-structured analysis Evidence of a structured investigation into a problem demonstrating consideration of the realistic needs of a real user Statement of measurable system objectives but lacking in scope	Evidence of an extensive well-structured analysis Extensive investigation of a demanding open-ended problem showing realistic appreciation of system needs and demonstrating a high level of perception of a real user's needs Clear and comprehensive set of measurable system objectives

Design			
Marks: 0 – 2	Marks: 3 – 6	Marks: 7 – 9	Marks: 10 – 12
Little or no evidence of design with detail and/or content insufficient to produce a useable system	Evidence of design but lacking the necessary detail to produce a usable system without further development	Evidence of a feasible design. Majority of aspects are documented so that a useable system could be developed	Design well-fitted to the situation and incorporating all the required aspects to support the development of a fully-working system

Technical solution			
Marks: 0 – 2	Marks: 3 – 6	Marks: 7 – 9	Marks: 10 – 12
Unstructured program that is trivial and/or incomplete with little evidence that it is working	A working program that produces some correct results but for a standard exercise and/or programmed in an unstructured way	Program showing reasonable structure, use of parameters and user-defined data structures	Well-structured program demonstrating methodologies appropriate to the programming language used

System Maintenance			
Marks: 0	Marks: 1 or 2	Marks: 3 or 4	Marks: 5 or 6
No samples of algorithm design. Program listing not self-documenting or with little annotation	Overall system design including information about modules / procedures. Some examples of algorithm design. Program listing clearly set out with some annotation	Overall system design including information about modules/ procedures. Representative samples of algorithm design. Program listing clearly set out - self-documented or clearly annotated	Same requirements as for 3 or 4 marks except that representative samples of algorithm design should use an appropriate standard method

Appraisal			
Marks: 0	Marks: 1	Marks: 2	Marks: 3
None provided or a few inappropriate comments	Little attempt made to relate achievement to the original objectives and / or shortcomings not identified	Achievement related to objectives. Analysis of and improvements needed and indication of how these could be achieved	As for 2 marks, plus… Analysis of feedback from user

Index